Key Concepts in
Social Work Practice

Recent volumes include:

Key Concepts in Anti-Discriminatory Social Work
Toying Okitikpi and Cathy Aymer

Key Concepts in Mental Health, Second Edition
David Pilgrim

Key Concepts in Learning Disabilities
Pat Talbot, Geoff Astbury and Tom Mason

Key Concepts in Family Studies
Jane Ribbens McCarthy and Rosalind Edwards

Key Concepts in Public Health
Frances Wilson and Andi Mabhala

Key Concepts in Palliative Care
Moyra A. Baldwin and Jan Woodhouse

Key Concepts in Health Studies
Chris Yuill, Iain Crinson and Eilidh Duncan

Key Concepts in Healthcare Education
Annette McIntosh, Janice Gidman and Elizabeth Mason-Whitehead

The SAGE Key Concepts series provides students with accessible and authoritative knowledge of the essential topics in a variety of disciplines. Cross-referenced throughout, the format encourages critical evaluation through understanding. Written by experienced and respected academics, the books are indispensable study aids and guides to comprehension.

Key Concepts in
Social Work Practice

Edited by

AIDAN WORSLEY, TIM MANN, ANGELA OLSEN
AND ELIZABETH MASON-WHITEHEAD

Los Angeles | London | New Delhi
Singapore | Washington DC

MT

Los Angeles | London | New Delhi
Singapore | Washington DC

SAGE Publications Ltd
1 Oliver's Yard
55 City Road
London EC1Y 1SP

SAGE Publications Inc.
2455 Teller Road
Thousand Oaks, California 91320

SAGE Publications India Pvt Ltd
B 1/I 1 Mohan Cooperative Industrial Area
Mathura Road
New Delhi 110 044

SAGE Publications Asia-Pacific Pte Ltd
3 Church Street
#10-04 Samsung Hub
Singapore 049483

Editor: Sarah Gibson
Assistant editor: Emma Milman
Production editor: Katie Forsythe
Copyeditor: Kate Scott
Proofreader: Kate Wood
Marketing manager: Tamara Navaratnam
Cover design: Wendy Scott
Typeset by: C&M Digitals (P) Ltd, Chennai, India
Printed and bound by CPI Group (UK) Ltd,
Croydon, CR0 4YY

Editorial arrangement and Editors' Preface © Aidan Worsley, Tim Mann, Angela Olsen and Elizabeth Mason-Whitehead 2013

Chapter 1 © Mike Thomas 2013
Chapters 2 and 21 © Jules Clarke 2013
Chapter 3 © Andrea Pepe and Dan Redfearn 2013
Chapter 4 © Jane Walker 2013
Chapter 5 © Patrick O'Byrne 2013
Chapter 6 © Debra Hayes 2013
Chapter 7 © Helen Fruin 2013
Chapter 8 © Terry Williams, Dorothy Carter and members of the Forum of Carers and Users of Services (FOCUS) 2013
Chapter 9 © Pat Higgins 2013
Chapter 10 © Angela Olsen and Liz Stevens 2013
Chapters 11 and 52 © Anne Keeler 2013
Chapters 12 and 41 © Elizabeth Harlow 2013
Chapter 13 © Jane Youell and Helga Stiborski 2013
Chapters 14 and 23 © Alice O'Sullivan 2013
Chapter 15 © Kate Cook 2013
Chapter 16 © Joanne Lewis 2013
Chapter 17 © Suryia Nayak 2013
Chapters 18 and 61 © Steven M. Shardlow 2013
Chapter 19 © Nicky Ryden 2013
Chapter 20 © Tim Mann 2013
Chapter 21 © Jules Clarke 2013
Chapter 22 © Mike Burt 2013
Chapter 24 © Jenna Murray de López 2013
Chapter 25 © David Nulty 2013
Chapter 26 © Aidan Worsley and Tim Mann 2013
Chapter 27 © Angela Olsen 2013
Chapter 28 © Marian Foley 2013
Chapter 29 © Denise Megson 2013

Chapter 30 © Bob Sapey 2013
Chapter 31 © Joanne L. Westwood 2013
Chapter 32 © Mandy Schofield 2013
Chapter 33 © Anna Beddow 2013
Chapter 34 © Julie A. Lawrence 2013
Chapter 35 © Mick Howarth 2013
Chapter 36 © Robin Miller and Jon Glasby 2013
Chapter 37 © Ali Gardner 2013
Chapter 38 © Jill Murphy 2013
Chapter 39 © Mike Blackmon 2013
Chapter 40 © Aidan Worsley and Lesley Littler 2013
Chapter 42 © Rachael Willis 2013
Chapter 43 © Tom Parr 2013
Chapter 44 © Mike Ravey 2013
Chapter 45 © Philip Gilligan 2013
Chapter 46 © Emma Kelly 2013
Chapter 47 © Shelley Briggs 2013
Chapter 48 © Karen Owen 2013
Chapter 49 © Noreen Maguinness 2013
Chapter 50 © Clare Stone, Lisa Malihi-Shoja, Mick McKeown and the Comensus Writing Collective 2013
Chapter 51 © Julie Bywater 2013
Chapter 53 © Bill Jordan 2013
Chapter 54 © Malcolm Payne 2013
Chapter 55 © Kate Bebe 2013
Chapter 56 © Ashley Weinberg and Michael Murphy 2013
Chapter 57 © Michael Murphy 2013
Chapter 58 © Simon Rogerson 2013
Chapter 59 © Sarah Kennedy and Valerie Houghton 2013
Chapter 60 © Pat Cox 2013
Chapter 62 © Neil Bateman 2013
Chapter 63 © Chris Sheehy 2013

First published 2013

Apart from any fair dealing for the purposes of research or private study, or criticism or review, as permitted under the Copyright, Designs and Patents Act, 1988, this publication may be reproduced, stored or transmitted in any form, or by any means, only with the prior permission in writing of the publishers, or in the case of reprographic reproduction, in accordance with the terms of licences issued by the Copyright Licensing Agency. Enquiries concerning reproduction outside those terms should be sent to the publishers.

Library of Congress Control Number: 2012937839

British Library Cataloguing in Publication data

A catalogue record for this book is available from the British Library

MIX
Paper from responsible sources
FSC www.fsc.org   FSC® C013604

ISBN 978-1-4462-0729-1
ISBN 978-1-4462-0730-7 (pbk)

6/5/13

Contents

contents

v

contents

key concepts in
social work practice

contents

ix

About the Editors and Contributors

EDITORS

Tim Mann, BA, B Phil, CQSW, PGCert, FHEA is Head of Social Work at the University of Chester.

Elizabeth Mason-Whitehead is Professor of Health and Social Care at the University of Chester.

Angela Olsen, MA (Learning Disability Studies), AASW, CCETSW Practice Teaching Award, CSS, HEA Fellow is Programme Lead BSc Integrated Practice in Learning Disability Nursing and Social Work at the University of Salford.

Aidan Worsley, MPhil, MA Social Work, BSc (Hons), CCETSW Practice Teaching Award and HEA Fellow is Professor of Social Work and Dean of the School of Social Work at the University of Central Lancashire.

CONTRIBUTORS

Neil Bateman, LLB, CQSW, Dip SA, DMS is a freelance welfare rights specialist (www.neilbateman.co.uk).

Kate Bebe, BA (Hons), DipSW, PQSW Practice Teaching Award is Lecturer in Social Work at the University of Chester.

Anna Beddow is Lecturer in Social Work at the University of Salford.

Mike Blackmon, BA, DipSW is a Senior Lecturer in the School of Social work at the University of Central Lancashire.

Shelley Briggs, DipSW, MASW, BA, History/Community and Public Affairs is a Senior Lecturer, Programme Lead Care Community and Citizenship at the School of Social Work, University of Central Lancashire.

Mike Burt, MA, BA, CQSW, Cert Ed, CIPD, Advanced Award in Social Work is Honorary Senior Lecturer at the University of Chester.

Julie Bywater, BA (Hons), Dip SW, FHEA is Senior Lecturer in Social Work at the University of Chester.

Dorothy Carter, Forum of Carers and Users of Services.

Jules Clarke, BA (Hons) Psychology, CQSW, Dip ASS, CCETSW Practice Teachers Award is Adoption Manager, Bolton Children's Services.

Dr Kate Cook, LLB, PhD is Feminist and Lecturer in Law at Manchester Metropolitan University.

Pat Cox, MA, BA (Hons), CQSW, Dip SA is a Reader at the School of Social Work, University of Central Lancashire.

Marian Foley, PhD, MBA is Lecturer in Social Work at the University of Salford.

Helen Fruin, MA, BA (Hons), CQSW, Dip Soc Admin, PGCE is Senior Lecturer in Social Work at the University of Chester.

Ali Gardner, BA (Hons), CQSW is a Senior Lecturer, BA and MA Social Work Programme at Manchester Metropolitan University.

Philip Gilligan, MA (Econ), BA (Hons), CQSW, CCETSW Practice Teaching Award, Postgraduate Certificate in Practice Teaching is Senior Lecturer at the Division of Social Work and Social Care, University of Bradford.

Jon Glasby, BA, MA/DipSW, PhD, PG Cert is Professor of Health and Social Care and Director of the Health Services Management Centre at the University of Birmingham, with an interest in health and social care partnerships, personalisation and community care.

Elizabeth Harlow, PhD, BA Hons, CQSW, Certificate of Coaching for Leadership and Professional Development, Introductory Certificate in Group Analysis is Professor of Social Work at the University of Chester.

Debra Hayes, MA, BA, CQSW is MA Social Work Course Leader at the Faculty of Health, Psychology and Social Care, Manchester Metropolitan University.

Pat Higgins, BA (Hons), CQSW, Practice Teacher Award, DASS, Diploma in Counselling is Visiting Lecturer at the University of Chester.

Valerie Houghton, RNMH, BSc (Hons), Specialist Practitioner for People with Learning Disabilities, PGDip (Community Care), PG Cert HERP Diploma Management is Lecturer in Nursing and Learning Disability Studies at the University of Salford.

Mick Howarth, MA, BA, CQSW is Former Head of Operations in Adult Social Care for Cheshire West and Chester Council.

Bill Jordan, MA Oxon, Grad Cert Social Work (Exon), with distinction, Doctorate, Kingston University (honoris causa) is Professor of Social Policy at the Plymouth University.

Anne Keeler, CQSW, BSc, Diploma in Counselling, Cert Ed is Senior Lecturer in Social Work at the University of Chester.

Emma Kelly, MSW, BA (Hons), DipSW is a Lecturer in Social Work (Safeguarding Children) at the University of Salford.

Sarah Kennedy, BA (Hons), DipSW, RNLD, MSc is Lecturer in Nursing and Learning Disability Studies at the University of Salford.

Julie A. Lawrence, MA Applied Social Studies, CQSW, CCETSW Practice Teacher Award, FHEA is Lecturer in Social Work and Learning Disability Studies at the University of Salford.

Joanne Lewis, BA (Hons) is a PhD Student researching Green Therapy – the potential for self-management of depressive symptoms – for the University of Hull and is also an Associate Lecturer in Education for Liverpool Hope University.

Lesley Littler, CQSW, CCETSW Practice Teaching Award is a Senior Lecturer at Edge Hill University.

Noreen Maguinness, CQSW, Child Care Award, BA (Hons) Health and Social Care, Postgrad Diploma in Teaching and Learning in Higher Ed, Masters (dis) Child Care Law and Practice is Senior Lecturer in social work at the University of Chester.

Lisa Malihi-Shoja, MA, BSc is the co-ordinator for Comensus and SUCAG, both of which are service user and carer involvement programmes based at UCLan.

Mick McKeown, BA (Hons), RMN, RGN is Principal Lecturer at the School of Health, University of Central Lancashire.

Denise Yuen Megson, MSc, BSc (Hons), RNT, RNMH, RN Adult is Senior Lecturer in Nursing and Learning Disability Studies at the University of Salford.

Robin Miller, BSc (Hons), DipSW, MA, MSc is a Senior Fellow, Health Services Management Centre, University of Birmingham and an Associate Fellow at the Third Sector Research Centre.

Jill Murphy, MBA, Diploma in Applied Social Studies, BA, CQSW is a Lecturer in Social Work at the University of Salford.

Michael Murphy is Senior Lecturer in Social Work at the University of Salford.

Jenna Murray de López, MA Social Anthropology, BA (Hons), DipSW is a Lecturer in Social Work at the University of Salford.

Suryia Nayak, CQWS, Ad Dip Psychotherapy is Senior Lecturer in Social Work, feminist and community activist at the University of Salford.

David Nulty, BA (Hons), MA, CQSW is Senior Lecturer in Social Work at the University of Chester.

Patrick O'Byrne, MA Applied Social Studies is Senior Lecturer in Social Work at the University of Huddersfield, 1980–2000, counsellor and family mediator.

Alice O'Sullivan, MA SW, BA (Hons) is a Senior Lecturer, School of Social Work at the University of Central Lancashire.

Karen Owen, BA (Hons), CSS is Adult Safeguarding Co-ordinator Cheshire West and Chester Council.

Tom Parr, BA (Hons), CSS, PGCE is Senior Lecturer in Social Work at the University of Chester.

Malcolm Payne, PhD, DipSS, BA is a Policy and Development Adviser, St Christopher's Hospice, London; Emeritus Professor at Manchester Metropolitan University; Honorary/Visiting Professor at Kingston University/St George's University of London, Opole University Poland; Honorary appointments at Helsinki University, Comenius University, Bratislava, Slovakia.

Andrea Pepe, MSc in Social Work, BA (Hons) is Lecturer in Social Work and Learning Disability Studies at the University of Salford.

Mike Ravey is Senior Lecturer in Nursing and Learning Disability Studies at the University of Salford.

Dan Redfearn, BSc (Hons) is a Lecturer Practitioner/Autism Specialist Nurse at the University of Salford/Tameside and Glossop Community Healthcare.

Simon Rogerson, MSC, MA, Ba, DipSw is Senior Lecturer, School of Social Work at the University of Central Lancashire.

Nicky Ryden, PhD, BA Jt Hons in Economics and SE Asian Studies, CQSW is a registered social worker with 30 years' experience, now a part-time tutor at Huddersfield University.

Bob Sapey, MA, PgCert, TLHE, CQSW is Senior Lecturer in Applied Social Science at Lancaster University.

Mandy Schofield, MA, BSc (Hons), CQSW is Deputy Head of Social Work at the University of Chester.

Professor Steven M. Shardlow, PhD is Chair of Social Work at the University of Salford.

Chris Sheehy Sociology, BA, CQSW Dip ASS is Senior Lecturer in Social Work, University of Salford and seconded to the role of President of the Salford UCU Branch.

Liz Stevens, MA, CQSW is Team Manager, Manchester Children's Services.

Helga Stiborski, BA Social and Community Studies, DipSW, Practice Teachers Award, Post Qualified Social Work Award and Deprivation of Liberty Safeguards Best Interest Assessor is an Independent Social Worker, Practice Educator and Deprivation of Liberty Safeguards (DOLS) Best Interest Assessor.

Clare Stone, MA, BA (Hons), CQSW, PG Dip Practice Teaching in Social Work, PTA, PG Cert Teaching and Learning in HE, FHEA is Senior Lecturer in the School of Social Work at the University of Central Lancashire.

Mike Thomas, PhD, MA (Law), BSc (Nurs), PGCert Ed, RMN, RNT, FHEA, MBPS is Professor, Pro-Vice-Chancellor and Executive Dean of the Faculty of Health and Social Care within the University of Chester.

Jane Walker, DipSW, BA (Hons) Post-qualifying Studies in Health and Social Work, Practice Teacher Award and the full PQ Award in Social Work is Lecturer in Social Work at the University of Chester.

Dr Ashley Weinberg, PhD is Senior Lecturer in Psychology at the University of Salford.

Joanne L. Westwood, PhD, MA, BA, PG Dip (Social Work) is Senior Lecturer and programme lead for the PG Cert Researching Social Care, School of Social Work at the University of Central Lancashire.

Terry Williams, CSW, DSWM, MBA, FAETC is the Development Worker for FOCUS North West (The Forum of Carers and Users of Services – a service user and carer led organisation which works in partnership with universities and colleges).

Rachael Willis, MSc Advanced Practice Management, PQ Advanced Award, AMHP, BA (Hons) Social Work and CQSW is a Senior Practitioner (Mental Health) with Lancashire County Council, member of the SWRB Practitioner Reference Group and CPD Advisory Implementation Group for the College of Social Work.

Jane Youell, BSc, PhD Student is researching the impact dementia has on intimacy in relationships at the Centre for Health and Wellbeing Research, University of Northampton.

Editors' Preface

Social work is characteristically a profession in change. Indeed, the one thing about the profession that can be relied upon is its constantly changing environment. It is therefore with some hesitancy that the editors make reference to the social work reforms, the nascent College of Social Work and the new structures being put into place for continuing professional development – simply because the landscape may have changed significantly in a few short months. Social work is undergoing what can only be described as a *precedented* period of transformation – a time when wholesale changes are affecting social work students, practitioners and managers alike – again. But underneath all this 'big picture' churn is the simple fact that through it all social workers are getting on with social work.

As they 'keep calm and carry on', social workers remain in a profession that makes high demands on knowledge, skills and understanding to carry out their duties. This book aims to support that process. The purpose of the book is to give the reader a broad, yet comprehensive perspective of the concepts that are relevant and significant in developing and maintaining knowledge and skills in the field of social work. While the book can be read in its entirety, readers may well use the book as a reference point and study one particular concept at a time. The sum of the entries will provide an overall view of the key theories, issues and practical considerations of social work professionals in the 21st century.

The book is aimed primarily at the qualifying social work student – on both undergraduate and post graduate courses. We feel its focus on practice helps the text speak clearly to both these groups. We also believe that the beginning practitioner will find the book useful – especially those Newly Qualified Social Workers who are embarking on their Assessed and Supported Year in Employment. Indeed, a range of workers from the vast array of social care roles will find many things in here that will be stimulating and relevant. We also draw attention to the appropriateness of this text for those colleagues in professions allied to social work who will find much in this volume to assist them – workers across the health and social care arena, health visitors, public health workers and so forth – who may connect with social work colleagues – and concepts – in their practice.

Some readers may be on placement or practising in the field and simply want to learn more about concepts that are connected to their own professional challenges. Others may be engaged in completing written assignments or generating their own knowledge through research and are interested in getting a better grip on some of the key concepts that apply to their study. The editorial team considers that all the essential concepts required by new and beginning social workers, and for the con- tinuing professional development of more experienced social workers, are covered.

Concepts can be described as general constructs derived from specific instances. In looking at the particular on different occasions we can begin to capture gener- alisations which help our understanding. Some concepts gather considerable weight as their relevance to practice and 'usefulness' mean they become common parlance in professional circles. But sometimes we can look at concepts uncritically without beginning to question their evidence base and their rationale. This book of 'key concepts' is our attempt to extract a group of concepts which are the most helpful for social workers. As with any list, we appreciate that some will argue for a concept that ought to have been included, perhaps at the expense of one that is – but we simply hope that the reader will forgive us for those that are omitted and enjoy the ones that are chosen. Our hope is that the reader will appreciate the writers' endeavours in constructing this outline of key concepts – moving far beyond brief dictionary and encyclopaedia type entries to offer a robust and in-depth look at each concept.

The chapters are presented in alphabetical rather than thematic order and each chapter follows a broadly similar structure. A *definition* gives the reader a quick insight into what the concept means but also what other interpretations might exist in terms of understanding. There follows a small number of *key points* that attempt to provide a quick résumé of the debate. The *discussion* section of each chapter explores the concept, looking at significant and contemporary contributions which aid the reader in understanding the concept fully. The *concept in social work practice* section applies the concept to a practice setting, often through a case-study approach, and aims to assist in looking at how the concept operates in the real world. *Cross references* are made to related chapters and each author offers a list of *suggested reading* to continue learning about the concept in more depth and detail.

In selecting our authors for each chapter we have drawn on a wide range of experience and expertise. You will find chapters by service users, carers, practitioners, students, lecturers and professors, all – in their own and different ways – experts in their field, although some are beginning authors and some very experienced. But all are able to bring an understanding of each concept from their experience and share it with the reader.

As noted at the outset of the preface, social work is, in every sense, about change. At the time of writing, the profession is getting to grips with one of the most significant periods of change in its history. The Social Work Reform Board and the Munro Review process have set challenging agendas for change. September 2012 will see the introduction of the Assessed and Supported Year in Employment which develops and builds upon the previous Newly Qualified Social Worker programme. Here we see requirements around levels of supervision for workers, opportunities for professional development and workload relief. There are also substantial changes to many elements of the qualifying provision affecting admissions, curriculum, placement length and assessment. Continuing professional development emerges from the old Post Qualifying Framework into a broader, academic base. Binding many of these developments together is the new Professional Capability Framework offering benchmark statements for the multiple levels of a social worker's career and attempting to move beyond a 'tick box' competency approach. Meanwhile, Munro seeks significant changes in social work within childcare – looking to free professionals from the burdens of an overly bureaucratised, defensive system. The responsibilities of the General Social Care Council (GSCC) will largely be shifted to the Health and Care Professions Council (HCPC) in the summer of 2012 – as the GSCC closes in the dying embers of the 'bonfire of the quangos'. With the loss of the GSCC goes the Code of Practice which will be replaced (for social workers at least – and as far as we understand at the time of writing) by the HCPC's Standards of Conduct, Performance and Ethics. Readers will need to be aware of this shift as they read through the book, especially where debates around values are examined.

Within this maelstrom of change, the profession looks to the newly established College of Social Work to act as its voice. The College will hold most of these new developments in social work and social work education and clearly has a challenging task in implementing them – and moving the profession forward through this period. In such times as these, it is more important than ever to hold on to the knowledge, skill and value base of the profession – remembering that it is those elements which, despite all these changes in infrastructure and policy, are the ones that most influence our provision to service users.

Social work is, as we have noted, a complex and challenging profession. Its knowledge roots draw from a vast array of disciplines; notably sociology, social policy, psychology, etc. whilst also generating its own knowledge and research base. Some believe that this makes social work an indistinct profession, struggling under the weight of its diffusion. However, we strongly believe that social work's eclecticism is one of its greatest strengths. Social work needs to draw on this wide range of ideas and knowledge and fashion an individual knowledge base that captures the complexity and uncertainty that characterise modern social work practice. Social workers are, we believe, the great unsung heroes of the public sector – dealing with difficult scenarios and making tough decisions within a strong value base – every day. Part of the strength to do the job lies in the foundations of knowledge that are deployed in shaping those decisions and we hope this book offers a contribution that supports good social work practice.

Aidan Worsley, Tim Mann, Angela Olsen, Elizabeth Mason-Whitehead

Acknowledgements

There are many people the editors wish to acknowledge in the development of the book, but we are especially indebted, of course, to all the talented authors who have worked with us – many of whom come from the North West of England with its strong tradition of social work practice and education. Thanks especially to the staff of the universities of Central Lancashire, Chester and Salford who have given so much of their time. The staff at Sage have, throughout the production of the book, been supportive, informative and helpful and we are very grateful for their input. Many thanks to Kathryn Clements for her administrative support.

Aidan Worsley would like to dedicate this book to his grandchildren, Malachy McDonnell, Thea and Megan Littler – and to his dear friend Tom Mason.

Tim Mann dedicates this book to his lifelong best friend and wife, Chris.

Angela Olsen dedicates this book to Peter Olsen and Pat Kemp and to the memory of Bob, with love always.

Elizabeth Mason-Whitehead would like to dedicate this book to Miss Rhiannon Worsley.

key concepts in
social work practice

1
Accountability

Mike Thomas

DEFINITION

Accountability means being answerable to others and is related to responsibility. Being accountable in the professional context means being personally liable or obliged to fulfil a duty to others. One *takes* responsibility for actions but one is *held* accountable.

Social work encompasses the core skills, values and characteristics that define a particular branch of knowledge and activity recognised by society as important to its general well-being. The public develops trust and confidence due to the activities of its practitioners and the state usually acts on behalf of the public via a governance structure which oversees these activities, usually through statutory legislation. Roles and responsibilities are aspects of accountability and governance and require clear clarification through role descriptors, expected activities and employment standards. According to Archer and Cameron (2009), such activities are more effective if each team member knows their role and is able to carry most of the role independently of others. Educators and practice managers oversee the level of competence required to join a profession or to maintain continuing membership. They are accountable to statutory agencies such as professional bodies and the government. Having a professional, statutory and regulatory structure bestows certain responsibilities on practitioners; in other words, social work practitioners are expected to protect and support users, carers and fellow professionals. The state allows the practitioner to have a protected title which only they are allowed to use.

Accountability is important for the social work professional as it supports a degree of autonomous action prohibited in other fields of social care activity. Brown (2011) spoke in the context of the future of universities but has relevance to accountability when he points out that practitioners are more effective and efficient when they have a considerable degree of control over their work. However, in order to protect public safety, autonomous choices are restrained by the responsibilities imposed by state control. This is carried out through professional accreditation for the practitioner and through institutional auditing for organisations.

Social workers are obliged to support their governing body (the General Social Care Council until 2012 and thereafter the Health and Care Professions Council), and are liable to fulfil its regulations in its Code of Practice for Social Care Workers and its Code of Practice for Social Care Employers (GSCC, 2010) and the Care

Standards Act (2000) (subject to changes in the forthcoming Health and Social Care Act). Social work is accountable to its professional body which in turn is accountable to government.

KEY POINTS

- Accountability is intrinsically related to responsibility and authority.
- Accountability means being obliged and responsible to others.
- Social work has professional, statutory and regulatory guidance for accountability.
- Social workers agree to uphold and maintain professional accountability which is enshrined in legislation and provides them with a protected title.
- Related concepts are responsibility, trust and obligation (see Thomas, 2008).

DISCUSSION

The General Social Care Council (GSCC) held responsibilities for regulating the social work profession until its transfer to the Health and Care Professions Council in 2012. The GSCC regulated the profession via registration. All social workers must by law register with the GSCC in order to practise and following implementation of Section 61 of the Care Standards Act (2000), the title of Registered Social Worker (RSW) has been protected in England since 2005. In terms of public accountability, individuals may be in breach of the law if they declare themselves to be social workers when not registered. Even an implied reference to the title social worker can fall foul of the protected title legislation so employers are also responsible and accountable to the GSCC for ensuring that if there is a substantial amount of social work in a given role then it must be filled by a RSW.

Employers and practitioners have a legal obligation to ensure social work registration, qualifications and roles are met. There are two elements of accountability here; personal accountability to meet role achievement by acting as a professional at all times; and public accountability, to act in a way that is ascribed by society. Social workers have to demonstrate that they are safe to practise by undertaking a series of tests on their competence, accountability and responsibility.

The register of and eligibility for the RSW status is via educational assessments. Employers have a legal duty to assess whether an individual is capable of entering the profession and is suitable to provide social care. Registration involves an annual fee, ensuring professional development and an obligation to inform the Council of any changes in circumstances such as, change in employers, or criminal/disciplinary issues. Most practitioners are perhaps unaware that failure to provide minor changes in circumstances 'promptly' can lead to charges of misconduct. To be more efficient and effective the GSCC launched its Code of Practice for Social Care Workers for Employers in September 2002 following Section 62 of the Care Standards Act (DH, 2000). The codes were updated in 2004 and 2010 and empowered the Council to remove an individual from the Social Work Register. A prerequisite condition for entering the profession is an obligation by, and a personal responsibility for, all practitioners to adhere to the codes.

There are five professional codes for employers (25 specific sub-headings) and six for social work practitioners (41 specific sub-headings). Employer codes include their accountability to the public with guidance for ensuring only suitable individuals enter the profession. Their professional accountability specifically states that they must have written policies and procedures in place which enable social workers to meet the code of practice for practitioners and that they must promote the code of practice and co-operate with the professorial body.

Social work practitioners have their public accountability stated with codes providing guidance on protecting the rights and promoting the interests of service users and carers as well as avoiding harm and being trustworthy and honest. Social workers are to uphold public trust and confidence whilst personal accountability means that the practitioner must be accountable for the quality of work and be responsible for maintaining and improving knowledge and skills.

Accountability for social workers is statutory and the practitioner, alongside the employer, is responsible for ensuring the codes of practice are upheld. This is a professional obligation for which they carry legal liability and is controlled by the state to protect the public.

THE CONCEPT IN SOCIAL WORK PRACTICE

Social work practice has been the subject of much central interference since the conservative government of Margaret Thatcher in the 1980s. The 1989 White Paper, *Caring for People*, stressed greater central monitoring of community care and was hugely influential in reinforcing central state control and the eventual marketisation of social and healthcare. It provided three guiding principles to make the state system more effective: the right service should be provided early enough to meet the most needs; individuals should have more choice and say over services; and people should receive care in their own homes or in as near a domestic environment as possible. Baggot (1998) suggested that the impact of the *Caring for People* White Paper (DH, 1989) led to control of local authority community plans through the mechanism of central funding and a national monitoring system by joint audit commission and social services inspectorate's evaluations. Central control stopped local community care being local, prevented the inclusion of service users and their carers in planning, and increased management focus on outcome targets. This led to blurred areas of accountability, particularly when the reductions in social services clashed with the role of advocate for the social worker. State interference eventually culminated in the Blair government's emphasis on targets and evidence based outcomes with many different regulatory bodies.

However, Pyne (2000) argued that this did not meet the public demand for a unified professional regulatory system compared to the reluctance of the different professional bodies in health and social care to work collaboratively and to public concerns over safety and competence. Differences over which was the most appropriate method of exerting state power over the health and social care professions and which was the most appropriate professional and regulatory body have increased public confusion and pressure on the professional responsibility of social work.

accountability

3

Thomas et al. (2010) point out that since the turn of the century social work has been subject to more public scrutiny with attempts to increase accountability of practice through research-based evidence with little regard for the complexity of the situations in which social workers find themselves. Increasingly, accountability and responsibility are viewed as being controlled through protocols and problem-based approaches rather than individualised and reflexive approaches. Rogers and Pilgrim (2001) argue that social workers bring important perspectives to care which stem directly from the occupational base it holds in local community structures. Front-line practitioners see and understand the impact of social causation in poverty and daily stress; are frequently engaged in supporting individuals who are labelled as deviant by others; and apply theoretical models from the social and psychological sciences. As such they are responsible for others, act as advocates within services, often with deteriorating resources, and liaise with a range of other professionals who hold different theoretical frameworks for practice. In terms of public accountability, the activities of social work are therefore difficult to measure using the more ortho-dox approaches to health with outcomes, evidence-based protocols and targets.

It is no surprise that there is some tension regarding to whom the social work practitioner is accountable; the code states to the service user, the contract of employment states to the employer and the registration to the Council. The RSW is responsible to stakeholders depending on situational demands and the practi-tioner must apply their judgements in each context to ensure priority accountabil-ity, or to apply simultaneous accountability to different authorities. Accountability is not a fixed concept but a dynamic guide for practice which alters as the situation – local, political and historical – alters.

Social work has traditionally resisted attempts to have a state-imposed, centrally driven approach to social care and the response to calls for the introduction of evidence-based protocol approaches may account for the resurgence of interest in social work supervision. Yet this is not a new concept. Most approaches are based on Kadushin's model (1976) which highlighted the three main functions of super-vision as educative, developing the skills, understanding and abilities of a social worker; supportive, focusing on relational development; and managerial, examin-ing quality control, processes, ethics and employment standards. There is a respon-sibility for social workers to work collaboratively with colleagues too (Code 6.5) which includes supervising others in the workplace, line managing staff and, for educators, acting as tutorial supervisors.

Social workers are accountable for their actions at all times, even outside the work situation. They also have to juggle complex situations to ensure they remain accountable to a number of different authorities simultaneously whilst applying independent and autonomous decisions. The employer has responsibilities for ensuring that a RSW is compliant with professional and regulatory codes of prac-tice. Accountability and responsibility is shared between the employer and practi-tioner, but in the final analysis personal accountability and responsibility rests solely with the practitioner.

Cross references: advocacy, empowerment, professional development, quality assurance, values

SUGGESTED READING

Pollard, K.C., Thomas, J. and Miers, M. (2010) *Understanding Interprofessional Working in Health and Social Care*. London: Palgrave Macmillan.

Mccarthy, J. and Rose, P. (2010) *Values-Based Health and Social Care – Beyond Evidence-Based Practice*. London: Sage.

REFERENCES

Archer, D. and Cameron, A. (2009) *Collaborative Leadership*. London: Elsevier.

Baggot, R. (1998) *Health and Health Care in Britain*, 2nd edn. Basingstoke: Palgrave Macmillan.

Brown, R. (2011) *Higher Education and the Market*. New York: Routledge.

DH (Department of Health) (1989) *Caring for People*. White Paper. London: DH.

DH (Department of Health) (2000) Care Standards Act. London: DH.

GSCC (General Social Care Council) (2010) *Code of Practice for Social Care Workers and Code of Practice for Employers of Social Care Workers*. London: GSCC.

Kadushin, A. (1976) *Supervision in Social Work*. New York: Columbia University Press.

Pyne, R.H. (2000) 'Professional regulation: shaken but not stirred', *Consumer Policy Review*, 10(5): 167–73.

Rogers, A. and Pilgrim, D. (2001) *Mental Health Policy in Britain*. Basingstoke: Palgrave Macmillan.

Thomas, M. (2008) 'Accountability', in E. Mason-Whitehead, A. McIntosh, A. Bryan and T. Mason (eds), *Key Concepts in Nursing*. London: Sage, pp. 9–14.

Thomas, M., Burt, M. and Parkes, J. (2010) 'The emergence of evidence-based practice', in J. McCarthy and P. Rose (eds), *Values-Based Health and Social Care: Beyond Evidence-Based Practice*. London: Sage, pp. 3–22.

2
Adoption

Jules Clarke

DEFINITION

Adoption is a means of providing a permanent family for children who cannot be raised by their birth parents. Adoptive parents become the child's legal parents upon the making of an Adoption Order, they acquire parental responsibility (PR) and the child will usually take on their surname. Unless ongoing support services are to be provided, the local authority ceases involvement upon the making of the order. An Adoption Order is the only order in childcare law which severs the birth parents' parental responsibility and makes the child a legal, life-long member of another family.

Although the child no longer has a legal relationship with members of their birth family, they may continue to have occasional contact with them, either indirectly by letter through the adoption agency or, more unusually, face to face. Such contacts are aimed at developing the child's sense of self and their identity, rather than promoting attachments. Indeed, the child's primary attachments will be with their adoptive parents. Generally, adoption is now expected to be an open process whereby children grow up with a developing knowledge of their background, with the reasons for adoption provided by their adopters in an age appropriate way. At 18, adoptees have the right to access information from their adoption records and if they wish they can initiate searches. Birth family members are also able to search for adopted adults but only through an intermediary service and identifying information such as the child's adopted name or their address would not be disclosed without their permission.

The legislative framework for adoption is governed by the Adoption and Children Act 2002 which came into force in December 2005. This Act modernised adoption practice, bringing it into line with the Children Act 1989, and ensuring that the child's welfare was the paramount consideration in all decisions relating to adoption, including whether to dispense with parents' consent. Additionally, a comprehensive set of amended Adoption Regulation, Guidance and National Minimum Standards came into force in April 2011. These, combined with the Care Planning Placement and Review Regulations 2010, will be shaping the future of adoption and permanence planning for looked after children.

In social work practice adoption is considered a positive option for children who require permanence outside their birth family.

KEY POINTS

- Adoption is a process not an 'event'. It has a lifelong and life changing impact on those involved: children, adopters and birth families.
- Contemporary adoption practice aims to meet the needs of a broader range of children than ever before.
- It is acknowledged in practice and in law that children, their adopters and birth families may need support with adoption issues at various points in their lives.
- Adoption must be an open process. Children need to grow up knowing they are adopted and with a positive sense of self and their identity.
- Drift and delay in the care planning process is prejudicial to securing a child's future in alternative family care.

DISCUSSION

Adoption and attachment

The terminology of attachment theory is perhaps the most used and yet misunderstood theory and rhetoric in childcare social work. Suffice to say that the concepts of attachment and adoption practice are inextricably linked and worthy of much greater attention than space here allows. In short, our perception of the quality of our lives is measured to a great extent by the quality of our relationships. As children and adults we are more content and more resilient to adversity if our lives are enriched by a hierarchy of secure, reciprocal relationships. We now have a wealth of research to affirm that the 'warm, intimate and continuous relationship' which Bowlby (1953:13) described as so important to the developing infant, continues to impact our growth, sense of well-being, and interpersonal experiences into adult life. Children who have not had the experience of a sensitive, available caregiver or a 'secure base' (Ainsworth et al., 1978; Fahlberg, 2001) during critical formative years will be impacted adversely, particularly where the deficiencies of the caregiver are compounded by exposure to abuse, neglect, or multiple moves in the care system. How children assimilate their parenting, trauma, loss and separation is individual but we know that symptoms of early adversity can manifest in some or many aspects of their being, from physiological and neurological development to overtly challenging behaviour or extreme compliance. More often it will be observed in their attachment behaviour, based on their 'inner working model' and expectations of how relationships are made and maintained.

Though the implications of early separation, loss and trauma are unsurprisingly adverse and potentially enduring, there is much within associated literature to suggest the potential for change given the right intervention. Where children are to be adopted, that intervention will often involve planning for the child to experience the parenting they have missed ('re-parenting' Fahlberg, 2001) and building their resilience (Gilligan, 2009). Though seeming simple, such approaches challenge the child's inner working model and will require resilience, insight and patience on the part of the parent. As Schofield and Beek (2006) note, attachment theory continues to offer a scientifically rigorous and yet practical framework for making sense of children's troubled and challenging behaviours and for supporting caregivers in providing them with a secure base. However, prospective adopters come to the process with hopes, expectations and attachment patterns of their own. Increasingly, prospective adopters are engaged in Adult Attachment Interviews as part of their assessment process so that the strengths, vulnerabilities and 'fit' of respective attachment styles can be explored at matching (Steele et al., 2003). However good the proposed match, prospective adopters will nonetheless need to accept that the road to the parent-child relationship they aspire to is likely to be very different to that for a birth child.

As our understanding of the relevance of attachment theory to adoption has grown, so too has its application. In the first instance it is used to help us understand the presentation of the child, assess their needs and identify therapeutic services. It applies to the nature of sibling relationships and enables us to address dilemmas about whether they should be placed for adoption together or separately. It has relevance to the history and perspective of the birth parents and is evident in tools to assess and educate adopters. Attachment is also a key element in the child's need for permanence.

Adoption and permanence

The permanency movement began in the 1970s, spurred by the infamous Rowe and Lambert (1973) study which highlighted the large numbers of children drifting in the care system who had lost connections (attachments) with their birth families but had no plans for alternative care. Since then legislation and practice has swung with uncertainty between emphasis on reunification to birth families and timely permanence planning outside. At times along the way 'a permanence plan' became synonymous with 'an adoption placement', though in reality the options were really much broader (Selwyn, 2010). The Adoption and Children Act 2002 grew from ongoing concerns about drift in care and a body of new research evidence indicating poor outcomes for children in the system. The Act promoted adoption as a 'positive option' rather than a 'placement of last resort'. It sought to reduce delay, ensure more children were considered for adoption, and welcome a broader range of prospective adopters. Importantly, it recognised that adoption had lifelong implications for all involved, including birth families, and made provision for a range of support services.

The Care, Planning, Placement and Case Review Guidance (DfE, 2010b) has recently given renewed attention to permanence planning, ensuring that 'permanence should be a key consideration from the day a child becomes looked after'. Although adoption is not promoted above other options, it suggests that three dimensions are to be considered: a child's emotional permanence (attachment); physical permanence (stability); and legal permanence (the carer has parental responsibility for the child). Assuming a pre-existing opportunity for attachment and stability, the *legal* stipulation that a carer should have PR means that permanence by this holistic definition could only be achieved by a return to parents, special guardianship, residence order or adoption.

Some argue the emphasis remains upon the making of these ideological legal placements whereas permanence should be viewed as a 'state of mind not of placement' (Selwyn, 2010:32–7) and the child's capacity and opportunity to make and sustain lifelong relationships (attachments) should be addressed as the primary objective in care planning (Selwyn, 2010).

Whatever the legal status, outcomes for children undoubtedly improve when they are raised in stable, loving family environments. Though for many reasons, disruption rates can be a crude indicator of outcomes, they are commonly cited to compare the relative merits of placement options. Children adopted as infants appear to fare particularly well in terms of stability. Disruption rates are low and psycho social outcomes are positive, comparing favourably with the general population. Non-infant adoptions have higher disruption rates (on average around 20 per cent rising to 50 per cent for 11–12-year-olds) but those who remain have generally better outcomes than their peers in care. There is a growing body of research to indicate predictive and protective factors in relation to the child, adopters and planning. Across all placement options there is clear consensus that age placement is the most powerful determinant of disruption. Similarly, the length and severity of abuse, challenging behaviour, previous disruption, and number of placement moves, all contribute to risk. These are research messages which should inform permanence planning. Clearly, difficult decisions about the probability of reunification with birth parents need to be made in a timely way if other options are to provide the child with the lifelong meaningful attachments, stability and sense of belonging that they need.

THE CONCEPT IN SOCIAL WORK PRACTICE

Please see Chapter 21 for a shared case study.

The route to adoption

In March 2010, there were 64,400 looked after children by local authorities in England, 73 per cent were in foster placements and 4 per cent were placed for adoption.

During the year, 3,200 children were adopted from care and 1,260 Special Guardianship Orders were granted (DfE, 2010a).

Children who are adopted from care are either 'relinquished' by their birth parents or the adoption plan is 'contested' by them. Very few newborn babies are now relinquished by their parents. Children adopted with parental agreement will usually be accommodated first with foster carers whilst their consent is legally obtained and witnessed by a Cafcass officer (Children and Family Court Advisory and Support Service).

Most adopted children come through the care system. During court proceedings, placement with birth parents, relatives or connected persons will always be assessed in the first instance, and a 'twin tracking' approach is often used whereby the authority progresses an adoption plan at the same time as considering permanence options within the birth family to avoid delay. In 'concurrent placements' a child is placed with their prospective adopters rather than foster carers whilst the assessments of birth family take place, though this specialist practice is still rare in most agencies. Once the assessments indicate a child has no viable family alternative, a Placement Order is sought from the courts, to give the authority leave to place with approved adopters. A child can only be placed for adoption if the agency has parental consent or a Placement Order and the proposed match with approved adopters has been agreed by the adoption panel. A child must be in placement for a minimum of ten weeks before the family can apply to court for the Adoption Order.

There are few restrictions on who can apply to adopt – only age (applicants must be over 21); domicile and certain criminal offences are automatic bars. However, applicants will go through a thorough process of training and assessment before their application will be considered for approval by the adoption panel.

Children who wait longest for adoptive families are often older, part of sibling groups or have complex needs or uncertain developmental futures. It also proves harder to find families who can meet the needs of children from minority ethnic backgrounds. It is estimated that as many as a quarter of children with adoption plans may not have families found for them. Agencies are increasingly becoming skilled in family finding and recruitment. Additionally, since 1997, all local authority and voluntary agencies have been able to exchange details of waiting children and adopters with the Adoption Register for England and Wales, with a view to identifying links across the country. Whilst there is much contested debate about political correctness, rigidity in approval and matching criteria – there undoubtedly still exists a national mismatch between children who wait and approved adopters.

CONCLUSION

Decisions to place children outside their birth families are some of the most difficult in social work and there are lifelong implications for all those touched by adoption. Agency responsibilities to children, their adopters and birth families will play a determining role in adoption outcomes. Though it has to be accepted that disruption cannot be eradicated, the emotional cost to those involved should not be underestimated. Workers should ensure that their permanence planning is legally compliant, best interests driven and research informed.

Cross references: direct work with children, fostering, law and social work, looked after children, safeguarding children

SUGGESTED READING

Fahlberg, V. (2001) *A Child's Journey Through Placement*. London: British Association for Adoption and Fostering (BAAF).
Schofield, G. and Beek, M. (2006) *Attachment Handbook for Foster Care and Adoption*. London: British Association for Adoption and Fostering (BAAF).

REFERENCES

Ainsworth, M., Blehar, M., Waters, E. and Wall, S. (1978) *Patterns of Attachment: A Psychological Study of the Strange Situation*. Hillsdale, NJ: Erlbaum.
Bowlby, J. (1953) *Child Care and the Growth of Love*. London: Penguin.
DfE (Department for Education) (2010a) 'Children looked after by local authorities in England: statistical first release September 2010'. Available from: www.education.gov.uk/rsgateway/DB/SFR/s000960/index.shtml (accessed 31 May 2012).
DfE (Department for Education) (2010b) *The Children Act 1989 Guidance and Regulations. Volume 2: Care Planning, Placement and Case Review*. London: HMSO.
Fahlberg, V. (2001) *A Child's Journey Through Placement*. London: British Association for Adoption and Fostering (BAAF).
Gilligan, R. (2009) *Promoting Resilience: A Resource Guide on Working with Children in the Care System*. London: British Association for Adoption and Fostering (BAAF).
Rowe, J. and Lambert, L. (1973) *Children Who Wait: A Study of Children Needing Substitute Families*. London: British Association for Adoption and Fostering (BAAF).
Schofield, G. and Beek, M. (2006) *Attachment Handbook for Foster Care and Adoption*. London: British Association for Adoption and Fostering (BAAF).
Selwyn, J. (2010) 'The challenges in planning for permanency', *Adoption and Fostering*, 34(3): 32–7.
Steele, M., Kaniuk, J., Hodges, J., Haworth, C. and Huss, S. (2003) *The Use of the Adult Attachment Interview: Implications for Assessment in Adoption and Foster Care*. London: British Association for Adoption and Fostering (BAAF).

3
Advocacy
Andrea Pepe and Dan Redfearn

DEFINITION

Social workers often work with people who are disempowered and disenfranchised. A core aspect of their role should therefore be to understand people's needs, and work with – and on – their behalf to help them achieve the best possible outcomes. Advocacy is a crucial part of this process; it is about taking action to help people say what they want, secure their rights, represent their interests and obtain services they need (Action for Advocacy, 2002).

Advocacy supports a variety of methods through which service user needs can be expressed and includes: self-advocacy – where individuals are empowered to speak for themselves; group advocacy – where people who share a common experience work together to bring about change; and citizen advocacy – where a paid advocate or befriender speaks up on behalf of an individual. These can contribute to change on many levels, for the individual, a defined group, or more structurally, impacting on policy, legislation and the upholding of basic human rights (Bateman, 2000).

For a young, migrant family with three children under five living in a one-bedroom shared house after having to leave an abusive family, it might mean support to apply for council housing, getting housing benefit and council tax credits, opening bank accounts and registering with a GP. For a group of older people who are all tenants of the same housing association, it could be working together to get their old, rotting and malfunctioning windows and doors replaced. For the organisation Mind, it may be its role as a partner in a national campaign to end the discrimination faced by people who experience mental health problems through community projects, anti-stigma campaigns and legal challenges to discriminatory practices.

KEY POINTS

- People who are structurally disadvantaged may need support to access services and/or bring about change.
- People may be discriminated against and require support to address that discrimination.
- Grouping together over a common issue gives a stronger voice to bring about change.

advocacy

11

- People may not have the mental capacity or communication skills to make decisions and express their views and may need an advocate to support them to achieve the best possible outcomes.
- There are inherent tensions and potential conflicts of interest within the role of a social worker acting as an advocate.

DISCUSSION

Advocacy can take many forms which can be divided into two broad types: people who take action for themselves as individuals, or groups; and volunteers or paid professionals speaking up on behalf of others who are unable to do so through difficulties in communication, capacity, discrimination or powerlessness. Key aspects of advocacy that relate to social work practice are self-advocacy, the role of independent advocates, and the social worker as an advocate.

Advocacy is seen as one of the key roles of social work – users and carers specify that they expect the social worker to challenge and lobby services (including their own) in order to ensure fair access and treatment. This is an example of professional advocacy and as such may have limitations and conflicts of interest.

Social workers are often state officials and must take into account their statutory obligations, budgetary and organisational policies, procedural guidance and their code of practice. All of these may constrain their ability to fully advocate on behalf of the person they are working with. Additionally, legal powers in child protection, mental health or mental capacity can require the social worker to intervene in a manner that directly disempowers the service user, leaving them unable to advocate for their wishes (Leadbetter, 2002).

These tensions are demonstrated by Anna, a social worker in Greater Manchester. Anna identified conflicts with social work values and the idea of workers and users 'competing' for limited resources in a private conversation:

> My social work training emphasised positive assessment – promoting the strengths and independence of service users – yet representing individuals at resource allocation panels requires an emphasis on the bleakest picture in order to get anything . . . You are also very aware that getting support for one service user means another will miss out, particularly in the case of residential placements. In some situations I have been asking for the same placement for two of my users making advocacy an impossible task.

Given these conflicts, social workers need to ensure that service users are represented independently, and the occupational standards highlight the need to recognise when and how an independent advocate should be involved. There is a clear legal basis for independent advocates in certain situations such as where a person is judged to lack capacity to make certain decisions (Mental Capacity Act 2005), or when detained under the Mental Health Act (2007). The social worker should also be aware of independent advocacy organisations that can act and represent individuals on either a long term, or case basis. The danger is that such advocates are viewed as barriers that obstruct the social worker from 'doing their job'. To prevent this, it is important to remember that they are in essence the voice of the user and should be used as a tool to overcome some of the conflicts that the social worker has in acting as advocate.

Another way of overcoming these conflicts is to support people to speak up for themselves. Self-advocacy is an approach that originates in learning disability services to enable people to do just that. Shaun Webster, who has learning disabilities, and works at CHANGE, a campaigning organisation for the rights of people with learning disabilities, describes the impact that this approach can have. He has been involved in making information on parenting skills accessible, to empower people with learning disabilities. 'People with learning disabilities worked on the booklets and DVDs, everyone had a lot of power, and I never thought I would see that in my life time', he explained.

People and groups who are oppressed, not listened to and simply told what to do, often get to the point where they don't know how to make a decision for themselves. Self-advocacy is about giving these people the support and skills to speak up, and also about ensuring that those who need to hear can understand. It is not just about responding to a particular issue; it includes the development of broader skills that promote self-awareness, confidence and determination. This can be achieved through: sharing experiences; supporting one another; learning to speak up; finding out about rights and speaking up to local services (People First, 2011). Supporting individuals to speak up for themselves should be seen as an inherent feature of all forms of advocacy and whilst People First (2011) emphasise the user-led nature, there is a recognition elsewhere that other advocacy processes can enhance independence (Gray and Jackson, 2002). This closely links advocacy to concepts of empowerment (Thomas and Woods, 2003) and in social work, advocacy must sit within this wider understanding and be utilised as a tool to create not just opportunity for expression of views, but real change that supports personal and societal development.

These developments can have an impact beyond the original focus of the advocacy activity and can perhaps be seen most clearly when group action brings about change on a political or structural level. This can have a profound impact on an individual's experience, but it is also possible that what starts as individual action, can lead to changes impacting on a much wider group of people through change to practice and/or structures (Bateman, 2000). This can be evidenced through consideration of Alan's story.

THE CONCEPT IN SOCIAL WORK PRACTICE

Alan is a 33-year-old man with learning disabilities, he has three children aged ten, eight and four. Six years ago he asked for support from the social services children and families team. The social worker from this team had no experience of working with people with learning disabilities and her assessment and interventions led to Alan feeling disempowered. Information about the process and assessment was not accessible to him; the assessment tool was not adapted for working with parents with learning disabilities and did not recognise his strengths. The support and advice that was recommended did not account for his needs; for example, he was referred to a general parenting group on nutrition but the information and pace of the session did not account for his learning needs.

Alan was on the brink of being taken to court by the local authority with the aim of taking the children into care when a community nurse suggested that Alan go to the Learning Disability Team. Amy, the Learning Disability social worker, was able to listen to Alan and understand that the assessment process was not suited to assessing the parenting skills of people with learning disabilities, and that Alan had not fully understood the process that was taking place around him.

Amy was able to advocate on Alan's behalf in the following ways:

- identifying a suitable assessment tool which she passed on to the children and families team;
- offering training to the children and families team on working with parents with learning disabilities;
- putting Alan in contact with other parents with learning disabilities;
- accessing appropriate support for Alan and his children;
- supporting Alan to find good legal representation.

Alan went on to join a group of parents with learning disabilities facilitated by CHANGE. This group enabled him to feel less isolated and to recognise that the difficulties he had experienced were not about him but about the oppression and discrimination faced by people with learning disabilities. The group campaigned for guidance and training to be provided to social workers and health visitors working with parents with learning disabilities. As a result of the campaign, national guidance was produced by the government.

The children and families social worker may have been experiencing a conflict of interest within her role – the needs of the children versus the needs of the parent. There may also have been resource constraints influencing what support she was able to provide.

Amy was able to advocate for Alan because she had detailed, up-to-date knowledge of the particular issues facing parents with learning disabilities and the services and support available. She was able to communicate effectively with the children and families team which ensured that Alan was treated fairly and that parents with learning disabilities will be fairly assessed in future by the children and families team.

Alan felt listened to and empowered by having contact with other parents with learning disabilities. This enabled him to understand that his difficulties were not about him personally but as a result of oppression and discrimination. Alan's involvement with the parents' group and the formulation of the National Guidance further increased his confidence and his understanding of the oppression and discrimination faced by people with learning disabilities.

In order to fully support people to bring about the change they want in their lives, social workers must fully understand the function of advocacy and embrace the potential tensions in order to provide the type of advocacy that would most empower the person they are working with.

Cross references: empowerment, learning disability, mental capacity, mental health, service user involvement

REFERENCES

Action for Advocacy (2002) *The Advocacy Charter*. London: Action for Advocacy.

Bateman, N. (2000) *Advocacy Skills for Health and Social Care Professionals*. London: Jessica Kingsley Publishers.

Gray, B. and Jackson, R. (eds) (2002) *Advocacy and Learning Disability*. London: Jessica Kingsley Publishers.

Leadbetter, M. (2002) 'Empowerment and advocacy', in R. Adam, L. Dominelli and M. Payne (eds), *Social Work: Themes Issues and Critical Debates*. Basingstoke: Palgrave, pp.200–8.

People First (2011) 'What is self advocacy?' Available from: www.peoplefirstltd.com/what-is-self-advocacy.php (accessed 17 May 2011).

Thomas, D. and Woods, H. (2003) *Working with People with Learning Disabilities: Theory and Practice*. London: Jessica Kingsley Publishers.

4
Anti-Oppressive Practice

Jane Walker

DEFINITION

Oppression involves the inhuman or degrading treatment of individuals or groups. Injustice and hardship are brought about by the dominance of one group over another utilising the negative and demeaning exercise of power. It arises out of unfair discrimination based on notions that the dominant group is the 'norm' and that their characteristics are valued highly. Any individuals or groups who do not share the same characteristics as the dominant group have a corresponding lack of value. Central to this is the concept of an 'ideal' human being. People who share the same characteristics as those in the dominant group enjoy the privileges that come from this, as the dominant group have the power to exercise control.

Clifford (1995) suggests that the term 'anti-oppressive practice' refers to an explicit position that recognises that social divisions, particularly race, class, gender, disability, sexuality and age, are matters of broad social structure, whilst at the same time being personal and organisational issues. Anti-oppressive practice considers the use and abuse of power not only in relation to individual and organisational behaviour, but also in terms of the impact of the wider society on individuals' lives. Healy (2005) proposes that the key principles of anti-oppressive practice involve critical reflection of self in practice and a critical assessment of service users' experience of oppression.

The process of location allows us to challenge those who see only our visible differences, such as, our race and gender, while failing to take into account our invisible differences, such as, our class and sexuality. It is important to recognise that people may experience oppression on several different levels. For example, for an older black woman who is a lesbian it is the interconnected nature of the social divisions to which we belong that ultimately defines who we are and the nature of the oppression that we may experience. Arriving at an understanding of the concept of anti-oppressive practice involves acknowledging and attempting to understand the complexity of the impact of oppression and discrimination in people's lives as highlighted within practice situations.

KEY POINTS

- Oppression and anti-oppressive practice are closely linked to other concepts, including empowerment, equality, values and the impact of prejudice, stereotyping and discrimination.
- Anti-oppressive practice is embedded in a commitment towards social justice and human rights for all citizens.
- Anti-oppressive practice involves the critical reflection of self in practice and a critical assessment of service users' experience of oppression.
- Anti-oppressive practice promotes minimal intervention and avoids a disempowering style of practice that can consciously or unconsciously promote dependency on the worker/service.

DISCUSSION

'Empowerment' is a contested concept; however, most would agree that it involves individuals taking or being given more power over decisions affecting their welfare. It involves taking some power away from professionals and service providers. The term 'working in partnership' refers to negotiated practice in which users are active participants engaged with professionals in deciding on a course of action. Research (SCIE Guide 23, 2008) suggests that most service users believe that professionals 'know best' and want access to professional expertise, but identifies that the most effective partnerships are those resulting from a negotiation between those with expertise gained through personal experience and those with professional expertise.

'Equality' is often seen as being synonymous with the term 'equal opportunities' which relates to various forms of anti-discrimination in terms of employment and recruitment and is closely linked to anti-discrimination and legislation underpinning it. The Equality Act (EA) (2010) superseded all previous legislation relating to equality and brought them together under one Act. The concept of 'protected characteristics' has been introduced and identified as age, disability, gender reassignment, marriage and civil partnership, pregnancy and maternity, race, religion and belief (including lack of belief), sex and sexual orientation. The EA extends protection to people who are *associated* with someone who has protected characteristics, for example, a disabled relative. Section 13(1) of the EA (2010) makes it clear that if a person discriminates against another on grounds of a protected characteristic and treats the person less favourably than they would others, it is direct discrimination and as such is unlawful. The EA defines indirect discrimination as involving acts, decisions or policies which are not intended to treat anyone less favourably, but which in practice have the effect of disadvantaging a group of people with a protected characteristic. Section 158 of the EA permits the use of positive action (measures to alleviate disadvantage experienced by people who share a protected characteristic), in order to reduce under-representation/encourage participation in relation to particular activities and to meet their particular needs. Employers must however reasonably think that there is disadvantage, different needs or disproportionately low participation (Wadham et al., 2010).

The term 'prejudice' refers to an opinion or judgement formed without considering the relevant facts or arguments. It is a biased and intolerant attitude towards particular people or groups of people based on an opinion or attitude which is rigidly and irrationally maintained in the face of strong contradictory evidence. It is a rigid form of thinking based on stereotypes and discrimination and stands in the way of fair and non-judgemental practice.

'Discrimination' involves unfair or unequal treatment of individuals or groups based on actual or perceived differences. It is a matter of social formation as well as individual or group behaviour. In order to understand how inequality and discrimination features in the social circumstances of service users and in the interaction between service users and the welfare state, Thompson (2006) argues that it is helpful to analyse the situation in terms of three levels. They are closely interlinked and constantly interact with one another:

- The **personal** level involves individual thoughts, feelings, attitudes and actions;
- The **cultural** level involves a sense of common values and shared understanding and meaning;
- The **structural** level refers to the network of social divisions and the power relations related to them.

PCS Analysis shows the different levels at which discrimination operates and how these levels reinforce each other. Thompson (2006) argues that we need to move beyond the personal level, not only in terms of understanding discrimination but also in terms of tackling it.

THE CONCEPT IN SOCIAL WORK PRACTICE

As a social worker, it is important to recognise that you will often be working with people who are less valued by society. You need to recognise this and its impact on the individual/family and be prepared to support them to gain more control over their circumstances, as your knowledge and understanding needs to be developed and continually reflected on over time.

The values that social workers are expected to promote and uphold are highlighted in the General Social Care Council (GSCC) (2002) Code of Practice – soon to be updated by the Health and Care Professions Council. Banks (2006) suggests that the GSCC codes are enshrined in the principle of self-determination. Workers are expected to promote service users' rights. The importance of the service user–social worker relationship is also emphasised and particularly the values of respect for a person's intrinsic worth, right to confidentiality and to make their own decisions, provided this does not involve risk to self/others.

The International Federation of Social Workers (IFSW) (2001) defines social work as a profession that promotes social change, problem solving in human relationships and the empowerment and liberation of people to enhance well-being. Informed by theories of human behaviour and social systems, social work intervenes at points where people interact with their environments. Principles of human rights and social justice are fundamental. It may be that it is this political dimension which distinguishes social work from other professions as it has a pivotal position in terms of relationships between the state and citizens. It is important to recognise that this relationship is double-edged, with potential for empowerment and potential for oppression, highlighting the importance of reflective practice as the individual worker will usually determine which aspect is to the fore, either consciously or unconsciously. Thompson (2006) warns us that the tide of discrimination is so strong that unless we actively swim against it, it is inevitable that we will be carried along with it, as intervention either adds to oppression or goes some way towards easing or breaking it.

Reflexivity involves taking account of our own social location, values and perspectives, and our membership of social divisions, in relation to the particular 'other' involved in a situation. In social work practice, for example, assessment, practitioners need to consider the ways in which their own social identity and values affect the information they gather. This includes their understanding of the social world as experienced by themselves and those with whom they work. It may be beneficial for you to think about any dominant attitudes present within the family in which you grew up about a range of social groups. Can you identify how these may affect the way you practise? Can you identify any ways in which the structure of society might affect service users, their circumstances and problems? In what ways can you take the structural factors into consideration in practice? McDonald and Coleman (1999) warn against the dangers of subscribing to 'hierarchies of oppression'. Hierarchies create social divisions and can stimulate conflict between oppressed groups; for example, creating competition for 'scarce resources', contributing further to their experience of oppression. This can lead to divisive 'us and them' thinking and beliefs. In-fighting between groups of people on the margins is clearly in the interests of those in 'the centre' who can maintain a 'divide and rule' position.

Oppression should never be ranked or compartmentalised. We need to locate and understand individuals within the context of their lived experiences. It is important to recognise the specificity of different forms of oppression, whilst acknowledging how they interconnect. One aspect of a person's being should not be used to define their whole self. Anti-oppressive practice addresses the whole person and enables a practitioner to relate to the individual in a way that takes account of the resources that both bring to the relationship. Anti-oppressive practice takes on board personal, institutional, cultural and economic issues and examines how these impinge on individual behaviour and opportunities to develop their potential (Dominelli, 2002).

Preston-Shoot (1996, cited in Thompson, 2000) reminds us of the importance of challenging oppression, suggesting that if we lose the ability to question injustice, we risk losing the empathy, values and practice skills which seek to counter the inequalities, internalised oppression, alienation and exclusion characteristic of contemporary social life. Although this is not always easy to achieve, it is important not to become overwhelmed by the enormity of the problems of inequality and injustice as a negative attitude is disabling. It is helpful to reflect from time to time on what it was that led one to undertake social work training. The chances are that 'wanting to make a difference' was high on a list of reasons. Social work *can* use its position to promote an empowering difference.

Cross references: empowerment, reflection, social justice, values

SUGGESTED READING

Dominelli, L. (2002) *Anti-Oppressive Social Work Theory and Practice*. Basingstoke: Palgrave Macmillan.
Laird, S.E. (2008) *Anti-Oppressive Social Work: A Guide for Developing Cultural Competence*. London: Sage.

REFERENCES

Banks, S. (2006) *Ethics and Values in Social Work*, 3rd edn. Basingstoke: Macmillan.
Clifford, D.J. (1995) 'Methods in oral history and social work', in R. Adams, L. Dominelli and M. Payne (eds) (2009) *Critical Practice in Social Work*. Basingstoke: Macmillan, pp. 209–19.
Dominelli, L. (2002) *Anti-Oppressive Social Work Theory and Practice*. Basingstoke: Palgrave Macmillan.
General Social Care Council (GSCC) (2002) *Code of Practice for Social Care Workers and Employers*. London: GSCC.
Healy, K. (2005) *Social Work Theories in Context: Creating Frameworks for Practice*. Basingstoke: Macmillan.
International Federation of Social Workers (IFSW) (2001) *Definition of Social Work, Ethics in Social Work: Statement of Principles*. IFSW. Available from: www.ifsw.org/policies/code-of-ethics (accessed 28 May 2012).
McDonald, P. and Coleman, M. (1999) 'Deconstructing hierarchies of oppression and adopting a "multiple model" approach to anti-oppressive practice', *Social Work Education*, 18(1): 19–33.
Preston-Shoot, M. (1996) in N. Thompson (2000) *Understanding Social Work: Preparing for Practice*. Basingstoke: Palgrave Macmillan, p.7.
SCIE Guide 23 (2008) *The Learning, Teaching and Assessment of Partnership Work in Social Work Education*. Social Care Institute for Excellence. Available at www.scie.org.uk/publications/guides/guide23/index.asp (accessed 12 June 2012).
Thompson, N. (2006) *Anti-Discriminatory Practice*, 4th edn. Basingstoke: Macmillan.
Wadham, J., Robinson, A., Ruebain, D. and Uppall, S. (eds) (2010) *Blackstone's Guide to the Equality Act*. Oxford: Oxford University Press.

5
Assessment

Patrick O'Byrne

DEFINITION

On reading a book on assessment, a colleague was heard to comment 'but all of social work is here' and, of course, that is true especially in terms of values, good engagement with service users, use of theory, helpful questioning, skills, etc. The reverse can also be true, in that all of social work involves some assessment thinking.

Crisp et al. (2005) found that there was no universally agreed definition of assessment. Kemshall (2002) said it is a process of professional judgement or appraisal of the situation, circumstances and behaviour. Compton and Galaway (1999) described assessment as the collection and processing of data to provide information for use in making decisions about the nature of a problem and what is to be done about it. Coulshed and Orme (2006) said it was an ongoing process in which the service user participates, the purpose of which is to understand people in relation to their environment.

Milner and O'Byrne (2009) define it as a five-stage process of exploring a situation by:

1 preparing for the task;
2 collecting data, personal details, reports relevant to the current situation including perceptions of the service user, the family and other agencies, of the problem and any attempted solutions;
3 seeking analysis, understanding and interpreting data by applying professional knowledge (practice wisdom as well as theory);
4 making judgements about the relationships, needs, risks, standard of care or safety, the seriousness of the situation and people's capacities for coping or potential for engaging in change;
5 deciding and/or recommending what is to be done, how, by whom, when, and how progress will be reviewed.

In practice, the concepts implicit in these five stages are not simply distinct steps: one's theories, beliefs about people, about causes of problems, about evaluating risk, affect all the stages. Stage 3 can affect the others. Our cultural norms and biases, for example, towards standards of childcare, influence judgements and decisions. Frameworks may set out details of the data to be collected, but these may cause some to use them as check-lists to be ticked off – they do not, in themselves, contribute to weighing the significance of the information, or to knowing what depth of understanding is required. The data collection in serious assessment is potentially endless, so there is an inevitable selecting, editing and prioritising, requiring professional judgement and a theoretical background, some 'maps' to help on the journey (see Milner and O'Byrne, 2009, for a selection of such maps).

KEY POINTS

- process
- collaboration
- reflexivity
- balance
- constructiveness

DISCUSSION

Process

The word 'process' is important in that assessment is more than a one-off event. It includes relationship-building, interviews, working through the five stages, reflection and re-assessment in consultation with colleagues and supervisors. Some so-called assessments may be just checking eligibility against set criteria, for example, eligibility for bath aids. That task is more accurately named 'one-off data collection only'. Munro (2011) makes the point very well, that social workers, except in acute emergencies, must be given the time they need to develop a working relationship with people and to develop user participation. In the recent past, the process has been over-managed and service user feedback sidelined. A service user is quoted in Munro (2011: preface) as saying:

> You have to know someone, trust them. They must be reliable and be there for you if you are going to talk about things you don't want to, things that scare you.

This cannot usually happen during a one-off contact.

Collaboration

Without collaboration the work will feel intrusive, and potential service users will feel we are intruding in their lives and will naturally become evasive. This can snowball into our moving up the scale of intrusiveness – a complex decision as it can carry losses as well as gains, especially in a complex situation. Collaboration means attempting to bridge the 'gaps' between social worker and service user, negotiating perceptions, being open and transparent about our agenda, about our reasons for seeing them, while showing that we are against the problem but *for* the person/s. Skills such as externalisation of problems (separating the person/s from the problem), circular questioning, exception-finding questions, and scaled questions help in promoting active participation and empowerment. Such empowerment promotes independence, support, protection and helps to balance rights with risks. This will not happen if people feel we see them as the problem – it helps in most cases to keep the problem as 'the problem' and get the person to be an ally in dealing with it. Collaboration also includes our being respectful and maintaining an anti-oppressive stance (see, for example, Thompson, 2006). Basic respect such as being on time for appointments, keeping our promises and showing people what we write about them in a meeting, makes for a good start. Nowadays, records are expected to show how partnership is developed in each case.

Reflexivity

This differs from 'reflection'. Reflection means thinking about an action afterwards, looking back on it and perhaps learning from a mistake. This however leaves the action unchanged. Reflexivity is taken to mean reflecting during an action and changing what we are doing as we do it – reflection in doing, rather than after doing. It also involves checking what is happening between people and us, and checking one's interpretations with others. Top-down regulation has contributed to what Munro describes as a 'compliance culture' (compliance with guidelines), whereas what is needed is a 'learning culture' that facilitates constant questioning of how we are doing, how we are perceived by service users and how well we are working with them and they with us.

We need to be reflexive enough to be able to make our hypotheses explicit at least to ourselves, so that we invite evidence for the opposite, for what might be needed in order to be able to see other outcomes as possibilities, so that the 'what to do' is fully considered before our thoughts move on to how and by whom it could be done.

Possibly the most important aspect of reflexivity is ensuring that we have more than one hypothesis, being aware of our theories and the assumptions on which they are founded, including ideas of our own which have developed through experience. We need to be on guard against shaping the data to fit our theory or to prove our one hypothesis. Better to consider whether it could be disproved. Perhaps seeking to improve it would be wiser?

Balance

This is closely related to reflexivity and greatly dependent on it. Simply put, it means keeping a balance of focus between problems/deficits on the one hand, and strengths/positives/possibilities, on the other. Most assessments contain more information about difficulties than about strengths. In our initial assessments especially, all the facts will naturally belong to the problem unless we make a constant effort to seek data that could belong to strengths and potentials or that could hold the seeds of solution or improvement.

THE CONCEPT IN SOCIAL WORK PRACTICE

Case study

A teacher once consulted me about a boy whom she described as the biggest problem in the school. The list of complaints was long, he was a problem to teachers and to other pupils, his parents were hostile to staff, he was abusive, a constant distraction and he was aggressive to everyone. She added several examples of these faults. I asked:

- What does he look like? – 'He is usually smart and he obviously looks after his clothes.'
- Do you know if he has any friends? – 'Yes, he comes to school with some other pupils, boys and girls, who are not problems.'
- Is there a teacher who gets on reasonably well with him? –'Yes, two of the younger members of staff.'
- Does he sometimes do his work satisfactorily? – 'Sometimes, usually for the teachers with whom he related better.'
- What were his parents like before the difficulties escalated? – 'I am not aware of any incidents with them.'
- Given this information, is it possible that there is more to him than meets the eye? – 'Possibly.'
- Who might be able to tell us more about his ability to behave well? – 'I suppose the two teachers to whom he relates well, and perhaps his parents.'
- Just to get started, could you try to catch him behaving well in school a few times, so you could compliment him and work out with him how he does it? – 'I will let you know how I get on.'

The 'problem-saturated story' had so dominated her thinking that she had been blind to, or had edited out, any positives and thereby could see no way of working with him, until these fairly obvious questions raised possibilities of other 'truths' about him and of strengths and abilities that sowed seeds of hope, allowing virtually a different boy to emerge.

In safeguarding practice, a balance between signs of danger/risk and signs of safety is important (see, for example, Milner and O'Byrne, 2009; Turnell, in press; Turnell and Essex, 2006). Prescribed frameworks such as the Single Assessment Process and the Common Assessment Framework ought to help with balance by requesting an examination of strengths as well as difficulties, but they fail to do so. They are more like a shopping list of deficits, so a deliberate effort is required to keep balance when using these frameworks. We will miss strengths unless we deliberately look for them under most of the headings. Meanwhile some social services departments are now developing their own balanced and constructive guidelines (see Munro, 2011).

Constructiveness

To some extent this flows from the first four points. It includes helpfully using any working relationship developed to test motivation, abilities and willingness to address the problem. It requires the integrity to honestly listen to the views of all concerned, not only about the difficulty itself but about the ideas of others, about various explanations, including ours, and about ideas concerning what needs to happen so that we can disengage. This could be described as planning or working with people towards the ending from the very beginning. It means not just thinking about to whom to refer the work, but directly working with people in considering and testing their ability to do more of what is helpful and not just less of what is not, and to start to build safety where it is needed.

It requires that we be sceptical about traditional positivistic thinking that sought to produce certain understandings of the nature of human difficulties and of what was normal. In the 21st century, when much of what is social is considered to be constructed by the language that describes it, we feel we cannot rely on such positivistic explanations. For this postmodern age, the subjective meanings of people who are experiencing difficulties are being seen as central, as are accounts of their world view. A constructionist approach considers that what is needed for change to happen is an awareness of these inner 'realities', some imagination on the workers' part, goal clarity, some willingness and confidence about attaining change. Needs, risks and resources are a consideration in any assessment. By resources I mean not only the ever more scarce external resources but the all-important internal resources of the service user/s, their family and others who could contribute. The last question put to the teacher in the above case study is an example of constructiveness.

Constructiveness therefore involves being creative about locating real evidence that backs up our judgements; for instance, judgements about people's ability and determination to change. It involves mobilising people's abilities. Where service users are willing to work on change we can negotiate time for them to prove they can do it, or to understand what help they might need towards that end, and whether that help can be successful. This is co-constructing with them new data for a positive story. Of course, where people are unable to do this, that information will be equally clarified. Parton and O'Byrne (2000: 188–200) offer a range of progress scales that help in measuring progress, or the lack of it, in a collaborative and constructive way.

CONCLUSION

Assessment is a complex, demanding and in some ways controversial activity. It is much more than collecting data by filling in a form. It is generally acknowledged to be crucial, particularly in statutory social work. But because it partly relies on positivist notions of being able to clearly know reality, it has invited practitioners to attempt to present data and judgements about them as if they were certain (see Parton and O'Byrne, 2000: Chapter 8). Courts and other public services expect a measure of certainty and clarity about social situations that is not always available.

Some of the judgements we are called upon to make are laden with moral and civic issues, such as responsibility taking, which are not easily defined. To pretend that there is certainty where there is none cannot be good practice. We can be open about the moral nature of assessment and avoid showing false certainty. We can also work with people in a way that provides sound evidence to support a judgement by testing possibilities in action. This could be described as assessment through helping, rather than before helping. Every extra hour spent on constructive assessment can save many hours of costly interventions.

Cross references: anti-oppressive practice, critical thinking, empowerment, risk assessment and risk management, theory and social work

SUGGESTED READING

Adams, R., Dominelli, L. and Payne, M. (2002) *Critical Practice in Social Work*. Basingstoke: Palgrave.
Milner, J. and O'Byrne, P. (2009) *Assessment in Social Work*, 3rd edn. Basingstoke: Palgrave.

REFERENCES

Compton, B.R. and Galaway, B. (1999) *Social Work Processes*. London: Brooks/Cole.
Coulshed, V. and Orme, J. (2006) *Social Work Practice: An Introduction*, 4th edn. Basingstoke: Palgrave.
Crisp, B.R., Anderson, M.R., Orme, J. and Green Lister, P. (2005) *Learning and Teaching in Social Work Education: Textbooks and Frameworks on Assessment*. London: Social Care Institute of Excellence.
Kemshall, H. (2002) *Risk, Social Policy and Welfare*. Buckingham: Open University Press.
Milner, J. and O'Byrne, P. (2009) *Assessment in Social Work*, 3rd edn. Basingstoke: Palgrave Macmillan.
Munro, E. (2011) *The Munro Review of Child Protection: Final Report – A Child Centred System*. London: Department of Education.
Parton, N. and O'Byrne, P. (2000) *Constructive Social Work*. Basingstoke: Palgrave Macmillan.
Thompson, N. (2006) *Anti-Discriminatory Practice*, 4th edn. Basingstoke: Palgrave Macmillan.
Turnell, A. (in press) *Building Safety in Child Protection Practice*. London: Palgrave.
Turnell, A. and Essex, S. (2006) *Working with 'Denied' Child Abuse: The Resolutions Approach*. Maidenhead: Open University Press.

6

Asylum Seekers and Refugees

Debra Hayes

DEFINITIONS

Providing definitions in the arena of immigration can be problematic. Historically, words like 'immigrant' and 'alien' took on additional meaning in the popular mind, becoming shorthand for 'black' or 'Jewish'. Today the term 'asylum seeker' conjures up an image which is predominantly male, poor and non-white. It is a phrase tied up with notions of illegality, negativity, social cost and welfare burden. It sits alongside the term 'refugee', the words often used interchangeably and unhelpfully.

In fact, the term asylum seeker is a relatively modern one and has only dominated immigration discussion since the 1990s. It is best understood by firstly unpacking the term 'refugee' which is enshrined in the UN Convention on the Status of Refugees of 1951. Article 1(A) lays down this status as pertaining to someone who is outside the country of their nationality or is unwilling to return to it and who must have a 'well-founded fear of being persecuted for reason of race, religion, nationality, membership of a particular social group or political opinion . . .'. The person becomes a refugee when recognised as such by the state whose protection they have sought. Whilst many flee and seek that refuge in the UK, only those who successfully claim political asylum are recognised formally and legally as refugees. This is then referred to as 'Leave to Remain' (Fell and Hayes, 2007: 149). The much larger number of those who apply for that protection and are in the decision-making process are those we refer to as 'asylum seekers'.

KEY POINTS

- Immigration status determines welfare eligibility. What you are entitled to in benefits and services, including those managed by social work, depends on who you are.
- Asylum seekers are supported through a completely separate and inferior welfare system emerging in the late 1990s and involving dispersal on a 'no choice' basis into particular communities.
- This asylum system has, over the last decade, created a new layer of 'failed' or 'refused' asylum seekers, many of whom then become outside ALL support. The destitution arising from this is now dominating agencies who work with asylum seekers.
- Asylum seekers may present in just about any social work practice arena, whether or not they are eligible for services. Asylum seekers may be older people, disabled people, have mental health needs, have children or indeed be children separated from their families or carers.

DISCUSSION

Immigration controls did not of course begin with asylum systems. They are the modern expression of a longer history of controlling 'outsiders'. Those controls have operated at borders managing who can gain entry to the UK but they also operate within the UK – managing what happens to those non-citizens who do enter and reside. Central to this is the concern that there should be constraints on access to the public purse and in particular to welfare provision (Cohen et al., 2002). These *internal* controls should be of concern to social work as they rely, not only on immigration officials or the police, but sometimes on the local state and welfare organisations to make decisions about eligibility for services.

Importantly, there are migrants legally resident in the UK who are neither asylum seekers nor refugees but who are subject to immigration control and consequently also face differential access to welfare. The 'no recourse to public funds' rule, central to UK immigration control, further illustrates the point that you may be allowed to enter and reside as long as you can prove you won't need access to public money. You may be given permission to live in the UK but will not be able to claim most benefits, tax credits or housing assistance that are paid by the state (Home Office, UK Border Agency, Public Funds).

The current asylum system as we know it rests on a key piece of legislation, the 1999 Immigration and Asylum Act. It is extremely significant in that it completely separated this group from access to normal welfare, creating a different and inferior system. This system involves a one-option only offer of accommodation in a specific area and subsistence level support while the claim for asylum is being processed. The concept of 'dispersal' and the creation of dispersal zones, managed by regional consortia, has been significant; firstly in constructing the asylum seeker as a burden to be spread, and secondly, in the creation of new communities of individuals and families who are living at subsistence level in areas not of their choice. No longer can they gravitate to pre-existing and well established migrant communities, but find themselves in poor quality accommodation, often in economically deprived areas and dependant on small cash payments (for a fuller discussion on this see Robinson et al., 2003: 123–47). Normally, asylum seekers are not allowed to work which adds to the poverty and social exclusion experienced within these dispersal communities. Later, I will explore the issues raised for social work by these new communities, but in concluding this section, I want to underline one further point. There has been a history of scaremongering in immigration discourse which uses statistics and focuses on numbers to create a sense of panic. The truth is, the UK, since 2005, receives around 25,000 asylum applications per year. This is less than many European countries and a fraction of the world's displaced people. In fact it amounts to far fewer people than attend a typical Premiership football match at a weekend. Of these, the overwhelming majority (72 per cent) will fail in their claim for asylum (Home Office, 2009: 15). Despite the fact that the countries producing the majority of asylum seekers to the UK are places we know to be in serious crisis, for example, Iraq, Afghanistan, Zimbabwe, the bulk of the claims for refuge will not be considered founded. To be clear then, the majority of those resident in dispersal zones will not be successful in their attempt to gain protection in the UK. Only a small percentage will gain refugee status and then access normal welfare entitlements. It is the vast majority of these refused asylum seekers who now pose the challenge to our profession.

THE CONCEPT IN SOCIAL WORK PRACTICE

In order to manage dispersal, statutory asylum teams have been created in those regions involved. Individuals and families being dispersed are allocated accommodation, doctors and school places if necessary. The systems which have emerged also engage voluntary organisations who have been contracted to undertake some of the work. We have seen what might have been small refugee organisations grow into large scale agencies involved in managing this dispersal. Additionally, there has been a blossoming of a wider layer of voluntary agencies, charities, churches, mosques, housing organisations and the like who have responded to the needs of these new communities and do invaluable work. Whether or not these agencies include qualified social workers, or indeed identify themselves as social work agencies, they do work which we recognise in our profession. Evidence of this can be seen in the plethora of social work practice placements in asylum agencies now used on social work degree courses.

In terms of the work of the mainstream statutory social work sector, the impact of asylum and dispersal has been uneven. In the context of marketisation and resource constraint, asylum seekers could not have been thrust into dispersal zones at a worst time. Underlining the separateness and ineligibility of this group, statutory services have resisted responsibility. In areas of mental health, older people, disability, we have seen the use of case law to clarify rights and entitlements. The Slough judgement (House of Lords, 2008) has been central in determining just when the needs of an asylum seeker become serious enough for access to mainstream services. This judgement clarified Local Authority responsibilities under Section 21 of the National Assistance Act 1948 and ruled that individuals had to have a care need above and beyond the provision of accommodation, such as personal care, to qualify for support.

One section of statutory social work which has not been able to escape responsibility has been the childcare arena. Unaccompanied asylum-seeking children (UASC) make up a small proportion of the asylum population. Around 3,000–4,000 children annually claim asylum in their own right (Crawley, 2007: 2). These children, unlike those in asylum-seeking families, are the clear responsibility of the local authorities where they present. They have rights therefore to Section 20 support under the Children Act which may also extend to support under Leaving Care Act provision. This group amongst all asylum seekers, have focused the attention of statutory social work. Unfortunately, over the last decade we have seen the escalation of challenges to childhood status within this group. Now up to half of all UASC face an age dispute with a systematic culture of disbelief permeating their relationship with childcare services. Where age disputes occur it becomes necessary to conduct age assessments to decide upon status. This imprecise and heavily criticised process (Crawley, 2007) has become a role and function provided by the social work profession. Again we find ourselves on contentious terrain and it may be the same local authority conducting the age assessment which then picks up the bill for support, potentially up to the age of 21. The consequences are obvious in an era of financial constraint and the culture of disbelief should be of concern if we are to work effectively with this vulnerable group (for a fuller discussion on working with UASC, see Kohli, 2007).

CONCLUSION

In conclusion I wish to focus on a growing challenge facing asylum communities. As the asylum system has become embedded over the last decade, appeal rights have been eroded and speedier decisions have brought claims for asylum to their conclusion, we are seeing large numbers of individuals and families at the end of the process. To reiterate points made earlier, the majority of those decisions will result in a refused claim for asylum. In these situations the next step involves the withdrawal of support, including eviction from accommodation. Some will agree to voluntary return and will then be allowed short-term emergency support (known as 'Section 4'), currently of around £35 per week in the form of vouchers. Many will simply go 'underground' and be left to the insecurities and dangers of the illegitimate economy. Some will present for help at the doors of homeless and asylum organisations (Lewis, 2009). Social work at its most basic level – the social work of food parcels, soup kitchens and sleeping bags – is alive and well in 21st century Britain. The challenge is a practical one of enormous proportions, but it is also a challenge to our ethics and values, a challenge to our profession's very purpose and function. How we face up to it will continue to illuminate both the best and worst of modern social work practice.

Cross references: equality and diversity, international social work, safeguarding adults, safeguarding children

SUGGESTED READING

Home Office, UK Border Agency, and Public Funds. Available from: www.ukba.homeoffice.gov.uk/publicfunds
Kohli, R.K.S (2007) *Social Work with Unaccompanied Asylum seeking Children.* Basingstoke: Palgrave Macmillan.
Newbigging, K. and Thomas, N. (2010) 'Good practice in social care for asylum seekers and refugees'. Available from: www.scie.org.uk

REFERENCES

Cohen, S., Humphries, B. and Mynott, E. (2002) *From Immigration Controls to Welfare Controls.* London: Routledge.
Crawley, H. (2007) 'When is a child not a child? Asylum, age disputes and the process of age assessment'. Immigration Law Practitioners Association. Available from: www.ilpa.org.uk (accessed 4 June 2012)
Fell, P. and Hayes, D. (2007) *What Are They Doing Here? A Critical Guide to Asylum and Immigration.* Birmingham: Venture Press.
Home Office (2009) 'Control of immigration statistics, UK'. Available from: www.homeoffice.gov.uk/publications/science-research-statistics/research-statistics/immigration-asylum-research/hosb1510/ (accessed 20 May 2012).
House of Lords (2008) 'R v Slough Borough Council, 2008'. Available from: www.publications.parliament.uk/pa/ld200708/ldjudgmt/jd080730/rmfc-1.htm (accessed 20 May 2012).
Lewis, H. (2009) 'Still destitute, a worsening problem for refused asylum seekers'. Joseph Rowntree Charitable Trust. Available from: www.jrct.org.uk (accessed 4 June 2012).
Robinson, V., Andersson, R. and Muster, S. (2003) *Spreading the Burden? A Review of Policies to Disperse Asylum Seekers and Refugees.* Bristol: Policy Press.
UN Convention on the Status of Refugees (1951) 'Article 1(A)'. Available from: www.unhcr.org (accessed 4 June 2012).

7

Care Management

Helen Fruin

DEFINITION

The term care management is linked more to adult care than children's, and was introduced via the NHS and Community Care Act 1990 (Brown, 2010), in conjunction with concepts such as service user choice, needs led assessments, a mixed economy of care, costing, and care in the community. Social work and nurse managers for the first time were given devolved budgets, and asked to cost care in units of hours or days (Netten and Beecham, 1993). Prior to this, services were largely 'in-house' with little or no costings required by social work staff. With this new budgetary responsibility, social workers were asked to devise 'care packages' which required more detailed assessments of service user and carer needs, to formulate individual care plans in partnership with service users, and to utilise a range of formal and informal support, which then had to be costed, monitored, and reviewed.

Hence, the management of these different tasks required a co-ordinator or 'care manager': Interestingly, the question then arose as to whether social workers in adult care should be known more as social workers or care managers. For the purpose of this chapter, care management will be discussed in terms of its application to adult care in England.

KEY POINTS

- Policy range and change: There are over 20 years of ongoing policy developments in care management.
- Initial care management processes: This involves prioritising and assessing the presenting needs, and then care planning with partners.
- Accessing, evaluating and adjusting a care package: This includes issues around commissioning services, and monitoring and reviewing the effectiveness of a care package.
- Choice: Consideration of personalised care arrangements alongside financial and practical constraints.

DISCUSSION

Care management policy development

Two decades of policy changes in this area would be difficult to explore in a short discussion, but a very brief selection for further research would be the NHS and

Community Care Act 1990, Fair Access to Care Services (FACS)' *Guidance on Eligibility Criteria for Adult Social Care* (FACS, 2002), and *Our Health, Our Care, Our Say* (DH, 2006).

The latter two policy guidance papers, alongside many others, have developed the care management concepts and application of the original NHS and Community Care Act 1990 in terms of key areas relating to how local authorities decide who is eligible for assessment and services (FACS, 2002), and how service users might manage or self-direct their own care package budgets (DH, 2006). These two examples underpin the above key points, which will be discussed below.

Initial care management processes: assessing priority needs and care planning with partners

The care management process begins at referral, where typically social care/workers or their manager prioritises whether the service user referred requires an immediate response, or whether they can wait a short time (days or even weeks) before they are assessed for services. FACS guidance outlines four main categories of urgency, briefly summarised below:

- Critical: The highest risk, where a person's life may be threatened due to acute illness, lack of personal care, neglect, or abuse;
- Substantial: Where abuse or neglect is probable, and where personal care is largely insubstantial;
- Moderate: Where several aspects of personal care are not carried out;
- Low: Where one to two personal care tasks are not carried out.

The 'gatekeeping' role of the social care/worker thus starts before any assessment takes place, as many referrals are deemed low or moderate, and councils may only choose to fully respond to referrals of critical or substantial risk.

Once service users are deemed eligible for assessment, they will be assessed by a qualified social worker or a social care colleague. Again, this will vary according to the complexity and urgency of the service user's situation and staffing responsibilities and availability. When an assessment is completed with as much input from the service user (and carer) as possible, the process of planning a care package continues. The philosophy of care management promotes a creative use of resources and individually tailored care arrangements, where skilled and experienced workers aim to utilise the strengths of service users and their existing support networks (carers, social groups, neighbours, etc.), as well as voluntary agencies, which are taking on increasingly diverse and complex supportive roles. When informal networks cannot support service users sufficiently, social work staff apply to managers for funding for services, as many are chargeable, whether they are with private agencies or still within the control of council services, such as day centres. The social worker may also refer to other statutory services such as those within the NHS, which may or may not be chargeable, in other words, an occupational therapy *assessment* may not be chargeable but the *aids* recommended by this service might be.

Finances are thus pivotal to care management, and assessments are crucial in determining levels of need and care, with encouragement to work in partnership with service users, carers and other professionals. Hence the promotion of multi-agency working and a single assessment process whereby a lead professional (typically a social worker or nurse) holds the main responsibility for holistically assessing the needs of a service user with appropriate colleagues, as opposed to lots of professionals carrying out their own separate assessments.

Accessing, evaluating and adjusting a care package: issues around commissioning and effectiveness

Social workers are often referred to as care managers or even care brokers, which emphasises the financial commissioning role of social workers working with adults. Many students and newly qualified social workers are often perturbed by the degree of financial 'mindfulness' that is now needed in adult social care management.

Accessing a good range and quality of services is a challenge for social workers. Services such as private domiciliary care agencies may have large 'block contracts' with councils, and thus social workers may only be able to use these agencies rather than other local suppliers who may be more appropriate or specialised. Conversely, social workers may have to search for non-contracted agencies, especially if they require specialist services or if the demand on contracted agencies is too great.

Monitoring a care package depends on its complexity, and any reviewing schedules set by councils. Where a high degree of risk and changing needs are present, social workers monitor and frequently adjust care arrangements. Costs will fluctuate with such changes, and again it will be the social worker's responsibility to apply for further funding as necessary. When agency funding ceilings are reached, social workers are then challenged to persuade fund holders/managers to find more money to fulfill statutory care obligations. Managers often need to be as creative as social workers in interpreting their agency's obligations and proposing the type of services that meet identified needs, but like social workers, they may not be successful in securing them. Staffing, finances and local service availability will thus determine the amount, speed of delivery, and often the quality and choice for service users, which may well be limited – despite the corresponding policy aspirations for consistently high standards of service and personalised care management.

Choice: personalisation and practical constraints in care management

Our Health, Our Care, Our Say (DH, 2006) further promoted individual budgets for service users, and brought the agenda of direct payments more directly into social work practice. This policy requires social workers to encourage service users to manage their own care arrangements as far as possible and to have more control over the money allocated directly to them for this.

For care management, the personalisation agenda can be seen positively in aiming to promote independence and choice for service users, but in practice, many social workers have found that service users are reluctant or simply unable to take on the 'responsibility involved in managing all aspects of a budget, for example, in becoming the employer of a care assistant' (DH, 2006). Additionally, the role of the social worker as care manager could be seen to be threatened or redundant as service users are encouraged to self-assess their needs, and broker and manage their own budget and care arrangements. However, many service users still prefer social workers to perform these care management roles which are often perceived as onerous and requiring expertise and knowledge of local services.

THE CONCEPT IN SOCIAL WORK PRACTICE

A social care worker, Emily, assesses Joan, who is 84, recently widowed, has limited mobility, but is mentally alert, sociable, and has a supportive family and church nearby. Emily deems Joan to have moderate needs (via FACS), and so will not be eligible, in her area, for funding for a care package. Joan could pay privately for care if she wishes, but cannot afford to. Joan has support from neighbours and her family, and carries out a lot of personal care for herself, and so she feels she can manage at present. Thus Joan does not receive any funding or services at this point from social services, and her case is closed.

Six months later, Joan's mobility is now poor and unsteady, her night time continence is proving difficult, and she has fallen twice recently, requiring hospital admission and physiotherapy prior to discharge. Joan is now assessed by a qualified social worker, Jane, and meets the criteria (via FACS) of having a substantial need. Jane refers to other agencies and seeks funding for possible services. She encourages Joan and her family to think about managing her own care/ budget, but they do not feel willing or able to do this. Jane and Joan plan a care package, for which Jane gets most of the funding she wanted agreed by her manager. Her package consists of:

- Assessment and input from the occupational therapy and falls prevention team, with them supplying rails and small aids (those under £20 are paid for by Joan).
- A domiciliary carer calling Monday to Friday each morning for one hour. This is to help Joan out of bed, get to the toilet, change her incontinence pad, remind her to take her tablets, make her breakfast, and leave a flask of tea and a sandwich for her lunch.
- A phone life line system is rented by Joan.
- The family are a crucial part of the care plan, phoning Joan daily, calling each evening to bring meals, checking if she has taken her medication, and taking her out at weekends.
- Socially, Joan also has a church visitor every Wednesday. She could join a local lunch club, but does not like the idea.

Jane would also like to arrange some 'pop in' 15-minute calls during the day time to check on her safety, toileting, medication, but the local application of FACS by her managers, and the cut in the department's budget, does not allow for this.

Jane will meet with Joan, her family, and any staff involved to review Joan's care. If no changes are needed, the care continues, and Joan's case file is pended as a case which is being funded by social services but is no longer actively managed by Jane (effectively 'closed' to the social worker). If Joan deteriorates, the case will be re-opened and allocated to Jane or another colleague for a re-assessment of Joan's needs.

Cross references: assessment, finance, multi-professional working, personalisation

SUGGESTED READING

Brown, K. (2010) *Newly Qualified Social Workers: A Handbook for Practice*. Exeter: Learning Matters Ltd.

Parker, J. and Bradley, G. (2007) *Social Work Practice: Assessment, Planning, Intervention and Review*. Exeter: Learning Matters Ltd.

REFERENCES

DH (Department of Health) (2006) *Our Health, Our Care, Our Say: A New Direction for Community Service*. London: HM Government, Department of Health.

FACS (Fair Access to Care Services) (2002) *Guidance on Eligibility Criteria for Adult Social Care*. London: HM Government, Department of Health.

Netten, A. and Beecham, J. (1993) *Costing Community Care*. Cambridge: Cambridge University Press.

8
Carers

Terry Williams, Dorothy Carter and members of the Forum of Carers and Users of Services (FOCUS)

DEFINITION

A carer is someone of any age who provides unpaid support to family or friends who could not manage without this help. This could be caring for a relative, partner or friend who is ill, frail, disabled or has mental health or substance misuse problems.

A young carer is a child or a young person under the age of 19 carrying out caring tasks and assuming a level of responsibility for another person, performing a role which would normally be undertaken by an adult (Princess Royal Trust for Carers, 2005).

Carers do not always recognise that they are carers, having often drifted into the role because of a loyalty to their cared for person. In shorter term caring, as in terminal illness, the role is often not recognised until it is too late, although the effects on the carer can be just as severe. It is important that carers are given support at the start of the caring role as it often transpires that without it the 'carer' becomes the 'cared for' or, as often happens there is the 'creaking gate' syndrome when the cared for outlive the carer. Recognition of the effect of the end of the caring role is not always as it should be. The caring role often ends with the death of the cared for or their being admitted to residential care. When this happens carers go through many emotions – loss of the person, loss of role, relief (which is often followed by feelings of guilt), anger and many others.

KEY POINTS

According to the 2001 Census:

- there were 5.2 million carers in England and Wales;
- 65 per cent of carers of working age give up work;
- 21 per cent of carers providing care for over 50 hours each week say they are not in good health;
- 40 per cent of people with learning disabilities are cared for by a parent over 60 years of age;
- carers save the economy an estimated £86 million per year (Office of National Statistics, 2001).

DISCUSSION

Consultations

Forum of Carers and Users of Services (FOCUS) members have been involved in meetings and discussions regarding their expectations of social workers and health professionals since 2005. These discussions have taken place at several universities in the North West of England. Many of the meetings involved carers and service users sharing ideas. The following is a summary of the key points made, although most issues cut across two or more of the categories.

Understanding the needs of carers

Carers want their needs to be properly addressed. They want professionals to understand the role of the carer and consider the carer as an individual rather than seeing them as just an extension of the cared for. It is easy to underestimate the help and support required. Social workers need to be able to 'read between the lines' as carers can often say they are coping when they are not. Social workers need to be realistic regarding what they expect from carers and should understand that all carers have their limits. The demands on carers can be considerable, even if the cared for enters residential care, the caring role does not finish. Furthermore, the loss of the person being cared for is not the end for the carer. There is a lot of emotion remaining. Emotional problems may commonly occur that include feelings of guilt.

Carers' needs are particularly likely to be underestimated when the person cared for has no physical problems; for example, caring for someone with drug abuse and drinking problems, or caring for people with mental illness such as depression and self-harming. Carers want social workers and other professionals to recognise the strain that all carers are subject to.

Young carers consulted felt their needs were often underestimated and many young carers were not identified as such by social workers. Relevant issues mentioned were: young people gradually drifting into the role of carer; the person cared for possibly fearing intervention; and a fear that the young person may be taken away from the person being cared for. Young carers felt that they got a 'raw deal' but were reluctant to do much about this as they worried about what could happen if there were any intervention. They felt that they did not have enough information and more ought to be told to them at school.

Professionalism

Carers expect practitioners to be competent and to have certain basic qualities and standards. They expect social workers and other professionals to be honest, patient and good listeners. Consultations highlighted the importance of treating everyone as an individual and showing respect for carers and families. Turning up on time for appointments was regarded as a basic way of showing respect. 'Doing what they say they will do' was also regarded as vitally important. Carers also felt that social workers and social work students should look at the person, not the condition, learn as much as they can before meeting service users and carers and gather as much relevant information as possible before meeting service users and carers. The ability to keep on learning was a theme at earlier meetings; qualities such as honesty, caring, patience, calm and empathetic were mentioned in all the discussions. Being open minded and not making assumptions were also common themes.

Communication

All professionals should be skilled communicators. One carer described this as being 'in tune with people'. Professionals should be able to explain what is happening in a way that can be easily understood. It is important to use plain English and avoid the use of jargon. Workers should talk to the family as well as the cared for and should try to avoid making assumptions. They need to ask and listen to fully understand. Listening properly is very important so that the worker genuinely hears what is said (failure to listen properly is a frequent criticism of health and social care professionals). Carers include a wide range of people including young carers and people with a learning disability and different ways of communicating should be used to cater for individual needs. Communication can most commonly go wrong during meetings. Professionals need to show patience, give extra time and take care to ensure they are understood.

Assessment and support

Carers consulted felt that it was important to get all the facts before judging a situation, particularly for formal assessments. Some carers referred to 'buck passing' and too much 'red tape'. Honesty and good communication are vital to ensure that the assessment is seen as a positive step rather than a meaningless exercise. It was generally felt that there should be a family assessment, rather than an assessment on an individual carer, as caring often involves the whole family. Carers of people with mental health needs, including those relating to drug or alcohol abuse, have similar assessment and support needs as those caring for someone with a physical disability

It is important that social workers are aware that carers are often loyal to the cared for and will not admit the need for support. Also, without support the carer can end up 'as bad as the cared for'. Some carers referred to difficulties arising when services are refused by the cared for regardless of the impact on the carer and carers not being able to access a social worker if the cared for does not have one. The value of care co-ordinators at social worker level was also mentioned. Carers' opinion as to the value of assessments is greatly influenced by the outcomes. Lack of respite services and other resources and lengthy waits for allocation of resources can have a devastating effect on people.

Several carers referred to the need for services to be more flexible:

> . . . transport is my issue. I can get my cared for into a day's respite without giving notice but I have to get him there. By the time I have got him ready and in and out of the wheelchair and car I don't feel like getting myself ready or going anywhere.

> Daily respite helps but I would love an evening out with my friend. She usually sits in if I go out so we don't go out together – to the cinema or the theatre would be wonderful.

Community resources, particularly organisations such as carers' centres and Crossroads (see www.crossroads.org.uk), provide both practical and emotional support. Carers expect professionals to know what is available in the community and to help carers access such services.

Young carers

Young carers said they deserved: the right to a good education; flexibility within their education to enable them to study and perform their caring role; respite or breaks from their caring role; someone to talk to; and the right to some life of their own. Young carers also felt that they should be entitled to a carers' allowance. We understand that carers' allowance is not paid if the carer is under 16. In addition, those over 16 only qualify if they care for 35 hours or more and are earning less than £100 per week (less expenses). If carers are in full-time education an allowance is not payable. Young carers' jobs and further education prospects suffer or are at risk and they feel there should be more legislation to protect them and give them equal opportunities.

The value of carers' expertise

Carers are probably in the best position to understand the needs of the person they are caring for. They are knowledgeable about his/her condition or disability, wishes and preferences. Social workers should recognise the expertise that carers have and learn from them. Some carers utilise this expertise by managing a budget to provide personal care on behalf of the person cared for. Their responsibilities include appointing and managing staff. Dealing with direct payments is challenging. Social workers and agencies should empower carers to draw upon their considerable experience and expertise so they feel confident dealing with the requirements involved. Appropriate guidance and support is vital. Young carers commented upon difficulties regarding the transition from being a young carer to becoming an adult carer. This can be a confusing and stressful time and they felt that they needed more help to prepare for this. Many carers, including young carers, are keen to share their expertise by contributing to the development of services and/or to participate in the education of students on professional courses. Others make a contribution at their local carers' centre. Although the demands of caring limits opportunities, many carers are able to contribute later in life when they no longer have caring responsibilities.

THE CONCEPT IN SOCIAL WORK PRACTICE

Case study

Jane, the student social worker, smiled as she rang the door bell. She had arranged respite for John and thought Mrs Evans would be pleased. Sue Evans opened the door. *Jane's late again*, she thought. She hoped Jane wouldn't be in such a hurry this time. After short pleasantries Jane told Sue about the respite care arrangements. *Strange*, thought Jane, *Sue doesn't seem to be appreciative; perhaps she doesn't realise how respite care is in short supply*. Jane glanced at her watch, *if I leave in the next ten minutes I will avoid the heavy traffic on the way home*, she thought.

That's the third time that Jane's looked at her watch since she arrived, observed Sue. *I wish she would ask me how I am. Doesn't she realise I am at the end of my tether and desperate for a break? I need respite now not in six weeks. Sometimes all I need is a day off but by the time I get it I have got through the problems. It makes me feel very much on my own. If only someone would take time to listen and understand. I don't know how I'll get through the next few weeks.* Jane waved goodbye. *Sue seems a bit down*, she thought. *Still, she didn't say anything so whatever is bothering her can't be that serious.*

Cross references: advocacy, empowerment, partnership, service user involvement, welfare rights

SUGGESTED READING

Bibby, A. and Becker, S. (2000) *Young Carers in Their Own Words*. London: Calouste Gilbenkian Foundation.

Clements, L. (2010) *Carers and Their Rights: The Law Relating to Carers*, 4th edn. London: Carers UKJ.

key concepts in
social work practice

REFERENCES

Office of National Statistics (2001) 'Census 2001'. Available from: www.ons.gov.uk/ons/guide-method/census/census-2001/index.html (accessed 15 October 2011).

Princess Royal Trust for Carers (2005) Available from: www.carers.org/what-carer (accessed 11 October 2011).

9.
Communication

Pat Higgins

DEFINITION

Communication is fundamental to human relationships. We communicate our thoughts, feelings and concerns in a number of ways. Communication forms the basis for relationships, social inclusion and engagement; however, for a number of reasons the people we work with may have difficulty both communicating and receiving information. This may be due to fear, anxiety, mental illness, sensory or learning disability, age and understanding, the use of drugs or alcohol or the stress of their current situation. It is therefore the responsibility of the practitioner to manage and overcome potential communication barriers for service users.

Communication is a complex process of giving and receiving information. The worker decodes the interaction and needs to be aware that information and understanding can easily be distorted in the process. Communication is one of the most complex yet important aspects of a social worker's role, it forms the most fundamental role in understanding the needs of service users and can provide the most basic service to service users, notably in the power of listening and validation.

KEY POINTS

- Communication is informed by a range of theoretical perspectives and disciplines; practitioners are required to maintain knowledge and application.
- Good self-awareness forms the basis of good communication, emotional intelligence and anti-oppressive practice. To be self-aware allows the practitioner to listen to another's pain, without judgement. The emotionally intelligent practitioner can assist the person to explore difficult, painful and often overpowering emotions.

- The ability to demonstrate empathy is informed by our own self-awareness and is communicated through active listening that contributes to establishing an effective working relationship based on trust and understanding. It validates a service user's experience and can provide an emphasis for service users on the value of exploring and dealing with their strong emotions which in itself can be both therapeutic and the start of the process of change.
- The ability to listen to service users' pain, distress and confusion can in itself offer individuals the opportunity to explore and identify their own issues and solutions within the process of active listening. It validates a service user's experience and informs further social work processes in terms of therapeutic engagement, assessment, planning and implementing strategies.
- There are different ways to communicate with children, service users and professionals.

As practitioners, we will work with a range of service users with varying needs and communication issues (Thompson, 2003). We need therefore to be able to develop our knowledge, understanding and application of skills in a range of different ways to communicate. We cannot say that there is one way of ensuring we can effectively communicate with all service users. Additionally, when communicating with other professionals, it is common for professionals to have their own language – jargon, acronyms, professional value base/perspective and pressures – and to ensure good inter-professional communication we need to be aware of this, and to aim to manage and overcome potential misunderstandings.

DISCUSSION

Communication is a basic skill which we all possess and as such we believe to be a simple process of sharing information. However, we do know that messages can get lost in translation, even when we speak the same language. Miscommunication can cause great distress, frustration and at times can be a very dangerous contributing factor to missing vital signs or communicating effectively to other professions in serious circumstances.

Social work draws on and applies a range of theoretical perspectives, such as a humanistic approach to communication and to understanding human relationships, counselling skills, models and approaches and more recently an emotionally intelligent approach to communication. Therefore, with a range of theories informing our knowledge and understanding of communication and social work practice, an eclectic approach to communication is required (Trevethick, 2005).

Communication is a complex process, and within this, the practitioner unpacks the interaction with knowledge and understanding that much within this interaction can be misunderstood, and as such the social worker needs to have emotional intelligence, and to be self-aware.

It is also important to acknowledge the need for good supervision and support for ourselves within the process of working with people. We need to ensure we are not over-identifying with our service users' painful emotions/experience; that we are not colluding or down playing risks to the service user, others or ourselves; and at times we need assistance to help us to see the 'wood for the trees' and as such supervision plays a vital role in reflection, support and guidance (Knott and Scragg, 2010).

The role of empathy and emotional intelligence demonstrates we are responding to another person's feelings. However, an important element to the use of empathy is: '. . . to be able to understand the confusion without becoming part of it' (Lishman, 2009: 84).

Sometimes, when we work with service users who are in emotional pain and distress, all we have to offer is ourselves. For example, as a hospital based social worker, I supported a family with the distress and loss of their two and a half year old son; I did not access a service, give advice or resolve the problem, but I was present, I was empathetic and supported the family through an extremely painful and distressing time.

Listening is not a simple process of listening; we can be easily distracted by a number of factors, such as noise, pressures of time, environment, unexpected content in what is being conveyed, and the impact on us personally by what is being said. Listening involves a range of appropriate responses to demonstrate that we are actively listening. We need to be able to discern as practitioners whether we can provide an appropriate and effective response here and now. We need to ask ourselves: Do I have to postpone other commitments? Can I pick this up at another point? All of which will impact on our response and engagement with the service user. What we do know and hear from service users is that service users feel valued when they have been listened to.

A student I was assessing on placement was providing support to a 34-year-old woman who had ongoing issues with alcohol. My student expressed her concern that she wasn't 'doing anything' for the service user, who returned again and again, to see my student. However, when we unpicked what the student was doing, she was listening, she was attentive, she validated the woman's experiences and she was encouraging this service user to continue in her attempts to reduce her use of and dependence on alcohol, and as such she was providing a valuable service for the service user.

THE CONCEPT IN SOCIAL WORK PRACTICE

On a basic level we need to use and apply good basic communication skills, to be knowledgeable about ourselves, our service, to possess local knowledge and to ensure we apply cultural awareness to practice. We must listen to service user groups, and ensure we inform ourselves with regard to the issues faced by service users and potential additional communication requirements.

We may need specialised training and at a very basic level to research approaches to communicating with different groups; for instance, to use age-appropriate language with children and tools to assist in the process which may be pictures or symbols. Koprowska (2008) has produced a helpful list of 'Do's and Don'ts' such as: to use simple language; to use short sentences; to be specific; to ask one question at a time; and to be aware that this takes time. All of this is good advice for communicating with a range of service users: those with a learning disability; those for whom English is a second language; and those who are overwhelmed by anxiety, fear or trauma. The emotionally intelligent practitioner is able to remain calm and grounded during communication which in turn will have a calming effect on the service user.

When we are communicating with a service user with communication difficulties, whether they be due to learning or speech difficulties, time will be of the essence as it will take longer to understand what the individual is telling us and it will take longer to ensure that we are being understood. We will need to work with the service users and their carers to ensure we can understand their communication, and the more familiar we become with the individual's communication the more we will understand and ensure their understanding of our communications.

We also need to be discerning in our application of the service user perspective. A group of young people in the care system came in to talk to a group of social work students. Afterwards, student feedback suggested some confusion, as some of the young people did not want social workers to have read their files before they met with them, whereas others complained about having to repeat their stories. This suggests that we listen to the messages we are receiving, and if an individual wants to tell you their experience of their life, we should be prepared to listen, but if the response we get is 'it's in the file isn't it?' then we certainly should have taken the time to prepare. We should not pre-judge the pertinent issues, and ensure we check with the service user what they think the priority is. However, we may need to apply professional judgement based on our knowledge and skills if we identify risk of harm.

When we communicate with service users who have experienced trauma, it may be too difficult to say or explain to others what that trauma is, and it may be that the use of other forms of communication are the best way of engaging with that person. It may be a child who does not have a language for what they have experienced and it may be the use of various communication methods which assist in that process, drawing, puppets, and play. However, we do need to be aware that it may be that a specialist therapist is the best practitioner to unlock the language of trauma.

When we work with other professionals we need to be mindful both of our own value base, professional priorities and pressures and use of jargon. Working with people is a complex business; it is pressurised, demanding and requires a range of approaches, knowledge and expertise. We cannot be expected to possess all that is needed to solve all human problems but what we can do is recognise the skills, knowledge and expertise of others. Some basic principles in inter-professional collaboration involves a good knowledge and awareness of our own professional value base, the ability to listen to and value other professional perspectives, and appreciate the pressures other professionals are experiencing.

In conclusion I would suggest that the important areas for good and effective communication, which is a core social work skill, include:

- a high level of self-awareness;
- effective listening skills;
- to work with and hear service users voice their knowledge and expertise of their experience and services;

- to use our judgement in applying our learning from service users in order to recognise and overcome communication barriers;
- to develop and apply sophisticated communications skills, which involve a high level of emotional intelligence and reflection.

This highlights the links to good quality supervision, good inter-professional working and continuing professional development.

Cross references: empowerment, professional development, reflection, service user involvement, supervision

SUGGESTED READING

Howe, D. (2008) *The Emotionally Intelligent Social Worker*. Basingstoke: Palgrave Macmillan.
Lishman, J. (2009) *Communication in Social Work*, 2nd edn. Basingstoke: Palgrave Macmillan.

REFERENCES

Knott, C. and Scragg, T. (2010) *Reflective Practice in Social Work*. Exeter: Learning Matters.
Koprowska, J. (2008) *Communication and Inter-Personal Skills in Social Work*. Exeter: Learning Matters.
Lishman, J. (2009) *Communication in Social Work*, 2nd edn. Basingstoke: Palgrave Macmillan.
Thompson, N. (2003) *Communication and Language: A Handbook of Theory and Practice*. Basingstoke: Palgrave Macmillan.
Trevethick, P. (2005) *Social Work Skills: A Practice Handbook*. Maidenhead: Open University Press.

10
Confidentiality

Angela Olsen and Liz Stevens

DEFINITION

Confidentiality has been defined by the International Standards Organisation (ISO 27001) as ensuring that information is accessible only to those authorised to have access. While this may at first reading appear to be a clear statement, it is worth examining it more closely and exploring whether it is a useful definition in terms of social work. A social worker might ask: 'Is all information in a service user's file accessible to the service user?' 'What about third party information about referrers or children or other professionals?' 'What is meant by "authorised", does it always include the service user, his or her carer, the social worker, other professionals?' All of these people might have a legitimate reason to want to see information.

KEY POINTS

- Access to personal and sensitive information and circumstances requiring intervention must be treated with respect.
- Breaching confidentiality without good cause can result in an investigation into professional misconduct.
- Confidentiality is not the same as secrecy. Withholding information relevant to safeguarding procedures can result in an investigation into professional misconduct.
- The person you are working with should be made aware from the outset and repeatedly, as necessary, that you will be keeping records of all involvement you have with them.
- A common dilemma in social work practice occurs when attempting to balance confidentiality with 'best interest' disclosure requirements.

DISCUSSION

Legislation, policy and codes of practice

The Department of Children, Schools and Families described confidential information as:

> personal information of a private and sensitive nature; information that is not lawfully already in the public domain or readily available from another public source; and information that has been shared in circumstances where the person giving the information could reasonably expect that it would not be shared with others. (DCSF, 2008: 15, para 3.12)

The term confidentiality can offer reassurance to service users that the information they are sharing is going to be used responsibly. However, it is important to be clear that the term is not synonymous with secrecy and that information may be shared with others if it is in the best interest of the individual or within the public interest.

The GSCC Code of Practice (2010) provides a framework for this in Code 2.3, which states that social care workers should respect confidential information and be able to clearly explain their agency's policy on confidentiality to the service user and/or their carer. However there is potential conflict with Code 4.4 which states that:

> As a social care worker, you must respect the rights of service users while seeking to ensure that their behaviour does not harm themselves or other people. This includes: Ensuring that relevant colleagues and agencies are informed about the outcomes and implications of risk assessments.

The Human Rights Act (see HRA, 2000, Schedule 8) states people have the right to privacy within social work practice; therefore, personal information about service users (including official records, photographs, letters, diaries and medical records), should be kept securely and not shared without the service user's permission, except in certain circumstances. The handling of such items, any information gathered and professional opinions expressed during assessment and intervention is subject to a duty of confidence. This is addressed within the Data Protection Act (1998) which requires the gathering and handling of information to be relevant and in relation to the purpose for which the information is to be used.

The final and perhaps most user friendly guidance for understanding confidentiality is provided by the Caldicott Review (DH, 1997). Although the language in the report is necessarily medical because it was primarily produced in response to information sharing within and between medical practitioners, the principles were quickly adopted by local authorities (LAs). In brief, the Caldicott principles are:

- justify the purpose of sharing patient identifiable information;
- don't use patient identifiable information unless it is absolutely necessary;
- use the minimum necessary patient identifiable information;
- access to patient identifiable information should be on a strictly need to know basis;
- everyone with access to patient identifiable information should be aware of their responsibilities;
- understand and comply with the Law (DH, 1997, 4.2: 16–17).

Good practice in maintaining confidentiality includes: not sharing information in casual conversations that may identify the person by name, location or details of their situation; using passwords on electronic documents; keeping paper documents secure; ensuring meetings are held where discussions cannot be overheard; and using codes or initials where possible but not to the extent as to lose the integrity and value of the discussion and resultant record of such.

It is important to remember that service users can apply to see personal records and that LAs can be required to disclose information if it is considered to be in the public interest. Applications to see files may be made under the Data Protection Act or under the Freedom of Information Act (2000). There are exemptions from requirement to disclose information but there is insufficient space to discuss access issues here. We would advise social workers to discuss any such applications with line managers or to seek advice from their legal departments should such a request be made.

THE CONCEPT IN SOCIAL WORK PRACTICE

Case study – confidentiality

Joe was social worker to the Gashir family. One lunch time he met Lydia, an out-of-hours social worker, in a supermarket. As this family had proved to be quite a stressful family to work with, Joe welcomed the chance to speak to someone else who had worked with them; Mrs Gashir had recently made contact with the out-of-hours service with concerns for her elderly mother who lives with her brother. As the colleagues began to talk they were careful not to refer to the family by name. They discussed the case in quiet tones. On returning to the office, Joe was asked to go into his line manager's office. Mrs Gashir's brother had coincidentally been in the supermarket at the time of Joe and Lydia's discussion. Although he had never met Joe he knew it was his family that were being discussed. The area, the family circumstance, ethnic sensitivities of the case confirmed to him that his and his family's personal information was being discussed in a public place. He had contacted Joe's line manager to make a complaint. He also demanded to know why he was the subject of safeguarding concerns regarding his mother's care.

DISCUSSION

Social work is a profession which means that the detail of day-to-day work cannot be discussed within the home environment; this can lead to social workers feeling isolated and in need of support from colleagues in deciding the direction a case should take. Joe was not gossiping about the case, he was looking for colleague support and wanted to learn more about their experience with the family. Joe and Lydia were careful to not use names and to not broadcast their discussion by speaking in loud voices; unfortunately the risks they took were clumsy, they discussed other identifiable details and discussed the planned intervention of the case in a public place which was then overheard. This therefore put a safeguarding investigation in jeopardy and also threatened the Gashir family relationships. Whilst there is no statutory right for one person to sue another over breaches of confidentiality; breaching rules of confidentiality can be seen as misconduct and may lead to de-registration by the professional body. Each team will have examples where they or colleagues have felt that conversations were being overheard or indeed had observers recognise the people they were discussing.

Case study – freedom of information

Sarah is 21, she was a looked after child, she moved between three foster homes over a ten-year period. Sarah asked her local authority for access to her files because she wanted to know why she and her sister had been placed separately. The local authority asked for some time to prepare the files so that they could remove third-party information. Sarah was distressed that the information that she eventually received revealed few details about the reasoning behind her separation from her sister.

DISCUSSION

Sarah's request to access the information held on her is a reasonable one; the local authority in agreeing to this are complying with legislation, via the Data Protection Act 1998 and the Freedom of information Act 2000; its response to remove all third party information was appropriate. It may be information on the person who reported Sarah's mother for neglecting her children, it may include information on research completed in the pursuit of finding Sarah's father, naming those thought to be but discounted as being, etc.

Social work records are made up of both accurate and factual detail as well as professional opinions based on the intervention, it is most important that professional opinions should be clearly identifiable within record keeping (ICO, 2008). This is in accordance with the Data Protection Act 1998 and also the Freedom of Information Act 2000. Practitioners should keep in mind that in the age of technology the records made are permanent, accessible to some degree by those people they are working with, and could have a lasting effect on people viewing the information held on them. In Sarah's case, her request to view her file was only a few years on from when the records were being made, in other circumstances the request to view files could be sooner or indeed many years after the records have been made.

CONCLUSION

Case work and the development of working relationships can be a difficult relationship for some service users; depending on levels of understanding a service user may become confused about the role of the social worker, considering him/her to be a confidante and friend. He or she might then disclose information that they later regret sharing. It is a social worker's responsibility to ensure that professional boundaries are maintained within the remit of the social work intervention.

Respecting the information of the people we are working with is a key part of being a social work practitioner; we must not share the information provided unless directly in relation to the intervention. This is a legal requirement and is integral to our professional codes of practice. This does not mean that we cannot share the information, as this can be done with the service user's agreement, or on an interagency basis in the process of completing the social work intervention; or indeed can be breached should there be identifiable risks, either to the person, a safeguarding issue for a child or vulnerable adult or when the person is considered to be at risk of harming themselves or other people.

It is generally accepted that all agencies will breach confidentiality when working with children and families where a child may be at risk and that they are expected to share information with other agencies where applicable, this risk overrides the agencies' duty of confidentiality toward the service user (Laming, 2009); social workers are duty bound to report this and also to report when a service user has threatened to hurt themselves or others.

Cross references: ethics, reflection, social justice, supervision, values

confidentiality

47

SUGGESTED READING

Department for Children, Schools and Families, and Communities and Local Government (2008) *Information Sharing: Guidance for Practitioners and Managers*. London: HM Government.

REFERENCES

Data Protection Act (1998) *Information Sharing: Guidance for Practitioners and Managers*. London: Department for Children, Schools and Families, and Communities and Local Government.

DH (Department of Health) (1997) 'The Caldicott committee: report on the review of patient-identifiable information'. Available from: www.dh.gov.uk/prod_consum_dh/groups/dh_digitalassets/@dh/@en/documents/digitalasset/dh_4068404.pdf (accessed 14 June 2011).

DCSF (Department for Children, Schools and Families) (2008) *Information Sharing: Guidance for Practitioners and Managers*. London: HM Government.

Freedom of Information Act (2000) Available from: www.legislation.gov.uk/ukpga/2000/36/pdfs/ukpga_20000036_en.pdf (accessed 12 April 2011).

GSCC (General Social Care Council) (2010) *Code of Practice for Social Care Workers and Code of Practice for Employers of Social Care Workers*. Available from: www.gscc.org.uk/codes/ (accessed 30 May 2011).

HRA (Human Rights Act) (2000) Available from: www.equalityhumanrights.com/human-rights/what-are -human-rights/the-human-rights-act (accessed 30 May 2012).

ICO (Information Commissioners Office) (2008) 'How does the Data Protection Act apply to recording and retaining professional opinions?' Available from: www.ico.gov.uk/for_organisations/data_protection_guide.aspx (accessed 14 June 2011).

Laming, Lord (2009) 'The protection of children in England: a progress report'. Available from: www.education.gov.uk/publications/eOrderingDownload/HC-330.pdf (accessed 14 June 2011).

11

Counselling

Anne Keeler

DEFINITION

A good starting point for this chapter may be to consider why we are looking at counselling in a book on social work when social work in the 21st century is a care/case management activity. The development of social work is charted by Brearley (1995), showing that the focus of intervention is mainly on the individual or their family. Whilst there was a period of radical social work during the 1980s in which social workers challenged the influences in society that created social problems, since then social work has become less of a political activity. Miller (2006) argues that social work focuses on single situations rather than social problems such as unemployment, poverty and 'delinquent' teenage behaviour. Consequently social workers aim to work with and support individuals and families who may be experiencing these issues.

Social casework since the 1900s has used the relationship between helper and helped to effect change. Paul Halmos's key text 'The faith of counsellors' (1965) introduced the counselling role into Britain and this was taken up by welfare officers (cited in Brearley, 1995).

The British Association of Counselling and Psychotherapy defines counselling and psychotherapy as 'umbrella terms that cover a range of talking therapies. They are delivered by trained practitioners who work with people over a short or long term to help them bring about effective change or enhance their wellbeing' (BACP, n.d.).

Counsellors make contracts with their clients where there is shared agreement about content, length of involvement, the aim of the work and how to define success in order to end the partnership. Nevertheless, good interpersonal skills are required for effective practice.

Core aspects of the counselling role are used within social work, and are often referred to as counselling skills. It is these skills, techniques and a shared value base that enhance social work practice. Thompson suggests that social work 'involves an element of counselling in terms of helping people to understand their situation, their feelings and their options' (2000: 66). For users of social work services they may experience a power imbalance and lack of choice about involvement in the process.

KEY POINTS

- Social work and counselling share a similar skills and value base.
- Core principles of person-centred counselling are key elements of social work practice.
- Supervision is an essential part of counselling and social work practice.

DISCUSSION

Key counselling models that can be seen to be useful to social work practice are: person-centred counselling, solution-focused counselling, and cognitive behavioural therapy (CBT). Many counselling techniques use problem-solving methods which are often adapted in social work. They also require both the service user and the counsellor to form a 'working relationship' or 'collaborative alliance' to be successful (Miller, 2006).

Three models of counselling are briefly described here.

Person-centred counselling

This approach is often attributed to the work of Carl Rogers who suggested in 1940 that the best way to help clients is to enable them to find solutions to their own problems. Individuals, according to Rogers, need to achieve self-actualisation and to be loved and valued by others (McLeod, 2009). If the love or approval expressed by parents is conditional on behaving in a certain way then this can result in the child/ person defining themselves by reference to these values. These 'conditions of worth' shape how we see ourselves, suggests Rogers (McLeod, 2009). The person-centred approach uses the client–therapist relationship in which the client feels accepted and valued. The therapist demonstrates 'core conditions' that enables the person to move towards self-actualisation. The core conditions are acceptance, congruence, empathy, and genuineness.

Cognitive behavioural therapy (CBT)

Integration of behavioural therapy and cognitive therapy form the basis of this approach. Behavioural therapies look at how behaviour can be controlled through positive and negative reinforcements and consequently this behaviour can be conditioned to respond to specific stimuli (Miller, 2006). However, a purely behavioural approach was seen to be limited as it did not take account of thought processes. Interpretation of events is filtered through past experience, history and the mood of the individual at that time. Early experience often shapes belief systems which shape thinking (Miller, 2006). Bringing the two approaches together in CBT seeks to help individuals deal with these patterns of thinking and behaviour.

Key elements of this approach include: collaboration between client and counsellor, a problem-solving focus, and time limited or brief intervention (McLeod, 2009). During the assessment phase, focus is on the problem that the client is seeking to change and explores information in four domains; cognition, emotions, behaviour and physical. Focusing on difficulties in the present rather than the past, the aim is to change those behaviours that can impact on feelings.

CBT can be offered by the NHS through GP practices. The methods used have also been adapted by social care providers and schools to manage behaviour, although there is some controversy over this if people are not being required to give their consent (Payne, 1991, cited in Higham, 2006). Motivational interviewing is influenced by CBT and the model developed by Prochaska and DiClemente is widely used in substance misuse services (Higham, 2006).

Solution-focused counselling

This approach focuses less on problem solving and more on 'seeking positive change with individuals or families' (Miller, 2006: 125). The focus is less on understanding the problem and looking at what needs to change and more on seeking the solutions to achieve this. Research in the 1960s and 1970s indicated that short-term interventions can bring about positive outcomes (Miller, 2006). Focusing on the future in contrast to looking at the past also contributed to changes. Miller suggests that 'experience can be interpreted as a result of an individual's social context and culture' (2006: 127) and is therefore socially constructed. What this approach does not do is consider any underlying issues and this is often the basis for criticism of this approach (Miller, 2006). It does however see the service user as the expert on their problem and it is the worker's role to assist them to define and identify how the situation could feel better. Early meetings should be used to set goals which are reviewed and renegotiated over time. This approach aims to help people feel they have control over their lives and therefore endings are as important as beginnings.

THE CONCEPT IN SOCIAL WORK PRACTICE

The last 30 years has seen social work take on a managerial role that draws on the statutory functions as the basis for intervention in people's lives. This does not sit comfortably with a counselling role. The Barclay Report (1982) identified two different activities in social work; social care planning and counselling (cited in Brearley, 1995). However, there was no further definition of counselling offered within the report. Yet it is evident that the essential skills for social work are connected to the humanist person-centred work of Carl Rogers. A key difference between counselling and social work is one of choice; social work service users are often required through legal interventions to engage with social workers with this being the only way to access services, whilst individuals are more likely to make a positive choice by accessing counselling services (Seden, 2005).

Key issues for this topic include: counselling skills, supervision and critical incident support.

Counselling skills

Seden (2005) argues that counselling skills are embedded within the six key roles of the National Occupational Standards for Social Work (TOPSS, 2004). Counselling skills can be seen to be at the heart of communication in social work and as Brearley suggests, they 'underpin . . . the whole range of social work . . .' (1995: 30).

Communication skills include: the ability to listen, hear and respond accordingly and are central to developing a good working relationship with the service user. The core conditions of person-centred practice are the basis for good communication (Seden, 2005). Warmth and interest in the service user help to form a positive relationship between worker and service user leading to effective practice.

Working with people who are vulnerable through age, disability or because of circumstances such as homelessness or domestic violence requires social workers to be aware of the power in their role and the need for flexibility when working with diversity. There is the potential to use communication inappropriately by manipulating or persuading someone to take a course of action that is not right for them. In contrast, social workers are required at times to give uncomfortable messages and need to be able to do this in a respectful and honest way.

Supervision

It is accepted that good quality counselling is enhanced by good quality and regular supervision of the counsellor. It is often a requirement of professional associations that the counsellor receives supervision for professional development both in training and during their working life. Unlike supervision in social work, which is a mainly management activity, counsellors draw on supervision sessions for education purposes, for support and to ensure that therapy offered is of good quality (Hawkins and Shohet, 2007, cited in McLeod, 2009). Supervision does not have to be on an individual basis and can be group case discussion or peer supervision.

Lord Laming (2003, cited in Simmonds, 2010: 214), in his report on the death of Victoria Climbié, stated that supervision is 'a cornerstone of all good social work practice'. In current social work practice, Simmonds (2010) suggests that supervision is used to audit social work activity, whereas it has previously focused on the relationship between service user and worker.

Critical incident support

A role shared by social workers and counsellors is that of providing support to individuals and families during or following unusual or traumatic events.

An organisational model of trauma was developed during the 1980s following a series of disasters in the UK such as the Bradford football stadium fire (1985) and the sinking of the Marchioness riverboat (1989). The aim of this model is to:

> deliver early psychological support that promotes normal recovery following a potentially traumatising event; to identify those who may go on to manifest long term symptoms of severe social and psychological impairment and help them access continuing specialist treatment; and to minimise any secondary trauma reactions. (Alderton, 2010: 20)

Traumatic events can lead to strong emotions and uncommon feelings of fear and distress. The reaction of individuals to the event is likely to be a mixture of the physical, emotional, cognitive and behavioural. Primary trauma is the distress caused by a traumatic event and is seen as a normal reaction to an abnormal event. However, secondary trauma can occur when individuals do not feel supported or properly looked after following a traumatic incident and this may lead to anger or resentment. Secondary trauma may also occur when individuals feel that organisations are not dealing with the situation promptly or skilfully.

Whilst the use of counselling skills may be central to good effective social work practice, many practitioners may feel that the managerial social work role that focuses on auditing, accountability and problem solving shares little in common with the roots of the counselling profession. Nevertheless social workers would do well to remind themselves that what service users value most is a social worker who has excellent communication skills and is able to listen to what is being said.

Cross references: communication, history of social work, supervision, values

SUGGESTED READING

Miller, L. (2006) *Counselling Skills for Social Work*. London: Sage.
Seden, J. (2005) *Counselling Skills in Social Work Practice*, 2nd edn. Maidenhead: Open University Press.

REFERENCES

Alderton, M. (2010) 'Debriefing in practice: assisting victims after traumatic incidents', *Healthcare Counselling and Psychotherapy Journal*, 10(2): 19–23.
BACP (British Association of Counselling and Psychotherapy) (n.d.) 'What is counselling?' Available from: www.bacp.co.uk/information/education/whatiscounselling.php (accessed 15 September 2011).

key concepts in
social work practice

Brearley, J. (1995) *Counselling and Social Work*. Buckingham: Open University Press.

Higham, P. (2006) *Social Work: Introducing Professional Practice*. London: Sage.

McLeod, J. (2009) *An Introduction to Counselling*, 4th edn. Maidenhead: Open University Press.

Miller, L. (2006) *Counselling Skills for Social Work*. London: Sage.

Seden, J. (2005) *Counselling Skills in Social Work Practice*, 2nd edn. Maidenhead: Open University Press.

Simmonds, J. (2010) 'Relating and relationships in supervision: supportive and companionable or dominant and submissive?', in G. Ruch, D. Turney and A. Ward (eds), *Relationship-Based Social Work*. London: Jessica Kingsley, pp. 214–28.

Thompson, N. (2000) *Understanding Social Work*. Basingstoke: Palgrave Macmillan.

TOPSS (2004) *National Occupational Standards for Social Work*. Skills for Care. Available from: www.skillsforcare.org.uk/developing_skills/National_Occupational_Standards/social_work_NOS.aspx (accessed 15 September 2011).

12
Critical Thinking

Elizabeth Harlow

DEFINITION

According to the 'Critical Thinking Community' (www.criticalthinking.org), the idea of critical thinking has been developing for the last 2,500 years, but the specific term has its roots in the mid- to late 19th century. Although there is no agreed definition (Coleman et al., 2002; Plath et al., 1999) the following might provide a valuable point for departure:

> Critical thinking is the intellectually disciplined process of actively and skilfully conceptualizing, applying, analysing, synthesizing, and/or evaluating information gathered from, or generated by, observation, experience, reflection, reasoning, or communication as a guide to belief and action. In its exemplary form, it is based on universal intellectual values that transcend subject matter divisions: clarity, accuracy, precision, consistency, relevance, sound evidence, good reasons, depth, breadth and fairness. (Scriven and Paul, 1987, Conference Paper)

The idea is important to education in general, but specifically to the education and practice of professionals such as social workers. During the course of their work social workers are confronted with complex situations. They have to gather information, assess its value, negotiate with stakeholders, decide on a course of action as a means of solving problems, as well as implement and review the action taken. Information gathered and the perspective of stakeholders might offer contested solutions or routes forward. Furthermore, planned actions have to be articulated and justified. In consequence, the ability to think critically; for example, to weigh up the evidence or the weight of argument, is of the utmost importance. It is important for the social worker, their managers and employing organisation, but particularly so for the service users whose lives will be affected by the decisions taken. Professional supervision is an important means through which social work practitioners reflect on their work, and in so doing engage in the process of critical thinking.

Whilst critical thinking might be associated with abstract reasoning, Brookfield points out that it is a 'lived and creative activity':

> Being a critical thinker involves more than cognitive activities such as logical reasoning or scrutinising arguments for assertions unsupported by empirical evidence. Thinking critically involves our recognising the assumptions underlying our beliefs and behaviours. It means we can give justifications for our ideas and actions. Most important, perhaps, it means we can try to judge the rationality of these justifications. We can do this by comparing them to a range of varying interpretations and perspectives. We can think through, project, and anticipate the consequences of those actions that are based on justifications. And we can test the accuracy and rationality of these justifications against some kind of objective analysis of the 'real' world as we understand it. (Brookfield, 1987: 13–14, cited in Brown and Rutter, 2008: 5)

KEY POINTS

- Critical thinking as a term has been used since the mid- to late 19th century.
- It concerns the ability to reason, and is important to making and justifying decisions that are taken in complex, contested and uncertain situations.
- Student social workers are encouraged to develop critical thinking capability and in consequence it is a component of educational programmes.
- Thinking critically is closely associated with the process of reflecting on work as a means of learning and achieving the best outcomes in practice.
- Supervision is one of the means through which social work practitioners might reflect and think critically about their work.

DISCUSSION

'Cogito ergo sum' or 'I think therefore I am' (Descartes, 1637) is probably the best known philosophical quotation (www.literature.org). According to Descartes, it is the ability to think that separates humans from animals, and its significance to humanity means that it is a crucial topic of investigation, not only for philosophers, but also social scientists. For example, psychologists working from a biological perspective may be interested in thinking as a function of the brain, whilst the development of thinking in humans is frequently associated with the work of the cognitive psychologist, Jean Piaget. However, critical thinking involves more than the process of 'thinking'. Thinking critically involves challenging, and challenging implicates the emotions. According to Brookfield:

> Asking questions about our previously accepted values, ideas, and behaviours is anxiety-producing. We may well feel fearful of the consequences that might arise from contemplating alternatives to our current ways of thinking and living; resistance, resentment, and confusion are evident at the various stages of the critical thinking process. (Brookfield, 1987: 7)

Given this, the idea of critical thinking may be applauded and encouraged, but in practice it might not occur as frequently as might be expected.

Within the social care and social work literature the concept is applied in a variety of ways. The emphasis may be on applying a critique of the social sphere or the specific process of day-to-day practice. In terms of the former, Jones-Devitt and Smith (2007) explore the way in which Marxism and feminism have challenged social arrangements and contributed to new ways of explaining, and in some instances re-organising, the world in which we live. The emphasis here is on the way in which critical thinking might lead to changes in legislation, policy and practice and how an appreciation of the social context is important for social care practitioners. Given the importance and complexity of the concept as well as its varied usage, it may be unsurprising that there is an overlap with related concepts such as 'reflective thinking'. The terms 'critical learning', and 'critical practice' are also in use. The different applications and overlapping concepts might be seen as encouraging confusion. Furthermore, Halonen (1995, cited in Coleman et al., 2002) argues that the concept of 'critical thinking' is over-worked and under-analysed.

On social work courses students are likely to be encouraged to critique the inequalities and injustices of social arrangements and develop 'critical practice' (see Adams et al., 2002) whilst attention may also be given to developing the specific reasoning skills (see Mumm and Kersting, 1997). In terms of the latter, this skill is encouraged by means of writing essays, research dissertations, and portfolios (Coleman et al., 2002), but specialist games have also been devised (see Gibbs and Gambrill, 1996, cited in Mumm and Kersting, 1997). These educational tasks allow students not only to acquire a body of knowledge, but to develop their skill in evaluating the arguments made by others and in practising their own ability in making and supporting a case. Active as opposed to passive learning is seen as encouraging critical thinking skills (Coleman et al., 2002).

THE CONCEPT IN SOCIAL WORK PRACTICE

Some social work theorists (for example, those working from a psycho-social perspective) might draw attention to the role played by emotion in the process of thinking and how it might impede reasoning. For Biestek (1957), an early contributor to social work theory, the role of the practitioner was to offer emotional support to his/her clients (service users) in order that thinking might be facilitated and solutions to problems found:

Frequently the release of feelings removes the blind spots, and enables the client to see his problem more objectively and move towards a solution. His mind is somewhat freed of certain impediments and inhibitions, thereby enabling him to think more clearly, reason more accurately, and act more surely. Ordinarily a constricting emotional involvement rather than a lack of intelligence is at the base of the problem. (Biestek, 1957: 46)

Although Biestek was writing about a form of social work that rarely applies in the 21st century, it is still appropriate that practitioners, in the pursuit of their goals, are advised to consider the emotional world of the service user as well as their ability to reason.

Similarly, from a psycho-social perspective, the poor emotional well-being of the social work practitioner might inhibit his/her ability to think critically or even engage in rational thought about a particular case. This situation might arise when a social worker is attempting to offer help and support to a service user who is experiencing a high level of emotional disturbance. This emotional disturbance will impact upon the relational dynamics and be experienced unconsciously by the practitioner. Agass (2005) examines this scenario and discusses the importance of supervision for social work practitioners.

Supervision, usually provided by a line manager, is the means by which the work of practitioners is managed, the practitioner's knowledge and skill is developed and the practitioner is provided with emotional support. It is the place where practitioners might be assisted to reflect on the thinking that has informed their approach to specific cases and the decisions that have been made. The supervisor, by means of a trusting relationship, is able to contain the worker's anxieties, facilitate critical reflection and new thinking on the situation. This process is therefore both conscious and unconscious. The social worker's ability to be aware of his/her emotions and the part they have played in the process of thinking is also considered to be important (see Howe, 2008). Supervision is therefore the place where conceptualising, analysing, synthesising and evaluating information might take place, but it is also the place where the emotional component of thinking and decision making is taken into account. It is important to note that there is a substantial body of literature on the process of supervision and discussion of this key concept will occur elsewhere.

Finally, it is important to note that social workers frequently plan and make decisions in partnership with an extensive network of stakeholders. These stakeholders include professionals from a range of different disciplines as well as service users themselves. The use of evidence, logical reasoning and the questioning of implicit and explicit assumptions is important. However, critical thinking is unlikely to constitute a panacea: it is unlikely to eliminate the emotional, interpretive and contested processes that remain at the heart of social work practice today.

Cross references: professional development, reflection, supervision

SUGGESTED READING

Brown, K. and Rutter, L. (2008) *Critical Thinking for Social Work*. Exeter: Learning Matters.
Howe, D. (2008) *The Emotionally Intelligent Social Worker*. Basingstoke: Palgrave Macmillan.

REFERENCES

Adams, R., Dominelli, L. and Payne, M. (eds) (2002) *Critical Practice in Social Work*. Basingstoke: Palgrave Macmillan.

Agass, D. (2005) 'The containing function of supervision in working with abuse', in M. Bower (ed.), *Psychoanalytic Theory for Social Work Practice: Thinking Under Fire*. London: Routledge, pp.189–200.

Biestek, F.P. (1957) *The Casework Relationship*. London: George Allen Unwin.

Brookfield, S. (1987) *Developing Critical Thinkers*. Milton Keynes: Open University Press.

Brown, K. and Rutter, L. (2008) *Critical Thinking for Social Work*. Exeter: Learning Matters.

Coleman, H., Rogers, G. and King, J. (2002) 'Using portfolios to stimulate critical thinking in social work education', *Social Work Education*, 21(5): 583–95.

Descartes, R. (1637) 'Discourse on the method of rightly concluding reason and seeking truth in the sciences'. Available from: www.literature.org (accessed 15 September 2011).

Gibbs, L.E. and Gambrill, E. (1996) *Critical Thinking for Social Workers: A Workbook*. Newbury Park, CA: Pine Forge Press.

Halonen, J. (1995) 'Demystifying critical thinking', *Teaching of Psychology*, 22(1): 75–81.

Howe, D. (2008) *The Emotionally Intelligent Social Worker*. Basingstoke: Palgrave Macmillan.

Jones-Devitt, S. and Smith, L. (2007) *Critical Thinking in Health and Social Care*. London: Sage.

Mumm, A. and Kersting, R. (1997) 'Teaching critical thinking in social work practice courses', *Journal of Social Work Education*, 33(1): 75–84.

Plath, D., English, B., Connors, L. and Beveridge, A. (1999) 'Evaluating the outcomes of intensive critical thinking instruction for social work', *Social Work Education*, 18(2): 207–17.

Scriven, M. and Paul, R. (1987) 'Defining critical thinking'. A statement by Michael Scriven and Robert Paul for the National Council for Excellence in Critical Thinking Instruction. The Critical Thinking Community. Available from: www.criticalthinking.org/about CT/define_critical_thinking.cfm (accessed 8 September 2011).

13
Dementia

Jane Youell and Helga Stiborski

DEFINITION

Dementia is an umbrella term used to describe various symptoms associated with cognitive ability; these include memory, decision making, comprehension, mood and language. There are many disorders which are commonly called dementia. The most common are Alzheimer's disease (approximately two thirds of cases), vascular dementia and Lewy Body dementia, although there are many other types. There is currently no cure for dementia, but some types can respond well to treatment

(Alzheimer's Society, 2011). Dementia is common. According to Alzheimer's Research UK (2011), there are approximately 820,000 people living with the diagnosis today. This figure is set to rise dramatically in the next 20–30 years. Dementia predominantly affects people over 65, but incidences of young onset dementia are now being recognised and diagnosed. The cost of dementia to the UK economy is almost more than the cost of cancer, heart disease and stroke combined. Prevalence rates increase with age. It is estimated that one in 1,400 will receive a diagnosis of young onset dementia. In the post-65 age group prevalence rates increase every five years, from one in 100 at 65–69 to one in six over the age of 80. Dementia is a progressive condition, but each person will experience dementia in their own unique way. Two thirds of those living with a diagnosis of dementia remain in the community (DH, 2009).

Dementia is a complex condition which impacts on relationships, employment, financial matters, mental capacity and end of life care. The right support at the right time by the right agency is crucial and every effort should be made to understand the wishes of the person with dementia. This chapter will briefly outline some of the key points around dementia care, in the hope that the reader will investigate dementia care and related social work practices more thoroughly.

KEY POINTS

- legislation, policy and guidance
- assessment
- specialist support
- funding and financial implications
- multi-disciplinary working

DISCUSSION

Dementia has risen up the UK Government agenda in response to the ageing population and the potential increase in the incidence of dementia and the associated costs in terms of health and social care needs. Two crucial Acts in the care of people with dementia are the Mental Health Act 1983 (MHA) and the Mental Capacity Act 2005 (MCA). The MHA affects those with a diagnosis of dementia in terms of assessment, treatment, safeguarding and care planning. A person with a diagnosis may be detained under the MHA if it is deemed in the person's best interests to do so as laid down within the MCA. The MCA aims to 'provide a statutory framework for people who lack capacity to make decisions for themselves' (Department of Constitutional Affairs, 2007: 1). A Code of Practice accompanies the MCA which offers guidance for workers and carers in relation to the legal duties set out in the MCA. As capacity is likely to be eventually lost or questioned in the course of the progression of dementia, or become variable/fluctuating depending on the decision to be made, the MCA is the core piece of legislation, which those working in dementia care must be familiar with and work within. The MCA works within five key principles. Capacity is presumed to be present unless proven otherwise, individuals have the *right* to make own decisions and should be fully supported to do so, individuals have the *right* to make an unwise decision, where decisions are made on behalf of another these decisions must be in the best interest of the individual person as laid down within the MCA, and where possible and appropriate basic rights and freedoms will be respected.

Capacity assessment is a decision specific test; a person may be capable of making decisions about some things such as their weekly shopping but unable to deal with large sums of money, for example. Who assesses capacity is dependent on the nature of the decision. If a person does not have capacity to make a specific decision, then the decision must be made in their best interests.

Case study

Mr Brown is 85 years old. He has dementia and lives alone in his own home. Mr Brown says that he no longer wants to have a daily bath. However, his district nurse feels that this would be good for him due to his bladder incontinence and risk of skin tissue breaking down. The district nurse asks for his social worker to get involved because of the risk to his well-being.

Although Mr Brown has dementia he is still able to make many decisions for himself, including those posing a risk which could be seen as unwise decisions. The social worker carries out a two-stage capacity assessment – the diagnostic test and the functional test. Mr Brown has a formal diagnosis of dementia so the diagnostic test is met. Mr Brown is able to understand and retain the relevant information; and communicate his decision. However, he is not able to weigh up the information such as considering the pros and cons of having a daily bath and the long-term risk to his tissue viability, so a best interest decision is made mindful of the principles of the MCA.

The best interest meeting/discussion concluded that, to be least restrictive, a daily wash may be more appropriate. The social worker discusses this with Mr Brown – which he agrees to. The district nurse also agrees to supply more incontinence pads and monitor his skin integrity.

Where a person's capacity in relation to a specific decision is in question but no other appropriate family member or friend is able to support, the Act states that an Independent Mental Capacity Advocate (IMCA) must act with and on behalf of the person. The IMCA role is fairly recent and came into effect with the MCA and shows a positive shift when supporting people who may lack capacity. In light of this shift in attitude, the then Government produced a National Dementia Strategy (NDS) entitled *Living Well with Dementia* (DH, 2009). The aim of the strategy was broadly threefold:

- to increase knowledge and understanding of dementia;
- to provide better training for professionals;
- to provide a range of support services.

The strategy cites 17 key objectives (an 18th was added later which related to the reduction in anti-psychotic medication) which set out to give guidance and address current shortfalls in service provision for local authorities.

Early diagnosis is a key objective of all those who work with dementia. The earlier the diagnosis is made the better the treatment plans and outcomes are likely to be. Dementia assessment can be difficult; symptoms can often lead to a variety of conditions. There is also the assumption that forgetfulness and confusion are a natural part of ageing in the general population, so some are reluctant to bother their doctor (GP). Generally, a GP would be the first contact and there has been some reluctance in the past by GPs to diagnose dementia, either because they are unsure of the accuracy of the diagnosis or feel that there is insufficient support available for those with the diagnosis. With the employment of Admiral Nurses and Dementia Care Advisors, support services are slowly growing, as is the confidence to make a diagnosis and assessment.

As dementia affects all aspects of life, specialist support is crucial. Admiral Nurses offer advice and support to those living with dementia. They are specialist mental health nurses, whose ethos is to promote living well and positively with dementia (Dementia UK, 2011). Dementia Care Advisors equally offer support particularly around treatment plans, planning future care and supporting carers.

Dementia can affect all aspects of a person's life. The financial implications of dementia are often cited by those living with the condition. For those living with young onset dementia, anxiety around losing a full-time income can be a major concern. But worries are also seen in older relationships. Often in partnerships one partner is responsible for financial matters; if this is the partner with dementia this can place the carer with added burden. Social workers need to be aware of the financial support available for those living with dementia and their carers, but would also need to be supportive of future financial implications.

The MCA offers guidance on advance directives and lasting power of attorney, in relation to financial as well as welfare matters which those living with dementia may need to consider. It is crucial that these considerations be made sooner rather than later as once a person is deemed to lack capacity, these options are no longer available. These can be difficult conversations to have for those living with dementia, their carers and professionals. The focus can appear to be on the more negative aspects of living with dementia and as such should be handled sensitively. The National Council for Palliative Care (2011) has recently produced a booklet called *Difficult Conversations* which offers advice to both professionals and unpaid carers on how to broach difficult subjects. The focus is around end of life care, but also mentions finances, future wishes, life after caring, etc. This is a useful tool for professionals to help open up those difficult conversations.

Case study

Janyce is a woman in her 70s who has just been diagnosed with the early stages of dementia. She lives alone but has two daughters who live locally. Janyce has always said that she would never want to be tube fed if ever that was an issue for her, as was the case with her own father. She was advised to make an Advance Directive that would stipulate her wishes should she lose capacity to make these types of decisions. If the use of the tube could be defined as life-sustaining treatment, the Advance Decision would need to be written, signed and witnessed and include a statement saying that it applies even if life is at risk in order to be valid.

This will ensure that the Advance Decision is legally binding. Her daughters agree with their mother's wishes.

As can be seen, dementia care is a complex and ever changing situation. Good communication between practitioners, carers and the person with the diagnosis is crucial. It is vital that multi-disciplinary working is achieved but this can be challenging for practitioners. A criticism of dementia care is that no one team 'owns dementia' and so support and care can be sporadic and inconsistent. A multi-disciplinary approach with good communication and involvement with the person with dementia and their carer should be the goal, as stated in the White Paper – *Our Health, Our Care, Our Say* (DH, 2006).

CONCLUSION

The challenges in dementia care are many, but this is an exciting time for researchers and practitioners. Dementia is finally being recognised and discussed, additional dementia specific training is being offered and the barriers such as stigma, perceptions and access to good care are steadily being removed, albeit quite slowly at times. Social workers will play an important role in the care of all of those affected by dementia and it is hoped that this chapter has given some insight into good practice.

Cross references: assessment, mental health, older people

SUGGESTED READING

DH (Department of Health) (2006) *Our Health, Our Care, Our Say*. London: The Stationery Office.
National Council for Palliative Care (2011) *Difficult Conversations: Making it Easier to Talk to People with Dementia about the End of Life*. London: National Council for Palliative Care.

REFERENCES

Alzheimer's Research UK (2011) 'Dementia statistics'. Available from: www.alzheimersresear-chuk.org/dementia-statistics (accessed 6 September 2011).
Alzheimer's Society (2011) 'What is Alzheimer's disease? Factsheet 401'. Available from: www.alzheimers.org.uk/site/scripts/documents_info.php?documentID=100 (accessed 6 September 2011).
Dementia UK (2011) 'Admiral nurses'. Available from: www.dementiauk.org/what-we-do/admi-ral-nurses (accessed 6 September 2011).
Department of Constitutional Affairs (2007) *Mental Capacity Act 2005: Code of Practice*. London: TSO.
DH (Department of Health) (2006) *Our Health, Our Care, Our Say*. London: The Stationery Office.
DH (Department of Health) (2009) *Living Well with Dementia: A National Dementia Strategy*. London: DH.
Mental Capacity Act (2005) (C 9). London: HMSO.
Mental Health Act (1983) (C 20). London: HMSO.
National Council for Palliative Care (2011) *Difficult Conversations: Making it Easier to Talk to People with Dementia about the End of Life*. London: National Council for Palliative Care.

14

Direct Work with Children

Alice O'Sullivan

DEFINITION

Much childcare social work involves working with the child's parent/s, the family group and co-ordinating other professionals' intervention. In its own right this non-direct work has a valuable place in social work but should not be confused with, or form a substitute for, direct work with children. Direct work with children has features and merits of its own and is best thought of as a spectrum. At one end of the spectrum direct work can include basic interactions with children. At the other end it is a distinct way of working with children which Hapgood defines as:

> a means of intervening directly in the lives of children and young people so as to enable them to understand significant events in their past, to confront feelings engendered by these events and to become more fully involved in the future planning of their lives. (Hapgood, 1988, cited in Ruch, 1998: 38)

At this end of the spectrum direct work is discrete time spent with children for the purpose of therapeutic support.

Within this chapter direct work with children covers the whole spectrum of structured child-centred time spent with a child on a one-to-one basis by a social worker for an array of purposes. The term 'child' is used here to denote any person aged under 18. The time spent with the child is 'structured' in that it is time put aside for such work. Structured does not denote that the time is necessarily led and structured by the worker but rather that the worker needs to have a clear goal or purpose. For effective direct work to take place social workers need to move into the child's world as opposed to staying in their own adults' world where activities such as interviewing and discussion take precedence.

KEY POINTS

- Direct work with children is used: to engage; as part of the assessment process; to communicate; to ascertain feelings and wishes; and for therapeutic reasons.
- Direct work with children should be child-centred and take place in the child's world, entailing the use of play, art, interactive media and stories.
- The activities involved in direct work must be appropriate in accordance to the child's development, language, culture and personality.

- The skills and personal qualities required to carry out direct work with children are those needed to be an effective childcare social worker and include interpersonal skills and patience.
- Direct work with children can be therapeutic but should not be therapy unless the worker is a trained therapist.

DISCUSSION

Direct work with children can take many forms, including play, games and fun activities and can incorporate any type of art. It might involve talking through an issue with a child whilst carrying out a non-threatening activity to 'take pressure off' the conversation. Direct work may entail a project that the worker and child undertake together such as forming a life story book or using interactive media. Direct work can involve writing, reading or discussing stories connected to the issues that the child is going through. The social worker may undertake direct work to engage and build a rapport with a child by using: 'getting to know you' games, 'finding out about you' worksheets or unstructured play. The format of any engaging work should centre around the child's interests and development. Social workers may use direct work methods in their assessments to involve the child in this process. Without direct work the social worker would need to rely merely on observation and questioning to gain the child's input, both of which are important elements of an assessment but in isolation they may not paint a full picture of the child's situation, feelings and views.

A social worker may also use direct work for therapeutic reasons. Some may have worries about social workers not being qualified to carry out therapeutic work. However, direct work should be thought of as therapeutic as opposed to therapy. Ruch (1998) discusses the difference between the work of a therapist and that of a social worker:

> Therapists focus on the inner world of the child, whilst social workers focus on and work with the external events in a child's life and how they affect the child's inner world. (Ruch, 1998: 39)

Both a social worker and therapist might use art as a means of working with a child, but their goal may be different. A social worker may use art to share information with a child about family members, whilst a therapist might want to ascertain the working of a child's inner thoughts about their family members by interpreting the art formed. Social workers need to be cautious when carrying out direct work because it is detrimental to encourage a child to delve into deep rooted issues that the worker and child are unable to manage. In the words of a child worker at Women's Aid: 'You mustn't open a box unless you know how to help the child shut it' (Mullender et al., 1997: 91). Therefore, social workers need to manage the boundaries of such work to ensure it is enhancing a child's well-being and that they incorporate direct questioning within their activities to ensure they remain in the child's external world. Alongside this, they should ensure the activities they plan involve appropriate imagery which is not threatening to the child.

Direct work is a central part of childcare social work. Social work practice is based on effective communication and communication with children takes a different form to communicating with adults. As stated by Goodyer, 'talk in children's own social worlds is often intrinsic to other activities, such as play' (2007: 738). Building a secure relationship with children is vital for effective social work. Bannister maintains that:

> A consistent and containing therapeutic relationship may start to meet children's needs for safety, recognition and reconnection with themselves and others. (Bannister, 2003, cited in Lefevre, 2004: 334)

Lefevre (2004) feels social workers are well placed to be this consistent and containing professional and such relationships can be formed through the use of direct work. McLeod found in her research with young people in care that they wanted more relationship-based social work from their allocated social worker. In their own words they asserted that there is 'too much corporate and not enough parenting' (McLeod, 2010: 772). McLeod asserts that a key ingredient of relationship-based social work with children is direct work.

A key role of some childcare social workers is collecting evidence for care proceedings. This poses a dilemma about what should be shared from what is 'discovered' in the direct work. Best practice here would be to clearly identify the purpose of each particular piece of direct work and ensure this is understood by the child, social worker, manager and other professionals. A further difficulty that can arise from direct work is the emotional impact such work can have on the worker. Supervisors need to be appropriately trained to ensure they are able to support social workers who undertake such work.

THE CONCEPT IN SOCIAL WORK PRACTICE

Case study – Jayne and Kay

Kay is a social worker supporting Jayne, a five-year-old, white British girl, who until recently lived with her mother and is now in foster care. Social workers have removed Jayne from the care of her mother due to concerns over her safety in relation to local gang members frequently staying at her house. Kay is undertaking a core assessment and a child protection conference has been called. Kay would like to talk to Jayne about whether she is happy at the foster carers; what her wishes are regarding where she would rather live; and to gain further information about her experience of living at her mum's.

Session 1

Kay encourages Jayne to draw images of herself and the significant people in her life and asks her to place a picture of herself in the centre of an eco-map and place the other people around her. Kay and Jayne use the map to discuss how close Jayne felt to each person.

Session 2

Kay encourages Jayne to use her toys to represent each of the significant people in her life. Kay uses the toys to play out and explain to Jayne why she was moved from her mum's home to the foster carers' home. Kay then encourages Jayne to use the toys to show what life was like at her mum's and at the foster carers'. Next Kay encourages Jayne to talk about her feelings about her situation using toys representing each of them.

Session 3

Kay shows Jayne two images, one of a happy face and the other of a sad face. Kay asks Jayne to point at the appropriate images to indicate her likes and dislikes. Kay begins with seemingly unthreatening subjects such as foods, animals, school and play and then moves on to the people in her life such as her mum, foster carers, extended family members and mum's friends.

Kay plans to use the information gained from these sessions in her core assessment and as part of the evidence at conference. Kay is very clear that she cannot take at face value or too literally all of what Jayne has shown her. She discusses with her supervisor her work with Jayne and how Jayne showed a very happy home life at the foster carers' and a less happy home life at her mum's. She showed she liked her mum by pointing at the happy face and did not like her mum's friends by pointing at the sad face. With further work through the toys Kay ascertained that Jayne would like to live with her mum but away from the friends and extended family members and do the fun activities she does with the foster carers with her mother.

There is concern about a lack of time childcare social workers have for direct work due to mounting caseloads and complying with bureaucratic procedures. Past serious case reviews have stated the need for social workers to see and talk to the child they are safeguarding. The fact that some social workers are not able to achieve this minimum suggests that direct work becoming a routine day-to-day practice remains a distant goal. Munro's statement in her review of child protection in England that social workers need be able 'to spend time with children and young people and develop a meaningful relationship' (Munro, 2010: 18) provides hope that social workers, frontline managers and policymakers will come to see direct work as a legitimate and essential social work task.

Cross references: communication, partnership, safeguarding children, supervision

SUGGESTED READING

Luckock, B. and Lefevre, M. (eds) (2010) *Direct Work: Social Work with Children and Young People in Care*. London: BAAF.

Willis, R. and Holand, S. (2009) 'Life story work reflections on the experience by looked after young people', *Adoption and Fostering*, 33(4): 44–52.

REFERENCES

Goodyer, A. (2007) 'Teaching qualifying social workers skills for direct work with children', *Social Work Education*, 26(7): 737–40.

Lefevre, M. (2004) 'Playing with sound: the therapeutic use of music in direct work with children', *Child and Family Social Work*, 9: 333–45.

McLeod, A. (2010) 'A friend and an equal: do young people in care seek the impossible from their social workers?', *British Journal of Social Work*, 40: 772–88.

Mullender, A., Debbonaire, T., Hague, G., Kelly, L. and Malos, E. (1997) 'Working with children in women's refuges', *Child and Family Social Work*, 3: 87–98.

Munro, E. (2010) *The Munro Review of Child Protection: Part One: A Systems Analysis*. London: Department of Education.

Ruch, G. (1998) 'Direct work with children: the practitioner's perspective', *Practice*, 10(1): 37–44.

15
Domestic Violence

Kate Cook

DEFINITION

Domestic violence is interpersonal abuse in intimate relationships. Some definitions limit this to partner/ex relationships whilst others include all violence within family-type settings (see Women's Aid, 2009). Both 'domestic' and 'violence' are terms which can mislead. This abuse is generally perpetrated by men against women as a means of control. In ongoing abuse situations, 89 per cent of the victims are women (Walby and Allen, 2004). Domestic violence can take place in other relationships such as between gay male partners or where an elderly relative of either sex is the victim.

Women who have experienced this 'violence' say that it may be physical but also includes: manipulation; restriction of access to family and friends; to money and other means of independence. It can also involve coerced sexual acts which the woman would not otherwise participate in. Common understandings of violent partners as driven by impulse, drink, stress and/or poverty do not explain the deliberate nature of much of this behaviour. Men may also be victims of female partners, however research shows that some abusers claim this as another means of retaining control (see Women's Aid, 2009). This control is rarely limited to the 'domestic'. An abuser can limit car use or lock their partner in the house. Even when a couple are out, perhaps for a social gathering, an abuser will still find ways of ensuring dominance, using threats and promises.

Within a family where there is a dominant violent male, children learn that women are not worthy of respect. They often witness violence and may become victims. 'Nearly three quarters of children on the "at risk" register live in such households' (Women's Aid, 2007). Abusers also use children as tools of control as women tend to submit, rather than risk their child's safety.

The term 'domestic abuse' is now favoured by some practitioners as more indicative of manipulative behaviour. The law does not contain specific offences for 'domestic violence' so that many other terms apply in legal contexts.

KEY POINTS

- Domestic violence can be understood as physical, sexual, emotional and financial abuse in intimate relationships, punctuated by periods of reprieve.
- Research suggests that around half of all women experience domestic violence, at least once.
- Domestic violence is easiest to approach, explain and understand as deliberate, controlling behaviour, designed to create and maintain dependence.
- For those who are victimised, domestic violence is difficult to discuss and harder still to escape.
- The woman is often striving to protect her children, so woman-protection is often synonymous with child-protection.

DISCUSSION

Research shows that women are killed during domestic violence (around two women each week, in England and Wales) and that the time at which a woman is most at risk, is when she attempts to leave (Women's Aid, 2006).

The women's sector remains the leading source of expertise, running women's safe houses (refuges) and providing access to talking support, over the phone, in groups and one-to-one. These agencies, headed by Women's Aid, aim to empower women and generally speak of women who escape violence as 'survivors' in preference to using the more stigmatising label of 'victim'.

Modern theoretical understandings of domestic violence also come from women's experiences. The idea of a 'continuum of violence' helps practitioners to see the connections between apparently different actions. There is a 'common character', 'the abuse, intimidation, coercion, intrusion, threat and force men use to control women' (Kelly, 1988: 78). This also shows links between domestic violence and child abuse.

The Duluth Domestic Abuse Intervention Project power and control wheel (Duluth, 2011), can help practitioners and survivors to understand the experience of being abused. This tool depicts the sexual and physical violence as the outer rim of a wheel which is made up of spokes, each of which describes a form of abuse. These cover emotional manipulation; using male privilege (behaving like an old-fashioned patriarch); isolation; using children; blaming; using economic power; coercion; and threats. The wheel also acknowledges the ways in which men play down the abuse, even using occasional indulgences as a part of their campaign. Being unpredictable is important for a successful abuser. The sum of this is the heart of the wheel, the violence, the unpredictability and the coercive behaviour together create power over the woman and control for the abuser (for more information see www.theduluthmodel.org). The wheel images help when discussing women's experiences with them.

Law often responds to domestic violence through civil law, as a private issue, positioning the problem between the two individuals. This means encouraging the victim to take out an injunction, requiring the violent partner to stay away. Thousands of injunctions are issued every year (statistics are given in Women's Aid, 2009) and they can sometimes be obtained with legal aid. The very fact that these injunctions, and domestic violence itself, are so common means that official responses are not always pro-active.

Criminal law responds to public legal issues. Many women see domestic violence as a public problem and want a response from the police. If an injunction is breached then the police are called to act on that and the police receive one call about domestic violence, every minute (Stanko, 2000). Despite this, official estimates state that only a quarter of domestic violence is reported to the police (Women's Aid, 2009).

The criminal law does not currently include separate offences relating to domestic violence. The offences often pursued following a domestic violence incident are the minor 'public order' offences. These are relatively easy to prove (generally without evidence being given by the victim) and carry minor penalties. More serious offences which may be committed include assault, wounding, sexual assault, rape and even murder.

The minor offences taken to court rarely reflect the reality of women who are facing daily violence and intimidation. Additionally, the police generally raise charges based on what took place without considering the effect of doing this on the woman involved. Consequently she may be too afraid to support the prosecution and often comes to court with her violent partner, apparently supporting his 'innocence'. In fact, she may have little real choice, believing herself to be better off within this relationship, than on her own/with her children.

Social workers may also become involved in very serious cases which result in a review under Section 9 of the Domestic Violence Crime and Victims Act 2004 (these provisions are also subject of a bill before parliament at the time of writing). Locally, councils often chair a multi-agency forum to discuss policy and practice on domestic abuse. However, the knowledge about domestic abuse often resides with the local Women's Aid group who may well run one or more refuges for women fleeing violence and provide a range of other services. Some localities may also have more than one refuge group and may have other women's groups (such as a Black or Asian women's group, a rape crisis centre or women's centre) all of whom may well have valuable knowledge, services and experience to offer.

The MARAC (Multi-Agency Risk Assessment Conference) aims to be a more focused meeting, considering cases where somebody is at serious risk, in order to ensure that local agencies (police, social workers, other care workers and voluntary agencies) act together to ensure safety. These depend on goodwill and partnership-working and so success is bound to vary. They also risk removing the woman's sense of control over her own actions even further and so care needs to be exercised to balance safety and women's rights.

Local councils may employ 'IDVAs' (Independent Domestic Violence Advocates or Advisers) who may be based in Women's Aid, Victim Support, with the police or in some other agency. Concerns are raised about the role, funding and 'independent' nature of these roles and so again, their usefulness probably varies.

The case study below considers a family where a MARAC-style intervention may have helped to avoid a death, in this case the husband's. Although it is usually the woman who is at risk, it is also possible to learn from the rarer cases where the woman fights back.

THE CONCEPT IN SOCIAL WORK PRACTICE

Case study

Kiranjit Ahulwalia came to Britain from India, in 1979 at the age of 24. She did not speak much English and moved in with her husband, Deepak's, family. They were married for ten years and throughout he was severely violent towards her. She tried to leave him on numerous occasions. She has reported that he used to leave her on the central reservation of the motorway, driving off with her two sons in the car, laughing at her. One night, after a particularly prolonged violent attack, Kiranjit poured petrol over Deepak's feet as he slept, and set it alight.

He died later, in hospital. She was sent to prison for murder, though eventually released on appeal, and her case helped to highlight the problems faced by women in abusive marriages, where their desperation drives them to take violent action (Ahluwalia and Gupta, 2008; Bindel et al., 1995). Kiranjit's story was later made into the film 'Provoked'.

Identifying who is most at risk is clearly a social worker's concern and it is important to think about those who, like Kiranjit, are vulnerable because they are not 'local' and so they do not have supportive networks. Perhaps these women lack English language skills, making them 'difficult to reach' and yet, meaning that the need to do so is enhanced. In some cases women may be smelly, bad-tempered, poorly clothed, have unruly children and appear to be drugged or drunk. Sustained violence does not produce attractive families, and so it is important that social workers are able to follow-up on the most intractable cases and not see these merely as 'unreachable'.

Other women's stories can help to illustrate the continuum of violence and encourage professionals to think about the relationship between child protection and domestic violence. Emma Humphreys also fought back. She fled a childhood home where ongoing violence was the norm. This led her to live in perilous circumstances as a youngster, making her way by selling her body. She eventually found a home with one of her clients, but then killed him, after repeated imprisonments, violations and a gang rape. Emma served a number of years in prison before being freed on appeal. Sadly her life ended in overdose, although she did live independently for a short time (Bindel and Wistrich, 2003).

All women can experience domestic abuse, but the young; those from poor families; who have disabilities and who have migrated, may be at increased risk. It is important that social workers strive to understand the lived experience of domestic violence, and learn enough to move beyond stereotypes.

domestic violence

Cross references: anti-oppressive practice, asylum seekers and refugees, empowerment, safeguarding children

SUGGESTED READING

Barron, J. (2009) 'The survivors handbook'. Women's Aid Federation. Available from: www.women-said.org.uk (accessed 2 June 2012).

Mullender, A. (1996) *Rethinking Domestic Violence: The Social Work and Probation Response*. London: Routledge.

REFERENCES

Ahluwalia, K. and Gupta, R. (2008) *Provoked: The Story of Kiranjit Ahluwalia*. Delhi: Harper Collins.

Bindel, J. and Wistrich, H. (2003) *The Map of My Life: The Story of Emma Humphreys*. London: Astraia Press.

Bindel, J., Cook, K. and Kelly, L. (1995) 'Trials and tribulations: "Justice for women"', in G. Griffin (ed.), *Feminist Activism for the 1990s*. London: Taylor and Francis, pp. 65–74.

Duluth (2011) *The Duluth Domestic Abuse Intervention Project*. Available from: www. theduluthmodel. org (accessed 5 September 2012).

Kelly, L. (1988) *Surviving Sexual Violence*. Minneapolis, MN: University of Minnesota Press.

Stanko, E. (2000) 'The day to count: a snapshot of the impact of domestic violence in the UK', *Criminal Justice*, 1: 2.

Walby, S. and Allen, J. (2004) *Domestic Violence, Sexual Assault and Stalking: Findings from the British Crime Survey*. London: Home Office. (Research, Development and Statistics Directorate.)

Women's Aid (2006) 'Why doesn't she leave?' Available from: www.womensaid.org.uk (accessed 8 May 2011).

Women's Aid (2007) 'Domestic violence statistics'. Available from: www.womensaid.org.uk (accessed 8 May 2011).

Women's Aid (2009) 'Domestic violence FAQ'. Available from: www.womensaid.org.uk (accessed 8 May 2011).

16
Empowerment

Joanne Lewis

DEFINITION

Empowerment, in this context, is the means by which social workers can enable or assist service users to exert an influence over the arrangements made for their social care provision. It is a process by which individuals, families and communities may have the opportunity to exercise a sense of control by being a key part of the process that will define their needs and ultimately shape their care provision. Adams deems 'empowerment' to be the capacity of the aforementioned groups to be afforded the opportunity to 'take control of their circumstances, exercise power and achieve their own goals' (2008: 17). Thompson considers empowerment to be 'a process of helping people gain greater control over their lives and the socio-political and existential challenges they face' (cited in Swain and French, 2008: 133).

KEY POINTS

- The importance of correctly identifying 'need' and the various factors that can influence what and how provision is applied thereafter.
- An awareness of the dilemma that choice presents, both for the service user and for the social work professional.
- The impact of the organisational model applied by management.
- Witnessing empowerment in practice.

DISCUSSION

In order for the social worker to effectively support those whose needs are greater, it is essential to ascertain their requirements as accurately as possible. In terms of empowerment that need can only be clearly identified by means of comprehensive communication with the individual, family or community concerned. Saleebey (2006) refers to the 'strengths perspective', in other words, what may at first appear to be a deficiency that perpetuates the need, may indeed hold within it a strength yet to be identified. Saleebey goes on to state that 'we best serve our clients by collaborating with them' (2006: 162). Indeed, within these discussions, although there may of course lie challenge, there may also lie the opportunity to correctly identify not only the need of the client but also their aspiration. The social worker is urged not to be so arrogant as to assume that they 'know the upper limits of the capacity to grow and change' and that furthermore, professionals must 'take individual, group and community aspirations seriously . . . every environment is full of resources' (Saleebey, 2006: 162).

Alongside the identification of need, it is imperative that in order to provide the correct and appropriate care, social workers must look to the finer details that will influence any care giving/support. These include: individual beliefs, cultural awareness, family beliefs and values and an understanding of the nature of the local community. Once the need and its finer details have been ascertained, the move towards empowerment continues with the provision of appropriate and adequate information and resources. Once again, empowerment is reinforced by means of 'choice'; the service user choosing (where they are able or where it is appropriate) what they consider to be the best course of action for them. As well as the social worker adhering to the General Social Care Council Code of Practice (GSCC, 2004), they must also ensure that the information they provide is clearly understood. More importantly, all options should be presented alongside those recommended by the social worker, in order for the service user to make an *informed choice*. Sensitive and accurate assessment of need by the social workers will hopefully lead to greater independence/empowerment on the part of the service user. When considering the assessment process, Griggs makes the very salient point that the procedure itself may prove for some clients to be an 'intrusive process' (2000: 23). Moreover, warns Griggs, this course of action may 'raise expectations of choice that agencies are unable to deliver' (Griggs, 2000: 23).

Of course, the social worker must also be aware that, whilst enabling the progression of their client/clients along the path towards 'self-actualisation' (Milliken and Honeycutt, 2004), the way is often fraught with possibilities for their personal and professional ethics to be challenged. Hunter and Ritchie highlight the potential for dilemma that may arise 'when people make choices which carry high risks or appear not to be in their best interest' (2008: 18). The General Social Care Council advise social workers that they *must* 'promote the independence of service users while protecting them as far as possible from danger or harm' (cited in Waine et al., 2005: 19). This is when detailed knowledge of all the aforementioned factors relating to the individual, family or community concerned can help to effect clear and pertinent guidance on the part of the social work professional.

A key factor in assisting the social work professional to enable empowerment on the part of the service user is the organisational model applied by management. The model employed should, ideally, be one that allows for various fundamental dynamics. By management employing clear, effective and ongoing communication at all levels, this will hopefully lead to an increase in social workers' involvement. When there is the need for change or improvement to (and implementation) of service provision, the management style should ideally consult with social workers and service users. The consummate management style should allow for an effective leadership that will enable the necessary changes to occur. The method adopted by the leader/leaders should enable them to become adept at motivating all departments. Moreover the effective leader should be able to facilitate all social workers in the devising and adopting a shared vision that is fully supported by all (Hunter and Ritchie, 2008).

THE CONCEPT IN SOCIAL WORK PRACTICE

It is only when empowerment is put into practice that social workers and their management can hope to gain a true insight into the scale of its effectiveness. One such example of empowerment in practice can be witnessed in the Sheffield and Children Young People's Empowerment Project (CHILYPEP). Its work revolves around children and young people living in areas and communities within Sheffield that have been identified as being highly deprived. The primary focus of the project is encouraging young people to become fully active in the decision-making process regarding the issues that impact upon their lives, 'to promote and facilitate the application of findings of consultation exercises with public services'

(Social Care Institute for Excellence, 2011). The project is based upon information garnered through questionnaires designed by the young participants as part of a peer research project. Although reports are analysed by staff at the project, this is done in direct discussion with the young people in the scheme. Participants develop questionnaires which, although evaluated by paid staff, are then written as reports in consultation with the young people. Of course, all forms of empowerment require assistance and this project's participants are further supported in their endeavours by a paid worker who assists the young people in the development of neighbourhood forums. These forums focus upon encouraging further discussion of the peer report's findings. The worker also co-ordinates the peer research projects. In addition to this, further support is lent in the form of a professional researcher, whose aim is to certify that the suggestions, topics and subjects proposed by the young people are adhered to.

The Social Care Institute for Excellence (SCIE) considered the achievements of this Sheffield-based organisation as being a good example of 'participation making a difference' (SCIE, 2011). The success of this form of empowerment can be measured through the information gathered by the report being employed by the local Youth Strategy Group in helping shape policy and practice in the Sheffield area. The scheme was also used as a means for the young people to develop consultation and research skills. In addition, and perhaps more significantly, the young people from these deprived areas, who may also have felt deprived of a 'voice' over the decisions that directly affected their lives, have now been presented with the means to counter this. This is further underpinned by the support they receive from the social workers to continue this process. For a further example of how empowering practice and research can provide a path for change for disadvantaged groups, the Shaping Our Lives Network's publication, 'We are not stupid' (Taylor et al., 2007), illustrates how empowering practice with people with learning disabilities can make a difference.

Cross references: advocacy, carers, partnership, service user involvement

SUGGESTED READING

Bell, M. (2011) *Promoting Children's Rights in Social Work and Social Care: A Guide to Participatory Practice*. London: Jessica Kingsley.
Taylor, J., Williams, V., Johnson, R., Hiscutt, I. and Brennan, M. (2007) 'We are not stupid'. London: People First Lambeth and Shaping Our Lives. Available from: www.shapingourlives. org.uk/documents/wansweb.pdf (accessed 20 May 2012).

REFERENCES

Adams, R. (2008) *Empowerment, Participation and Social Work*, 4th edn. Basingstoke: Palgrave Macmillan.
Griggs, L. (2000) 'Assessment in community care', in M. Davies (ed.), *The Blackwell Encyclopaedia of Social Work*. Oxford: Blackwell, pp. 22–3.
GSCC (General Social Care Council) (2004) *Code of Practice for Social Care Workers*. London: GSCC.

empowerment

Hunter, S. and Ritchie, P. (2008) 'With, not to: models of co-production in social welfare', in S. Hunter and P. Ritchie (eds), *Co-Production and Personalisation in Social Care and Changing Relationships in the Provision of Social Care*. London: Jessica Kingsley, pp. 9–18.

Milliken, M.E. and Honeycutt, A. (2004) *Understanding Human Behaviour: A Guide for Health Care Providers*, 7th edn. New York: Delmar Learning.

Saleebey, D. (2006) *The Strengths Perspective in Social Work Practice*, 4th edn. Boston, MA: Pearson/Allyn and Bacon.

SCIE (Social Care Institute for Excellence) (2011) 'SCIE guide 20: participation – finding out what difference it makes: practice site 5'. CHILYPEP (Sheffield Children and Young People's Empowerment Project). Available from: www.scie.org.uk/publications/guides/guide20/sites/site05.asp (accessed 20 May 2012).

Swain, J. and French, S. (2008) *Disability on Equal Terms*. London: Sage.

Taylor, J., Williams, V., Johnson, R., Hiscutt, I. and Brennan, M. (2007) 'We are not stupid'. London: Shaping Our Lives and People First Lambeth. Available from: www.shapingourlives.org.uk/documents/wansweb.pdf (accessed 20 May 2012).

Waine, B., Tunstill, J., Meadows, P. and Peel, M. (2005) *Developing Social Care: Values and Principles*. Bristol: Policy Press.

17
Equality and Diversity

Suryia Nayak

DEFINITION

The concepts of equality and diversity are at the heart of Sojourner Truth's speech delivered in 1851 at the Women's Convention on equal rights in Ohio, where baring her breasts, she asked a curious question, 'Ain't I a woman?' This situation has more resonance with social work than is first apparent. Sojourner Truth challenged notions of equality that did not recognise and excluded her on the basis of racial and social differences – she was a black slave. In terms of social work the question is, who represents the metaphorical Sojourner Truth? Or, which people and communities are not recognised, marginalised and excluded by social work and why?

This chapter examines how the relationship between inclusion and exclusion is contingent on recognition and lack of recognition of the 'interdependency of difference' (Lorde, 1979: 111). Sojourner Truth's identity as a black slave was recognised, but this became a basis for not recognising other aspects of her identity, such as her gender and eligibility for particular rights. She was seen as 'Other'. The concept of the 'Other' produces a false binary of 'us and them'. This is a tension that social work must guard against if it wants to adhere to the BASW (2012) code of ethics (para. 3.2), which states that one of the primary objectives of social work is: 'The fair and equitable distribution of resources . . . Equal treatment and protection under the law . . . seeking to alleviate and advocating strategies for overcoming structural disadvantage.'

Within the GSCC Code of Practice (2010), non-discriminatory practice is intrinsic to public trust and confidence, maintaining, regulating and raising national standards in social care services (Sections 1 and 5). Promoting and respecting equality of opportunity, dignity and diversity is not an arbitrary matter of the personal beliefs or values of individual social workers; it is enshrined in professional codes of practice, conduct and ethics.

The Equality Act 2010, followed on 5 April 2011 with the public sector Equality Duty, includes age, sexual orientation, religion or belief, pregnancy and maternity, and gender reassignment. Public bodies including social work are legally bound to consider all individuals in developing policy, delivering services and in relation to their own employees.

The Equality Act defines equality as 'everyone having the same chances to do what they can. Some people may need extra help to get the same chances' (Home Office, 2010: 3). The Equality Act identifies two particular duties, namely the socio-economic duty and the equality duty. The Equality Act recognises that positive action may need to be taken in order to achieve the socio-economic and equality duty.

KEY POINTS

- Social work must grapple with the complexity of the interdependency of difference.
- Social work must resist the notion of a hierarchy of oppression because 'the master's tools will never dismantle the master's house' (Lorde, 1979: 112).
- Concepts of equality and discrimination are socially, historically and culturally contextualised.

DISCUSSION

Political thinkers including Aristotle, Rousseau, Hegel and Marx articulate theories of equality, rights and liberty on the principles of what is relational, distributive and proportionate. Deconstructing the relational or distributive aspect of equality and discrimination includes asking: how can a deeper understanding of the intersubjective encounter of difference form a basis for anti-oppressive and anti-discriminatory social work practice?

Audre Lorde states, 'Much of Western European history conditions us to see human differences in simplistic opposition to each other: dominant/subordinate, good/bad, up/down' (Lorde, 1980: 114). This construction of difference along binary divisions is problematic. It masks the complexity of the interdependency of difference. Butler explains, 'This means we are not separate identities in the struggle for recognition but are already involved in a reciprocal exchange, an exchange that dislocates us from our positions, our subject positions' (Butler, 2004: 44). The anxiety of being dislocated from our positions of inclusion and recognition prevents acknowledgement that we are constituted through relations to the 'Other'. Laclau (1977) argues that power relations between groups are configured in terms of difference which paradoxically forms the rationale for exclusion and subordination. The identity category of being white is contingent on the existence of non white identities, heterosexuality is contingent on the foreclosure of gay, lesbian and bisexual identities, the reification of youth on the denigration of being old, the notion of being able bodied on the notion of being disabled and so on.

Hall exposes the contradiction of binary positions:

> identities are constructed through, not outside, difference . . . it is only through the relation to the other, the relation to what it is not, to what has been called its 'constitutive outside' that the positive meaning of any term – and thus its identity – can be constructed. (Hall, 1996: 17)

In terms of social work, the concept of the 'constitutive outside' mobilises a realignment of binary divisions as fundamental as social worker/service user. The notion of a stable, unified identity and identification is destabilised because it is constituted by what is outside, what it is not.

Application to social work

The question by Sojourner Truth, 'Ain't I a woman?' illustrates that the act of recognition simultaneously involves a dynamic of misrecognition. The question becomes, who for social work personifies the 'constitutive outside'? Just as the women in the 1851 Ohio convention did not recognise that their identification or commonality was based on what is excluded and what is 'Other'; social work must question how it articulates, positions and represents service users and carers. Social work needs to take proactive action to address why certain groups, identities and communities are not accessing services.

Sampson states:

> We know that the self needs the other in order to be a self at all. We know that when those selves are dominant in a given society, they can construct the other so as to affirm a particular kind of self for themselves . . . If I find myself in and through you, but no longer control the you that grants me myself, then I am forced to deal with a self that is beyond my control, and I may not enjoy this self with which I must now contend. (Sampson, 1993: 153)

The tension for social work is what position of affirmation is dislocated, when service users assert their right to self-determination, define their own needs and resist paternalistic, resource-led interventions? Beyond the rhetoric of reductionist acronyms such as AOP and ADP, social work must engage in sustained work on questioning the machinery used to constitute a known, stable, authentic 'Other'.

Equality should not be confused with treating everyone the same, indeed this could result in discrimination and inequality. A simple example of this would be to serve everyone the same meal so that everyone has equal portions, quality and content of food. However this may ignore cultural, political and religious prohibitions of not eating pork, non-halal meat and dairy products. A focus on equality of outcome and capabilities provides a more sophisticated lens of analysis.

Service design and delivery in health and social care operate on the prioritisation of need. Implicit is a ranking of those who are more or less oppressed where the competing demands are rationalised on ideological and economic grounds. McDonald and Coleman (1999) argue any hierarchy of oppressive experiences, where some are assessed to be more oppressed than others, serves to replicate the inequality inherent in hierarchical structures that cause oppression.

Mcdonald and Coleman's 'multiple model' of the cumulative effects of discrimination and oppression resonates with the Crenshaw's theory of intersectionality. Intersectionality argues that identity is formed by interconnecting forces of race, gender, class and sexuality. Crenshaw disrupted notions of adding and subtracting or hierarchical ranking of categories of oppression demonstrating that the 'intersectional experience is greater than the sum of racism and sexism' (Crenshaw, 1989: 140–9). Understanding and applying this social work practice, theory and research must take into account that one form of oppression leads to the reinforcement of another.

THE CONCEPT IN SOCIAL WORK PRACTICE

Case study

Raja is a mixed raced 70-year-old woman referred to social services by the Albert Kennedy Trust. Raja is homeless and in poor physical health. Recently, her partner of 30 years died and Raja was excluded from the funeral and forced to leave the home she had shared with her partner because of racist homophobic attitudes. Making an appropriate referral is proving difficult due to a lack of culturally sensitive residential provision, budget cuts and little understanding of the complexity of Raja's needs. Assessment forms, referral procedures and systems to enable intervention, do not represent and address Raja's complex multiple needs and this is reflected in service design and delivery.

Raja's case demonstrates how a lack of understanding of the intersection of simultaneous multiple oppression leads to a lack of appropriate mechanisms in service design and delivery to address complex needs. Raja's needs are inextricably bound up with her identity; she is not just her age, her race, her socio-economic situation, her sexuality, poor health or her bereavement. To construct a hierarchy of oppressive experiences in assessment and intervention would be to replicate the very discrimination and oppression that has left her homeless and socially excluded. Any fragmentation or categorisation of Raja's needs in relation to her identity must be resisted to enable a holistic approach based on equality of outcome and capabilities. Notions of partnership, empowerment, respect, dignity and self-determination must take account of the 'constitutive outside' so that false binaries of 'them and us', do not collude with ideology and mechanisms that marginalise, reject and constitute an authentic 'Other'. In representing or advocating for Raja or indeed any service user, carer or community, it is imperative to acknowledge that, 'Representation is never merely descriptive; it serves also a constitutive and regulatory function which is obscured in (but not absent from) accounts relying upon the conventions of representational realism' (Wilkinson and Kitzinger, 1996). Representation in itself cannot be avoided, this would be impossible; however, conventions of representation mobilised through discourse and social constructions must be questioned. Social workers must engage in non-defensive, personal professional scrutiny of values, attitudes and behaviour:

> As Paulo Freire shows so well in *The Pedagogy of the Oppressed*, the true focus of revolutionary change is never merely the oppressive situations which we seek to escape, but that piece of the oppressor which is planted deep within each of us, and which knows only of the oppressors' tactics, the oppressors' relationships. (Lorde, 1980: 123)

Cross references: anti-oppressive practice, ethics, sexuality, social exclusion, social justice

SUGGESTED READING

Brown, W. (2006) *Regulating Aversion: Tolerance in the Age of Identity and Empire*. New Jersey and Oxford: Princeton University Press.
Lorde, A. (1984) *Sister Outsider*. New York: Crossing Press.

REFERENCES

BASW (British Association of Social Workers) (2012) *Code of Ethics*. Birmingham: BASW.
Butler, J. (2004) *Precarious Life: The Powers of Mourning and Violence*. London and New York: Verso.
Crenshaw, K. (1989) 'Demarginalizing the intersection of race and sex: a black feminist critique of antidiscrimination doctrine, feminist theory, and antiracist politics'. University of Chicago Legal Forum, 139.
Equality Act 2010. London. The Stationery Office.
GSCC (General Social Care Council) (2010) *Code of Practice*. London: GSCC.
Hall, S. (1996) 'Who needs identity?', in P. du Gay, J. Evans and P. Redman (eds) *Identity: A Reader*. London: Sage, pp. 15–30.
Laclau, E. (1977) *Politics and Ideology in Marxist Theory: Capitalism, Fascism, Populism*. London: Left Books.
Lorde, A. (1979) 'The master's tools will never dismantle the master's house', comments at 'The Personal and the Political Panel' Second Sex Conference, New York, 29 September 1979, reprinted in Lorde, A. (1984) *Sister Outsider*. New York: Crossing Press, p. 112.
Lorde, A. (1980) 'Age, race, class and sex: women redefining difference', delivered at the Copeland Colloquium, Amherst College April 1980, reprinted in Lorde, A. (1984) *Sister Outsider*. New York: Crossing Press, p. 114.
McDonald, P. and Coleman, M. (1999) 'Deconstructing hierarchies of oppression and adopting a "multiple model" approach to anti-oppressive practice', *Social Work Education*, 18(1): 19–32.
Sampson, E.E. (1993) *Celebrating the Other: A Dialogic Account of Human Nature*. New York: Harvester Wheatsheaf.
Truth, S. (1851) Speech at the Women's Convention on Equal Rights in Akron, Ohio.
Wilkinson, S. and Kitzinger, C. (1996) *Representing the Other: A Feminism and Psychology Reader*. London: Sage.

18
Ethics

Steven M. Shardlow

DEFINITION

The term 'ethics' derives from the Ancient Greek 'ethos', which combined two notions, 'custom' and 'character'. This etymology is helpful for modern interpretations of 'ethics', which may be understood as 'the science of good behaviour'. Within this domain of knowledge, core questions to be addressed are, for example: 'How should a person act in particular situations?' or 'How should good people best live their lives?' Aristotle, perhaps the first philosopher to fully address such questions (sixth century BC), framed answers in terms of the moral virtue of the individual, which included motives. Since Aristotle, many philosophers have suggested answers based upon different fundamental principles. For example, Kant (18th century German philosopher) argued that we should treat others as we wish to be treated ourselves (categorical imperative); while John Stuart Mill (19th century English philosopher) argued that the rightness or wrongness of an action be determined by the outcome (utilitarianism). Professional social work draws upon these ideas; hence the term 'ethics', in social work, refers to questions about how social workers should behave in professional situations, for example, with: service users, carers, colleagues, other professionals, students, etc. In many countries, where professional social work is practised, the answers to the question 'How should a social worker act?' are addressed by professional codes of ethics that describe prohibited and desired behaviours.

KEY POINTS

- The domain of ethics is centrally concerned with the exploration of questions about how we should behave.
- Desirable behaviour in our personal and professional lives may be governed by different ethical principles.
- There are different approaches as to how to make decisions about which behaviours are right or good.
- Most professions have a code of ethics that both requires certain actions and proscribes other actions.

DISCUSSION

Of the major philosophical approaches about how to behave morally, perhaps the most significant for social work are the following.

Faith-based ethical codes

Many major religions contain prescriptive statements about behaviour. In Christianity, Judaism, and Islam, for example, these statements are laws, believed by followers to have been handed down by a deity. As such there is an imperative for believers to adhere to these statements, in other words, the justification for ethical behaviour is belief in a particular deity. The rise of faith-based social work raises possible conflict between the requirements of a secular professional code of ethics and 'faith-justified' laws.

Deontological theories

Deontological theories purport to provide rational justifications for moral behaviour that is secular and applicable to all irrespective of religious belief. Originally, these arose as part of the European Enlightenment, notably in the work of Kant (1785). He developed the so-called 'categorical imperative' – a maxim, which approximately states that you should treat others as you would wish to be treated yourself. This approach to moral decision making about desired behaviours does not list prescriptions but requires social workers, or anyone else, to reflect using this maxim to guide principled action.

Consequentialist theories

According to consequentialist theories, the rightness or wrongness of a proposed action is determined by its consequences. The most well known being utilitarianism, first developed by Bentham (1970[1822]) and Mill (1970[1861]). In its crudest form, utilitarianism rather brutally implies that actions are right if more people will be made happy than will be made unhappy. Various problems exist with this form of moral theory, not least that actions of which most would disapprove, for example, lying, is not *prima facie* regarded as wrong. In the less sophisticated versions of consequentialism, making one individual suffer for the benefit of many is permissible, in other words, it is acceptable to punish the innocent to satisfy the crowd. As a broad generalisation, welfare policy in modern societies, of which social work forms a part, is most likely to be grounded loosely on a consequentialist morality, in other words, the improvement of the general level of happiness in society. For social workers involved in any form of social protection or risk management, consequentialist moral theories can be unwelcome. Hence, the rightness or wrongness of an action to remove or not to remove an individual from the community may only become apparent by the action's consequences; hence a form of 'moral luck' applies (Hollis and Howe, 1990). For example, a decision may have been taken to leave a vulnerable child with carers who may not be able to provide acceptable levels of care. Subsequently, if no harm befalls the child the decision was correct. If, on the other hand, the child is seriously abused or even killed then the social worker will face the media opprobrium and the decision not to remove the child will be judged *post hoc* to have been wrong.

Virtue ethics

Recent years have seen a resurgence of virtue ethics (Clark, 2006) and (McBeath and Webb, 2002) challenged by Houston (Houston, 2003). For social workers this would imply that the period of professional education had in combination with the social workers pre-existing character traits combined to create a virtuous individual able to use these personal characteristics, such as, a sense of justice and fairness to develop what might be termed moral intuition. This resonates with the Munro Report (Munro, 2011) about social work with children and families in England, which set forward the notion of developing an authoritative and confident social worker able to take personal responsibility for decisions.

THE CONCEPT IN SOCIAL WORK PRACTICE

Ethical requirements apply in two broad areas of social work, professional practice and the conduct of research. First, regarding professional practice, in many countries social work is a regulated profession, that is, only those with designated qualifications and/or registration with the competent professional body may term themselves legally as 'social workers'. In addition, social workers would normally be expected to conduct themselves according to a code of practice (UK) or codes of ethics as specified by the competent professional body, for example, in Australia (AASW, 2010) and the United States (NASW, 2008). In the four countries of the UK there are very similar, if not identical codes of conduct: England (GSCC, 2004), Northern Ireland (NISSC, 2004), Scotland (SSSC, 2004), and Wales (CGC/CCW, 2004). At a global level, the International Federation of Social Workers has published *Ethics in Social Work: A Statement of Principles* (IFSW, 2004). Non-compliance with the requirements of the code of practice in the UK, or code of ethics elsewhere, amounts to professional misconduct for which the social worker may be disciplined by the professional body and may be removed from the register and therefore no longer able to practise.

Second, the approach to research ethics varies significantly by country. In the UK, social work research must conform to ethical and governance requirements specified by the organisation that conducts the research (frequently a university) and the site of the research (frequently a service provider organisation). In England, certain kinds of research, for instance, research that is particularly complex or refers to aspects of social care, must be referred to the Social Care Research Ethics Committee managed by SCIE. While studies that involve staff or service users in healthcare must be approved by the Local Research Ethics Committees (run under the auspices of the Department of Health). In addition, there is a code of research ethics that has been widely adopted across the UK (Butler, 2002).

There are several types of ethical problems that social workers may face in day-to-day practice, these may include:

1 Ethical dilemmas where a social worker is confronted by a choice between two or more actions, such as whether to promote a vulnerable older person's *independence* by enabling them to live in the community or by assisting them to move to

residential accommodation to prioritise their *safety*. Acting in accord with the need to promote someone's safety may be in conflict with drive to promote independence; this is unlikely to be a simple choice. In day-to-day practice there are likely to be many complicating factors, paramount among these will be the requirement to listen to and take full account of the wishes of the older person.

2 Boundary issues define the nature of appropriate behaviour with service users. An understanding of where the boundary lies that delineates the nature of ethical behaviour with service users is essential for professional practice. In part this is defined by the professional codes of practice. However, such codes are frequently quite general and leave considerable areas of discretion for the practitioner. Some forms of behaviour are clearly prohibited by the codes of practice, others are not. A particular type of boundary issue concerns the distinction between personal and professional relationships. What may be acceptable in a friendship is not necessarily acceptable in a professional relationship.

3 Confidentiality and data protection are key concerns for all social workers. It is inevitable that social workers acquire detailed knowledge about the people with whom they work. Using that information ethically can present considerable challenges. An initial presumption is that the information is confidential to the social worker and the person that has provided that information. However, concerns over the safety or the need to protect vulnerable people may entail that information can no longer be kept confidential between the social worker and the provider.

4 The ethical issues that social workers face are made more complex by virtue of that fact that most social workers (certainly in the UK) work in large organisations, whether in the state, not-for-profit or private sectors. As a part of such an organisation, the social worker has to reconcile the needs of the person with whom they are working, organisational requirements, the requirements of the professional code of ethics and the individual's conscience. These complexities compound the difficulty of decisions that have to be made by social workers on a day-to-day basis when working with people with complex social problems.

Cross references: anti-oppressive practice, confidentiality, empowerment, equality and diversity, partnership

SUGGESTED READING

Beckett, C. and Maynard, A. (2005) *Values and Ethics in Social Work: An Introduction*. London: Sage.
Parrott, L. (2010) *Values and Ethics in Social Work Practice*, 2nd edn. Exeter: Learning Matters.

REFERENCES

AASW (Australian Association of Social Workers) (2010) *Code of Ethics*. Canberra: Australian Association of Social Workers.

Bentham, J. (1970[1822]) 'An introduction to the principles of morals and legislation', in M. Warnock (ed.), *Utilitarianism*. London: Fontana, pp. 33–77.

Butler, I. (2002) 'A code of ethics for social work and social care research', *British Journal of Social Work*, 32(2): 239–48.

CGC/CCW (Cyngor Gofal Cymru/Care Council for Wales) (2004) 'Codes of practice for social care workers and employers'. Available from: ww.ccwales.org.uk/eng/conduct/pdf/final_codes_workers.pdf (accessed 29 October 2008).

Clark, C. (2006) 'Moral character in social work', *British Journal of Social Work*, 36(1): 75–89.

GSCC (General Social Care Council) (2004) 'Codes of practice for social care workers and employers'. Available from: www.gscc.org.uk/NR/rdonlyres/041E6261-6BB0-43A7-A9A4-80F658D2A0B4/0/Codes_of_Practice.pdf (accessed 23 March 2008).

Hollis, M. and Howe, D. (1990) 'Moral risks in the social work role: a response to Macdonald', *British Journal of Social Work*, 20(6): 547–52.

Houston, S. (2003) 'Establishing virtue in social work: a response to McBeath and Webb', *British Journal of Social Work*, 33(6): 819–24.

IFSW (International Federation of Social Workers) (2004) *Ethics in Social Work: A Statement of Principles*. Berne: International Federation of Social Workers.

Kant, I. (1785) 'Groundwork of the metaphysic of morals', in H.J. Paton (ed.), *The Moral Law*. London: Routledge, pp. 53–123.

McBeath, G. and Webb, S.A. (2002) 'Virtue ethics and social work: being lucky, realistic, and not doing one's duty', *British Journal of Social Work*, 32(8): 1015–36.

Mill, J.S. (1970[1861]) 'Utilitarianism', in M. Warnock (ed.), *Utilitarianism*. London: Fontana, pp. 251–321.

Munro, E. (2011) *The Munro Review of Child Protection: Final Report A Child-Centred System*. London: Department of Health.

NASW (National Association of Social Workers) (2008) *Code of Ethics*. Silver Spring, MD: National Association of Social Workers.

NISSC (Northern Ireland Social Care Council) (2004) 'Codes of practice for social care workers and employers of social care workers'. Available from: www.niscc.info/content/uploads/downloads/registration/Codes_of_Practice.pdf (accessed 28 October 2008).

SSSC (Scottish Social Services Council) (2004) 'Codes of practice for social service workers and employers'. Available from: www.sssc.uk.com/NR/rdonlyres/761AD208-BF96-4C71-8EFF-CD61092FB626/0/CodesofPractice21405.pdf (accessed 28 October 2008).

19
Family Work

Nicky Ryden

DEFINITION

Family work in social work terms means the working with a 'family' to promote the welfare and well-being of one or more family members. All social work activity will be associated with aspects of 'family'. The family can be a source of support or of distress for its members. Family work is not the same as 'family therapy' which has its own theoretical framework and practitioners. It can be helpful to conceptualise the family as an interactive system, between at least two related generations who expect trust and loyalty from each other (Bell and

Wilson, 2003). In seeking to work with families, social workers are required by policy and principle to work in partnership, that is, to identify the strengths of the family and find solutions which will promote the healthy functioning of the family system. This is complex work, particularly as a family can appear benign, with abuse and neglect well concealed except from the most persistent inquiry (Ferguson, 2011; Munro, 2011).

KEY POINTS

- partnership – a guiding principle of the Children Act 1989
- family life cycle –the length of the relationship and the age and stage of development of any children (Murgatroyd and Wolfe, 1985)
- an interactive system – striving for equilibrium
- solution-focused approaches – seek to share power with families and use the family's own strengths to achieve change (Milner and O'Byrne, 2002)
- respectful uncertainty – the stance that social workers need to maintain in order to challenge families who may seek to hide behaviour that endangers vulnerable family members (Laming, 2003)

DISCUSSION

Generally 'family work' is thought of in relation to social work with children, but it should be borne in mind that adult service users also have families who may be a source of support, or of potential harm. In respect of children, the Children Act 1989 places a duty on the local authority to facilitate the upbringing of children by their own families, whilst safeguarding and promoting their welfare. The prevention of family breakdown is a central social work task, as is the prevention of harm to children, harm which often arises from parental ill health, violence within the home, parental use of drugs and alcohol, as well as the structural pressures of poverty, racism and social inequality.

> The purpose of social work involvement is to assist families, to assess their dilemmas and to provide necessary and skilful help as well as protection. (Iwaniac, 1996: 187)

The Labour government (1997 to 2010) initiatives on family support have given little attention to the social work role with families, and one of the effects of this has been to locate the responsibility for preventive work with children and families to other agencies, such as Sure Start children centres, extended schools, and the voluntary sector.

Family life has a cycle, and where the family is on the cycle can have implications for their ability to cope with additional stresses. There is a difficult balance to be achieved between supporting parents in their parenting and protecting children from harm. Sinclair et al. (1997) suggest that preventive services and family support should minimise the hazards associated with the child's journey through childhood. Preventive services can be universal or targeted, depending on the degree of need or the level of risk identified for the family and the child. Social work with families will bring practitioners into contact with an array of family groups that will require understanding, sensitivity, trust, genuineness, warmth and empathy and effective communication skills together with the ability to work on specific problems.

Murgatroyd and Wolfe (1985) suggest that a family is a system striving for equilibrium; it might be a re-constituted family, striving to integrate the emotional needs and aspirations of family members who have not grown up together. Cohesive families share activities, demonstrate warmth and are low on criticism of family members. They are effective communicators, share favourable views of each other and are optimistic about the future, whilst non-cohesive families demonstrate the opposite characteristics.

Conceptualising the family as a system remains useful to current practitioners: '. . . the family is an interactive system, consisting of a group of people which includes at least two generations who are related by biological and/or legal ties and expectations of loyalty and trust' (Bell and Wilson, 2003: 8).

To deliver work that will meet the challenges and diversity of family life in a working environment that promotes short-term interventions requires a theoretical model that will guide the process. This may be 'task-centred' or 'solution-focused'; a choice that may be a matter of personal preference, although some agencies encourage a specific approach and provide training to support the development of the necessary skills.

Solution-focused practice assumes that families and individuals have problem-solving skills and the focus is on creating stories of success and competence (Milner and O'Byrne, 2002). This is based on social construction theory that suggests we construct our understanding of reality through the language and stories that we use to name and explain events (see Fook, 2002, for a discussion on discourse, language and narrative). The language we use generates powerful discourses that shape our beliefs and understanding about self and others. Solution-focused theory, by encouraging people to create narratives of success rather than failure, seeks to empower individuals in finding solutions to issues that cause distress and unhappiness (Parton and O'Byrne, 2000).

Task-centred work is a problem-solving technique: 'It offers an optimistic approach that moves the focus away from the person as the problem, to practical and positive ways of dealing with difficult situations' (Coulshed and Orme, 2006: 157). It was developed during the 1970s in reaction to the unfocused long-term involvement of many helping agencies with 'problem families'. In the United States, Reid and Shyne (1969) explored the effects of a time-limited intervention, eight sessions, compared to the usual open-ended casework. They found the people working with a time limit were more likely to change and to maintain that change than people who were worked with over a longer period. Reid and Epstein produced their seminal text *Task-Centred Casework* in 1972. They identified a range of problems where task-centred practice can be effective including: personal relationships; transitions; inadequate resources; behaviour problems; some forms of emotional distress; difficulties in maintaining social relationships; or dealing with organisations. Research by Goldberg (Goldberg et al., 1985) also identified those situations where it did not work, when problems were deep seated and long term, or where people were not in touch with reality, such as substance misusers or people with serious mental ill health. It is not a model that addresses social change (Payne, 2005).

Task-centred and solution-focused approaches recognise the capacity of families to solve their own problems with appropriate advice and support. Milner and O'Byrne (2002: 16) write of 'respectful uncertainty' being a useful stance for the worker engaging in solution talk.

THE CONCEPT IN SOCIAL WORK PRACTICE

Once the initial and core assessment have been completed how should one proceed? Having a clear theoretical model for practice is necessary when undertaking work on the issues identified by the assessment. Each piece of work will have a life and process of its own, which can be characterised by the acronym ASPIRE (Herbert, 1993: 13):

- **AS**   **AS**sess, identify the issues, any risks, and agree the aims and objectives, that need to be addressed.
- **P**   **Plan** to meet those needs, whether providing services and resources or engaging with the family on a plan of work that will reach the agreed aim.
- **I**   **Implement** the plan, a series of meetings to discuss aspects of the problem, solutions and tasks, designed to change the situation within an agreed time frame.
- **R**   **Review** with the family if aims have been met, or whether further work is needed on existing or new aims. If met then **an end** to the relationship should be negotiated, if not another agreement should be made for further work.
- **E**   **Evaluate** the intervention by asking the family for their views on the process, for feedback on your performance, if anything could been done differently, was especially valued or disliked by the family.

The skill in family work lies in establishing a shared understanding of the problem, why it is problematic to the family or the individual and then working out specific goals and tasks. Supporting the family in addressing the tasks, and so creating change in the family system, will be most effective when these are changes the family want to implement. The social work role is to encourage and manage the process, providing information as appropriate and undertaking tasks which are not within the family's remit. Task-centred practice is not compiling a 'to do list' for the family, but developing a working partnership that shares power with the family and encourages them to recognise their own problem-solving skills.

The style of interviewing for solution-focused work called 'solution building' by de Jong and Berg (2002), begins with the worker asking: 'How can I be helpful to you?' – immediately indicating a partnership approach. Solution building interviewing recognises the service user as the expert. If the service user is the expert then the worker can be curious about the problem and take a position called 'not knowing'. Berg calls this listening with solution building ears (de Jong and Berg, 2002: 21). Milner and O'Byrne (2002) argue that the combination of solution-focused problem solving and the attention paid to narrative make this approach effective and generally very quickly helps service users arrive at a satisfactory solution. 'Signs of safety', an Australian approach developed by Turnell and Edwards, has been promoted as a constructive approach to safeguarding children in the UK (Turnell and Edwards, 1997; Turnell and Essex, 2006).

Cross references: assessment, communication, partnership, theory and social work

SUGGESTED READING

Collins, D., Jordan, C. and Coleman, H. (2010) *An Introduction to Family Social Work*, 3rd edn. Belmont, CA: Brook/Cole Cengage Learning.

Featherstone, B. (2004) *Family Life and Family Support: A Feminist Analysis*. Basingstoke: Palgrave Macmillan.

REFERENCE LIST

Bell, M. and Wilson, K. (eds) (2003) *The Practitioner's Guide to Working with Families*. Basingstoke: Palgrave Macmillan.

Coulshed, V. and Orme, J. (2006) *Social Work Practice*, 4th edn. Basingstoke: Palgrave Macmillan.

de Jong, P. and Berg, I.K. (2002) *Interviewing for Solutions*, 2nd edn. Pacific Grove: Wadsworth.

Ferguson, H. (2011) *Child Protection Practice*. Basingstoke: Palgrave Macmillan.

Fook, J. (2002) *Social Work, Critical Theory and Practice*. London: Sage.

Goldberg, E.M., Gibbons, J. and Sinclair, I. (1985) *Problems, Tasks and Outcomes: The Evaluation of Task Centred Casework in Three Settings*. London: George Allen and Unwin.

Herbert, M. (1993) *Working with Children and the Children Act*. Leicester: British Psychological Society Books.

Iwaniac, D. (1996) 'Competence in working with families', in K. O'Hagan (ed.), *Competence in Social Work Practice*. London and Bristol, PA: Jessica Kingsley Publishers, pp.191–213.

Laming, H. (2003) *The Victoria Climbié Inquiry*. London: TSO.

Milner, J. and O'Byrne, P. (2002) *Brief Counselling: Narratives and Solutions*. Basingstoke: Palgrave Macmillan.

Munro, E. (2011) *The Munro Review of Child Protection: Final Report. A Child Centred System*. (Cm 8062). Norwich: The Stationery Office.

Murgatroyd, S. and Wolfe, R. (1985) *Helping Families in Distress: An Introduction to Family Focussed Helping*. London: Harper and Row Ltd.

Parton, N. and O'Byrne, P. (2000) *Constructive Social Work: Towards a New Practice*. Basingstoke: Palgrave Macmillan.

Payne, M. (2005) *Modern Social Work Theory*, 3rd edn. Basingstoke: Palgrave Macmillan.

Reid, W.J. and Epstein, L. (1972) *Task-Centred Casework*. New York: Colombia University Press.

Reid, W.J. and Shyne, A.W. (1969) *Brief and Extended Casework*. New York: Colombia University Press.

Sinclair, R., Hearn, B. and Pugh, G. (1997) *Preventive Work with Families*. London: National Children's Bureau.

Turnell, A. and Edwards, S. (1997) 'Aspiring to partnership: the signs of safety approach to child protection casework', *Child Abuse Review*, 6: 179–90.

Turnell, A. and Essex, S. (2006) *Working with Situations of 'Denied' Child Abuse: The Resolution Approach*. Buckingham: Open University Press.

20
Finance

Tim Mann

DEFINITION

The concept of finance underpins almost all aspects of social work practice, whether it relates to the amount of money allocated for the provision of social work services, the resources available to social workers to carry out their job, or the financial circumstances that service users and carers find themselves in. Social workers have often been in the unenviable role of having to ration scarce resources, but the current global financial crisis has brought into much sharper relief the financial context of the social work task. As Birkenmaier and Curley note, 'while the concern about credit and assets may appear to be outside the realm of traditional social work, the ability of low income families to build good credit and wealth impacts on their use of the social service system' (2009: 264). Glasby talks about the 'anti-financial tendencies of social work' (2009: 494) and I would suggest that it is crucial for qualified social workers to have a sound grasp of the financial landscape in which they operate. The current National Occupational Standards for social work (TOPSS, 2002) specifically state that social workers should 'contribute to the management of resources and services' (Key role 5, Unit 15) and the emerging capabilities framework for social workers arising from the work of the Social Work Reform Board (2010) specifically refers to the 'economic well-being' of service users.

KEY POINTS

- The majority of users of social work services are poor.
- Social work services, and the resources they use, have to be paid for, and their availability depends on the prevailing economic and political climate.
- The personalisation agenda in adult services is significantly changing the way that money is allocated and used by vulnerable adults.
- Demographic changes are having a significant impact on the demands for social care services as are the increasing level of expectations from an older population.
- Decisions about resources are ultimately tested in the courts, where the relevant law is applied to specific situations.

DISCUSSION

Social workers operate at the interface between the needs of vulnerable adults and children, and the resources available to meet them. This is influenced by the national and local political context as well as enduring policy initiatives of successive governments. The majority of funding for such services comes to local authorities through the allocation of grants and business rates from central government. Council tax represents only about 25 per cent of local government spending, and so the ability of councils to make spending decisions is limited because of this; thus, when a council decides to prioritise a particular area of public service, then it has to make political choices about how this will be funded and so reduce spending in another area. Social care spending on both adults' and children's services represents a large proportion of a council's total budget, so whilst you may read in your local paper about decisions to close a library to fund overspending in social care, it would require the council to close quite a few libraries to have any impact on a seriously overspent social care budget. The other key source of revenue for care services is income (charges) from service users which for a typical council represents many millions of pounds and is one of the key differences with NHS services in the UK. Some service users may be eligible for continuing healthcare funding and similarly, service users who are subject to Section 117 (aftercare) of the 1983 Mental Health Act cannot be charged for their services. It is worth remembering that perhaps the biggest contribution to supporting vulnerable people is provided by informal carers – family members and friends.

The 1990 National Health Service and Community Care Act led to significant changes in the financial arrangements for care services from 1993. This transfer saw a big increase in the budgets of local authorities, but of course, also transferred the responsibility to meet assessed needs under the Act from a finite amount of money. Thus, as demands and expectations have increased over time, councils have to balance needs with limited resources. The advent of the community care reforms of the early 1990s also left a legacy that private and voluntary providers of services made an increasingly large contribution to the 'mixed economy of care'. Carey (2008) argues that this process of 'privatisation' has had 'a considerable impact upon the experiences of service users' (2008: 918), and for Lymbery and Postle, 'The financial imperatives of community care have therefore wrought a substantial shift in the role of social workers, even if there is continuity concerning the skills that they have to exercise'(2010: 2505).

However, social workers have had to learn new skills in this context including contracting and commissioning which for many workers can feel like a managerialist nightmare.

The issue of demographic pressures has already been referred to and successive governments have attempted to confront this challenge with the appointment of various Royal Commissions and other bodies to look into how best to pay for the future care needs of an increasingly ageing population. There are some who argue that like NHS services, care services should be provided free to the user and paid for by the state, which is the current position in Scotland, although the Scottish government are finding this increasingly difficult to afford. In England, the coalition government appointed the Dilnot Commission (2011) to look again at this issue and although their report was widely accepted as drawing the right balance between the needs of the individual and the tax payer, it is not clear if their proposals will be taken up as similarly to all previous suggestions, it would require additional long-term investment by the state in the provision of care services. Turning now to some of the legal issues in social care finance, local authorities find themselves caught between what the law says you must do, and finite resources which mean you cannot. Of course it depends if what the local authority is being asked for is subject to a 'power' or a 'duty' in law, although a local authority is not allowed to set a deficit budget. Within adult services, one of the main ways that costs can be constrained is by the setting of eligibility criteria (see Chapter 7 on care management) although even this is increasingly being subjected to legal challenge if not in terms of the level set, then by the process that was followed in setting the eligibility criteria. The government has recognised the complexity of the law in relation to adults and the Law Commission (2011) has recently reported on proposed changes to the legal framework for adults, although it is highly likely that even if the changes were implemented it would still be down to the courts to establish the legal basis of individual decisions. It goes without saying that social workers should seek legal advice within their organisations when these issues are confronted.

THE CONCEPT IN SOCIAL WORK PRACTICE

Social workers support the most vulnerable people in our society, many of whom rely heavily on state benefits to sustain their independence. Whilst the complexity of welfare benefits is rightly left to specialists (see Chapter 62 on welfare rights), social workers should know the basic entitlements and where to refer people for the more specialist help. They should also be concerned with aspects of welfare reform that would have a significant impact on service users and carers as part of their advocacy role. Many families supported by social workers are in significant debt and a good awareness of local credit union facilities, for example, may reduce the reliance on loan sharks and other high-interest loan arrangements. As Glasby observes (2009) it is social workers who often have to communicate difficult decisions about money to individual service users, and not the managers or policy makers who are responsible for those decisions.

This chapter has focused on the financial arrangements for vulnerable adults, but money is no less significant for work with children and families. Preventative services for families at risk are often determined by the financial circumstances of a local authority or the political priorities of national or local government. Particularly in services for children with a disability, social workers need to manage the complexity of funding between different agencies, usually with health and education. The availability of direct payments for children has meant a huge increase in spending on children with a disability in recent years. Within children's safeguarding services, whilst a poor Ofsted inspection inevitably leads to significant turmoil within the local authority, one of the positive outcomes is invariably increased investment in safeguarding services.

The personalisation agenda is changing the way that social workers work with vulnerable adults, and research (Leece and Leece, 2011) suggests that these changes leave people 'confused' and with 'loyalties torn' (2011: 219). Many local authorities are using this new agenda to reduce the number of social workers working in adult services and using unqualified 'social care assessors' instead, in part to reduce the costs of assessment services. One of the key challenges with personalisation is how to effectively safeguard people at risk of abuse, and with power and money being increasingly and rightly given to service users, the risk of financial abuse also increases.

Social workers also have to manage the balance between preventative services and focusing scarce resources on those most in need. There is great variety across local councils in their per cent-spend of community care budgets on residential and nursing care for older people. Of course in part this will reflect historical patterns of spending that are hard to shift, but it will also be linked to the actions of social workers seeking to do what they regard as the best for their service users, and yet leading to very different outcomes for the people they are working with. Using such information, and the cost consequences of other decisions that are made, can better inform the actions of social work.

There is a 'more for less' culture that is impacting on the work of all public services, and whilst social workers should always be looking for the most efficient ways of doing things – 'best value' if you will – perhaps more than ever they are having to face some tough choices in their work with individuals and families. To bring this even closer to home, social workers across the UK are currently facing pay cuts as part of the attempt by local councils to reduce their spending.

Cross references: accountability, care management, law and social work, personalisation, political context of social work

SUGGESTED READING

Hafford-Letchfield, T. (2009) 'Resource management in social care organisations', Chapter 5, *Management and Organisations in Social Work*, 2nd edn. Exeter. Learning Matters.

White, R., Broadbent, G. and Brown, K. (2009) 'Community care law: an introduction', Chapter 8, *Law and the Social Work Practitioner*, 2nd edn. Exeter: Learning Matters.

REFERENCES

Birkenmaier, J. and Curley, J. (2009) 'Financial credit: social work's role in empowering low-income families', *Journal of Community Practice*, 17(3): 251–68.

Carey, M. (2008) 'Everything must go? The privatization of state social work', *British Journal of Social Work*, 38(5): 918–35.

Dilnot Commission (2011) *Fairer Funding for All: The Report of the Commission on Funding of Care and Support*. London: Department of Health.

Glasby, J. (2009) 'Money talks: the role of finance in social work education and practice', *Social Work Education*, 20(4): 493–8.

Law Commission (2011) *Adult Social Care, No 326*. London: The Stationery Office.

Leece, J. and Leece, D. (2011) 'Personalisation: perceptions of the role of social workers in a world of brokers and budgets', *British Journal of Social Work*, 41(2): 204–23.

Lymbery, M. and Postle, K. (2010) 'Social work in the context of adult social care in England and the resultant implications for social work education', *British Journal of Social Work*, 40(8): 2502–22.

Social Work Reform Board (2010) *Building a Safe and Confident Future: One Year On*. London: Department for Education.

TOPSS (Training Organisation for the Personal Social Services) (2002) *National Occupational Standards*. Leeds: TOPSS.

finance

21
Fostering

Jules Clarke

DEFINITION

Fostering is a means of providing family care for children who cannot remain with their birth parent(s). It takes many forms and children can stay with approved foster carers for varying periods of time. It is most commonly used to provide temporary care for children 'looked after' whilst their permanence plans are developed. Some will return to their birth parents or relatives, others will stay in foster care long term and move onto independent living. A small proportion will be adopted.

The key difference between adoption and fostering is that adoptive parents become the child's legal lifelong parents upon the making of the Adoption Order and they acquire sole Parental Responsibility (PR). Foster carers never have PR for children in their care, no matter how long they stay, nor does the birth parent lose it. The only way a foster carer can obtain PR is by seeking a Special Guardianship Order, a Residence Order or an Adoption Order, by virtue of which the child would cease to be looked after or fostered. Indeed, where social work involvement is no longer necessary in stable foster families, applications for such orders will often be supported by the authority to remove children from the care system, and promote family independence. In these instances ongoing financial support may be agreed.

Where children are looked after in foster care on a voluntary basis, PR remains entirely with the birth parent. If there is statutory involvement (e.g. a Care Order), the local authority shares PR with the birth parent and has a duty to involve the parents in care planning arrangements. In all cases, authorities have a regulatory duty to visit the child, supervise, support and review a fostering placement for its duration. All foster carers are paid allowances, whereby they are *reimbursed* the estimated cost of care at an agreed national rate. Most are additionally paid fees as a *reward* element for the care they offer.

The regulatory framework for fostering providers is the Fostering Services Regulations (2011), which sets out the duties and responsibilities for assessment, approval, supervision and review of fostering placements. New Guidance and National Minimum Standards for fostering came into force in April 2011 along with specific guidance relating to 'kinship care' (approval of family, friends or 'connected persons' as a child's foster carer). Practitioners should also be mindful of the impact of the Care Planning, Placement and Review Regulations 2010, on both fostering provision and placement decisions.

KEY POINTS

- Foster care is considered the primary resource for those children who cannot remain with their relatives or friends.
- Foster care is the preferred placement for a wide range of children, who cannot live at home, many of whom might previously have been placed in residential care.
- There is recognition that caring for children who have a range of complex and challenging needs is a demanding task which requires training, support and supervision in addition to personal qualities and attributes.
- Where it is considered in children's best interests, a relative or friend may go through a process of assessment to become their approved foster carer.
- The national shortage of foster carers means that some children are in placements that do not meet their needs.

DISCUSSION

The professionalisation of foster care

Foster care is now largely considered to be a professional occupation. Indicative of this is the terminology in general use. The reference to foster 'parents' has been abandoned in practice, reinforcing the fact that birth parents retain their responsibilities, and carers do not take their place. In foster families children are therefore more often encouraged to call carers by their first names. The term 'foster parent' is however retained in the regulations, in recognition of the expectation that carers are part of the overarching 'Corporate Parenting' strategy. They are expected alongside all other professionals to adhere to the five principles of *Every Child Matters* (DfE, 2003) and promote best outcomes, by acting in the manner of a 'good parent' in their provision of day-to-day care.

Juxtaposed with the professionalism of fostering services is the fact that an increasing number of foster carers are now 'kinship carers', in other words, relatives or friends of the child in care, who have been approved as foster carers by the local authority under the Fostering Regulations (2011). Their motivation to foster is not a considered career choice; it usually arises from crisis and a desire to keep the child in their familiar family network. Kinship carers broadly follow a similar process of assessment, training and approval as non-related carers once a child is in their care.

Some argue that assessment of kinship carers requires a different criteria and approach given their motivations and circumstances (Broad and Skinner, 2005) whilst others contend that our threshold expectations of care for looked after children should not be compromised by 'relative benefits'. Keeping a child in their family and community is an ambition supported in a good deal of legislation and regulation. Whilst it must be an option to consider in every case, it is not without

fostering

93

its vulnerabilities. For some children it will not be appropriate and for others it will not be viable, as a proportion of prospective carers, be they kinship or unrelated, will not meet the regulatory requirements to allow panel approval. Talbot and Calder (2006: 31) contend that 'fostering panels are inflexible processes that have the potential to exclude relatives who offer the best placement choice'. They suggest that this is 'class bias' 'ignorant of the outcomes for children who live in kinship placements' (p.31).

The research outcomes for children in kinship foster care give mixed messages but many suggest outcomes do compare favourably with those in unrelated foster placements (Farmer and Moyers, 2008; Hunt et al., 2008), and on some dimensions they appear to fare particularly well. Kinship carers present as more resilient, with placements lasting longer when under strain. Children report a stronger sense of stability, contentment and integration into the family.

Fostering as a permanence plan

The majority of looked after children (73 per cent) are in foster care placements. The legal relationship between carers and foster children is by definition insecure. For many children this is inconsequential as their experience of foster care is destined to be short term, perhaps because they are able to return to birth parents. However, foster care is the long-term plan for some, particularly for older children who do not want to be adopted and for those who benefit from regular contact with relatives, even though they cannot live with them. There are those children too, for whom adoption is desirable but not achievable because a suitable family cannot be found. Where children are not afforded legal security then attention should focus on the emotional permanence and placement stability that can be achieved in foster care.

Biehal et al. (2009) found that disruption rates for children fostered compared unfavorably for those adopted; however, fostered children were usually older at the point of placement and age is a known disruption indicator across all placement types. There was positive evidence that some children in long-term foster care expressed a strong sense of emotional security and stability and fared as well as adopted children in terms of education and mental health. The quality of care and relationships (attachments) seemed to be the key in achieving the best outcomes.

THE CONCEPT IN SOCIAL WORK PRACTICE

Fostering services are provided by local authorities and independent fostering providers (IFPs); both are inspected and regulated by Ofsted. All carers go through a process of training and assessment and their application for approval must be considered by a fostering panel. A decision is reached about the numbers of children they should care for and the duration of placements, be it short breaks, bridging or long term. Post approval, in line with their professional status, they are allocated a 'supervising social worker' and are required to engage in a process of ongoing training and development. Dependent upon their level of knowledge, skills and experience, carers will be paid allowances and fees. Some develop areas of significant expertise and are able to offer care to children who have complex physical or emotional needs. The impetus to keep children out of residential care has led to huge demand for foster placements and the private sector has grown significantly to meet the needs of local authorities who may struggle to recruit and retain carers in the required numbers.

The Fostering Network, a charity in support of carers and providers, estimates there is a current need for 10,000 new foster carers nationally, to offer a range of fostering services. For this reason the regulations have imposed 'sufficiency duties' upon local authorities to identify the range of provision they may need. Nonetheless, recruiting and retaining foster carers remains a primary challenge for agencies nationally. The ongoing development of a skilled, dedicated and professional fostering workforce is imperative and the focus should not just be on those who offer permanence. Short-term and bridging carers can be key agents of positive change in children's lives, as illustrated in this case study of bridging to adoption.

Case study

Simon and his sister Lucy lived with their birth mother, Anna, until the age of four and three when they were placed in foster care, with Maureen. Both children had experienced neglect and Lucy showed significant developmental delay. The children had previously spent time with their grandmother because of Anna's chaotic lifestyle and drug dependency. Support services had failed to bring about any lasting change and a parenting assessment of Anna during care proceedings indicated she was unable to prioritise their needs above her own. Their grandmother reported that she could not care for the children permanently due to her failing health. No other relatives or friends could be identified as prospective foster carers. The children's social worker prepared Child Permanence Reports (CPRs) for consideration by the adoption panel and the care plan for adoption was supported. A Placement Order was sought from the courts to allow the children to be placed with an adoptive family and a Family Finder was allocated from the adoption team to search for suitable approved adopters. A couple was finally identified some distance away, through the Adoption Register for England and Wales, and the match was agreed at adoption panel.

Maureen played a key role throughout the permanency planning process. Mindful of the attachment training she had received, she provided nurturing day-to-day care and established consistent routines and boundaries for the children. She acted on advice from health professionals and her supervising social worker to promote their development, sibling relationships and emotional well-being. She liaised with social workers, teachers and the children's guardian appointed by the court and reported on the children's progress at meetings and statutory reviews. Maureen transported the children to contact and supervised some of the visits with their mother and grandmother. She made relationships with both and included them in decisions about the children's care. Using direct work techniques, Maureen worked alongside the social worker to help the children understand that they would not be returning home, and prepare them for their new family. She assisted with their life books and memory boxes. Maureen provided information for the Family Finder to identify the adoptive family best suited to meet their needs and welcomed the adopters into her home over several days so they could transfer routines and get to know the children, before they moved permanently to their adoptive family.

CONCLUSION

In support of concepts of resilience Gilligan writes 'children can do well in difficult circumstances, given favourable opportunities. Without exception, vulnerable children do well because of the interest and commitment of at least one concerned adult' (2009: 32). The importance of relationships is a key theme that runs throughout research and theory in relation to childcare planning. Foster carers' role in this respect should be valued and promoted.

Cross references: adoption, direct work with children, law and social work, looked after children, safeguarding children

SUGGESTED READING

Broad, B. and Skinner, A. (2005) *Relative Benefits – Placing Children in Kinship Care*. London: British Association for Adoption and Fostering (BAAF).
Schofield, G. and Beek, M. (2008) *Achieving Permanence in Foster Care*. London: British Association for Adoption and Fostering (BAAF).

REFERENCES

Biehal, N., Ellison, S., Baker, C. and Sinclair, I. (2009) *Characteristics, Outcomes and Meanings of Three Types of Permanent Placement: Adoption by Strangers, Adoption by Carers and Long-Term Foster Care*. DCSF: University of York.
Broad, B. and Skinner, A. (2005) *Relative Benefits – Placing Children in Kinship Care*. London: British Association for Adoption and Fostering (BAAF).
DfE (Department for Education) (2003) *Every Child Matters*. London: The Stationery Office.
DfE (Department for Education) (2010) *Statistical First Release*. London: The Stationery Office.
Farmer, E. and Moyers, S. (2008) *Kinship Care-Fostering Effective Family and Friends Placements*. London: Jessica Kingsley.
Fostering Services Regulations (2011) Available from: www.legislation.gov.uk/uksi/2011/581/contents/made (accessed 15 June 2012).
Gilligan, R. (2009) *Promoting Resilience: A Resource Guide on Working with Children in the Care System*. London: British Association for Adoption and Fostering (BAAF).
Hunt, J., Waterhouse, S. and Lutman, E. (2008) *Keeping them in the Family: Children Placed in Kinship Care Through Care Proceedings*. London: British Association for Adoption and Fostering (BAAF).
Talbot, C. and Calder, M. (eds) (2006) *Assessment in Kinship Care*. Lyme Regis: Russell House Publishing.

22

History of Social Work

Mike Burt

DEFINITION

Emerging in the second half of the 19th century, the practice of social work, as currently understood, established a place in social policy and led to the formation of occupational groups. Payne (2005) and Pierson (2011) have provided the most complete accounts of the history of social work in the United Kingdom. Payne (2005) found the roots of social work in the Poor Law charity organisation and the settlement movement. Pierson (2011) identified the wide range of groups of social workers which became established from the end of the 19th century in voluntary organisations and the municipal authorities. Cree argues that '[t]he history of social work reflects an number of interweaving and at times contradictory themes' (1995: 10). Because of this diversity a significant issue in the writing of social work history is that of determining which developments should be included and which should be afforded pre-eminence. Some interpretations of the history of social work have contested the relevance of certain strands. They have emphasised those aspects which the writer considers to be the most significant and which should be retained in the future development of social work.

KEY POINTS

- The study of history involves an understanding of what took place in the past, in the context of its time, events themselves being part of a continuing process (Tosh and Lang, 2006).
- History can be distorted by nostalgia which involves looking back at the past in a way which draws attention to what are regarded as positive elements and suggests that change has been for the worse. Similarly, the perception of history may be distorted by a belief in progress which suggests that things are continually improving (Tosh and Lang, 2006).
- The diverse origins of social work mean that a number of strands lay claim to significance in its development.
- The development of social work in the United Kingdom was particularly influenced by the 'welfare state' legislation in 1948 which required local authorities to provide health, welfare and children's services.
- Social work has experienced difficulty in identifying its function and establishing itself as a recognised profession.

DISCUSSION

The history of social work can be studied from the perspective of theoretical approaches, the examination of archival records and oral history. Howe (1994) has argued that the movement towards creating a single social work profession with a common theoretical base, which took place between the 1950s and 1970s, represented a modernist approach. He suggests that the forces of postmodernism have subsequently proved more dominant, social work has become fragmented and has found it difficult to establish a clear identity. Theorisation can be helpful because of the way in which it can provide an overview of a particularly complex range of factors. However, it can result in an over-simplification of historical events. An approach which examines the archival records of, for example, voluntary organisations, local authorities and government, is able to identify changes in particular aspects of social work and achieve an understanding of the way in which priorities in the provision of individual services have changed. However, historians recognise the limitations of this approach, that the original records were themselves selective and subject to the original bias of the writer. Nevertheless, the advantage is that significant details can be recalled which might be overlooked by a broader theorisation of changes. An example is the consistency of workload studies in the late 1960s which show that social workers only spent about a quarter of their time in direct contact with clients. Subsequent reductions have not been as significant as is sometimes suggested. Some authors have captured the experiences of social workers in the past through individual oral histories (Burnham, forthcoming; Prynn, 2011).

Social work has not been the subject of much extended historical analysis. Lorenz argues that:

> [t]here has been far too little in the way of serious historical research in our profession . . . Only when we engage in open-minded, critical historical research can we hope to find meaning in this confusing diversity, to define our place in the diversity of histories with which we are interwoven. (2007: 599)

Other than the complete texts previously referred to, there are single chapters which provide a summary of the historical development of social work. For example, Parrott (2002) explores the history of social work from the perspective of conflicting ideologies. There has been a limited amount of material written by historians about social work. With a few exceptions, relating mainly to historical accounts of the voluntary sector, their work is confined to broader accounts of the personal social services in the development of the welfare state. Lowe (2005), for example, outlines the way in which fewer resources for the personal social services were provided by the post-war welfare state compared to other provisions. The Social Work History Network has been established to promote interest in the history of the profession.

A study of historical developments in social work and the cultural, social, economic and political influences which shaped them enables the practitioner to gain a perspective on the process which has led to the current configuration of services and the role of the social worker. It provides an opportunity for the individual practitioner to locate their own orientation towards their profession. It makes it possible to understand the influences on practitioners and managers and achieve some appreciation of why many plans and aspirations for social work have often been slow in being realised. The notion that we should 'learn the lessons of history' should be approached with some caution by the individual practitioner. The practice of individual social workers is constrained by resources. Governments shape wider social conditions and employing organisations have a responsibility to provide a work setting in which individuals and teams of practitioners can be effective. Nevertheless, individual practitioners are responsible for their own post-qualifying professional development and contributing towards the future development of the social work profession.

THE CONCEPT IN (HISTORICAL) SOCIAL WORK PRACTICE

Social work was a generic term used increasingly from the beginning of the 20th century to describe a wide range of tasks of workers who carried individual titles, for example; friendly visitor, probation officer, housing manager, health visitor, care committee organiser, relieving officer, club leader, hospital almoner. During the inter-war period, local voluntary organisations became associated with the National Council for Social Service which was established in 1919. Local authorities employed an increasing range of health and welfare staff or engaged voluntary organisations to act as their agent, to meet the requirements of legislation, for example, the Mental Deficiency Act 1913. In 1930, the responsibilities of the Poor Law Guardians were transferred to local authorities. During this period social workers were considered to be trained if they had studied for a social studies diploma. Professional training was first provided for hospital almoners in 1907 followed by psychiatric social workers in 1929. The post Second World War legislation required local authorities to provide a separate Children's Department, and a range of mental health and welfare services in Public Health Departments. This legislation, together with the introduction of a national system of welfare benefits made it possible to differentiate social welfare more clearly from its earlier association with education, health and charitable provision. A professional qualification in childcare started in 1947. The creation of the National Health Service meant that medical and psychiatric social workers became state employees and they were particularly influential in drawing on the increasing knowledge of psychology and psychiatry in developing social casework as a method of intervention. Following the Younghusband Report in 1959, two-year qualifying courses in social work were introduced in colleges.

By the beginning of the 1960s the term social worker was more usually restricted to occupational groups in local authorities, the health service, the courts and voluntary organisations involved in the support or supervision of people in institutions or in the community. For example, there were childcare officers, mental welfare officers, medical social workers, psychiatric social workers, welfare officers, and probation officers. These services were fragmented between different local authority departments, hospitals and the courts with limited communication between them. Following the recommendation of the Seebohm Committee which reported in 1968, the Local Authority Social Services Act 1970 required local authorities to establish a single social services department. The British Association of Social Workers was formed in 1970. The different routes to achieving a qualification in social work were merged in 1971 with the introduction of the Certificate of Qualification in Social Work. The generic term social worker was widely applied to workers in case-holding roles, over half of whom were still unqualified. In the late 1960s and 1970s, the earlier development of professional social work on the basis of social casework was challenged by a radical approach which argued that it was the structures of society which should be the focus of change, not individuals and families. The polarisation which this conflict produced proved particularly unhelpful to the development of social work at a time when it faced numerous challenges. These arose from organisational issues following the introduction of social services departments, new legal responsibilities, an increased demand for social care services and the continuing higher priority given to work with children and their families compared with other groups of clients.

Throughout its history, social work has been subject to the identification of social policy priorities as expressed in government circulars and legislation. The post-war concern about the negative effects and cost of institutionalisation resulted in the development of preventive work by children's departments and, following the Mental Health Act 1959, some increase in the community based work of mental welfare officers. Media and public concern about child abuse in the mid 1970s resulted in the government requiring social workers to expand their work of investigating child abuse. The closure of institutions, including children's homes and mental hospitals was accelerated during the 1980s. Social workers became increasingly involved in the assessment of the needs of children, young people and adults and of the relationships which were significant to them. Indeed, social work has been more successful in developing formal methods of assessment compared with methods of intervention. The Children Act 1989 and National Health Service and Community Care Act 1990 both extended the assessment role of social workers and subsequent legislation included the assessment of carers' needs. These changes reflect the readiness of governments throughout the 20th century to increasingly involve the state in the regulation of family life.

Cross references: assessment, law and social work, political context of social work, professional development, social work

SUGGESTED READING

The History of Social Work (Special Issue) (2008) *British Journal of Social Work*, 38(4).
Pierson, J. (2011) *Understanding Social Work: History and Context*. Maidenhead: Open University Press.

REFERENCES

Burnham, D. (forthcoming) *The Social Worker Speaks: A History of Social Workers in the Twentieth Century*. Farnham: Ashgate.

Cree, V. (1995) *From Public Streets to Private Lives: The Changing Task of Social Work*. Aldershot: Avebury.

Howe, D. (1994) 'Modernity, postmodernity and social work', *British Journal of Social Work*, 24(5): 513–32.

Lorenz, W. (2007) 'Practising history: memory and contemporary professional practice', *International Social Work*, 50(5): 597–612.

Lowe, R. (2005) *The Welfare State in Britain*, 3rd edn. Basingstoke: Palgrave Macmillan.

Parrott, L. (2002) *Social Work and Social Care*, 2nd edn. London: Routledge.

Payne, M. (2005) *The Origins of Social Work: Continuity and Change*. Basingstoke: Palgrave Macmillan.

Pierson, J. (2011) *Understanding Social Work: History and Context*. Maidenhead: Open University Press.

Prynn, B. (2011) 'The world of the child care officer 1948–1972'. Available at: www.swhn.chester.ac.uk (accessed 9 October 2011).

Tosh, J. and Lang, S. (2006) *The Pursuit of History*, 4th edn. Harlow: Pearson Education.

23
HIV and Social Work

Alice O'Sullivan

DEFINITION

Three decades on from the emergence of HIV, there is still widespread ignorance about the condition. There are estimated to be around 86,500 people living with HIV in the UK, a quarter of whom are undiagnosed (HPA, 2010). There are around 1,645 children and young people diagnosed with HIV in the UK (CHIPS, 2010). Some of these people for various reasons are likely to come into contact with social workers. Non-specialist social workers, who have limited HIV knowledge, may be affected by the stigma that still surrounds HIV and the widely held misconceptions about the condition. This chapter therefore outlines basic information about HIV and highlights issues that people living with HIV face.

HIV (Human Immunodeficiency Virus) is defined as a manageable, chronic condition (CHIVA, 2011a). The virus gradually reduces the number of white blood cells, weakening a person's immune system, leaving them susceptible to opportunist infections. However, antiretroviral medication slows down or stops this process and represses the levels of HIV in the body. Medication needs to be taken daily throughout a person's life, and enables people to live 'more or less a normal life span' (NAM, 2006: 36). The term AIDS has been historically used in the UK to describe when a person's immune system is extremely compromised. This term is no longer used by professionals, and instead 'living with HIV' is used to describe people who are HIV+.

HIV is present in the blood, sexual fluids (semen and vaginal) and breast milk of HIV+ people (NAM, 2006). HIV is passed on from one person to another when one of the above bodily fluids gets into another person's blood stream. HIV is passed on through sex (where different sexual activities hold different levels of risk of transmission), sharing hypodermic needles, blood transfusion where blood is not screened for HIV and from mother to baby. HIV transmission may be prevented in the following ways: using condoms, avoiding sharing/reusing needles, screening blood for HIV (conducted in the UK since 1985) and by HIV+ mothers adhering to appropriate medication. HIV cannot be passed on through everyday activities and therefore service users living with HIV pose no risk of infection to social workers.

KEY POINTS

- People living with HIV in the UK are likely to live relatively healthy lives in a normal life span.
- Under the Equality Act 2010 all HIV+ people are considered to have a disability and are legally protected from 'discrimination, harassment and victimisation by business and service providers' (NAM, 2010: 23).
- People living with HIV may experience difficulties relating to HIV medication and HIV-related secondary conditions.
- HIV stigma and discrimination remain in today's society and create many social difficulties for people living with HIV.
- A person's HIV status is highly confidential medical information and a person's consent is needed before sharing this information.

DISCUSSION

People living with HIV who are taking medication can now live healthy, full lives. Despite medical advances however, HIV stigma remains prevalent in the UK and presents multiple social issues to people living with HIV (Bravo et al., 2010; Prost et al., 2007). HIV+ people are more likely to be marginalised, isolated and less likely to access services, leading to poor mental and emotional well-being. HIV stigma means that people living with HIV often have to decide to whom they want to disclose their HIV status (Bravo et al., 2010). HIV disproportionally affects some minority groups in the UK such as gay and bisexual men and people from BME communities (HPA, 2010). Therefore, the stigma surrounding HIV can be related to homophobia and racism.

Testing, medication, stigma, disclosure to others and limited support networks are all issues that may affect adults living with HIV. Adults living with HIV may require care packages if their HIV is currently unmanaged or if they have a secondary condition or disability. Bywater and Jones assert that 'as HIV-related illnesses can fluctuate it is essential that care needs are responded to flexibly' (2007: 102). There are concerns that adults living with HIV with additional needs are not able to access support from adult services because 'critical need' is now 'the only criteria to be eligible for generic social work services in most local authorities' (Cairns, 2011: 6). There may also be further health complications as people reach older age (Vance et al., 2008).

Testing children for the virus can present issues for parents; however, all children born to HIV+ mothers should be tested. 'Disclosure' is a term often used to describe the process of building up a child's understanding of their own HIV status. In the UK children are given 'partial, truthful information' about their condition but are often not told their condition is called HIV until they are around 11 years old (Melvin et al., 2008: 5). This is due to fears that, firstly, children will tell others about their HIV status and secondly, that children will not be able to cope with this information. Parents frequently find the process of disclosure difficult and require support before, during and after the disclosure (Waugh, 2003). Research has found that children benefit from early disclosure, especially where children are given support during and after the naming event (Wiener et al., 2007). Children living with HIV may have issues forming friends as there are challenges in disclosing their HIV status with their peers (CHIVA, 2011b).

Any social workers practising in the UK may come across HIV+ service users. Non-HIV specialised social workers are likely to have received little training in HIV and may hold misconceptions. Despite this, the social work profession could be argued to be well placed to support people living with HIV with the issues discussed above and other non-HIV related issues (Cannon Poindexter, 2010). Social work values such as social justice, social change and human dignity all resonate with the needs of those living with HIV. Social work models such as empowerment, group work, and the social model of disability are all valuable when supporting those living with or affected by HIV. Social work knowledge in areas such as oppression, human development and social relationships aids the understanding of the complexities of HIV and has the potential to transform the perceptions and misconceptions of wider society regarding HIV. Social work skills in interpersonal communication, advocacy and relationship-building can be drawn upon to work effectively with people living with and affected by HIV. As part of anti-oppressive practice, social workers should counteract HIV stigma and discrimination.

THE CONCEPT IN SOCIAL WORK PRACTICE

Case study

Elizabeth is the single mother of Sara (aged ten), and both mother and daughter are living with HIV. The family are Black African. Sara's school made a referral to children's services, after Sara told a teacher that her mum often shouts at her and recently hit her during an argument. In the referral, the teacher states that Sara's behaviour is extremely negative and she has experienced difficulties in engaging Elizabeth in the CAF process.

Jen, a social worker, makes a home visit to undertake an initial assessment where she speaks to Elizabeth and Sara separately. During their conversation Elizabeth discloses her own and Sara's HIV status to Jen. Elizabeth explains that Sara continues to refuse to take her medication, which has severe health consequences. This causes arguments between the two, leading to a few occasions where Elizabeth became so frustrated that she has hit her daughter. Elizabeth explains that she has felt unable to ask for help as she worries about people finding out her HIV status. Elizabeth explains that Sara is not aware of her HIV status, and nor is her school. They both attend a clinic for their HIV treatment locally.

Sara informs the social worker that her mum often shouts at her about her medication and has hit her a few times. Sara does not understand why she needs to take medication, which she dislikes as it gives her strange dreams. Sara is worried about her mum as she cries frequently, has no friends and does not leave the house.

Jen is aware that the family's HIV status needs to be treated confidentially. Jen explores with Elizabeth who else should be given this information and they agree that Jen will inform her line manager. It is often considered good practice for just two people to know someone's HIV status in an organisation (Conway, 2005). Jen will also need to consider where and how to store the family's information (electronically and in paper files) to maintain confidentiality. Jen recognises that the clinic Elizabeth and Sara attend will have expertise in this field and she therefore agrees with Elizabeth to liaise with them. Jen and Elizabeth decide that Jen should get advice from a national charity that specialises in working with children living with HIV.

Jen makes the following assessment: Sara is a child with a disability, and there is an immediate need for her to continue taking her medication or her physical health will deteriorate. There is concern for Sara's current emotional well-being and extreme negative behaviour at school. Sara's relationship with her mum is currently strained and appears to be deteriorating. Sara's emotional and physical well-being will suffer if her mum keeps using the methods of shouting and hitting to get Sara to take her medication, and there is a need to safeguard Sara against this. Sara needs to develop a clearer understanding of her health condition but this process needs to be carried out by her mother and HIV specialists. The family are isolated and Sara is being parented by a mother currently experiencing low mood and possibly depression. The family may be affected by HIV stigma and racism. Elizabeth appears to have her own physical and mental health issues with which she is currently not coping.

Jen and her manager decide that Jen should carry out a core assessment and co-ordinate a meeting of a multi-agency team to create a plan to support Sara as a 'child in need' and Elizabeth as a parent. Jen will also speak to Elizabeth about making a referral to Adult Social Services, her GP and any local HIV voluntary organisations. Jen will need to manage the complexity of maintaining HIV confidentiality whilst working in partnership with others who are unaware of the family's HIV status.

Cross references: asylum seekers and refugees, confidentiality, ethics

SUGGESTED READING

NAM (2006) *Living with HIV*. London: Lithospher.
Bywater, J. and Jones, R. (2007) 'Sexuality, HIV and social work', Chapter 6, *Sexuality and Social Work*. Exeter: Learning Matters.

REFERENCES

Bravo, P., Edwards, A., Rollnick, S. and Elwyn, G. (2010) 'Tough decisions faced by people living with HIV: a literature review of psychosocial problems', *AIDS Reviews*, 12(2): 76–88.
Bywater, J. and Jones, R. (2007) *Sexuality and Social Work*. Exeter: Learning Matters.
Cairns, G. (2011) 'Is there life after death for HIV social care', *HIV Treatment Update*, 207: 4–9.
Cannon Poindexter, C. (ed.) (2010) *Handbook of HIV and Social Work Principles, Practice and Population*. Hoboken, NJ: Wiley.
CHIPS (2010) 'Summary date'. Available from: www.chipscohort.ac.uk/summary_data.asp (accessed 21 June 2011).
CHIVA (2011a) 'HIV and AIDS'. Available from: www.chiva.org.uk/parents/understanding/hivandaids.html (accessed 21 June 2011).
CHIVA (2011b) 'Psychosocial issues'. Available from: www.chiva.org.uk/professionals/social-care/psychosocial.html (accessed 13 June 2011).
Conway (2005) *HIV in Schools: Good Practice Guide to Supporting Children Infected and Affected by HIV*. London: NCB.
HPA (2010) 'HIV in the United Kingdom: 2010 report 4(47)'. Available from: www.hpa.org.uk/web/HPAwebFile/HPAweb_C/1287145367237 (accessed 28 June 2011).
Melvin, D., Donaghy, S. and Conway, M. (2008) 'Talking to children about their health and HIV diagnosis'. Available from: www.chiva.org.uk/guidelines/2009/pdf/talking-to-children.pdf (accessed 13 June 2011).
NAM (2006) *Living with HIV*. London: Lithospher.
NAM (2010) *Social and Legal Issues for People with HIV*. London: NAM.
Prost, A., Elford, J., Imrie, J., Petticrew, M. and Hart, G.J. (2007) 'Social, behavioural, and intervention research among people of sub-Saharan African origin living with HIV in the UK and Europe: literature review and recommendations for intervention', *AIDS Behaviour*, 12: 170–94.
Vance, D.E., Struzick, T.C. and Masten, J. (2008) 'Hardiness, successful aging and HIV: implications for social work', *Gerontological Social Work*, 51(3/4): 260–83.
Waugh, S. (2003) 'Parental views on disclosure of diagnosis to their HIV-positive children', *AIDS Care*, 15(2): 169–76.
Wiener, L., Mellins, C.A., Marhefka, S. and Battles, H.B. (2007) 'Disclosure of an HIV diagnosis to children: history, current research and future directions', *Journal of Developmental and Behavioural Paediatrics*, 28(2): 155–66.

24

International Social Work

Jenna Murray de López

DEFINITION

Social work is an intriguing professional and academic discipline because it straddles both the local and the global (Dominelli, 2010). Domestic and international social work practice involves various related activities such as providing services for migrants, refugees and asylum seekers, working on international health projects, responding to crisis situations and influencing change in global policies.

At a joint congress in 2000 of the International Federation of Social Workers (IFSW) and the International Association of Schools of Social Work (IASSW) a new definition for international social work was created. The core definition contained in a one page document stated that:

> The social work profession promotes social change, problem solving in human relationships and the empowerment and liberation of people to enhance well-being. Utilising theories of human behaviour and social systems, social work intervenes at the points where people interact with their environments. Principles of human rights and social justice are fundamental to social work. (IFSW, 2001)

The various social, economic and environmental consequences of globalisation have culminated in the internationalisation of social problems where problems that begin in one country swiftly impact upon another. This chapter discusses international social work, not as a unique type of practice in itself, but as conscious professional action in an interdependent world (Healy, 2001). By analysing the interface between international and domestic practice we are able to see how the global and the local are intrinsically linked in both positive and negative ways.

KEY POINTS

- Social work is professional action in an interdependent world.
- Social work is best understood as 'social professions' in order to incorporate all types of social work occurring in an international context.
- All social workers must be aware of the impact of globalisation on local practice.
- Theories associated with international social work are: globalisation, international development, human rights, political economy and cross-cultural perspectives.

DISCUSSION

A brief history of international social work

International social work as recognised professional action is certainly not a new phenomenon. Three core international organisations were founded in Europe in 1928, not long after the profession of social work itself was born. Since its creation, the International Association of Schools of Social Work (IASSW) has maintained the strategy of holding international conferences and seminars to facilitate the interchange of information and ideas on an educational, policy and practice level (Healy, 2001; Lyons et al., 2006). In 1956, the International Federation of Social Workers (IFSW) was born. The primary aim of the IFSW is to promote social work as a profession with professional standards and ethics (Healy, 2001). Their definition of social work and code of ethics have been adopted around the world; in the UK their affiliated organisation is the British Association of Social Workers (BASW).

In the UK, the philanthropic and charitable history of social work pre-welfare state also branched out along international lines with the work of NGOs – today one can find charity based organisations such as Oxfam, Save the Children, Action for Children and Age UK International working in all continents contributing to both long-term development and crisis situations. Many of these organisations are practising social work, although they do not necessarily identify with the profession. Dominelli (2010) attributes this to both the relative low status of the profession and its porous professional borders. An alternative reason for this may also be culture-specific notions of 'social work' and, depending on the country, a wish to separate any community based action from those of the state. Lyons et al. (2006) propose that for all of these reasons international social work should be discussed as 'social professions', and people undertaking this type of work as 'social professionals'.

The work of social professions in the international development field and the influence of development theory from the 1970s onwards have been greatly criticised by social activists, political commentators and academics (Bristow, 2008; Harvey, 2005; Lewellen, 2002). International development has historically been misdirected and tied up with complex political economic motives, laying it open to accusations of strategic investment that benefits the global North and increases inequality in the global South (Gledhill, 2009). Development initiatives that have failed to balance the needs of people and the environment in both rural and urban areas has intensified people's vulnerabilities in a globalising world (Dominelli, 2010).

Professional action in an interdependent world

Contemporary social work practice must provide a space for the local to engage with the global on a meaningful level, and vice versa. Social work in an international context should be rooted in respect for local knowledge systems as the basis for problem solving. When writing about the positive by-products of globalisation,

Appadurai (2000) argues that knowledge is created by people participating in the world they live in, he calls this 'collective imagination'. The wider dissemination of local knowledge is key to social workers' understanding of how people react to the environment they find themselves in. The rapid advancement in and access to communication technologies in recent years has given voice to many marginalised populations, empowering them to challenge previous representations of themselves as the 'exotic other', and in doing so has contributed to empowerment as a grassroots process. The demands of indigenous peoples in particular have heightened aspirations for new theoretical understandings that take into account their spiritual needs and the reclaiming of traditional rights and heritages, and their dreams of developing not simply as consumers in the global market place. Social professionals working in the health and social care global sectors have a duty to inform themselves of global and local issues and at all times seek social justice for the people who seek their assistance. Due to their direct contact with people, social professionals are in the position to uphold the principles and ethics set by the IFSW and are well placed to advocate the needs of people at a global policy level.

THE CONCEPT IN SOCIAL WORK PRACTICE

Globalisation has dramatically increased international aspects of domestic social work practice. Migration, whether permanent or transmigration, means that social workers are much more likely to come into contact with international populations as part of domestic social work practice. It is important here to highlight transmigration: the circular movement of people back to their original country, migration to a second or third country before settlement and technological advancements that help to maintain contact with family networks in the migrant's country of origin are all aspects that have greatly enhanced global interdependence.

As migration continues to bring large numbers of refugees and immigrants to new countries, social workers encounter them in schools, hospitals, child welfare agencies and community organisations. Many professionals are ill-prepared to provide informed and skilled assistance to individuals and families from other countries and cultures because of the amount of knowledge required for cross-cultural competence. Drachman (1992) has developed a stage-of-migration framework to support social professionals who work with migrants. This framework enables social workers to collect critical information on an individual that is vital towards understanding their situation and how best to support them. The framework has generic and specific usefulness because it can be applied to all immigrant groups and individuals (Drachman, 1992). The stage-of-migration framework suggests that assessment and intervention must take into account the following three stages: premigration and departure; transit; and resettlement. Table 24.1 illustrates the critical variables that a social professional must take into account.

The case study that follows is that of an asylum seeker who was originally referred to an independent support service for refugees and asylum seekers from a primary care mental health team.

Table 24.1 Stage-of-migration framework

Stage-of-migration	Critical variables
Premigration and departure	• Social, political and economic factors
	• Separation from family and social networks
	• Decisions regarding leaving family members behind
	• Consequences of leaving a familiar environment
	• Life-threatening circumstances
	• Experience of violence
	• Loss of significant others
Transit	• Aspects of safety throughout journey
	• Legal status in arrival location
	• Consequences of waiting for decision to be made on status
	• Loss of significant others
Resettlement	• Cultural issues
	• Reception from host country
	• Opportunity structure of host country
	• Discrepancy between expectations and reality
	• Consequences of cumulative stress throughout the process and ongoing support available

Source: Adapted from Drachman's stages-of-migration framework, 1992: 69

Case study*

Jean-Gabriel (22) was from Cameroon and he was referred to Revive by the primary care mental health team. He had applied for asylum on arrival to the UK but was refused and was approaching an appeal hearing. He was extremely traumatised because he had lost both of his parents in tragic circumstances and had suffered ill-treatment in his country of origin. He did not speak much English. He came several times to our outreach advice service where we formed a supportive relationship and I helped him with housing issues and assisted him to access Revive's allotment project. I accompanied Jean-Gabriel on the day of his appeal hearing. He was distraught when he had to replay the story of how he had come to the UK and he broke down whilst giving his evidence. I supported him throughout the day. On this occasion the judge allowed his appeal and he was granted refugee status.

Since then he has continued to access a lot of assistance from Revive in the areas of benefit applications, housing and education. I advocated on his behalf

---

*Revive social worker (adapted with kind permission from Revive project, Salford, UK)

to assist him to obtain council housing on health grounds and arranged for a volunteer to accompany him to interviews with the council's homelessness department. He is now much more settled and he is actively looking for work and has recently started English classes. He is a 'mentor' to another young man from the same country who is also a service user and an asylum seeker. He has given him a lot of support and encouragement to believe that there is also hope for his future.

The case of Jean-Gabriel illustrates how the critical variables of Drachman's three stages can be taken into account to ensure an individual receives the support they need. The stage-of-migration framework works from the philosophy that migration is a recurring phenomenon and so promotes the need for an established service response, rather than short-term crisis management of isolated cases. In doing so it further emphasises the need for all social workers to be aware of the impact of globalisation and international issues on local practice as part of their ongoing professional development.

Cross references: asylum seekers and refugees, equality and diversity, ethics, multi-professional working, social justice

SUGGESTED READING

Dominelli, L. (2010) *Social Work in a Globalizing World*. Cambridge: Polity.
Healy, L.M. (2001) *International Social Work: Professional Action in an Interdependent World*. Oxford: Oxford University Press.

REFERENCES

Appadurai, A. (2000) 'Grassroots globalization and the research imagination', *Public Culture*, 12(1): 1–19.
Bristow. K. (2008) *Transforming or Conforming? NGOs Training Health Promoters and the Dominant Paradigm of the Development Industry in Bolivia. Can NGOs Make a Difference? The Challenge to Development Alternatives*. London: Zed Books.
Dominelli, L. (2010) *Social Work in a Globalizing World*. Cambridge: Polity.
Drachman, D. (1992) 'A stage-of-migration framework for service to immigrant populations', *Social Work*, 37(1): 68–72.
Gledhill, J. (2009) 'The rights of the rich versus the rights of the poor', in S. Hickey and D. Mitlin (eds), *Rights-Based Approaches to Development: Exploring the Potential and Pitfalls*. Sterling, VA: Kumarian Press, pp. 31–46.
Harvey, D. (2005) *A Brief History of Neoliberalism*. Oxford: Oxford University Press.
Healy, L.M. (2001) *International Social Work: Professional Action in an Interdependent World*. Oxford: Oxford University Press.
IFSW (International Federation of Social Workers) (2001) 'Definition of social work'. Available from: http://ifsw.org/resources/definition-of-social-work (accessed 3 April 2012).
Lewellen, T.C. (2002) *The Anthropology of Globalization [Electronic Resource]: Cultural Anthropology Enters the 21st Century*. London: Bergin & Garvey.
Lyons, K., Manion, K. and Carlsen, M. (2006) *International Perspectives on Social Work: Global Conditions and Local Practice*. Basingstoke: Palgrave Macmillan.

key concepts in
social work practice

25

Law and Social Work

David Nulty

DEFINITION

Laws are the rules and principles that govern aspects of a community's action, in this case social work and its related disciplines, and which are created and enforced by political and legal authority.

Of all of the chapters you may read in this book this is the most likely to become obsolete. This is for two reasons. First, whilst there appears to be no immediate plan to change the broad framework of social work law for children and adults, incremental changes to key pieces of law arise from the cycle of consultative and law making activity in UK governments. New regulation and guidance is published on a frequent basis. There is also a plethora of reports ranging from those sponsored by government departments, special interest groups and major charities. This abundance of new publications makes it impossible for this chapter to offer a comprehensive or timely guide to the law, regulation and guidance that applies to the care and welfare of children and adults.

The second reason for obsolescence is that paper-based books are least well adapted to meet the volume of online publication and legal change. The major social work law reference works such as Brammer (2010) and Brayne and Carr (2010) respond to the exponential growth of online information by offering a blend of paper-based information, analysis, online updates and learning.

KEY POINTS

- Information about law and how to put it into the context of day-to-day social work practice is readily available online.
- We should think about law outside of the silos we work in.
- Does law construct social work practice in its image?
- Social work ignores law at the peril of its service users.

DISCUSSION

law and social work

111

Information on law is immediately available

The first key concept of this chapter is that with any device that can access the internet it is possible to find with relative ease all of the prime social work legislation, case law, regulations and guidance from government websites. Add to this the online presence of the Social Care Institute of Excellence, this constitutes a comprehensive resource. Analysis is offered by the national press with Guardian Society, specialist social work/social care press sites such as Community Care and CYP Now who support daily news coverage with specialist features and blogs. Organisations such as the Joseph Rowntree Foundation, Research in Practice, MIND, Family Rights Group, the Children's Legal Centre and the Centre for Mental Health provide a deeper level of analysis and vehicles for the voice of service users to be heard. It is likely that following the publication of any major piece of legislation, report or social care scandal that there will be an analysis available *within hours*.

We should think about law outside of silos

Braye and Preston-Shoot (2006, 2010a, 2010b, 2011) emphasise the complexity of both learning about law and social work. They challenge the approach that social work law should be taught in isolation from practice favouring integrative approaches that reflect the realities of the ways that people live.

The traditional approach to thinking about social work law is to set up a triangular framework (with the inclusion of the Human Rights Act and Equalities Act 2010 at the centre as essential guiding principles) to provide a way of identifying key pieces of law and associated guidance by service user groups.

We could think about law by considering other triangular configurations such as familial violence, substance misuse and mental health or independence, choice and mental capacity. These triangulations would reorder the naïve framework (laws listed by service user group) so that laws about child protection and safeguarding vulnerable adults would be grouped under familial violence and their contradictions placed in clear focus. An analysis of serious case reviews would show that legislation covering these two groups is divergent, creating anomalies and dangers depending on the location of the social worker within a local authority's workforce. Although people for the most part live together in families different assessment frameworks will be used according to the age of the service user. The consequence of this fragmented approach is that mistakes arising from poor inter-professional communication and co-operation can have profound, often fatal impacts for service users (CYP Now, 2011).

Does law construct social work practice?

A third key concept to be considered is that different forms of law have created workplace structures to help deliver the expectations of that legislation. As an example, the single assessment process (2002) in adult social care has in theory created a model of team working that is inter-professional but not necessarily social work led. Contrast this with the explicitly social worker led framework of assessment (2000) in children's services or the intentionally inter-professional common assessment framework (2004) for early intervention with children. Each assessment system, driven by the legal right established by case law of service users to have their needs assessed, uses a different configuration of bureaucratic systems.

Johns (2009), Brammer (2010) and Brayne and Carr (2010) explore areas of conflict between the value base of social work. These lie in the fields of youth justice, immigration and dealing with the needs of refugees. This raises questions about how social work practice in these areas can stay consistent with the Code of Practice (GSCC, 2011) that relate to the nation where social workers practice.

A good example of law seeking to reengineer practice is the Children Act 1989 which seemed at the point of implementation in October 1991 as comprehensive enough in scope and in the regulation contained within it to stand the test of time. However the failure of social work to implement the Act effectively led to the introduction of the Looked after Children System in 1993 (Garrett, 1999), Quality Protects (2000) and the Framework of Assessment (2000) as methods imposed from the Department of Health to ensure the Act was followed effectively. An analysis of the contents of the 1989 Act would show that these initiatives did not constitute anything more than a way of getting the spirit and letter of the original act implemented.

There does seem to be an observable tendency for there to be more law and more guidance and more systems to monitor the adherence to law; so has law constructed social work in its image, or has social work forced law to intervene more and more to resolve some of the tensions it is creating? To some extent both assertions are true.

Social work ignores law at the expense of service users

The concept that service users should have a say in how services are delivered to them, and wherever possible should manage their own care packages is embodied in adult social care legislation and guidance. This approach reflects two dominant trends in mid to late 20th century life. The first is the rejection of paternalistic/authority based interventions by the state and the second is that of consumer power. These principles to some extent are embodied in the Code of Ethics (BASW, 2011) that social workers espouse and that underlie ideas of anti-discriminatory practice detailed at great length in the social work literature (Thompson, 2006). However, an analysis of the specialist social work press (Community Care, 2011) shows distrust of personalisation because it appears to be tied to process re-engineering of the social care workforce, loss of professional status and autonomous decision making (Community Care Special Report, 2011).

In 2011 there is a growing body of evidence that suggests that the failure of social work to be able to protect service users or safeguard their human rights could lead to a further consolidation of legislation that governs the provision of services to children. Eileen Munro's long running analysis of social work services for children highlights serious deficiencies in both methods and outcomes (Munro, 2011). The Family Justice Review (Ministry of Justice, 2011) identified that: children are trapped in the legal system with uncertain outcomes; that there needs to be revision of civil law relating to the application of parental responsibility; and that the use of expert witnesses needs to be limited to speed up the legal process. These appear to mirror concerns expressed before the implementation of the Children Act 1989.

A similar consolidation could be required in adult services. The Law Commission review on Adult Social Care (Law Commission, 2011) highlights the need to develop adult safeguarding services within a statutory framework similar to children's safeguarding services. A recent report into home care services (*Guardian*,

2011) identified that the human rights of service users to not experience demeaning treatment was routinely violated as a result of inflexible, minimal or inadequate service provision. Andrew Dilnot in his recent commission report (Dilnot, 2011) identifies that we need to adapt the way we fund residential care for older people as the current system will collapse if we do not. Witness the recent demise of the Southern Cross residential care group as immediate evidence of what this crisis may be like (BBC News, 2011).

In addition to these reports, serious case reviews undertaken by both adults and children's safeguarding boards continue to provide extensive biographies of the degradation and sometimes avoidable deaths of service users.

Law currently exists to prevent these gross violations of human rights. It is a reflection of the potential obsolescence of this chapter that I mentioned at the start that whilst the names of the scandals that affect social work and social care may change the impact on service users does not.

Cross references: history of social work, managing change, political context of social work

SUGGESTED READING

Brammer, A. (2010) *Social Work Law*, 3rd edn. Harlow: Longman.
Brayne, H. and Carr, H. (2010) *Law for Social Workers.* Oxford: Oxford University Press.

REFERENCES

BASW (British Association of Social Workers) (2011) 'Code of ethics'. Available from: www.basw.
co.uk/about/code-of-ethics (accessed 15 August 2011).
BBC News (18 July 2011) 'Southern Cross sees third of care homes rescued'. Available from:
www.bbc.co.uk/news/business-14191177 (accessed 15 August 2011).
Brammer, A. (2010) *Social Work Law*, 3rd edn. Harlow: Longman.
Braye, S. and Preston-Shoot, M. (2006) 'SCIE Guide 13: learning, teaching and assessment of law
in social work education'. Available from: www.scie.org.uk/publications/guides/guide13
(accessed 15 August 2011).
Braye, S. and Preston-Shoot, M. (2010a) 'On the evidence for viruses in social work systems: law,
ethics and practice', *European Journal of Social Work*, 13(4): 465–82.
Braye, S. and Preston-Shoot, M. (2010b) *Practising Social Work Law.* Basingstoke: Palgrave Macmillan.
Braye, S. and Preston-Shoot, M. (2011) 'On administrative evil-doing within social work policy
and services: law, ethics and practice', *European Journal of Social Work*, 14(2): 177–94.
Brayne, H. and Carr, H. (2010) *Law for Social Workers.* Oxford: Oxford University Press.
Community Care (25 May 2011) 'Social workers say personalisation will fail most service users'.
Available from: www.communitycare.co.uk/Articles/2011/05/25/116868/social-workers-los-
ing-faith-in-personalisation.htm (accessed 15 August 2011).
Community Care Special Report (2011) 'The state of personalisation'. Available from: www.
communitycare.co.uk/static-pages/articles/the-state-of-personalisation (accessed 15 August 2011).
CYP Now (2011) 'Serious case review: be alert to mental health of parents'. Available from: www.
cypnow.co.uk/news/1024524/Serious-Case-Review-alert-mental-health-parents/?
DCMP=ILC-SEARCH (accessed 15 August 2011).
Dilnot, A. (2011) 'Commission on funding of care and support'. Available from: www.dilnotcom
mission.dh.gov.uk (accessed 15 August 2011).

Garrett, P.M. (1999) 'Questioning the new orthodoxy: the "looking after children" (LAC) system and its discourse on parenting', *Practice*, 11(1): 53–65.

GSCC (General Social Care Council) (2011) *Code of Practice*. London: GSCC.

Guardian (20 June 2011) 'Home care of elderly "abuses basic human rights"'. Available from: www.guardian.co.uk/society/2011/jun/20/home-care-elderly-human-rights (accessed 15 August 2011).

Johns, R. (2009) *Using the Law in Social Work*. Exeter: Learning Matters.

Law Commission (2011) 'Review of adult social care'. Available from: www.justice.gov.uk/lawcommission/areas/adult-social-care.htm (accessed 15 August 2011).

Ministry of Justice (2011) 'Family law review interim report'. Available from: www.justice.gov.uk/about/moj/independent-reviews/family-justice-review (accessed 15 August 2011).

Munro, E. (2011) 'Review of child protection'. Available from: www.education.gov.uk/munroreview (accessed 15 August 2011).

Thompson, N. (2006) *Anti-Discriminatory Practice*. London: Palgrave Macmillan.

26
Leadership and Management

Aidan Worsley and Tim Mann

DEFINITION

Management is generally concerned with the co-ordination of the actions and performance of an organisation in line with the policies, procedures and objectives of that organisation. Within social work, perhaps the most visible unit of management is the team leader and typically senior management teams are led by directors and their assistants. One of the many ideas of management, but one which is particularly relevant to contemporary analysis is that of 'scientific management'. Frederick Taylor coined the phrase, which embraced now familiar notions of efficiency and effectiveness and the control of work tasks. The work of Weber (Weber et al., 1991) is also relevant to the tasks of management, particularly his notion of bureaucracy which included a formal administrative hierarchy and a prescribed system of rules and procedures.

Leadership is an aspect of management but the two are rightly differentiated. Management, as noted, is to do with the planning and organisation of tasks whereas leadership is connected with creating, coping and helping to adapt to change (Hafford-Letchfield, 2009). Thus, leadership becomes transformational as it is designed to help people make and manage changes. This can be done by role modelling, articulating goals and influencing others through good communication.

leadership and management

115

These two ideas overlap most closely when we look at the idea of strategic planning where senior managers construct aims as a means of guiding a course of actions that deliver the business of the organisation (Payne, 2009).

KEY POINTS

- Management is the process of organising resources to get things done, leadership offers a sense of direction and a good leader may spearhead the movement in that direction.
- Management and leadership overlap but are concerned with different elements. Both will struggle to achieve results if one is absent.
- Managerialism is a significant issue in social work, impacting on services considerably. There is some evidence that it is having a deleterious effect on service delivery (Munro, 2011).
- All social workers are managers and as the role develops, the line between practitioner and manager is becoming blurred.

DISCUSSION

Social workers capture many aspects of management in their daily work – care management, workload management, etc. Looking inwards towards the organisation, they operate within structured policy and procedures, outwards by taking into account the interests of service users and politicians. Social workers also ensure their work is monitored and reviewed appropriately. Every social worker is having to learn to think on a much broader canvas than has ever been the case before: 'Thinking like a manager also enables social workers to bring a critical eye to bear on their own organisations, the services they provide and the standards they set' (Coulshed et al., 2006: 12).

One of the difficulties with the concept of the social worker as manager/leader is the level of control they are able to deploy over their working practices. There are two elements to this debate that we would like to consider: professional discretion and managerialism. Looking first at the issue of autonomy and discretion, social work is an interesting example where its level of professional power compared to, for example, the professions of medicine and law is relatively weak. However, it is equally clear that social workers operate within increasingly complex, multi-problem scenarios open to various interpretations which require high levels of skill, knowledge and a well-developed value base. Thus, as professionals operating in complex environments, one of the tasks of managers becomes the exercise of control over working processes – a balance must be struck. Clearly we would not want a state to be reached where professional discretion was given free reign, as this would run many dangers such as personal prejudice affecting judgement. The balance to be struck should not, however, err into over-controlling bureaucracy as this can have its own dangers. As Friedson notes, 'professional failure is marked by the dissolution into pure discretion, while administrative failure is marked by the petrification of forms' (Friedson, 1994: 70). The Munro review of child protection services describes a situation that has evolved where social workers have become constrained by the rules and timescales that have been set for them to the detriment of the needs of the child (Munro, 2011). Managerialism is largely concerned with the tendency to take the controlling aspects of managing an agency and its employees and focus on compliance, performance management and target setting. Thus, rather than encouraging diverse forms of response within a flexible use of professional discretion, managerialism often uses business techniques centred on compliance rather than allowing professional judgement to shape the organisational response (Payne, 2009). This is not new and Howe notes specifically how this can apply to social work:

> Managers seek to create regular and predictable task environments so that routine responses can be prescribed in set situations. They attempt to define both the work and the way the organisation functionaries will react. Thus, in a predefined situation, the social worker is expected to act in a pre-programmed way. Work becomes both fragmented and standardised. By increasing rules, routines, procedures, the manager diminishes the area of professional discretion available to the social worker (Howe, 1991: 204)

Indeed, as many social workers will attest today, managerialism is alive and well and perhaps constitutes one of the major flaws of contemporary social work management. Tied with links to risk aversion driven policy, social workers across the UK face more and more bureaucratic procedure curtailing their discretion and autonomy. This process, whilst perhaps inadvertently de-professionalising, is in danger of damaging the role and function of social work. Authors such as Sue White drive home not just the problem for the profession but also for service users who are more likely to become casualties of practice limited in such a fashion. White argues how the Integrated System for Children's Services serves such a policy:

> ... the ICS, by attempting to micro-manage work through a rigid performance management regime, and a centrally prescribed practice model, has disrupted the professional task, engendering a range of unsafe practices and provoking a gathering storm of user resistance. (White et al., 2010: 405)

One of the more severe challenges facing leaders and managers in the current social work context is the fragmentation of services and the ever more complex construction of function that characterises contemporary multi-disciplinary and multi-provider services. In terms of organisational theory, *differentiation* is characterised as the splitting of organisations in a number of component parts. *Integration* is concerned with the mechanisms that hold the organisation together. The greater the degree of differentiation, the greater the need for effective integration mechanisms. Thus, for social work, its endless divisions, specialism and re-organisation create such a degree of differentiation that copious methods of integration are required. The appropriate leadership style is also dependent on the situation and the balance between the use of authority by the leader and the authority given to team members.

As we have noted, one of the real difficulties facing social work is that its structures are inherently mechanistic – tasks are broken down into specialism, workers have clear job descriptions, lines of accountability and there is a hierarchy of authority. This is the kind of bureaucracy that Weber (Weber et al., 1991) envisaged, but it is far better suited to routine and stable tasks and not the complex world of social work. It could be argued that the challenge is to develop more organic structures to offer a better response to the conditions in which social work finds itself. In organic structures, activity is organised around specialism rather than function to facilitate communication and information gathering. Horizontal communication is highly valued and is seen as important as vertical accountability. Organic structures emphasise team work and staff flexibility. One of the more severe tests for the future of the profession appears to be finding a way to develop a more organic approach to management in social work.

THE CONCEPT IN SOCIAL WORK PRACTICE

Case study

Christy is a team leader in a small adult services team that delivers a range of services primarily to adults with physical and learning disabilities. The team consists of six members of staff, three of whom are newly qualified. Of the remainder, only one has been a social worker for more than four years. The team is stretched with its workload and struggles to manage the work it has to allocate. Christy is aware of these tensions and puts effort into team meetings – trying to ensure that the team bonds and works together. Because of the pressures, team relationships are poor and the office struggles to maintain a positive atmosphere. New guidelines have been introduced which affect a range of assessment processes and it feels like the last straw for the team. Christy decides that something must be done. She arranges a team away day to look at the new processes, as people prefer to be led and not driven, and participation produces a greater level of commitment to achieve the goals of the team. Leadership requires people to follow, and the social workers in the team have a valid contribution to make to responding to the pressures faced by the team. She ensures the staff feel valued and encourages them to think through new ways of working together to meet the new challenges ahead. One of the activities that she introduces to the team is a team skills analysis using the work of Belbin (2010) who identified nine team roles that need to be undertaken for the team to be successful. The model states that nobody is perfect but a team can be, and by looking at the specific skills and preferences of the team, Christy is able to utilise the expertise of the team and identify where there may be areas for further development within it. Given this new opportunity, the team come together and realign themselves into two main groups dealing with different aspects of the work. Christy ensures the two groups work in harmony by setting up a weekly case discussion forum which she asks a member of the team to chair on a weekly basis. Christy also tries to help the team become more strategic in their thinking by connecting them into broader organisation structures and policy developments to help shape future changes. Whilst Christy still has a management responsibility for the work required of the team, she also has a leadership role; for example, to represent the needs of the team within the local authority and possibly to advocate for support with their work pressures.

Cross references: accountability, managing change, quality assurance, supervision

key concepts in
social work practice

SUGGESTED READING

Broadhurst, K., Hall, C., Pithouse, A., Peckover, S., White, S. and Wastell, D. (2010) 'Risk, instrumentalism and the humane project – identifying the informal logics of risk management in children's statutory services', *British Journal of Social Work*, 40(4): 1046–64.

Lawler, J. and Bilson, A. (2010) *Social Work Management and Leadership: Managing Complexity with Creativity*. Abingdon: Routledge.

REFERENCES

Belbin, R.M. (2010) *Team Roles at Work*. London: Butterworth Heinemann.

Coulshed, V., Mullender, A., Jones, D. and Thompson, N. (2006) *Management in Social Work*, 3rd edn. Basingstoke: Palgrave Macmillan.

Friedson, E. (1994) *Professionalism Reborn: Theory, Prophecy and Policy*. Chicago, IL: Polity Press.

Hafford-Letchfield, T. (2009) *Management and Organisations in Social Work*, 2nd edn. Exeter: Learning Matters.

Howe, D. (1991) 'Knowledge, power and the shape of social work practice', in M. Davies (ed.), *Sociology for Social Work*. London: Routledge, pp. 202–21.

Munro, E. (2011) *The Munro Review of Child Protection: Final Report: A Child Centred System*. Department of Education. London: HMSO.

Payne, M. (2009) 'Strategic planning and leadership', in R. Adams, L. Dominelli and M. Payne (eds), *Practising Social Work in a Complex World*, 2nd edn. Basingstoke: Palgrave Macmillan, pp. 179–85.

Weber, M., Turner, B., Gerth, H. and Wright Mills, C. (1991) *From Max Weber: Essays in Sociology*. London: Routledge.

White, S., Wastell, D., Broadhurst, K. and Hall, C. (2010) 'When policy o'erleaps itself: the "tragic tale" of the children's integrated system', *Critical Social Policy*, 30(3): 405–31.

27
Learning Disability

Angela Olsen

DEFINITION

Learning disability (LD) is the term used in many UK services to describe a condition recognised by the World Health Organization (WHO) as – intellectual disability. The WHO's International Classification of Functioning, Disability and Health (ICF) formerly known as ICD-10 defines intellectual disability as:

> . . . a significantly reduced ability to understand new or complex information and to learn and apply new skills (impaired intelligence). This results in a reduced ability to cope independently (impaired social functioning), and begins before adulthood, with a lasting effect on development. (WHO 2011)

In the UK, the Department of Health used the same definition in the White Paper, *Valuing People* (VP) (2001). Learning disability is typically measured in the first instance by testing the individual's intelligence quotient (IQ). The average IQ for the adult population is 100. An IQ of less than 70 indicates that a person may have intellectual disabilities. IQ measurement is a contested tool and is generally supported by the use of other assessment tools that gather information about an individual's social functioning; however, these are also contested. A person with an IQ of 20 or less is defined as having profound intellectual and multiple disabilities (PMLD). People in this group are likely to have difficulty in walking unaided and will often have significant health needs. They may also have sensory disabilities, rely on non-verbal means of communication, such as signs and symbols, and may engage in self-injurious behaviour; see 'Raising our sights' (DH, 2010a).

Although VP (2001) estimates that there are 210,000 people with severe LD and 1.2 million with mild or moderate LD in the UK the real figure is unclear because many other hidden disabilities such as dyslexia inhibit a person's ability to learn in some situations. Conditions such as cerebral palsy, which can affect the speech and co-ordination of an individual, can sometimes lead to a misdiagnosis of learning disability when in fact the individual might have an IQ in excess of 100.

KEY POINTS

- People with learning disabilities can lead productive lives, gain qualifications, hold down paid jobs and become good parents. People who have LD may also have epilepsy, autism or mental health problems.
- Approximately 16,000 people have PMLD. Developments in healthcare and support mean that the population of people with PMLD is increasing by 1.8 per cent per year (DH, 2010a).
- People with LD might live in the family home; in properties with other people who have LD and be supported by care staff; or on their own. Some people need 24-hour support in adapted properties that are fitted with assistive technologies to help them to live as independently as possible; whereas others live in ordinary dwellings only needing occasional support with bills, etc.
- 20–30 per cent of prisoners have LD or conditions that make it difficult to cope in the criminal justice system (Prison Reform Trust, 2008)

DISCUSSION

The terminology used to label people who have a low IQ has changed throughout history. Terminology generally reflects the social, political and economic imperatives of the time during which it was used. The concept of Learning Disability (LD) is relatively recent and reflects the privileging in the 20th century of academic achievement. The term LD, although recognised by politicians and service providers, is contested by some people who may be labelled in this way. There is a current move amongst academics to change the preferred terminology to Intellectual Disability (Olsen, 2009).

Readers will be aware of sociological debates around the medical and social models of disability. The medical model of disability locates the cause of disability in the condition of the person, thus LD becomes a 'personal tragedy' for the individual because they are considered innately unable to learn new things; thus the problem is theirs, not one for society. The social model assumes that the person is disabled not by their 'impairment' but by a society that does not allow for difference or diversity. Thus a person may be categorised as disabled by an employment system that requires potential workers to gain academic qualifications before starting a job rather than assessing individuals in work to see if they are competent enough to carry out the tasks required.

Key legislation

The publication of the White Paper *Valuing People* (2001) raised the profile of people with LD and set out the principle that people should have rights, choice, control and independence over their own lives. However, a subsequent series of high-profile reports revealed that human rights violations continued to occur in services (see Sutton and Merton Report, 2007).

Valuing People Now (VPN) (DH, 2009a) and *Valuing Employment Now* (VEN) (DH, 2009b) set out strategies and implementation plans to improve life chances for people with LD. Both papers recognised the importance of giving positive messages to parents of babies with LD; starting from an assumption of competence and achievement. Implementation plans required local authorities, schools, health services, housing and transport providers to work together to make their services accessible to people with LD. VEN states that children should be included in work experience placements while still in school, with individual budgets being used to pay for job coaching to enable youngsters to develop work skills. VEN proposed the development of a Sustainable Hub for Innovative Employment for People with Complex Needs (SHIEC) (see Cooper and Ward, 2011).

The push towards making housing, transport and work more physically accessible may eventually help to reduce the current situation of social disenfranchisement that exists for many people with learning disabilities. However, the majority of people with LD are still excluded from ordinary school life, meaningful employment and commonly enjoyed leisure activities. Fear of bullying and hate crime continues to prevent many people with LD from travelling on public transport and employers' perception of competence to work prevents many of them from recruiting people with LD.

Autistic spectrum disorders

(See the Autism Act 2009 and the Autism Strategy [DH, 2010b]
Autism is a lifelong developmental disability that affects how a person communicates with, and relates to, other people. It also affects how they make sense of the world around them. They might also experience over- or under-sensitivity to light, sounds, touch, tastes, or colours. People who have autism may take longer to process information and may take speech very literally; for instance, it would be unwise to offer someone a piece of cake and call it 'to die for'.

THE CONCEPT IN SOCIAL WORK PRACTICE

Case study: supporting a person through transition

Sue had moderate LD, epilepsy and used a wheelchair. When she was young her epilepsy was unpredictable, causing nocturnal seizures during which she sustained multiple injuries. She had limited verbal communication skills. As she grew up her seizures became more frequent. Her mother found it increasingly difficult to care for her. At the age of 11 it was decided that Sue could no longer remain at home and she moved into a residential school, where her health and educational needs could be met. When she was 14, Sue's social worker, Nancy, encouraged her to think about her future. By this time her epilepsy was under control and she was able to communicate in an easily understandable way. Sue was able to make a bigger contribution to the discussions about her future than she had as a child. She and Nancy invited all the people that were important to her to contribute to the plan; these included Sue's teachers, residential workers, mother, and community nurse. Sue moved into a supported tenancy with three other people the week after her 18th birthday and Nancy ceased to have any involvement in Sue's life. Annual reviews were held and when she was 23 she asked the reviewing social worker, Richard, if he could help her to move in with her boyfriend, Steven, who had autism but did not have any formal support.

Sue's life is typical of many people with LD. Assessment and funding are often complicated by joint funding arrangements; there is often disagreement about the funding of what are often expensive educational placements that are sited many miles away from the family home. In Sue's case the local authority (LA) children's services and local education authority (LEA) funded her schooling, although in some areas it would have been funded by the LEA and health authority. There is often a debate about whether the residential component of schooling meets social or medical needs.

An important aspect of Nancy's role was to prepare Sue and her mum emotionally for the move. Parents often experience feelings of loss and guilt about their perceived inability to continue to care for their children at home. Some families find that short break services, sometimes called 'respite care', enable them to recharge their batteries and support their children well into adulthood. Short breaks can be provided in specialist care facilities or in family homes, sometimes known as shared care (or adult placement if the person is over 18). A person with LD might also be supported at home while their parents take a holiday. Sue's LA did not provide this service, prompting Sue's move. Nancy encouraged Sue and her mother to create a life-story book and memory box so that Sue could show staff at the residential school things from her life that were important to her; these encouraged the development of communication skills.

Once Sue turned 18 the LA became responsible for the assessment of her needs. Her tenancy was jointly funded through Supporting People (which funded her housing costs) and LA adult services (funding her care costs). Sue's request to move in with Steven was put to Richard who was dually qualified as a social worker and learning disability nurse and so able to undertake an holistic health and social work assessment.

During the time in the tenancy Sue had been supported to develop life skills and integrate into her local community, thus developing a network of supporters who could help her to think about living a more ordinary life outside 'services'. Richard suggested to Sue that she might formalise this and develop a 'Circle of Support' (CoS). Sue's circle comprised Richard, Steven, her key worker at the tenancy, her mum and a local taxi driver whom she had got to know well. CoS enable people with LD to surround themselves with informal supporters who help them to make important decisions and share tasks; thus decision making is taken away from the social worker whose primary role becomes one of advisor or advocate. Living independently of services does not necessarily mean living alone. Sue was enabled to live with her boyfriend and their home was adapted so that she could reach kitchen and bathroom equipment easily from her chair. Their CoS helped the couple to consider their ability to manage money and run a household.

CONCLUSION

The trend towards personalisation and individual budgets is leading to fragmentation of services and loss of the collective voice; potentially leading to the isolation of people with LD. Assessments in support of independent living need to take into account safeguarding issues such as the person's ability to understand and balance risks. The key tasks for social workers include balancing risk and opportunity while promoting opportunities for independence.

Cross references: advocacy, empowerment, personalisation, physical disability

SUGGESTED READING

Grant, G., Goward, P., Richardson, M. and Ramcharan, P. (eds) (2005) *Learning Disability: A Life Cycle Approach to Valuing People*. Maidenhead: Open University Press.
Race, D. (2007) *Intellectual Disability: Social Approaches*. Maidenhead: Open University Press.

REFERENCES

Autism Act (2009) The Stationery Office. 439510 19585. Available from: www.legislation.gov.uk/ukpga/2009/15/contents (accessed 30 May 2012).
Cooper, V. and Ward, C. (2011) 'Valuing people now and people with complex needs', *Tizard Learning Disability Review*, 16(2): 39–43.
DH (Department of Health) (2001) *Valuing People: A New Strategy for the 21st Century*. London: HMSO.
DH (Department of Health) (2009a) *Valuing People Now: A New Three-Year Strategy for People with Learning Disabilities*. London: Department of Health.
DH (Department of Health) (2009b) *Valuing Employment Now: Real Jobs for People with Learning Disabilities*. London: Department of Health.
DH (Department of Health) (2010a) 'Raising our sights: services for adults with profound intellectual and multiple disabilities'. Available from: www.dh.gov.uk/prod_consum_dh/groups/dh_digitalassets/@dh/@en/@ps/documents/digitalasset/dh_117961.pdf (accessed 30 May 2012).

learning disability

DH (Department of Health) (2010b) *Fulfilling and Rewarding Lives: The Strategy for Adults with Autism in England*. 13521, 14307. Available from: www.dh.gov.uk/en/Publicationsandstatistics/Publications/PublicationsPolicyAndGuidance/DH_113369 (accessed 30 May 2012).

Olsen, A. (2009) 'The changing of the guard: groupwork with people who have intellectual disabilities', *Groupwork*, 19(3): 39–56.

Prison Reform Trust (2008) *No One Knows: Police Responses to People with Learning Disabilities and Learning Difficulties*. London: Prison Reform Trust.

Sutton and Merton Report (2007) Available from: www.positive-options.com/news/downloads/Commision_for_Healthcare_Audit_and_Inspection_-_Investigation_-_Sutton_and_Merton_PCT_-_2007.pdf (accessed 12 April 2011).

WHO (World Health Organization) *International Classification of Functioning, Disability and Health (ICF)*. (2011) Available from: www.euro.who.int/en/what-we-do/health-topics/diseases-and-conditions/mental-health/news2/news/2010/15/childrens-right-to-family-life/definition-intellectual-disability (accessed 2 March 2011).

28
Looked After Children

Marian Foley

DEFINITIONS

In England, the term 'looked after' was introduced by the Children Act 1989, and is the legislative term for children in public care:

> A child is looked after by a local authority (LA) if s/he is in their care by reason of a care order, or is provided with accommodation under section 20 of the Act for more than 24 hours with the agreement of the parents, or of the child if s/he is aged 16 or over (section 22 (1) and (2) of the 1989 Act). (DCSF, 2010a: 6)

Unaccompanied asylum seeking children, those subject to court orders with residence requirements (secure or remand), and those looked after on a planned basis for short breaks or respite care are looked after children (DCSF, 2010a). When a child is voluntarily accommodated under Section 20 of the Children Act 1989, the LA does not have parental responsibility for the child. Here, accommodation may be provided as part of a broader range of support services to help children in need (Rowlands and Statham, 2009). When a child is subject to a care order, the LA acquires parental responsibility and the parent retains their parental responsibility.

The Children Act 1989, as amended by the Children (Leaving Care) Act 2000, Adoption and Children Act 2002, Children Act 2004 and the Children and Young Persons Act 2008 (DCSF, 2010a: 6) provides the legal framework for working with looked after children (LAC) and sets out the duties and responsibilities of LAs. It brings an increased emphasis on improving the experience of care for LAC through earlier identification of permanence options, improving their school experience, supporting them to do well in school and improving the transition from care to independent living.

Numbers of looked after children

On the 31 March 2011, there were 65,520 LAC in England, 60 per cent of whom were looked after under a care order and 31 per cent looked after under a voluntary agreement. The majority (48,530) were cared for in a foster placement. During the year ending 31 March 2011, 27,310 children started to be looked after. Of these children, 54 per cent were provided with a service because of abuse or neglect and 18 per cent because of family dysfunction (DfE, 2011a). These figures are dynamic as many children in care will eventually return home. Historically, trends in the numbers of LAC in England have been explained as a complex relationship between policy, social work practice and legislation (DfE, 2011b; Rowlands and Statham, 2009) and media attention (DfE, 2011b). Following publication of the serious case review into the death of Peter Connelly in November 2008, there was an increase in LA Section 31 applications in England continuing into 2010. However, MacLeod et al. (2010) noted that the publicity surrounding Peter's death was only a partial explanation for the increase in applications.

KEY POINTS

- The legislative framework and contemporary practice indicate that children are generally best cared for within their families.
- Children are likely to be taken into care on a court order because of abuse and neglect, and to have had prior contact with children's services, before becoming looked after.
- For most children, care is temporary and they will return home.
- The effective care planning and review process for LAC is critical in ensuring timely and appropriate care, and for permanence options to be identified at the earliest opportunity.
- Care can, and does, make a positive contribution to children's welfare.

DISCUSSION

Care planning and reviews for looked after children

An allocated social worker must ensure the needs of LAC are assessed, and that they have a timely and appropriate care plan identifying their needs, which stipulates how they will be met, and by whom. The care plan brings together information from assessments and the child/young person's developmental needs, including health, education, identity and contact with family and friends. The care plan must include the child/young person's wishes and the views of their parents. A key aim is to ensure appropriate long-term permanent plans are made for LAC. The concept of permanency for a child includes ensuring their emotional, physical and legal needs are met (DCSF, 2010a).

Reviews and the role of the independent reviewing officer

Children may wait some time before final decisions on permanency can be made (Beckett and McKeigue, 2010), although attempts to reduce the delay in care proceedings through the introduction of the Public Law Outline have been made (Ministry of Justice, 2008). To avoid 'drift' and ensure the care plan is being implemented, all LAC have regular statutory reviews chaired by an Independent Reviewing Officer (IRO). The minimum statutory requirements require the first review to be convened within 20 days of a child becoming looked after, the second within a minimum of three months, and then others at six-monthly intervals. The role of the IRO is to quality assure the care planning and review process for LAC, giving full consideration to the child's wishes and feelings and ensuring permanency options are considered at the earliest possible stage (DCSF, 2010b). The IRO must monitor the performance of the LA to ensure the care plan for the child reflects their current needs and is consistent with the LAs legal responsibilities towards that child.

The corporate parent

The concept of 'corporate parenting' was introduced in 1988 with the launch of the 'quality protects' agenda aimed at improving the life chances of LAC. LAs have a legal and moral responsibility to promote the well-being and life chances of LAC by ensuring children in their care are given every opportunity to reach their full potential. Initially regarded as the responsibility of children's services, increasing emphasis has been placed upon 'corporate parenting' as the shared responsibility of all local services, including: health, education, police and housing.

Improving the educational achievement of LAC

The 2007 *Care Matters* White Paper (DfES, 2007) set out to improve the attainment of LAC. It was acknowledged that whilst some LAC do well in school, most do not compared to children on average and educational achievement is unacceptably low. To improve this situation, Section 52 of the Children Act 2004 placed a duty on LAs to promote children's educational achievement. All LAC of school age are required to have a Personal Education Plan (PEP) which records what needs to happen in order for a child to reach their full educational ability. It is the social worker's responsibility to ensure that all actions recorded in the PEP are acted upon and reviewed as part of the statutory review of the care plan. Prior to the statutory review, the social worker is responsible for several actions, including completing the review record and recording relevant information on a child's educational progress. They must ensure that the child's carers and birth parents, where appropriate, and education professionals contribute to the PEP and notify the IRO of any significant changes to it. This duty extends to young care leavers who are continuing their education. Where the child has a Statement of Special Education Need (SEN), the PEP review needs to be linked to the annual review of the SEN.

THE CONCEPT IN SOCIAL WORK PRACTICE

Case study

Katie (seven) and Gemma (eight) lived with their mother until they were aged five and six respectively, when they moved into a temporary foster home. Prior to coming into care the children had been known to children's services for two years following a school referral concerned about neglect. The children often arrived at school hungry, were inadequately dressed for the weather and their attendance was poor. Their mother, Mary, was known to misuse alcohol. Following an initial and core assessment, family support services were provided. There was some improvement in the children's appearance and school attendance. Their mother attended alcohol services and there was some evidence of reduction in her alcohol use. Mary began a relationship with Kevin and initially things went well, but when Kevin ended the relationship Mary's alcohol use began to increase and she stopped attending all appointments with alcohol services. There was a marked deterioration in the children's appearance and school attendance. Gemma appeared to be losing weight and Katie was becoming more withdrawn in school. An initial child protection conference was held; the children were registered under the category of neglect and a child protection plan was drawn up. Unfortunately, Mary's drinking continued to increase. The children's care continued to deteriorate, so the LA applied for an interim care order and the children were placed in LA foster care with Brenda and Mike.

Katie and Gemma missed their mother, but had contact with her three times a week at a local family centre. Their social worker visited them regularly to ensure their needs identified in the care plan were being met. Katie and Gemma were happy within the placement and that future plans were explained. Katie and Gemma quickly settled into their new routines. They continued to attend their local school and see their friends. Gemma quickly put on weight and Katie stopped being withdrawn and made local friends. They regularly attended school and began to make real progress in their schoolwork. They expressed a wish to return home to live with their mother if she stopped drinking. Mary appeared motivated to stop drinking and wanted the children to return home. She was attending alcohol services and significantly reduced her alcohol intake, but this was still in the early stages. Court assessments are ongoing but it is likely that if the assessments of Mary are positive, and she can evidence a sustained period of change, the children will return home subject to a care order.

The children remain anxious about the future but they have a good relationship with their social worker and their foster carers, who are able to support and reassure them through this process. Their wishes and feelings are considered within the court process by the appointment of a children's guardian from Children and Family Court Advisory and Support Service (CAFCASS), who appoints a children's panel solicitor to directly convey the children's wishes and feelings in the court process.

This case study highlights the fact that the welfare of children often improves in care (Forrester et al., 2009) but for children involved in care proceedings the wait for permanency decisions is often an anxious one. Close supportive relationships with social workers and carers can help them through this process. The decision to return children home, especially in neglect cases, is complex, with success dependent on a number of variables (Farmer and Lutman, 2010).

Cross references: adoption, fostering, substance misuse, youth justice

SUGGESTED READING

DCSF (Department for Children, Schools and Families) (2010a) *The Children Act 1989 Guidance and Regulation Volume 2: Case Planning, Placement and Case Review*. London: DSCF.

REFERENCES

Beckett, C. and McKeigue, B. (2010) 'Objects of concern: caring for children during care proceedings', *British Journal of Social Work*, 40(7): 2080–101.

DCSF (Department for Children, Schools and Families) (2010a) *The Children Act 1989 Guidance and Regulation Volume 2: Case Planning, Placement and Case Review*. London: DSCF.

DCSF (Department for Children, Schools and Families) (2010b) *IRO Handbook: Statutory Guidance for Independent Reviewing Officers and Local Authorities on Their Functions in Relation to Case Management and Review for Looked After Children*. London: DSCF.

DfE (2011a) *Children Looked After by Local Authorities in England (Including Adoption and Care Leavers) – Year Ending 31 March 2011. SFR21/2011*. London: DfE.

DfE (2011b) *The Munro Review of Child Protection: Final Report. Cm 8062/2011*. London: DfE.

DfES (2007) Care Matters: Time for Change. London: The Stationery Office.

Farmer, E. and Lutman, E. (2010) *Case Management and Outcomes for Neglected Children Returned to Their Parents: A Five Year Follow-Up Study. RB214*. London: DSCF.

Forrester, D., Goodman, K., Cocker C., Binnie, C. and Jensch, G. (2009) 'What is the impact of public care on children's welfare? A review of research findings from England and Wales and their policy implications', *Journal of Social Policy*, 38(3): 439–56.

MacLeod, S., Hart, R., Jeffes, J. and Wilkin, A. (2010) *The Impact of the Baby Peter Case on Applications for Care Orders* (LGA Research Report). Slough: NFER.

Ministry of Justice (2008) *The Public Law Outline: Guide to Case Management in Public Law Proceedings*. London: Ministry of Justice.

Rowlands, J. and Statham, J. (2009) 'Numbers of children looked after in England: a historical analysis', *Child and Family Social Work*, 14(1–2): 79–89.

key concepts in
social work practice

29

Managing Change

Denise Megson

DEFINITION

Change management has been defined as 'the process of continually renewing an organisation's direction, structure, and capabilities to serve the ever-changing needs of external and internal customers' (Moran and Brightman, 2001: 111). This chapter will put change management within the current professional and socio-political context and highlight the links it has with leadership.

Change in social work is constant, as the profession responds and adapts to external factors such as:

- new training programmes, based on the capabilities framework (Social Work Reform Board, 2010);
- working in partnership with service users to identify commissioning and evaluation of services in form of partnership boards;
- the personalisation agenda and the change in the roles of social workers from expert professional service provider to facilitators and care navigator;
- the current economic situation leading to cutbacks in services and job losses. Information technology – use of electronic records, data protection and freedom of information.

KEY POINTS

- Change is essential to keep improving.
- The changes are likely to affect an organisation's direction, structure and capabilities.
- Strong leadership is necessary to affect the change and in a way that is beneficial to the people who work in the organisation and its users.
- Within social work the changes in the next few years will be national and external to organisations but will have a big impact on individual organisations.

DISCUSSION

There have been various theories and models published on the management of change. Two of the more commonly known models are Kotter's eight-steps change model (Kotter and Cohen, 2002) and Lewin's (2011) three-step model of change.

Each model describes stages of the change process and the leadership and tasks needed to effect change.

Briefly, Kotter's eight-steps model is as follows:

1 **Create the urgency**

Communicate why change is needed – maybe legislative, improving quality of service, improving skills of workforce, competition in the market.

2 **Form a powerful coalition**

Get people who are instrumental in driving the change through; leadership is required and can be from grass roots. Get commitment from these individuals; the team should have members from different levels.

3 **Create a vision for change**

Determining the values that are central to the change, have a short summary of the vision and a strategy for achieving the vision. The people responsible for driving the changes need to be able to describe the change succinctly.

4 **Communicate the vision**

Discuss and talk about the change at all levels of operation within the organisation. Tie the discussions back to the vision. Listen to concerns and anxieties. Lead by example.

5 **Remove obstacles**

Identify what processes and structures may be impeding change. Identify people who are responsible for delivering the change, reward those making the change. Identify people who are resisting and see what the barriers are.

6 **Create short-term wins**

Have short-term targets that are achievable or start on an area that can get relatively quick results. Reward those who have helped in getting the results.

7 **Build on the change**

Improvements to be part of the continual process of change and long-term goals to ensure momentum does not get lost.

8 **Anchor the change in corporate culture**

Embed the values central to the change in the day-to-day operation of the organisation. Celebrate the successes to date. New people who support the vision may have to replace those who leave.

Lewin's three-step model is often described using the analogy of changing the shape of a block of ice. To change a solid square block of ice to a cone, you have to first melt the square block, reshape the water and then refreeze it to form the new solid shape.

1 **Unfreeze**

Identify the compelling reasons for change, what needs to change, and the current state of the organisation. Is there support from the people at the top of the organisation? Create the need for change. Use evidence to support this and share this with all concerned within the organisation, developing the vision and strategy to deliver the change. There are tools that can be used to develop some of the evidence, for example, a Strengths Weakness Opportunities and Threats (SWOT) analysis.

2 **Change**

Communication is important throughout the period of change, including being honest and open. Describe the benefits; involve people by providing opportunities for participation. Generate short-term wins and negotiate with external stake-holders as necessary.

3 **Refreeze**

Anchor the change into the culture by identifying what supports the change and the barriers. Then develop ways to sustain the change. Training will have to be provided to keep everyone informed and supported. For a critique of Lewin's model see Burnes (2004).

Leadership qualities to facilitate effective change

Both models acknowledge that leadership is needed to deliver change, however leadership does not necessarily have to come from people with a conferred role to manage or lead. Research with successful women from British Ethnic Minority communities (Champayne et al., 2007) suggests a different model of change man-agement can be equally effective.

There are eight factors that form the basis of the model, which can be assessed to identify a baseline. The eight factors are:

- *Values driven leadership*: having a set of values and principles which are consist-ently practised to improve relationships within teams, organisations and com-munities. These leaders make decisions that are true to themselves and build the trust of people they work with. Some of the values are openness, inspiring trust and hope. These leaders have an attitude that is inclusive by creating struc-tures and processes that enable others to succeed.
- *Spiritual belief*: the ability to use and supply spirituality, faith and/or belief in a way that positively empowers, inspires and motivates self and others.
- *Self-mastery*: total belief in and control of oneself in an outcomes driven approach to personal growth and leadership development.
- *Presence, passion and power*: the ability to communicate with conviction, impact and authority.
- *Bi-cultural competence*: the ability to effectively function in and lead across more than one culture, switching and shifting seamlessly within different national contexts and across geographical boundaries.
- *Multiple perspectives*: the ability to look at issues and make decisions drawing from and informed by a variety of alternative perspectives.
- *Cultural capital*: the capacity to accumulate non-monetary and relationship capital generated outside the workplace.
- *Transformational leadership*: the ability to consistently combine the best ele-ments of transformational (inspirational/strategic) leadership with transactional (task-focused) leadership.

THE CONCEPT IN SOCIAL WORK PRACTICE

Case study

Using the personalisation of care as an example of managing change in practice, the scenario will serve as an example to illustrate the concepts. Louise is the manager of a respite unit providing short stays for children with profound learning disabilities and challenging behaviours. There are 28 families who use the service currently and most of the families have been using the service for a minimum of six years. In line with new policies and best practice guidelines, she wants to change some of the working practice in the unit to be more child-centred and family focused. From the assessments Louise identifies that families book the children's stays based on historical factors and do not consider the children's friendships. She would like families to work together so they can book stays based on the children's needs and so that staff will be able to facilitate activities to further develop existing friendships.

Using Kotter's eight-steps change model described above, Louise holds meetings with staff and families to discuss changes in policies and best practice guidelines. She uses some person-centred tools at the meetings to introduce the concept and to gauge the feelings from participants. She asks the participants for ideas and asks for expressions of interests to form a working party. After the meetings, notes are circulated to all staff and families to keep them informed of outcomes and decisions.

At the second stage, she communicates with those who have expressed interest and motivates those who have shown interest to join the discussions.

In order to create a shared vision for change, Louise does some work on mining values and collates the core ones. She leads the working group to develop a vision statement and a short narrative to help her and others to articulate what they are doing and how they are going to do it.

The group also develops a newsletter to tell other existing and potential service users about the work. A suggestion box is made available for comments and expressions of concerns. These are looked at fortnightly and replies are posted on the newsletter after the working group have discussed them. For example, families are concerned about the number of days they will be able to book if their children come together with friends as each family's need is different. Similarly, staff are anxious about being able to provide care in a person-centred manner if all the individuals booking in at certain times have very different and complex needs.

It is decided to run a pilot with interested families first. A discussion meeting with these families identify some of the barriers in the booking process in that some families book for the whole year whilst others will do so every three months. As a compromise, a six-month period is agreed. Staff members are then able to plan for the individuals coming up to six months in advance and they start suggesting ideas for activities that the children would enjoy and participate in. A date for evaluating after three months is agreed and the sorts of information that are important for the evaluation and how it is to be gathered is considered. Louise agrees to lead on some of the areas like the paperwork but asks staff and families to consider what links they have with their own communities that can be used to facilitate different experiences for the children. Staff members are allocated different tasks like looking at what is in the community generally and what skills they have as individuals and want to develop as part of delivering a more person-centred service.

Achievements in these small tasks are recognised as the information is pooled and attributed to the individuals in the newsletters. Staff are pleased to see their names in print and to be recognised for their contributions. The momentum is maintained as staff continue to meet with families to evaluate the changes and feedback on experiences. New members of staff are inducted into the system and once the focus on spending time at respite with friends is achieved, a new theme will be the next focus.

The above scenario incorporated the leadership skills necessary to manage the change in a way that benefits children and families and develops capacity of staff and family members. It highlighted some of the barriers that may impede progress when changing service is delivered. The example used other key concept, person-centred care to illustrate the interconnection of key concepts.

Cross references: leadership and management, multi-professional working, reflection, team working

SUGGESTED READING

Kotter, J.P. and Cohen, D.S. (2002) *The Heart of Change: Real Life Stories of How People Change Their Organizations*. Boston, MA: Harvard Business School Press.
Paton, R. (2008) *Change Management: A Guide to Effective Implementation*, 3rd edn. London: Sage.

REFERENCES

Burnes, B. (2004) 'Kurt Lewin and the planned approach to change: a re-appraisal', *Journal of Management Studies*, 41(6): 977–1002.
Champayne, C., Harper Juantah, C. and Peters, J. (2007) *Different Women Different Places: A Study of the Lives and Experiences of Black and Minority Ethnic Women Leaders*. Cheam: The Diversity Practice Limited.
Kotter, J.P. and Cohen, D.S. (2002) *The Heart of Change: Real Life Stories of How People Change Their Organizations*. Boston, MA: Harvard Business School Press.
Lewin, K. (2011) 'Kurt Lewin change management model'. Available from: http://currentnursing.com/nursing_theory/change_theory.html (accessed 5 October 2011).
Moran, J. W. and Brightman, B. K. (2001) 'Leading organizational change', Career Development International, 6(2): 111–18.
Social Work Reform Board (2010) *Building a Safe and Confident Future: One Year On*. London: HMSO.

30
Managing Technology
Bob Sapey

DEFINITION

Adjective or verb – is this technology for managing the activities of the social worker or vice versa? Whilst this could be taken as a simple linguistic question, it also reflects an important issue that has arisen in the use of new technologies for some time. In the second half of the 19th century, business managers sought ways of maintaining control over the increasing activity of their organisations. Yates (1993) describes how they did this by formalising internal communication and by 1920 she says that control of such communication had become a fact of life in the workplace. Managers' decisions in choosing technologies were influenced by their need to have control over how their workforce operated and what it was aiming to achieve.

Beniger (1990) likens information and communication technology to organisations which consist of people behaving in an ordered manner, processing data and information so as to achieve a common goal. Computing technologies undertake the same activities and can therefore be understood as an integral part of the organisation, not simply an additional tool. As with people working in any other organisation, social workers experience the technologies in their workplace as sometimes assistive and sometimes controlling. Much will depend upon the extent to which they are permitted to make choices about its use.

Service users can be similarly affected, but they may find it difficult to separate the actions of the social worker and the computer as they are both part of the same organisation. Some may prefer the privacy afforded by the call-centre approach while others will wish to be valued in a face-to-face setting. Whichever, the experience of receiving social work services will be affected by the relationship social workers have with the technology in their organisation.

KEY POINTS

- An action understanding of organisations is of value to understanding the relationships between social workers and technologies.
- Informationalisation is impacting on the nature of the social work task.
- The modernisation of social work and social care decontextualises human beings, both social workers and service users.

DISCUSSION

The idea that technology is a form of organisation is a rational approach to understanding the role of information and communication systems. Beniger (1990) observed that early businesses became organised as their activities grew and the owners required some way of ensuring that the individuals they employed communicated with each other so as to serve their best interests. Imports, exports, sales, purchases, deliveries and payments all needed to be co-ordinated and this involved both the communication and processing of information between people. The computer can undertake the same tasks and in the right situations can replace people. However, as the complexity of the information increases the limitations of the role of the machine becomes apparent. Computers are much better than the human brain at storing and retrieving large amounts of complex data, but they are unable to replace the inferential knowledge that comes from experience that may be required to make sensitive decisions. In human services this is particularly the case as decisions almost always involve making assessments of how service users and other people are responding to suggestions and ideas. According to this approach, the task then is for people to determine the appropriate use of technology according to the business to be conducted. Providing counselling would require face-to-face communication while notifying people of the time of a meeting might be best done by email. A database may be effective at supporting the work of registration staff in terms of recalling a multitude of due dates for various actions, whereas a case conference might be better suited to an inter-professional negotiation of safeguarding plans.

However, a rational approach to using technology assumes that people have similar responses to its use which is not the case. Our experience of organisations – the people and the technology – varies, as does our competence with different technologies. Singer (1999) points out that while face-to-face communication may be difficult for people with Asperger's syndrome, online discussion groups appear to enable greater participation. Similarly, the experience of the Patient Voices project (www.pilgrim.mysen.co.uk/patientvoices/) shows that many people with mental distress may find it empowering to be able to produce digital stories to put over their views at case conferences. On the other hand, we probably all know people who find computers intimidating and who would not use them given the choice. As such our experiences affect our interactions with technologies and organisations.

It may be helpful therefore in considering the role of technology in organisations to reconsider how we theorise organisations. Silverman (1970) argues that we tend to make the mistake of reifying organisations, to construct them as entities which exist in their own right rather than seeing them as the combined activity of the people within them. This action approach acknowledges that people are socialised into particular modes of behaviour, that they are actors performing to a script. However, individuals may step outside their prescribed roles and at such times organisations are affected and they may change. ICTs tend to conform more rigidly to their scripts (or programming) and as such may create the greater rigidity we have all experienced from time to time – 'Computer Says No'.

So the computer may well be limited to rational models of activity while people have a greater potential for improvisation. But which would be the best choice in specific situations will also depend on the way they are perceived by the person being served.

Whilst ICTs have become an integral part of our lives, historically their use is relatively recent and we are still in the process of learning just how to manage them. Castells (1996) has argued that since the late 20th century, we have been going through a process of informationalisation, much the same as the industrialisation which began some 200 years earlier. Such revolutions create immense change, much of which requires a paradigm shift in the way we understand what is happening. Central to this new economic mode is the value we now place on the production and ownership of data. In this way, technology moves from being an effective way of achieving the production of existing goods and services, to constructing its own new products. Modern databases have opened up new demands and expectations, for example, CRB reports in employment or census data in genealogy.

There is a tendency amongst public sector managers and policy makers to view ICTs as providing the solution to almost any failure imaginable. There is now no limit to the complexity of the procedures that civil servants design and put into our legislation as they expect that the systems they create can be managed using computers. Poor services are often deemed to be the result of failures to communicate and the solutions proffered are more and better communication systems. Expectations are set very high with managers and politicians aiming to have integrated information systems covering health, education and welfare services, with potential to include police, immigration and security where necessary. Some of this will rely on people knowing when to communicate what to others, but the aim is to reduce the number of different systems that have been unable to communicate without a reliance on humans who are prone to error. The computer is expected to be accurate and up to date, yet this is often not the case.

In her interim report on child protection, Munro (2011) is critical of ICT systems which are designed without consideration of how they might alter the human task of social work. Her concern is that the role of the social worker may be altered to such an extent that they become ineffective at achieving the desired outcome, the protection of a child. She recommends the necessity to take a different approach to the design of ICT systems used in childcare agencies; that they should support the skilled, professional activities of the social worker rather than dictate how that work is done. This clearly gets to the heart of the question as to whether 'managing', in the context of managing technology is an adjective or a verb; but Munro's recommendations would require a significant reversal of the trends of organisational development since the mid-19th century of 'control through communication' (Yates, 1993) and since the late 20th century of replacing the inferential knowledge of professionals with algorithms in social work decision making (Ravetz, 1993).

Beyond the issue of how technology affects the capacity of social workers to undertake their roles in a professional manner is the issue of how it impacts on people in need of welfare support. Informationalisation is more than simply working with data; it is about using that data to produce information and knowledge. Social workers may have found their roles changed and perhaps limited to working with data, but those who need welfare services have been re-contextualised as the source of that data. While budget cuts may lead to fewer services and higher thresholds of eligibility, even those people who do not qualify are required to provide the information that will lead to their failed assessment of need. That data is stored and used to analyse how to allocate services in the future. The virtual world of the 'managing technology' must be fed its data if it is to exist. A computer without data is of no value, and it is the welfare applicants who fail to access the services they require who help keep it living.

Managing technology – as an adjective the technology may serve the interests of those in control, as a verb it requires social workers to compete with other vested interests to ensure the technology is supportive of effective practice. For service

key concepts in
social work practice

users however, this question may be academic as the technology, be it managing or being managed, may simply be another indicator of their unmet need.

Cross references: accountability, managing change, record keeping

SUGGESTED READING

Harlow, E. and Webb, S. (2003) *Information and Communication Technology in the Welfare Services*. London: Jessica Kingsley.
Sapey, B. (1997) 'Social work tomorrow: towards a critical understanding of computers in social work', *British Journal of Social Work*, 27(6): 803–14.

REFERENCES

Beniger, J. (1990) 'Conceptualizing information technology as organization, and vice versa', in J. Fulk and C. Steinfield (eds), *Organizations and Communication Technology*. Newbury Park, CA: Sage, pp. 29–45.
Castells, M. (1996) *The Information Age: Economy, Society and Culture: Volume 1 – The Rise of the Network Society*. Malden, MA: Blackwell Publishers.
Munro, E. (2011) *The Munro Review of Child Protection. Interim Report: The Child's Journey*. London: Department of Education.
Ravetz, J. (1993) 'Information technology support systems in the human services', in B. Glastonbury (ed.), *Human Welfare and Technology: Papers from the HUSITA 3 Conference on IT and the Quality of Life and Services*. Assen: Van Gorcum and Comp, pp. 45–54.
Silverman, D. (1970) *The Theory of Organisations: A Sociological Framework*. London: Heinemann.
Singer, J. (1999) '"Why can't you be normal for once in your life?" From a "problem with no name" to the emergence of a new category of difference', in M. Corker and S. French (eds), *Disability Discourse*. Buckingham: Open University Press, pp. 57–67.
Yates, J. (1993) *Control through Communication: The Rise of System in American Management*. Baltimore, MD: John Hopkins University Press.

31
Media and Social Work
Joanne L. Westwood

DEFINITION

It has been well established that the media helps shape public concerns about social problems and specifically about the issues with which the social work professions contend (Franklin and Parton, 1991). Whilst social work is variously represented in the media as being about the protection of the vulnerable, social work is also concerned with promoting the rights and interests of marginalised and vulnerable groups (General Social Care Council, 2011 [GSCC hereafter]). Research in this field suggests that media representation would have us believe that social workers only protect, and not always very well (Franklin and Parton, 1991).

The 'social work' which is defined in media-constructed discourses, social workers will quickly come to realise, is just that – a media construction. Social work education encourages students to embrace knowledge about the profession, society and the people they work with from their engagement with a broad range of academic disciplines, rather than from the media – however influential it may be.

The social work profession is primarily accountable to the people who use social work and care services through the requirement for their registration with the GSCC. Social workers are also accountable to their employers. Both the GSCC and its apparent successor, the Health Professions Council (HPC) regulate the way in which confidential information is reported and investigated by the media. There are certain precautionary measures which social workers need to be aware of related to the engagement of the media and social work practice. The confidential nature of the information – and the rights of people using social services to have their personal information protected – makes communications with the press in relation to specific cases a difficult task. This usually comes within the remit of a press or communications officer, rather than being the responsibility of an individual social worker.

It is nonetheless important for the profession to have some understanding and awareness of the way in which social work and social workers are represented both *in* and *by* the media, and to have the tools to question these perceptions and challenge the 'common sense' arguments which newspaper and broadcast editors promote about social issues and their causes and remedies. It also needs to be acknowledged that the growth in media forms creates opportunities for the social work profession to promote itself.

KEY POINTS

- The media play an important role in constructing social work and social workers.
- These constructions are often linked to failings which have been highlighted in public inquiries.
- Social workers are accountable and thus need to carefully align themselves in accordance with their professional regulatory body and their employers in matters concerning media reporting of cases.
- On certain issues the media are well situated to lead the public-awareness campaigning element of social problems.
- Social work is challenged to engage with a wide range of evolving media.

DISCUSSION

The news media, social work and child abuse

Aldridge urges us to acknowledge that, 'media organisations are driven by considerations of costs and profits' (1990: 612) and suggests that '. . . social work's bad news provides sex and violence in abundance' (1990: 617), the bread and butter, arguably, of the press media. It is also clear that the press inculcate immediacy and drama which 'slant the selection of stories towards the more sensational' (Ayre, 2001: 889).

Media interest in social work and specifically child abuse can be traced back to the death of Maria Colwell in 1973. Media constructions of social work are often linked to failings which have been highlighted in public inquiries, or, as in the case of the Cleveland crisis, the press and broadcast media actually leading the public-awareness campaigning element (Aldridge, 1990; Kitzenger, 2000). Franklin and Parton (1991) argue that, 'child abuse inquiries have been the major triggers of media interest as well as their primary focus' (1991: 12). In the Cleveland public inquiry into the way in which children were removed from their parents, the press reporting of the issues was discussed in an entire section of the published report (Franklin and Parton, 1991) which criticised the press for their role in continuing the crisis.

In the media reporting of the Beckford, Carlile and Henry cases the media:

> . . . constructed an extremely negative stereotype of social workers which presented them as incompetent, non-judgemental and indecisive individuals . . . extremely reluctant to intervene in the private realm of family life even to protect children from a suspected abusing adult. (Franklin and Parton, 1991: 14)

These media constructions gain valuable currency in the aftermath of child deaths and social work itself arguably comes to represent all that is wrong with public services, whilst social workers are represented as being all that is wrong with social work. Media reports often stereotype and provide simplistic but enduring constructions which do little to reflect the complexity and uncertainty which characterises social work practice.

Broadcast television and social work

The television broadcast media also play an influential role in portraying the profession and its workforce. Social work and social workers have been represented in television drama serials many times over the last 40 years or so (Henderson and Franklin, 2007). Social workers tend to be depicted ambiguously, in other words, as both intrusive and neglectful and, more explicitly although less frequently, as incompetent bungling pseudo-professionals – as the following examples illustrate.

When it was originally broadcast, the now classic *Cathy Come Home* (Loach, 1966) provoked a storm of media and public interest. Questions were asked in parliament regarding the problem of children being taken into care because they were living in inadequate housing. This broadcast, along with the publication of Abel-Smith and Townsend's (1966) *The Poor and the Poorest* attracted a largely supportive media response to housing problems in the UK post-war welfare state. Whilst the importance of addressing housing and poverty issues were raised broadly sympathetically, the characterisation of the social workers was less so. In *Cathy Come Home* the social workers are depicted as both 'child-snatchers' and 'heartless bureaucrats'. This theme is also evident in the powerful Channel 4 film *Ladybird Ladybird* (Loach, 1994) which tells the story of a single mother who leaves a violent relationship and, following a fire in her home, has her children taken into care.

In contrast the recent television (BBC1) drama *Exile* (Brocklehurst, 2011) tells the story of a family struggling under the pressure of caring for an elderly parent with dementia. There was, however, very little evidence of social work involvement depicted in this drama – the social worker and any social work intervention was conspicuous by its absence. In *Exile*, when the female carer felt unable to continue caring for her father she was almost magically able to put him into immediate respite care. A dramatic and imaginative feat on the part of the writers no doubt, but one which certainly gives a false and altogether unrealistic impression of how carers and service users struggle to access social support when they need it without going through a sometimes lengthy process of referral and assessment.

Henderson and Franklin (2007) discuss findings from a study which charted the ways in which social care professionals were characterised in popular UK television drama. Although the portrayal of social carers was reasonably frequent, their role is largely peripheral; many were depicted sympathetically, but they were outsiders and remained as such throughout the programmes. Nonetheless, Henderson and Franklin (2007) remain optimistic about the opportunities for promoting the social work profession. They argue that the television serial drama is, 'an important cultural resource which could be targeted by those seeking to change public perceptions of the profession' (Henderson and Franklin, 2007: 151).

THE CONCEPT IN SOCIAL WORK PRACTICE

Whilst there is undoubtedly an overemphasis on child abuse and social work in the media, this has a long history and it is not necessarily going to change swiftly. It might be better to ensure that efforts are directed at developing a critical perspective on the way in which the media constructs social workers and the profession. Previously, it has been argued that social work needs to develop relationships with the press (Ayre, 2001). Although generally supportive of this, Aldridge, as far back as 1990, argued that this is challenging given that the press is focused on economic gain at the expense sometimes of presenting unbiased reports. However, it is clear that those agencies, who work alongside or in concert with the values of social work, use the media to promote social issues and raise public awareness and so it is important to remain attuned to the potential of relationships between the social work profession and the media.

Social work educators increasingly draw on a range of media based resources to inform teaching including Social Care TV (SCIE, 2011). These interactive resources illustrate the complexity involved in decision making which is clearly at odds with the simplistic and 'common sense' mantra which frequently characterises press reporting about social work. They are also valuable tools for students to engage with at an early stage of their training. In the training of social workers multi-disciplinary working between other professionals including journalism can, 'provide concrete strategies through which both social workers and journalists can collaborate in raising public awareness about socially vulnerable populations' (Stone et al., 2008: 169). There is limited research into such collaborations, but there is little doubt that such initiatives are potentially helpful developments in social work education in the current economic climate.

More recently changes have led to the establishment of the College of Social Work (CoSW), which aims to promote the profession. A key communication strategy of the CoSW is to disseminate public information about what social work 'is' and who it works with – and to encourage social work professionals to promote good news stories about the work they do. This strategy was published in direct response to the recommendations made by the Social Work Task Force Reform Group (College of Social Work, 2012). *Community Care* magazine also ran a campaign to promote good news stories about social work (Community Care, 2009) although there has been criticism that this tends to focus on child protection social work rather than the range of social work practice with adults and communities.

Finally, it falls to the regulatory bodies to promote the social work profession and to individual social workers to align themselves and familiarise themselves with the communication procedures available to them. Social workers need to recognise that the media is an economic rather than a welfare enterprise and thus using the media critically is an important developmental objective for student social workers and new entrants to the profession.

Cross references: communication, ethics, the political context of social work, safeguarding children

SUGGESTED READING

Aldridge, M. (1990) 'Social work and the news media: a hopeless case?', *British Journal of Social Work*, 20(6): 611–25.

Franklin, B. and Parton, N. (1991) *Social Work, the Media and Public Relations*. London: Routledge.

REFERENCES

Abel-Smith, B. and Townsend, P. (1966) *The Poor and the Poorest*. London: G. Bell & Sons.

Aldridge, M. (1990) 'Social work and the news media: a hopeless case?', *British Journal of Social Work*, 20(6): 611–25.

Ayre, P. (2001) 'Child protection and the media: lessons from the last three decades', *British Journal of Social Work*, 31(6): 887–91.

Brocklehurst, D. (2011) 'Exile'. Available from: www.bbc.co.uk/programmes/b0110cpy (accessed 27 May 2011).

College of Social Work (2012) *Speak up for Social Work: A Profession of Principles*. Available from: www.collegeofsocialwork.org/index.asp (accessed 24 April 2011).

Community Care (2009) 'Stand up now for social work – what you can do'. Available from: www.communitycare.co.uk/Articles/2009/07/06/110972/Stand-Up-Now-for-social-work-what-you-can-do.htm (accessed 12 September 2011).

Franklin, B. and Parton, N. (1991) *Social Work, the Media and Public Relations*. London: Routledge.

GSCC (General Social Care Council) (2011) 'What is conduct?' Available from: www.gscc.org.uk/page/5/Conduct.html (accessed 24 April 2011).

HPC (Health Professionals Council) (2011) *Professionalism in Healthcare Professions.* Available from: www.hpc-uk.org/ (accessed 24 April 2011).

Henderson, L. and Franklin, B. (2007) 'Sad not bad: images of social care professionals in popular UK television drama', *Journal of Social Work*, 7(2): 133–53.

Kitzenger, J. (2000) 'Media templates: patterns of association and the (re)construction of meaning over time', *Media Culture and Society*, 22(1): 61–84.

Loach, K. (1966) *Cathy Come Home*. Available from: www.screenonline.org.uk/tv/id/438481/index.html (accessed 27 May 2011).

Loach, K. (1994) *Ladybird, Ladybird*. Available from: www.imdb.com/title/tt0110296 (accessed 27 May 2011).

SCIE (Social Care Institute for Excellence) (2011) 'SCIE TV'. Available from: www.scie.org.uk/socialcaretv (accessed 27 May 2011).

Stone, S., Ekman, E., English, D. and Fujimori, S. (2008) 'Teaching notes: collaboration among social work and journalism students and faculty: an instructional model', *Journal of Social Work Education*, 44(1): 163–72.

32
Mental Capacity

Mandy Schofield

DEFINITION

Mental capacity can be defined as the ability to make autonomous decisions; a highly valued attribute amongst adults in democratic society (Dunn et al., 2007). Historically, particular groups of people have been classed as lacking decision-making capacity simply due to the presence of mental disorder or disability (Boyle, 2008). Viewing capacity in such global terms can deprive people of exerting any agency in decision making, thus denying their right to self-determination and autonomy. The Mental Capacity Act (MCA) 2005, covering England and Wales, was implemented in October 2007 and provides a statutory framework for people over the age of 16 who lack capacity to make decisions for themselves. The Act clearly sets out the steps to be taken in making decisions for people who have lost their decision-making abilities and is intended to protect and empower vulnerable adults in relation to decisions about their healthcare, welfare or finances.

KEY POINTS

- A person must be assumed to have capacity unless proven otherwise.
- All practicable steps must be taken to enable someone to make a decision.
- Assessment of capacity is time and decision specific.
- Decisions made on behalf of someone must be in the person's best interests.
- Social workers must have full regard for the provisions of the Mental Capacity Act 2005 and its Code of Practice.

DISCUSSION

The promotion of an individual's right to self-determination is one of the fundamental principles of social work practice (Banks, 2006). Social workers must 'support service users' rights to control their lives and make informed choices about the services they receive' (GSCC, 2002: 1.2). Achieving such standards becomes more complex when there are concerns about a person's capacity to make decisions. The maximisation of freedom and autonomy may conflict with a need for care and protection. With an emphasis on presumption of capacity, supported decision making and best interests decisions, the provisions of the MCA 2005 attempt to balance adults' rights with the need to protect them from harm (Johns, 2007).

Principles

There are five key underpinning principles which must be followed when using the MCA 2005. The principles are set out in Section 1 of the Act, as follows:

1 A person must be assumed to have capacity unless it is established that he lacks capacity.
2 A person is not to be treated as unable to make a decision unless all practicable steps to help him do so have been taken without success.
3 A person is not to be treated as unable to make a decision merely because he makes an unwise decision.
4 An act done, or decision made, under this Act for or on behalf of a person who lacks capacity must be done, or made, in his best interests.
5 Before the act is done, or the decision is made, regard must be had to whether the purpose for which it is needed can be as effectively achieved in a way that is less restrictive of a person's rights and freedom of action.

The principles can be seen as a set of rights for people who lack decision-making abilities, offering a level of protection for some of the most vulnerable in society (Richards and Mughal, 2009). The presumption of capacity ensures that people are no longer considered as lacking capacity purely on the presence of some kind of mental disorder. Similarly, decisions that may appear irrational or eccentric must be accepted as long as the person has the capacity to make the decision. This offers a much greater level of autonomy, allowing people to make decisions that carers or professionals may disagree with (Williamson, 2007).

Assisted autonomy

The overall aim of the MCA 2005 is to promote and facilitate decision making. Principle 2 requires that those assessing a person's capacity must provide the person with as much support as possible to participate in the decision-making process. Boyle (2008) uses the term 'assisted autonomy' to describe the way in which people should be enabled to express their wishes and preferences in order to have some level of influence (however limited) on decisions that affect them. The MCA Code of Practice (Department of Constitutional Affairs, 2007) gives helpful guidance about the kind of support that people might need. Social workers are legally required to 'have regard' for the guidance and to take relevant practical steps to support the person. This may include the use of alternative forms of communication, consideration of the person's immediate environment and the use of expert help.

Assessing capacity

If there is reasonable belief that a person lacks capacity to make a particular decision, a two-stage test of capacity must be undertaken. The first stage is a diagnostic test (Section 2 MCA 2005) to determine whether the person has an impairment of, or a disturbance in the functioning of the mind or brain. Such a definition automatically includes people with mental health problems, learning disability, brain injury and those experiencing temporary confused states. However, the second part of the test assesses how the 'diagnosis' affects the person's actual ability to make a specific decision at a particular time, reinforcing the requirement that a lack of capacity cannot be established merely by reference to a person's age, appearance or diagnosis. Section 3 of the Act provides that a person is unable to make a decision for himself if he is unable:

a   to understand the information relevant to the decision;
b   to retain that information;
c   to use or weigh that information as part of the process of making the decision; or
d   to communicate his decision (whether by talking, using sign language or any other means).

If a person is unable to satisfy any of the above conditions, they will be assessed as lacking the capacity to make the particular decision.

Whilst the Act does not specify the person responsible for an assessment of capacity, the MCA Code of Practice indicates that this will normally be the person who is directly concerned with the decision at the time it is to be made (Department of Constitutional Affairs, 2007: 4.38). Social workers have an integral role in welfare decisions related to a wide range of care, support and treatment, and are inevitably expected to carry 'the burden to demonstrate a person lacks capacity' (Leyshon and Clark, 2005, cited in Johns, 2007: 559). Social workers need to ensure that information is provided in a way that is most appropriate to help the person understand, retain and use it in order to make the decision.

Best interests

Where someone is found to lack capacity to make a decision, the Act authorises decisions in relation to 'acts in connection with care or treatment' to be made on someone's behalf as long as it is in their 'best interests'. As a term it is not succinctly defined but Section 4 offers the 'best interests' checklist which substitute decision-makers are required to follow.

All relevant circumstances which affect the particular decision must be considered and every effort must be made to establish the person's view of the decision. There is a legal obligation to ascertain the person's past and present wishes and feelings through consultation with family members and others involved in their care. The person's beliefs and values must also be taken into account. Even those deemed as lacking capacity to make a decision, may still be able to express a preference. This level of support incorporates a 'positive dimension of autonomy' (Boyle, 2008: 533) and must be encouraged to enable the exercise of autonomy. Substitute decision making in a person's best interests must also be the least restrictive alternative and must consider whether there is a need to act or make a decision at all (Dunn et al., 2007).

The principle of best interests decision making has long been established within the common law but the Act now offers a 'general model of substitute decision making' (Dunn et al., 2007: 131), ensuring that certain steps are followed in the determination of best interests. Whilst this 'codification' (p. 131) helps to focus objectively on the person for whom the decision is being made rather than the decision maker's views, it does not solve all practice dilemmas. Boyle (2008) presents the dichotomy of supporting outcomes that enable people to follow their lifestyle choices against approaches that can be seen to improve the person's situation. Such dilemmas highlight the complexity of working in adult social work and the need for a high level of skill in both communication and assessment.

Further safeguards

The Mental Health Act 2007 amended the Mental Health Act 2005 by introducing the Deprivation of Liberty Safeguards (DOLS) which allows the lawful detention of people who lack capacity to make decisions about their care or treatment. The safeguards provide a process of authorisation for the deprivation of liberty in both care home and hospital settings.

THE CONCEPT IN SOCIAL WORK PRACTICE

Case study

Betty is an 82-year-old white British woman, diagnosed as being in the advanced stages of dementia. She has been married to Ted for 60 years and they have two grown-up children. When Betty was first diagnosed, at the age of 68, she discussed her future care with her family and was adamant that she would never want to go into residential care. The family agreed that they would do all they could to enable her to remain at home. They currently have domiciliary care workers visiting twice a day but over the past few months concerns have been raised about Ted's ability to continue caring for his wife. His health is deteriorating and he is about to be admitted to hospital for an urgent operation.

Betty should not be considered unable to make decisions about her care whilst Ted is in hospital purely on the diagnosis of dementia. If there is reasonable belief that Betty may lack capacity to make such decisions, an assessment of capacity must be undertaken by the social worker involved. A written record showing that, on the balance of probabilities, Betty may or may not lack the capacity to make the decision will be required. Appropriate ways of communicating with Betty will need to be explored to ascertain whether she is able to understand, retain and use information to communicate a decision. Any decisions taken in Betty's best interests must reflect her expressed wishes, beliefs and values. This will involve consultation with Ted, wider family, health and social care professionals and anyone with an interest in her well-being. Practical steps must also be taken to enable Betty to express her preferences and any decision made on behalf of Betty must also have regard for the least restrictive alternative. Despite the potential risks, the option of Betty remaining at home will need to be given serious consideration.

Cross references: assessment, mental health, safeguarding adults, social work in healthcare settings

SUGGESTED READING

McDonald, A. (2010) 'The impact of the 2005 Mental Capacity Act on social workers' decision making and approaches to the assessment of risk', *British Journal of Social Work*, 40: 1229–46.

Manthorpe, J., Rapaport, J. and Stanley, N. (2008) 'The Mental Capacity Act 2005 and its influences on social work practice: debate and synthesis', *Practice: Social Work in Action*, 20(3): 151–62.

REFERENCES

Banks, S. (2006) *Ethics and Values in Social Work*, 3rd edn. Basingstoke: Palgrave Macmillan.

Boyle, G. (2008) 'The Mental Capacity Act 2005: promoting the citizenship of people with dementia?', *Health and Social Care in the Community*, 16(5): 529–37.

Department of Constitutional Affairs (2007) *Mental Capacity Act 2005: Code of Practice*. London: The Stationery Office.

Dunn, M.C., Clare, I.C.H., Holland, A.J. and Gunn, M.J. (2007) 'Constructing and reconstructing "best interests": an interpretative examination of substitute decision-making under the Mental Capacity Act 2005', *Journal of Social Welfare and Family Law*, 29(2): 117–33.

GSCC (General Social Care Council) (2002) *Codes of Practice for Social Care Workers*. London: General Social Care Council.

Johns, R. (2007) 'Who decides now? Protecting and empowering vulnerable adults who lose the capacity to make decisions for themselves', *British Journal of Social Work*, 37: 557–64.

Richards, S. and Mughal, A.F. (2009) *Working with the Mental Capacity Act 2005*, 2nd edn. North Waltham: Matrix Training Associates.

Williamson, T. (2007) 'Capacity to protect – the Mental Capacity Act explained', *The Journal of Adult Protection*, 9(1): 25–31.

33

Mental Health

Anna Beddow

DEFINITION

The legal definition of mental disorder is 'Any disorder or disability of the mind' (DH, 2007). This broad definition encompasses mental illness, personality disorder and learning disability. The work of the mental health social worker is diverse and firmly rooted within a multi-disciplinary and legislative context. Mental health problems are common amongst the population, 25 per cent of people will experience some kind of mental health problem during the course of a year, and of those 2–4 per cent will have a severe illness with estimates varying from 0.3 to 1.4 per cent for this being enduring (Gilbert, 2003). It is this latter group of people with whom the vast majority of mental health social workers will come into contact.

This chapter will focus on the role of the statutory social worker working within a multi-disciplinary service. It is imperative that mental health social workers have an understanding and appreciation of the differing understandings of what it is that we mean by mental health. There is no one common understanding of the phrase mental health. There are differing understandings and expressions to describe the same experiences of one individual. As a mental health social worker it is important that you are aware of the various 'models' of understanding and how they may be applied to each individual with whom you work (Golightley, 2008).

KEY POINTS

- People who use mental health services are often stigmatised and discriminated against. The legal framework offers protection and support as well as the powers to detain.
- Mental health services have been subject to extensive reform and are driven by social policy. Negative media attitudes have perpetuated stereotypical societal ideas about people with mental health problems.
- Research and evidence have informed and shaped the ways in which mental health social work has developed.
- The mental health social work role has a distinct history within social work. It offers many challenges in terms of interventions and practice which can be against the wishes of the people who are subject to it.

The legal framework

The Mental Health Act 1983 as amended by the Mental Health Act 2007 is the key piece of legislation for mental health social workers to understand the parameters in which they work. It sets out the conditions whereby an individual can be subject to the provisions of the Act and detained either in hospital or in the community. It defines mental disorder and sets out the conditions that must be met for an individual to be sectioned. In conjunction with the Act is the Code of Practice which is crucial for the safe and appropriate operation of the Act (DH, 2008). Social workers can act as approved mental health professionals who have a legal duty to undertake mental health act assessments.

The care programme approach

Originally introduced in 1991, the care programme approach ensured a unified care co-ordination approach for users of services with a named care co-ordinator (Lester and Glasby, 2010). Service users who are subject to the care programme approach are holistically assessed and from that assessment a comprehensive care plan is established. The care plan will take account of every area of a person's life and will also include a risk assessment. Each care plan will name the care co-ordinator. The role of care co-ordinator can be taken on by nurses, social workers, occupational therapists and psychologists. The plan will be regularly reviewed by the members of the multi-disciplinary team working with the person.

Service configuration

As a mental health social worker you could be working in a variety of settings. Many mental health social workers are employed by NHS trusts. Each team will have a particular focus to reflect the needs of the users of the services. The current approach favours targeted intervention with specific goals and aims in mind. Social workers also work in forensic settings within a multi-disciplinary context, assuming the role of social supervisor once someone is discharged from the secure setting. In this capacity it is their responsibility to provide regular reports to the Ministry of Justice as to the progress of the person in the community.

Social work values and ethics

Mental health social workers (particularly those who are also approved mental health professionals) must be aware of the need to exercise the legislative role appropriately and with due regard to the Code of Practice (GSCC, 2002). Mental health social workers often face the challenge of coercion (Campbell, 2010) as they carry out the statutory function. This can create ethical dilemmas and debates which must be resolved within their multi-disciplinary contexts, whilst holding fast to their own professional standpoint.

The users of services and their carers

The needs of service users and carers are now firmly embedded into legislation and policy. However there is still a discernible 'gap' or 'disconnection' (Gilbert, 2003: 22) between the lived experience of using mental health services and the views of many professionals. As professionals it is imperative that we are alert and receptive to the voice of the service user however that may be articulated.

DISCUSSION

> The liberty of madness can only be heard from the fortress in which it is imprisoned. (Foucault, 2006: xxxii)

This quotation serves as a useful starting point for a discussion of the nebulous concept of mental health. By implication Foucault tells us that in the act of labelling we create the conditions for oppression. The structures around mental health would here refer to psychiatry and what we could describe as a medical model. Within this perspective the individual is labelled or categorised as suffering from a mental illness, this then is delineated as a formal diagnosis (Archambeault, 2009). This diagnosis or label becomes pivotal in the life of the individual as it is often the indicator as to whether or not they will be eligible for services.

The process of labelling can epitomise the perspective of social construction. That is, that mental disorder is a social category, a means of describing or ordering an understanding of the world. It could also be an ontological position that would claim mental disorder merely as a category that does not refer to any 'objective reality' at all (Busfield, 2001: 5). This though may be at odds with the lived experience of those within the mental health system, for whom mental illness is a distressing reality. Many service users find themselves in the uncomfortable position of having to accept or comply with a label with which they do not agree as a gateway to both fiscal and service based support. They may agree that they need support but would not want to endorse a medical understanding or model.

Even though there are divergent views as to the definition and description of what is described as mental illness, mental disorder or mental distress, what cannot be equivocated are the potentially devastating consequences of these experiences in the lives of individuals (Lester and Glasby, 2010). The dominance of the medical profession and the power that psychiatrists in particular can exert in the lives of individuals has been of consistent concern to users of the services.

In practice, mental health social workers often develop pluralistic understandings of mental health that seek always to place the user of the service at the forefront. Users of mental health services are very often stigmatised, which is reflected in what is commonly referred to as social exclusion. Mental health social work is dominated by a need to mitigate the effects of social exclusion whilst promoting the need for social inclusion. An example of how collective action in mental health services can be a catalyst for change can be seen in the work of the Mental Health Alliance; a pressure group that formed in response to the proposals that were first put forward for a new Mental Health Bill by the Labour government in 2001. This unlikely alliance which included: the Royal College of Psychiatrists; Sainsbury Centre for Mental Health; British Association of Social Workers; and Mind (a mental health charity), worked together to force changes in what they all considered to be a seriously flawed Green Paper.

THE CONCEPT IN SOCIAL WORK PRACTICE

The following case study illustrates some of the dilemmas that professionals must resolve.

Case study

Ruth is a mental health social worker who is also approved as a mental health professional. She works on an assertive outreach team in a busy inner city team. She has been managing the ongoing crisis of a service user of hers, Paul. Paul's mental health has been deteriorating but unusually he remains in contact with Ruth. Paul is subject to a community treatment order but has said that this is not the reason why he is staying in touch, it's because he trusts Ruth. He has a diagnosis of schizo affective disorder and is prescribed anti-psychotic medication. He has had several previous hospital admissions. On previous occasions when Paul has become psychotic he has harmed himself as he hears voices telling him that he is evil. He harms himself as a punishment. He has never tried to commit suicide. Paul does not wish to take medication due to the side effects. One of the side effects is weight gain and as an ex-athlete Paul is keen to remain physically fit. Paul has been warned that as a condition of his community treatment order he must keep his appointments with Ruth.

Ruth is due to see Paul one morning at 10am. Unfortunately, a colleague of hers is off sick and as an emergency she is asked to cover the duty rota for her colleague. Already by 9.30am there is one referral in for a mental health act assessment.

As an Approved Mental Health Professional (AMHP) Ruth has a statutory duty to make an assessment. There is no one else available to see Paul.

This example highlights where the dilemmas and difficulties will need to be resolved. The key points to be noted are:

- As an AMHP Ruth has a statutory duty to undertake mental health act assessments.
- Community treatment orders can require that people make themselves available for visits and if they fail to comply they can be recalled to hospital. The implications of a visit not been made could be potentially very difficult for the service user. Ruth has established a relationship with Paul which could be jeopardised if he perceives her to be inconsistent.

The resolution of these difficulties is dependent upon key social work skills which will include:

- *Assessment*: Ruth will need to carefully assess the dilemma she has, gathering as much information as she can. She will need to use comprehensive risk assessment skills that will determine how she acts.

- *Time management*: This practical skill is absolutely crucial to effective conflict resolution.
- *Negotiation*: Ruth will need to liaise, plan and co-ordinate with other colleagues.

The decisions that are made will be contingent upon a number of factors and will change. This is the mercurial nature of social work.

Cross references: advocacy, assessment, empowerment, mental capacity, multi-professional working

SUGGESTED READING

Golightley, M. (2008) *Social Work and Mental Health*, 3rd edn. Exeter: Learning Matters.
Lester, H. and Glasby, J. (2010) *Mental Health Policy and Practice*. Basingstoke: Palgrave Macmillan.

REFERENCES

Archambeault, J. (2009) *Reflective Reader: Social Work and Mental Health*. Exeter: Learning Matters.
Busfield, J. (ed.) (2001) *Rethinking the Sociology of Mental Health*. Oxford: Blackwell.
Campbell, J. (2010) 'Deciding to detain: the use of compulsory mental health law by UK social workers', *British Journal of Social Work*, 40: 328–34.
DH (Department of Health) (2007) *Mental Health Act*. London: Department of Health.
DH (Department of Health) (2008) *Mental Health Act 1983: Revised Code of Practice*. London: Department of Health.
Foucault, M. (2006) *History of Madness*. Abingdon: Routledge.
Gilbert, P. (2003) *The Value of Everything*. Lyme Regis: Russell House Publishing.
Golightley, M. (2008) *Social Work and Mental Health*, 3rd edn. Exeter: Learning Matters.
GSCC (General Social Care Council) (2002) *Codes of Practice for Social Care Workers*. London: General Social Care Council.
Lester, H. and Glasby, J. (2010) *Mental Health Policy and Practice*. Basingstoke: Palgrave Macmillan.

34
Multi-Professional Working

Julie A. Lawrence

DEFINITION

There are numerous definitions of multi-professional working. For the purposes of this chapter, multi-professional working is seen as collaborative practice which is the collection of perspectives, knowledge, skills, values and motives applied by a number of practitioners (Weinstein et al., 2003). This underpins the formation of more formal working arrangements such as joint working within a multi-professional or multi-disciplinary team. This is further enhanced by the fact that the team of individuals has different training backgrounds, but share common objectives and makes a different but complementary contribution (Marshall et al., 1979).

KEY POINTS

- Multi-professional working has become a key feature of social welfare across the UK since the late 1980s.
- Clear governance arrangements are important for effective multi-professional working.
- Organisations need a shared understanding and commitment to the vision of multi-professional working.
- Social work as a discipline is well placed to facilitate the co-ordination of services where more than one agency or worker is involved and across agency boundaries.

DISCUSSION

A brief history of multi-professional working

The nature of social work practice in relation to health and social care is such that, for many, the quality of the service received is dependent upon how effectively different professionals work together (Barrett et al., 2005). Social work in the United Kingdom (UK) has been identified with local authority social services departments since the 1970s. Such departments provide advice and information and arrange support to individuals, families and groups in local communities. Significant numbers of social workers are also employed by voluntary and independent organisations (Barrett et al., 2005). This chapter asserts that the knowledge, skills and abilities of a social worker are not practised in a vacuum, but rather that effective social work practice is only attained with full multi-professional co-operation.

Multi-professional working has become a key feature of social welfare across the UK since the late 1980s. While collaborative methods of working have been promoted in all areas of public policy, nowhere are they more evident than in the planning and delivery of health and social care (Heenan and Birrell, 2006). Working across the boundary between health and social care in the UK has come to dominate debates about the future provision of healthcare services (Glendinning and Coleman, 2003); while attempts to co-ordinate the planning and delivery of health and social services through national strategies can be traced back to the 1960s (Hudson, 1998). However, in the last decade, working together at the health and social care interface has been relentlessly endorsed and advocated in government documents. The strategy document, *Partnership in Action*, (DH, 1998) stressed the need to look at the whole system and focused on making joint working between health and social services easier. The subsequent Health Act in 1999 enabled flexible approaches to the overcoming of obstacles to more integrated working through pooled budgets, lead commissioning and integrated provision.

The NHS Plan (DH, 2000) advocated stronger alliances through working together by health and social care agencies and called for fundamental change.

Key legislation and policy drivers

Legal and policy requirements now formalise expectations for 'joined-up' provision (Children Act 2004). The Act gave local authorities a duty to ensure that children in need are identified, and their needs met by arrangements established between statutory and voluntary services. The Act and subsequent guidance placed an emphasis upon parental responsibility, the participation of children and the importance of multi-agency working.

The National Health Service and Community Care Act (DH, 1990a) gave a duty to the local authority to assess and, where applicable, provide community services, in co-operation with other agencies. Subsequent policy guidance emphasised the importance that local collaboration is the key to community care (DH, 1990b). The Health and Social Care Act (DH, 2001) created new powers to establish care trusts by building on existing health and local authority powers to develop partnerships and provide integrated care.

Munro's report of child protection services highlighted the fact that government policy in recent years has been designed in recognition that the services children and families receive have often been limited, in part because of the failure of professionals to understand one another's roles or to work together effectively (Munro, 2010). Munro also recognised that increased bureaucracy also impacted on workers' ability to work effectively.

THE CONCEPT IN SOCIAL WORK PRACTICE

One way of conceptualising multi-professional working is by considering how effectively services are co-ordinated and delivered. Social workers, for example, have traditionally emphasised the importance of co-ordination of services where more than one agency or worker is involved. This occurs in areas such as key aspects of mental health work, community care and in child protection, thus reiterating the move towards 'specialist' social work practice. Morris et al. (2008) also highlight the fact that the changing landscape for social work practice means that there are few settings for social work where some form of joint agency activity is not a requirement for effective provision and practice. In relation to children's services, one of the main elements of the Green Paper, *Every Child Matters* (Department for Education and Skills, 2003) was its recognition that improved multi-agency and inter-professional working is required if we are to avoid a repeat of the tragic events that characterised the Victoria Climbié case.

It is acknowledged that some professionals may view engaging in multi-professional practice as a risky business. However, being able to agree identifiable roles and responsibilities can overcome some of the conflicts which may arise for professionals (Prothero and Bennion, 2010). Stewart et al. (2003) suggest that joint training and cross agency secondments can help staff to appreciate each other's roles and responsibilities.

Case study: North East England

An important study undertaken by Hudson (2007) illustrated that the literature on inter-professional working tends to be dominated by explanations for lack of progress, rather than an account of achievements. The research developed two models – termed optimistic and pessimistic models respectively. To understand the factors that may underpin different rates of inter-professional achievement, a case study of the Sedgefield Integrated Team in County Durham, England, was used to test out aspects of the models. Three separate agencies joined forces to establish a more integrated front line approach – Sedgefield Primary Care Trust, Sedgefield Borough Council and Durham County Council. These established five locality-based, co-located, front-line teams across the borough, each consisting of social workers, district nurses and housing officers.

A key theme which emerged was that integrated teams will work because the service professionals (nurses and social workers) were not far apart in relation to the promotion of their particular professional values:

> It's great when you have got someone with health needs and you are working with the nurse – you can do the social bit and they can do the health bit. It's really helpful. SW (Hudson, 2007: 11)

In addition to this, the socialisation to an immediate work group can override professional or hierarchical differences. The author concludes by stating that much of the success in Sedgefield had been down to the presence of the right people in the right place at strategic and operational levels – a theme that could vanish in Sedgefield and could not be expected to be replicated in other locations and contexts. The other major factor was the funding for the project, which made an important difference to what could be achieved.

Barriers to multi-professional working

There are recurring themes which emphasise the fact that the orientation of research to date has focused upon the relationships between agencies (health and social care), rather than on how the delivery of services is realised through the collaborative efforts of localised policies and operational practices between health and social work professionals. Illustrated below are the main factors which may affect social work practice when engaged in multi-professional working.

Examples include:

- geographical boundaries between teams;
- communication boundaries across services and between professional staff;
- status inequalities between professional groups;
- a miss-matching of cultures and/or understanding of services which might create a divide between disciplines;
- organisational boundaries and a lack of an overall strategic vision to multi-professional working;
- a lack of clarity regarding others' roles and responsibilities;

- a lack of clarity regarding management roles and responsibilities leading to conflict between managers;
- financial limitations as to what can be provided and by whom with the resources available.

Carers' and service users' perspectives

It seemed like quite a few people had pieces of the jigsaw but no one had the picture on the box. (Hudson, 2006: 5)

This remark from an older person illustrates that, generally, what people are interested in is whether services join up and do what they need them to do, in the right way, at the right time. Evidence from a variety of sources confirmed that both carers and service users considered that problems with multi-professional working made a direct impact on their support (Leathard, 2009).

It is important to assert, however, that whilst both carers and service users have a voice and views about the issues of multi-professional working, it would be too simplistic to present their collective views. Each group has distinctive interests and perspectives about the need for greater collaborative working between professional groups.

CONCLUSION

It is clear that what emerges from health and social care research, academic literature and professional practice is that, despite being difficult to achieve, multi-professional working is necessary. Legislation and government policy requires it. Most importantly, users need, want and deserve access to a wide range of holistic services that respond to their needs as a whole person. A team's collaborative efforts are essential for the planning and provision of good quality services, regardless of whether the focus is children and families, or vulnerable adults living primarily within a community setting.

Cross references: partnership, practice education, social work in healthcare settings, team working,

SUGGESTED READING

Leathard, A. (2009) *Interprofessional Collaboration: From Policy to Practice in Health and Social Care*. London: Routledge.

Morris, K. (ed.) (2008) *Social Work and Multi-Agency Working*. Bristol: The Policy Press.

REFERENCES

Barrett, G., Sellman, D. and Thomas, J. (2005) *Interprofessional Working in Health and Social Care*. Basingstoke: Palgrave Macmillan.

Children Act (2004) London: HMSO.

Department for Education and Skills (2003) *Every Child Matters: Change for Children*. London: HMSO.

DH (Department of Health) (1990a) *The National Health Service and Community Care Act*. London: HMSO.

DH (Department of Health) (1990b) *Community Care in the Next Decade and Beyond*. London: HMSO.

DH (Department of Health) (1998) *Partnership in Action: Discussion Document*. London: HMSO.

DH (Department of Health) (2000) *The NHS Plan*. London: HMSO.

DH (Department of Health) (2001) *The Health and Social Care Act*. London: HMSO.

DH (Department of Health) (2004) *The Children Act*. London: HMSO.

Glendinning, C. and Coleman, A. (2003) 'Joint working: the health service agenda', *Local Government Studies*, 29(3): 51–72.

Heenan, D. and Birrell, D. (2006) 'The integration of health and social care: the lessons from Northern Ireland', *Social Policy and Administration*, 40(1): 47–66.

Hudson, B. (1998) 'Circumstances change cases: local government and the NHS', *Social Policy and Administration*, 32(1): 71–86.

Hudson, B. (2006) 'Whole systems working: a guide and discussion paper', *Care Services Improvement Agency, Integrated Care Network*. www.csip.org.uk.

Hudson, B. (2007) 'Pessimism and optimism in inter-professional working: The Sedgefield Integrated Team', *Journal of Inter-Professional Care*, 21(1): 3–15.

Leathard, A. (2009) *Interprofessional Collaboration: From Policy to Practice in Health and Social Care*. London: Routledge.

Marshall, M., Preston, M., Scott, E. and Wincott, P. (eds) (1979) *Teamwork For and Against: An Appraisal of Multi-Disciplinary Practice*. London: British Association of Social Workers.

Morris, P., Perry, C., Peebles, R., Fearns, K., Bartlett, N. and Webster, K. (2008) 'Interagency work', *Community Care*, 27(89): 1–8.

Munro, E. (2010) *The Munro Review of Child Protection Interim Report: The Child's Journey*. Department of Education. London: HMSO.

Prothero, S. and Bennion, A. (2010) 'Integrated team working: a literature review', *International Journal of Integrated Care*, 10: 1–10.

Stewart, A., Petch, A. and Curtice, L. (2003) 'Integrated working in health and social care in Scotland: from maze to matrix', *Journal of Integrated Care*, 17(4): 335–50.

Weinstein, J., Whittington, C. and Leiba, T. (eds) (2003) *Collaboration in Social Work Practice*. London: Jessica Kingsley.

35

Older People

Mick Howarth

DEFINITION

The notion of an ageing population is old news. It is, of course, good news – and increasing longevity is a cause for celebration. This 'old news', however, represents the single and most significant impact on adult social care and indeed society as a whole for the foreseeable future. In England today there are 8.5 million people over the age of 65, some 17.5 per cent of the population. By 2034, there will be 16.4 million people over 65, an increase of 93 per cent, with older people representing 23 per cent of the population (Office for National Statistics [ONS], 2008). The over 65s will increase by 650,000 each year for the foreseeable future. It is this definition, 65 years and over, which most adult social care departments work to as opposed to a 'pensioner' definition of old age.

The impact for social care services becomes clear when it is realised that two thirds of all adult service users, 1.2 million, are older people and just over half the budget is typically spent on this group. The challenge for the future will be how to keep pace with this increasing demand.

KEY POINTS

- The demographic challenge – understanding the implications of an ageing society.
- The funding challenge – how are adult social care services responding to the economic downturn.
- Support service options – best practice trends in provision including reablement, extra care housing and assistive technology.
- The shape of things to come – the future for social work with older people.

DISCUSSION

The demographic challenge

The bald statistics of the increasing number of over 65s only tells a partial story of likely future demand. The increasing number of those over 75 years, and in particular those over 85 years, indicate even greater demand. Those over 85 years doubled in number between 1984 and 2009 to 1 million, and will more than double again to 3.5 million by 2034 (ONS, 2008). These very elderly individuals are likely to be in poorer health and to live alone. Morbidity also increases with age. This is best illustrated by the increasing number of people with dementia. It is estimated there are 750,000 people with dementia today, rising to 1.5 million by 2034. One in 100 people between 65 and 69 years has dementia but this increases to one in three for those over 90 years. One study predicts a 67 per cent increase in the need for health and social care services in the next 20 years – double this for people aged over 85 (Age UK, 2011a, 2011b). The number of people from black and ethnic minority groups is also set to change. Although such groups represent 16 per cent of the overall population at present, only 9 per cent are over 60 years. This percentage will increase and services will also need to further sharpen their responsiveness to cultural needs.

These facts paint a sobering picture of future demand for older people's services going forward despite the 'success' story they equally spell out. Finally, regarding increasing expectations, although satisfaction levels with social care provision are generally high, we do know that currently of all those who meet Fair Access to Care (FACS) eligibility criteria only 30 per cent reported receiving all the support they needed, with around 50 per cent getting some help (Commission for Social Care Inspection, 2008). Expectations from the 'Baby Boom' generation (those born between 1946–63) are likely to be far more challenging.

The funding challenge

A real growth in adult social care funding of 40 per cent over the past decade sounds comforting. This looks less impressive when it is realised that other key public sectors faired significantly better. The health service increased by 100 per cent over the same period, transport by 70 per cent, and education by 60 per cent (HM Treasury, 2008). If adult social care is the poor relation in the public sector, then older people are the poorest relation of all. Just 13 per cent of the growth was spent on older people (Information Centre for Health and Social Care, 2009), the lowest of all service user groups, despite it having the fastest rising demographic. The current £8.4 billion spent on older people's services is faltering and will also have to meet increasing demand. How have local authorities responded to manage both growing demand and diminishing resources? In 2005, half of councils provided support to those with 'moderate' needs under the FAC's criteria. By 2011 this had fallen to just 18 per cent, as providing services to only those with critical and substantial needs became the norm. Councils have also become much firmer with 'self-funders', those with (currently) over £23,250 savings who are supported to make their own private arrangements. To offset falling resources many councils have looked to raise additional income through increased charging. Whilst charging for residential care is governed by national guidelines (CRAG), local authorities are free to set their own arrangements for community care services, and such charges have increased by 10 per cent above inflation in the last decade. In this climate, maximising resources becomes more critical and developing preventative services which can defer or delay older people needing long-term support and finding more cost-effective interventions are a key plank to maximise value for money.

Support Service Options

the landscape of provision for older people has remained very familiar over the last 40 years, dominated by residential, home care, day services and meals provision. The ratio of residential care to community based care has remained stubborn at around 1:3.8 – an often surprisingly low figure. Over 50 per cent of spending is on the 20 per cent of individuals in long-term care settings. It is suggested that the target should be a maximum of 40 per cent on meeting this need but most authorities are well adrift of this assumption (DH, 2009). Although the shape of provision is broadly familiar, there has been a key change in who provides services. Local authorities have steadily withdrawn from provision in residential care and home-care markets due to the perceived high cost of 'in house' services and the independent sector is now the dominant provider – a trend set to continue as local authorities embrace a 'commissioning only' role.

The emergence of Direct Payments is a new option allowing individuals to purchase their own care. Not only has this helpfully extended choice and control such options are often more economic than local authority services. There are, however, some genuinely new service options which can be effective in supporting older people in the community – the place they want to be.

Reablement: Such intensive support services, provided free for up to six weeks, are increasingly being used both to facilitate hospital discharge (step down care) and prevent hospital admission or deterioration in the community (step up care). Some local authorities are seeing reablement as the 'first offer' for all eligible older people on the evidence (DH, 2009) that up to 50 per cent of individuals do not need support after such an intervention and that it can delay care for up to two years. Not only is this better support for older people maximising independence it helps support a switch away from continued investment in long-term residential care.

Extra Care Housing (ECH): Although there is no single definition of ECH, the key feature is that there is a 24-hour on-site care team, who can offer flexible and responsive care. Individuals live in their own apartment (rented or owner occupied), invariably purpose built to meet the needs of older people and access care and support as needed. Some schemes also provide communal facilities and activities to encourage health and well-being. Older people are supported in their local community and the cost to local authorities is just the care element; housing costs are met by the individual (or housing benefit) and food, fuel costs, etc are also met by the individual compared to residential care.

Assistive technology: Using assistive technology to support people in their own homes was given a significant boost by the Preventative Technology Grant in 2006–8. Varying from simple call systems to services which trigger an alarm in a variety of situations such as a fall or wandering behaviour, the technology gives older people, and their family carers, confidence that assistance can be summoned if needed. Telecare is a relatively low cost service but can provide much needed reassurance to enable someone to remain in their house and can also sometimes replace actual care visits, for example, medication reminders or 'safe and well' short calls.

THE CONCEPT IN SOCIAL WORK PRACTICE

The 'big idea' for public sector services is that services are 'Personalised' according to the needs and preferences of users, where 'Choice' and 'Control' are the watchwords (Gardner, 2011). However the Audit Commission (DH, 2009) has highlighted that more work is needed to close a range of gaps if individual budgets for older people are to become a reality. It seems that processes and systems have not kept pace with policy aspirations. These barriers must be overcome if self-directed support is to be a reality for often frail and vulnerable customers.

The Dilnot Report (2011) proposes a shift in the financial threshold at which individuals pay for their social care. The report recommends this be increased to £100,000, and that individual's maximum contribution to their care costs be capped at £35,000. It is estimated this would cost an initial £1.7 billion per annum. This represents significant investment and although the report would impact on what is perceived as a great unfairness in how charging works, what this 'investment' would not do is fund one more residential place or an extra hour of domiciliary care. Some tough choices lie ahead if this report is to be implemented.

The Dartington review on the future of adult social care (Humphries, 2010)

In considering the key demographic, economic, social and modernisation trends this review suggests four possible future scenarios:

- *A residual service*: Here current trends continue and services focus only on the poorest. Bleak economic prospects mean even tighter rationing of publicly funded services. Self-funders increasingly find themselves outside the 'care system'.
- *Incremental betterment*: Some modest improvements are made as individual budgets slowly prompt the development of alternatives to traditional services but more significant reform is held back due to lack of resources.
- *The care crunch*: Despite some possible improvements the economic pressure and demographic demands finally bring the current system to the point of collapse. Attempts to restrain demand by tighter eligibility simply create even more pressure. This scenario envisages the introduction of more national rather than local guidelines for social care support as central government seeks to take control of the crisis and loss of public confidence.
- *Transformed well-being*: Here social care is superseded by a new universal offer and a new funding model brings additional resources supporting the creative use of personal budgets and more investment in early investment in early intervention and prevention. A new national operating and charging system is established with self-directed support as a key feature.

Whilst the modernisation agenda including reablement, ECH, assistive technology and individual budgets offers much hope for truly personalised services for older people, the deepest recession for 60 years and demographic demands presents both policy makers and social workers with their most challenging task for a generation.

Cross references: assessment, care management, finance, personalisation, social work in healthcare settings

SUGGESTED READING

Gardner, A. (2011) *Personalisation in Social Work*. Exeter: Learning Matters.
Humphries, R. (2010) *Dartington Review on the Future of Adult Social Care*. Research in Practice for Adults. Available from www.ripfa.org.uk/publications/darlington-review (accessed 20 May 2012).

REFERENCES

Age UK (2011a) 'Care in crisis: causes and solutions'. Available from: www.ageuk.org.uk/Documents/EN-GB/Campaigns/Care%20in%20Crisis%20-%20FINAL.pdf?dtrk=true (accessed 20 May 2012).
Age UK (2011b) 'Older people facts and figures'. Available at: www.ageuk.org (accessed 28 May 2012).

Commission for Social Care Inspection (2008) *Cutting the Cake Fairly*. London: CSCI.

DH (Department of Health) (2009) *Use of Resources in Adult Social Care*. London: HMSO.

Dilnot Report (2011) *Commission on Funding of Care and Support: Fairer Funding for All*. London: Department of Health.

Gardner, A. (2011) *Personalisation in Social Work*. Exeter: Learning Matters.

HM Treasury (2008) *Pre-Budget Report 2008*. London: HMSO.

Humphries, R. (2010) *Dartington Review on the Future of Adult Social Care*. Research in Practice for Adults. Available from: www.ripfa.org.uk/publications/dartington-review (accessed 20 May 2012).

Information Centre for Health and Social Care (2009) *Personal Social Services Expenditure and Unit Costs 2007–8*. London: HMSO.

Office for National Statistics (2008) *Population Estimates 2008*. London: HMSO.

36
Partnership

Robin Miller and Jon Glasby

DEFINITION

Although partnership is an important concept, it has been described as a 'terminological quagmire' (Leathard, 1994: 5) and as an example of 'definitional chaos' (Ling, 2000: 83). Part of the problem is that the term can apply to a range of different relationships, including between:

- professionals and people using services;
- different professionals;
- different organisations;
- the public, private and voluntary sectors.

Although Leathard (1994) identifies 52 separate terms in common usage, many definitions focus on a number of underlying themes (Glasby and Dickinson, 2008):

- The *added value* of working together (the idea that 'the whole is greater than the sum of its parts').
- The idea of sharing or of *reciprocity* – with mutual risks and benefits.
- A *formal* and *ongoing* relationship. Often, partnerships have an 'agreement' to bind them together and practitioners often find the metaphor of a journey helpful – we cannot be fully sure exactly where we are headed but we recognise we need to travel together for at least part of the way.

Partnerships between services and people accessing their support, and between professionals from different disciplines, are covered in other chapters of this book. This chapter therefore focuses on partnerships between agencies.

KEY POINTS

- Social care has always worked closely with other sectors but over recent times there has been a greater focus on the potential benefits of partnerships between agencies.
- There are a variety of reasons why agencies form partnerships but the outcomes that are anticipated are not always clear upfront.
- Partnerships vary in their 'depth' and 'breadth' and can be arranged through 'hierarchies', 'markets' and 'networks'.
- The evidence for the impact of partnerships is not clear.

DISCUSSION

Partnership is not new – adult social care has traditionally worked closely with health, housing and independent care providers, while children's services have had close ties with education, youth services, the police and paediatric healthcare. Recently, the emphasis on partnership has increased, principally as a means to address 'wicked issues' within society that single agency responses seem powerless to tackle (Audit Commission, 1998). There is much common sense behind such hopes – agencies working together must surely be a more effective way to organise our resources than agencies working in isolation, as the latter risks duplication of effort, gaps in provision or even conflicting approaches. There are dissenting voices, though, regarding both the reality of and motivations behind partnerships. Sullivan and Skelcher (2002) provide a useful framework for considering why agencies enter collaborative arrangements:

- *Optimistic perspectives* are based on *exchange theory* in which agencies recognise that only by working together can they achieve desired outcomes within available resources. This relies on partners prioritising the interests of the whole and not only those that advance their own objectives.
- *Pessimistic perspectives* are underpinned by *resource-dependency theory* in which agencies enter partnerships to exert control over their partners and so acquire the necessary resources to achieve their own priorities.
- *Realistic perspectives* draw on *evolutionary theory* and see partnerships as a means through which agencies can survive changing political and economic environments.

The concept of 'forced partnerships', in which agencies are required to work together by a more powerful part of a hierarchical system, can be added to these perspectives (Glasby and Dickinson, 2008).

Whatever the motivations of individual agencies, it is vital that partnerships are clear about the *outcomes* to be delivered (Dickinson, 2008). Without this there is a danger that agencies become focused on the *process*, and view the smooth functioning of administrative and governance systems as evidence that a partnership has been successful even if it has had no discernible impact on their recipients. Having agreed the outcomes to be delivered, agencies need to decide on how best to structure their partnerships. There are three main approaches to organising partnerships: as a 'hierarchy' (in which the partnership is delivered through a bureaucratic structure); a 'market' (which is driven by trading and/or incentives); and a 'network' (in which agencies come together informally to achieve a common vision) (Glasby and Dickinson, 2008).

Partnerships commonly face a number of challenges, which Robinson et al. (2008) summarise as: 'contextual barriers and political climate' (e.g. co-terminosity, financial pressures and changes in political leadership); 'organisational challenges' (e.g. incompatible policies/procedures); and 'cultural issues' (e.g. professional stereotyping). Addressing these issues requires softer or *transformational* aspects such as leadership, culture and developing a common narrative, as well as *transactional* aspects such as performance, processes and financial systems (Audit Commission, 2010).

Despite their prevalence, evidence for the positive impact of partnerships is lacking. Dickinson (2007) attributes this partly to difficulties of 'attribution' (i.e. being clear that the partnership, rather than other factors, has led to the impact), 'causality' (i.e. being clear how the components of the partnership have caused the changes) and the long-term 'time spans' before partnerships address the 'wicked issues' in question. Atkinson et al. (2007) report that the impact on professionals is much better established than the impact on people accessing services, and this may in part be due to the former being easier to evaluate. They also note that negative impacts (such as greater workload for professionals and increased demands for services) have been identified.

THE CONCEPT IN SOCIAL WORK PRACTICE

Partnership by hierarchy: care trusts – Northern Ireland

Unlike other parts of the UK, Northern Ireland has traditionally had a more integrated health and social care system (Heenan and Birrell, 2006). Following devolution this integrated approach has been further developed, with statutory health and social care services delivered through five health and social care trusts. These are commissioned by a single integrated commissioning body (the Regional Health and Social Care Board). These trusts are responsible for employing children and adult health and social care staff and managing the connected budgets.

The new Northern Ireland Trusts report positive changes following the total integration of health and social care within single organisations (Heenan and Birrell, 2009). These include improvements in hospital discharge, development of integrated multi-disciplinary teams and processes, and the resettling of people with a disability and/or mental health difficulties from long-stay hospitals. In England there are indications that Torbay Care Trust has been able to positively impact on issues such as hospital admission rates (Thistlethwaite, 2011). However there is no evidence that the English Care Trust model was successful in general (Miller et al., 2011) and Heenan and Birrell (2009) also note challenges from an integrated organisation (notably the danger that social care perspectives/priorities will be secondary to the concerns of health professionals and services).

Partnership by networks: managed care networks – Scotland

The WHO describes a network as a 'grouping of individuals, organisations, and agencies organised on a non-hierachical basis around common issues or concerns'. Within the UK 'managed clinical networks' are used to denote healthcare clinicians from primary and secondary care working together in relation to a particular condition such as cancer or diabetes (Hudson, 2011). In Scotland, Managed Care Networks (MCNs) have been promoted by the Joint Improvement Team (www.jitscotland.org.uk) to address broader and more complex issues than a single condition such as 'promoting well-being'.

As an example, Lanarkshire has used its experience of a managed clinical network for stroke to develop the Older People Network (LOPN). Incorporating professionals from social care, acute and primary healthcare services, the network initially grew 'organically' by engaging champions drawn from frontline practitioners and people who access services in a form of 'distributed leadership'(Hendry, 2010). It has subsequently developed a more formal constitution with a steering group and a network manager and provides guidance and support to operational staff working with older people.

Partnership by incentive: delayed discharge payments – England

Difficulties in relation to hospital discharge have been a longstanding policy issue due to the negative impact both on individuals and on services. Poor partnership working is often cited as a key factor in such delays (Glasby, 2003). The New Labour government introduced a range of initiatives in England to address these issues, including additional funding for intermediate care services and a new protocol setting out the discharge pathway. The most controversial was the Delayed Discharges Act 2003, which gave acute hospitals a duty to notify social services of patients who were ready to be discharged and were potentially in need of community care services. Social services then had defined time scales to undertake assessments and arrange the discharge – failure to do so would lead to a charge being made by the hospital for each further day that the person remained in hospital.

This system was attempting to incentivise partnership working through financial penalties, and there were considerable concerns at the time that this would 'reinforce a negative blame culture' rather than be a positive driver for better working relationships (House of Commons Select Committee, 2002). Henwood (2006) reviews the evidence of the impact on hospital discharge, and notes in the 18 months following its introduction there was a decline in the number of older people whose discharge was delayed. She notes, though, that there had been a steady decline in numbers in previous years due to other initiatives and the increased focus on this issue, and it was therefore not possible to clearly attribute this to the new charging arrangements.

Cross references: learning disability, multi-professional working, older people, personalisation, safeguarding adults

SUGGESTED READING

Barratt, G., Sellman, D. and Thomas, J. (eds) (2005) *Interprofessional Working in Health and Social Care*. Basingstoke: Palgrave Macmillan.

Glasby, J. and Dickinson, H. (2008) *Partnership Working in Health and Social Care*. Bristol: Policy Press.

REFERENCES

Atkinson, M., Jones, M. and Lamont, E. (2007) *Multi-Agency Working and its Implications for Practice*. Reading: CfBT Education Trust.

Audit Commission (1998) *A Fruitful Partnership: Effective Partnership Working*. London: Audit Commission.

Audit Commission (2010) *Working Together Better? Managing Local Strategic Partnerships*. London: Audit Commission.

Dickinson, H. (2007) 'Evaluating the outcomes of health and social care partnerships: the POET approach', *Research, Policy and Planning*, 25(2/3): 79–92.

Dickinson, H. (2008) *Evaluating Outcomes in Health and Social Care*. Bristol: Policy Press.

Glasby, J. (2003) *Hospital Discharge: Integrating Health and Social Care Divide: The Experiences of Older People*. Bristol: Policy Press.

Glasby, J. and Dickinson, H. (2008) *Partnership Working in Health and Social Care*. Bristol: Policy Press.

Heenan, D. and Birrell, D. (2006) 'The integration of health and social care: the lessons from Northern Ireland', *Social Policy and Administration*, 40(1): 47–66.

Heenan, D. and Birrell, D. (2009) 'Organisational integration in health and social care: some reflections on the Northern Ireland experience', *Journal of Integrated Care*, 7(5): 3–12.

Hendry, A. (2010) 'Lanarkshire's managed care network: an integrated improvement collaborative', *Journal of Integrated Care*, 18(3): 45–51.

Henwood, M. (2006) 'Effective partnership working: a case study of hospital discharge', *Health and Social Care in the Community*, 14(5): 400–7.

House of Commons Select Committee (2002) *Delayed Discharges, Third Report of Session 2001–2002*. London: House of Commons Health Committee.

Hudson, B. (2011) 'Ten years of jointly commissioning health and social care in England', *International Journal of Integrated Care*, 11(7): 1–9.

Leathard, A. (ed.) (1994) *Going Inter-Professional: Working Together for Health and Welfare*. Hove: Routledge.

Ling, T. (2000) 'Unpacking partnership: the case of health', in J. Clarke and S.M.E. Gewirtz (eds), *New Managerialism, New Welfare?* London: Sage, pp.82–101.

Miller, R., Dickinson, H. and Glasby, J. (2011) *The Vanguard of Integration or a Lost Tribe? Care Trusts Ten Years On*. Birmingham: HSMC.

Robinson, M., Atkinson, M. and Downing, D. (2008) *Supporting Theory Building in Integrated Services Research*. Slough: NFER.

Sullivan, H. and Skelcher, C. (2002) *Working Across Boundaries: Collaboration in Public Services*. Basingstoke: Palgrave Macmillan.

Thistlethwaite, P. (2011) *Integrating Health and Social Care in Torbay*. London: Kings Fund.

partnership

165

37
Personalisation

Ali Gardner

DEFINITION

Personalisation is an umbrella term used to describe both an ideology and a way of delivering services which recognises service users as central to designing, planning, implementing and reviewing the services they receive. Although officially introduced in government policy in December 2007 with the publication of *Putting People First* (DH, 2007) it is not specific to social care and started as a cross government agenda in 2003.

KEY POINTS

* Personalisation is about more than personal budgets.

For many social workers, personalisation means personal or individual budgets and whilst this is a key feature of the government's agenda for transformation of adult social care, it is only one part of the process of change. Personalisation refers to individuals having as much choice and control in the way support is designed and delivered and ensuring that universal and community support and services are available and accessible to everyone.

* It has its roots in the disabled people's movement.

Disabled people were instrumental in making personalisation a reality as far back as the early 1970s and the work of the Union of the Physically Impaired against Segregation (UPIAS, 1976). An opportunity arose following the introduction of the Independent Living Fund (ILF) in 1988. For the first time, disabled people had a taste of choosing and controlling their own support and services. The ILF was only ever intended as a transitional grant for those who had lost out financially through new benefit changes. However, disabled people campaigned to keep this popular form of support, believing it gave them choice, flexibility and control and was closely aligned to principles of independent living and the social model of disability (Glasby and Littlechild, 2009).

* Personalisation is about thinking and doing.

Personalisation is both a way of *thinking* and a way of *doing*. It cannot be viewed solely as a new system which social workers need to learn to operate (Gardner, 2011).

key concepts in social work practice

166

It must be understood at a more fundamental level which acknowledges the complex relationships social work and social welfare provision has with those who are in receipt of services.

DISCUSSION

There are many strands and layers to personalisation as a concept. Subsequently, the level at which one engages with this concept will to some degree determine one's understanding and analysis of personalisation. From an academic perspective, the interest may be in tracing and analysing the history of changing ideology and theory, particularly with reference to the shifting relationship between the individual and the state. From a political perspective, one may engage with personalisation in relation to its potential to provide better value for money given the current financial context and the changing demographic profile in particular, the increasing number of people requiring long-term support or care. From a social work practitioner perspective, one is more likely to consider whether and how personalisation will work in practice, how service users might benefit from this approach and how it may affect their own role. From a service user perspective, one is likely to focus on the direct benefits or challenges personalisation will bring to their life. In this sense personalisation is multi-dimensional and can mean different things to different people.

Some of the shared values in relation to personalisation focus on increasing choice and control and promoting self-determinism for individuals. Duffy (2006) describes personalisation as a transition from a 'professional gift' model, whereby service users are positioned at the bottom of a chain controlled by the state with professionals providing expert knowledge and controlling service delivery, to a 'citizenship' model, whereby individuals are viewed as central to the process, valued as experts in their own lives and empowered to negotiate and direct support and services (all of which reflects a closer link to the social model of disability). There are concerns, however, that personalisation may not work for all service users and that it will threaten social work as a profession (Ahmed, 2008).

Service users and self-assessment

A key change to the self-directed support model is the notion of self-assessment whereby greater emphasis is placed on service users identifying their own needs. The underlying principle to self-assessment is that individuals understand their own needs better than social workers (Renshaw, 2008). Disabled people have argued that they should be able to assess their own needs and have power and control over service provision. Morris (1993) suggests that professional resistance to self-assessment based on an assumption that it will lead to *insatiable demand* is insulting and ignores evidence that service users are quite capable of rationing their own services if they are given clear criteria.

Research concerns relating to brokerage

The key debate in relation to support brokerage and social work relates to whether it should be independent or part of the social work role. In their research, Leece

personalisation

and Leece (2010) found that participants were overwhelmingly in favour of independent brokerage and that the conflict of interest was too great for social workers to undertake this role. Scourfield (2010) stresses the importance of where brokerage is situated – both organisationally and ideologically. In his research, he found that whilst some welcomed the independence of brokerage situated outside of the statutory sector, others were more cautious of this role being transferred given the lack of regulation and professionalism within support brokerage.

Loss of a collective voice

Research from several different strands has stated the potential threat of fragmenting communities, services and support. In research carried out by Flynn (2006), focusing on personal assistants and safeguarding, respondents commented on the potential of people becoming isolated and were concerned that the power of the collective voice on commissioning and regulation may be lost. Similarly, Spandler (2004) identifies the potential dangers and threat to collective voice and action in fragmenting services and support relating to direct payments.

THE CONCEPT IN SOCIAL WORK PRACTICE

Case study

Sam is a 45-year-old man with learning disabilities. He has lived with his mother for all of his life in a small house near a local town. His mother died some months ago and Sam's sister has moved in with him on a temporary basis to support him through this loss and transition. Sam's sister needs to return to her own home and Sam is adamant that he wants to remain in his home. Financially this may be possible as the house is paid for and has been left to Sam in his mother's will.

Self-assessment

The social worker visited Sam to complete a self-assessment questionnaire. With his sister and some help from the social worker, Sam was able to identify the support he needed. The self-assessment questionnaire focused on key areas including personal care needs, daily living needs, relationships, risk, choice and control. The aim of self-assessment is that service users fully participate in the process based on the principle that they are most likely to be the best experts in relation to their own needs. During the assessment, the social worker and Sam's sister have some concerns about Sam's perception of his own needs and levels of risk to himself. The social worker and Sam's sister work sensitively with Sam to address these issues. Further discussions reveal that Sam does have an awareness of the risks but has tried to cover them up as he is worried he will have to leave his home.

Resource Allocation System (RAS)

Once the assessment has been completed the local authority needs to decide how much money a person is entitled to for them to stay healthy and safe. The

Resource Allocation System was developed by *In Control* in 2003 and continues to be refined by *In Control* and local authorities who adapt it to their own systems and structures. The RAS is a framework to understand and describe needs and provides a methodology for the conversion of needs to money. The self-assessment questionnaire leads to a number of points which are then converted into an amount of money which is referred to as the indicative amount.

Support planning

The social worker informs Sam of the amount of money available to meet his needs. The social worker and Sam's sister work together to identify how the money can be spent. Sam needs to make sure that the outcomes link to the assessed needs and that he can demonstrate how they will improve his health and well-being. Some people decide to complete the support plan themselves or seek independent support through a support broker but Sam has decided that he would like to do this with his social worker and sister. In the support plan Sam decides to recruit a personal assistant to help him with some of the daily living skills such as budgeting, cooking, house safety and developing independence outside the home. Sam decides to involve his sister and an independent broker to help manage the money and the personal assistant. Once the social worker is satisfied that there are clear outcomes related to the assessed needs, the money can be managed, risks have been addressed and Sam is in control of his support, she can organise the release of the money to Sam. He can then employ a support broker and begin the process of recruiting a suitable PA with the support of his sister.

Review process

Once Sam has his support plan in place, the social worker must arrange an out-come focused review. The social worker will support Sam to consider whether the outcomes identified in the support plan have been met. The social worker must review how the money has been spent and the brokerage arrangements that have been set up. Duffy (2010) suggests that the reviewing stage offers the best opportunity to help people make improvements in their lives as they are in a better position to review what is working. The social worker's role is to support Sam to identify, recognise, understand and articulate his needs and to support him to take the lead in designing, arranging and reflecting on any support and services.

Cross references: advocacy, anti-oppressive practice, empowerment, partnership, values

personalisation

169

SUGGESTED READING

Gardner, A. (2011) *Personalisation and Social Work*. Exeter: Learning Matters.
Glasby, J. and Littlechild, R. (2009) *Direct Payments and Personal Budgets: Putting Personalisation into Practice*. Bristol: Policy Press.

REFERENCES

Ahmed, M. (2008) 'Social workers vague on personal budgets'. Available from: www.community care.co.uk/Articles/2008/10/22/109755/social-workers-lack-knowledge-of-personalisation-survey-finds.htm (accessed 21 October 2011).

DH (Department of Health) (2007) *Putting People First: A Shared Vision and Commitment to the Transformation of Adult Social Care.* London: Department of Health.

Duffy, S. (2006) *Keys to Citizenship: A Guide to Getting Good Support for People with Learning Disabilities*, 2nd edn. Birkenhead: Paradigm.

Duffy, S. (2010) *New Script for Care Managers: A Discussion Paper from the Centre of Welfare Reform on Behalf of Paradigm and Blackburn with Darwen.* Sheffield: Centre of Welfare Reform.

Flynn, M. (2006) 'Developing the role of personal assistants: researched and compiled for a skills for care pilot project examining new and emerging roles in social care', University of Sheffield, 28 March 2006, LSE.

Gardner, A. (2011) *Personalisation and Social Work.* Exeter: Learning Matters.

Glasby, J. and Littlechild, R. (2009) *Direct Payments and Personal Budgets: Putting Personalisation into Practice.* Bristol: Policy Press.

Leece, J. and Leece, D. (2010) 'Personalisation: perceptions of the role of social work in a world of brokers and budgets', *British Journal of Social Work*, 41 (2): 204–23.

Morris, J. (1993) 'Key task 1: criteria motives', *Community Care*, 14 January: 17.

Renshaw, C. (2008) 'Do self assessment and self directed support undermine traditional social work with disabled people?', *Disability and Society*, 23(3): 283–6.

Scourfield, P. (2010) 'Going for brokerage: a task of independent support or social work?', *British Journal of Social Work*, 40(3): 868–77.

Spandler, H. (2004) 'Friend or foe? Towards a critical assessment of direct payments', *Critical Social Policy*, 24(2): 187–209.

UPIAS (1976) *Fundamental Principles of Disability.* London: UPIAS.

38
Physical Disability

Jill Murphy

DEFINITION

. . . a physical or mental impairment that has a substantial and long-term adverse effect on ability to carry out normal day-to-day activities. (Equality Act 2010: C15, Part 1, p. 5)

KEY POINTS

- long term – effect is likely to last for at least 12 months;
- must affect one of the 'capacities' – mobility, manual dexterity, speech, hearing, seeing and memory;
- people with HIV, cancer and multiple sclerosis are covered from the point of diagnosis;
- legal rights are provided in employment, education, access to goods services and facilities, buying and renting land or property, functions of public bodies.

DISCUSSION

Models of disability

The 'medical model' of disability stereotypes people with physical disability, promoting notions of pity, fear and patronising attitudes. The 'medical model' creates a cycle of dependency and exclusion, which is difficult to break as professional practices and attitudes disable individuals, and powerful and pervasive views of disability are reinforced in the media, language and literature. Many disabled people internalise negative views of themselves creating feelings of low self-esteem and achievement, further reinforcing non-disabled people's assessment of worth.

The 'social model' of disability sets the disabling factors within contemporary social organisation which takes little or no account of individuals with physical impairments thereby excluding them from participating in mainstream society. The social model is a reaction to the dominant medical model, focusing on barriers (attitudinal, environmental and organisational), which prevent disabled people from having equality of opportunity. Disabled people's disadvantage is thus due to a complex form of institutional discrimination as fundamental to our society as sexism, racism or homophobia. The 'cure' to the problem is in the restructuring of society which is an achievable goal benefiting everyone. Prejudicial attitudes toward disabled people and all minority groups are not inherited, but learned through contact with the prejudice and ignorance of others.

THE CONCEPT IN SOCIAL WORK PRACTICE

Case study

Tim is nine, has cerebral palsy and uses a wheelchair. He loves cricket, can hold a bat and ball and wants to play at school. After a risk assessment determines the risk as too great because Tim cannot move out of the way quickly he is not allowed to play. His parents have asked you to negotiate with the school. What could you negotiate to allay the school's fears and give Tim an equal opportunity to participate?

Negotiated plan:

- Tim couldn't use a full-sized bat so used a smaller one.
- The arms of the wheelchair were in the way, but without them he fell out, so Tim agreed to wear a tummy strap.

- At nine, probably all children should not face a hard ball so a tennis ball was used.
- A shorter distance for bowling was implemented.
- Tim could have a runner to run for him or someone to push him. He chose a pusher.
- For fielding, Tim used a hanging basket cardboard liner.
- To be inclusive, it was the same for everyone.

Everyone could choose to have a smaller bat, bowl underarm with a softer ball, and could run or have a runner.

The PE teacher said: 'No one will want to play with Tim'. We said 'Why don't we ask them if they want to play this new game called short cricket?'

Two weeks later the PE teacher rang. Out of the 30 children, 22 wanted to play short cricket with Tim. After three months she told us that: 'We don't seem to have as many absentees for PE lessons, or notes from Mum excusing their child from taking part. The children who normally avoid PE due to weight or other issues are joining in'.

Risk taking is part of being alive and children need to take healthy risks in a controlled setting to develop. Controlling risk is not the same as eliminating risk. Participation is a major factor in learning and we need ways to understand and control risk while enabling children to participate.

By becoming inclusive everyone benefited from Tim's love for cricket.

The psycho-social approach recognises that individuals need respect and encouragement in the face of disability. Keeping hope alive is vital, and this is particularly relevant with acquired brain injury (ABI) which occurs when a sudden assault damages the brain. It is one of the most common causes of disability and death in adults.

Box 38.1	
Cognitive deficits	• coma
	• confusion
	• reduced attention span
	• memory problems and amnesia
	• problem solving and judgement deficits
	• inability to understand abstract concepts
	• loss of sense of time and space
	• decreased awareness of self and others
Motor deficits	• decreased endurance
	• delays in initiation
	• inability to plan motor movements
	• paralysis or weakness
	• spasticity (tightening and shortening of the muscles)
	• swallowing problems
	• poor balance
	• tremors
	• poor co-ordination

Perceptual or sensory deficits	• changes in hearing, vision, taste, smell, and touch • loss of sensation or heightened sensation of body parts • difficulty understanding where limbs are in relation to the body • vision problems, double vision, limited range of vision
Communication and language deficits	• difficulty speaking and understanding speech (aphasia) • difficulty choosing the right words to say (apraxia) • slow, hesitant speech and decreased vocabulary • difficulty forming sentences that make sense • problems identifying objects and their function • problems with reading, writing, and numbers
Functional deficits	• impaired ability with daily living • problems with organisation, shopping, or paying bills • problems with vocational issues • inability to drive a car or operate machinery
Social difficulties	• impaired social capacity resulting in self-centred behaviour • difficulties in making and keeping friends • difficulties understanding and responding to social interaction
Regulatory disturbances	• fatigue • changes in sleep and eating patterns • dizziness • headache • loss of bowel and bladder control
Personality or psychiatric changes	• apathy • decreased motivation • emotional changes • irritability • anxiety and depression • disinhibition, temper flare-ups, aggression, swearing, lowered frustration tolerance, and inappropriate sexual behaviour (Certain psychiatric disorders are more likely to develop if damage changes the chemical composition of the brain.)
Traumatic epilepsy	Epilepsy occurs in 2–5 per cent of all people with ABI. Occurring immediately after the injury, within the first year, or years later.

Communication skills, information provision and removal of attitudinal and environmental barriers that prevent full participation in life are paramount. Professionals have a key role as sources of information.

Rehabilitation

All phases of rehabilitation have psychological aspects and emotional and cognitive reaction to events can influence future events. Professionals need to be sensitive to these socio-emotional aspects of disability. Interagency and interdisciplinary co-ordination of services is essential and close respectful relationships need to be cultivated with avoidance of making organisational and professional priorities for efficiency the priority. Co-ordination and advocacy are central.

Genuine respect demands service users' right to make informed decisions about their own lives, enhancing self-respect and ability to act on their own initiative. Effort needs to be made to understand a client's wishes and the right to be individual. Grouping people together with the same disability must avoid stereotyped inferences about them. Difference in needs, wishes, abilities and circumstances require diverse approaches, not inflexible agency services and procedures, allowing individuals to challenge the rule rather than prove it.

Coming to terms with disability follows a bereavement process for lost identity and grief symptoms following functional loss can lead to depression. Gender and ethnicity affect the manner in which grief symptoms are reported and require supportive attitudes of society, professionals, family and friends and opportunities for satisfactory living within the community. Social and emotional concerns need time and attention to resolve and over-emphasis on pathology can be replaced with a focus on assets (Rathus, 2008).

Positive reinforcement helps recovery by improving self-esteem and promoting independence. The significance of disability is influenced by the individuals view about themselves and their situation and the following concerns recognised:

- resentment, inferiority, guilt, loneliness, feeling a burden;
- will I still be loved and accepted?
- worries about the future – will I manage?

Key professional skills include:

- showing empathy;
- helping individuals find a balance in energy levels;
- giving clear information supporting decision-making processes;
- encouraging individuals to learn to cope with their limitations and changes in their lives and to discover their strengths;
- respecting and noticing needs and perspectives without imposing ideas;
- supporting expressions of emotions and communication;
- accepting individuals' identity values and views on autonomy;
- supporting individuals in directing their lives even if this conflicts with professional views;
- providing support and information to relatives.

Supported living

Supported living is a special variant of services delivered to a person in their own home, and characterised by a focus on normalisation. An individual focused approach, as opposed to task orientation, facilitates and supports the changing needs of individuals.

Occupational therapy

Occupational therapy is concerned with treatment of disease by working with individuals through engaging the mind and attention on occupation, and focuses holistically on contributing to and hastening recovery. Physical, social and psychological functioning is considered to assist development and recovery. Advocacy focuses on client-identified goals, collaborative relationships and involvement in decision making (Maitra and Erway, 2006). This achieves greater engagement, motivation, improved satisfaction and intervention outcomes. Self-care, home management, community re-integration, vocational, academic, and leisure skills, functional mobility, and written communication are all addressed.

Assisted technology (AT)

Assisted technology (AT) is any device or system that allows an individual to perform a task that they would otherwise be unable to do, or increases the safety and ease with which the task can be performed.

ATs contribute to independence and autonomy for individuals with either acquired impairments or developmental disorders, and address a range of functional activities requiring cognitive skills as diverse as complex attention, executive reasoning, prospective memory, self-monitoring for either the enhancement or inhibition of specific behaviours and sequential processing. They have also been developed to address the needs of individuals with information-processing impairments that may affect visual, auditory and language ability, or the understanding of social cues (McCreadie and Tinker, 2005).

ATs improve the efficiency of traditional rehabilitation practices by enhancing a person's ability to engage in therapeutic tasks independently and by broadening the range of contexts in which those tasks can be exercised. AT interventions can represent entirely new methods of treatment that can reinforce a person's residual intrinsic abilities, provide alternative means by which activities can be completed, or provide extrinsic supports so that functional activities can be performed that might otherwise not be possible (Phipps and Richardson, 2007).

Examples of AT applications are: environmental control (voice activated controllers); low vision (text to speak software); hearing loss (assisted listening devices); and communication (speech generating devices).

Cross references: advocacy, anti-oppressive practice, empowerment, equality and diversity, learning disability

physical disability

175

SUGGESTED READING

Murphy, J. and Pardeck, J. (2005) *Disability Issues for Social Workers and Human Services Professionals in the Twenty-First Century*. Binghampton, NY: Haworth Press.

Priestley, M. and Shah, S. (2011) *Disability and Social Change: Private Lives and Public Policies*. Bristol: Policy Press.

REFERENCES

Equality Act 2010. London: The Stationery Office.

Maitra, K. and Erway, F. (2006) 'Perception of client-centered practice in occupational therapists and their clients', *American Journal of Occupational Therapy*, 60: 298–310.

McCreadie, C. and Tinker, A. (2005) 'The acceptability of assistive technology to older people', *Ageing and Society*, 25(1): 91–110.

Phipps, S. and Richardson, P. (2007) 'Occupational therapy outcomes for clients with traumatic brain injury and stroke using the Canadian Occupational Performance Measure', *American Journal of Occupational Therapy*, 61(3): 328–34.

Rathus, S. (2008) *Childhood and Adolescence: Voyages in Development*. Wandsworth: Thompson.

39
The Political Context of Social Work

Mike Blackmon

DEFINITION

Deriving from the Greek 'polis', relating to 'communities' or 'city-states', the term 'politics' is, today, subsumed in a plethora of understandings. Variously described as 'the science or art of government', 'a particular set of political beliefs or principles' and 'factional scheming for power' (Merriam Webster, 2011), difficulty remains in providing any one definitive meaning to the word 'politics'. Yet, however defined, it is clear that 'politics' impacts at personal, cultural and structural levels, on every citizen of a nation state, daily, across all aspects of life.

From small 'p' politics relating to personal world viewpoints informed by value bases, through cultural 'politics' relating to professional lives, to bigger 'P' structural politics of local, regional and national government, politics fundamentally underpins the way in which society is organised and how 'social justice' is dispensed.

KEY POINTS

- Politics and social work are intrinsically linked activities.
- Politics link to the value base and societal values of practitioners.
- Social work is itself a politically created and controlled activity.
- Social work as a profession has no clear universally accepted 'political' identity beyond a broad commitment to social justice.
- Political decision making affects social workers' ability to achieve professional objectives.

DISCUSSION

Within contemporary society politics has, by significant sections of the public, come to be considered a remote activity with limited relevance to the everyday life of citizens. This retreat from mainstream politics is perhaps explained as a product of creeping limitations, imposed by globalisation, on the ability of nation states to direct their fiscal and social affairs independently. The role of 'politician' is effectively reduced to that of 'business manager' and political choice to differing shades of the neo-liberal consensus (New Right/New Labour) underpinning current free market thinking. Certainly, post-1979, unrestrained growth in globalisation has seen seismic shifts in political thinking, away from a broad post-Second World War 'welfare consensus' towards new political landscapes embracing 'residual welfare' approaches.

Such changes in 'political' direction ultimately impact upon the rights, freedoms, welfare and social justice afforded to citizens, as moving political landscapes herald changing social policy developments, amid shifting social priorities. It is within such political contexts, located in the operational zone between state and individual, that the profession of social work, itself a product of political responses to societal difficulties, exists.

The actions of social workers are guided by policy and legislation enacted by governments of differing political hues, according to prevailing ideologies. Increasingly, policy makers and employers have favoured understandings of social work as, ideally, an administrative/executive activity focusing solely on delivering prevailing policy directions whilst adopting an 'apolitical' stance in the execution of its statutory duties. In recent years, moves toward 'managerial' approaches within the workplace and what Jones (1996) identifies as creeping 'anti-intellectualism' within social work training requirements, has seen what Rogowski (2010) considers a concerted drive towards the de-professionalisation of the social work role. In placing accountability and control above that of autonomy and professional judgement, social workers are increasingly reduced to administrative gate keepers of resources and identifiers of 'risk'. Under such a model, a future perhaps awaits the profession, less as independent champions for social justice, and more as state administrators managing fall out 'problems' of failed, or failing, social policy initiatives.

The social work profession has long been associated with deeply held beliefs in the pursuit of social justice to address problems within society. Indeed, despite a 'contested and ambiguous nature' (Parton and O'Byrne, 2000) there remains a

the political context of social work

177

general commitment to social justice values across the social work landscape, albeit with conflicting perspectives on the means of achieving social justice and explanations for inequality itself.

It is clear most social workers are drawn to the profession by underlying motives to assist and improve the lives of others. That much, by and large, appears a universal characteristic of the social work practitioner. However, achievement of those improvements requires ability to not only practically orchestrate change through, say, accessing of appropriate resources, but also requires practitioners to appreciate explanations underpinning 'need' so as to inform intervention approaches. Coulshed and Orme (1998) identify that most social work decisions are based on 'values', dominated by moral codes transmitted across society and developed through individual experiences of socialisation. Politics, driven by ideological beliefs in fundamental approaches to societal organisation, clearly links to value bases and societal values. For example, the location of poverty in pathological failings of individuals continues to hold 'popular' political currency, and maintains some, if limited, influence within social work practice. Yet, social work has also developed strong, contrasting, 'collectivist' voices throughout its history, firmly locating poverty at the door of structural inequality within society, not individual weaknesses of a perceived feckless 'underclass'. And therein lies a conundrum for the profession.

Far from wholly encompassing stereotyped 'left wing, do-gooders', social work comprises practitioners of varying political hues, whose agreement is around relatively broad commitments to social justice rather than widespread adoption of more radical practice manifestos (see Jones et al., 2010). This internal uncertainty weakens any clear professional identity and plainly presents opportunity for 'political' moulding of a workforce more suited perhaps to meeting employer priorities than service user needs. As such, social work threatens to become a profession, less charting an independent course in stormy seas, but more a profession moving with prevailing political winds and potentially collaborating in the delivery of policies that further exclude the vulnerable or, indeed, seek the very demise of the profession itself.

THE CONCEPT IN SOCIAL WORK PRACTICE

Placing above discussions within current social work practice contexts, it is worth turning to assess the political fall-out occurring in response to the international banking crisis that unfolded in 2008 and consider resultant ramifications for social work practice.

In 1997, a revitalised Labour Party, having reassessed its long standing 'socialist' ideological perspectives and embraced a blend of social democracy and neo-liberalism described as a 'Third Way' of politics (Giddens, 1998), swept to power under a massive mandate for change. The 'New Labour' project, focused on tackling social exclusion, set about injecting huge investment into a somewhat depleted public sector, overseeing an expansion of services across the care sector and introducing numerous publicly funded initiatives, including key programmes such as Sure Start and Connexions. In response, gradual improvements in many care sector services were noted as NHS waiting lists and levels of both crime and unemployment fell significantly. Whilst welcoming services expansion, New Labour's project also embraced 'market' and 'managerial' approaches favoured by its predecessors, implementing a 'modernising agenda' for public services, resulting in the promotion of initiatives such as PFIs and Internal Markets.

A period of prolonged, frenetic legislative activity around social care followed, seeing the introduction of new statutory roles/duties (Children Act 2004, Mental Capacities Act, 2007) and changing working agendas such as 'personalisation'. Managerial approaches to the workplace saw increasing demands for the 'evidencing' of practice, perversely resulting in social workers reporting 60–80 per cent of their time consumed in administration (White et al., 2010), as the costs of accountability drained resources from front line service delivery.

The sustained economic growth overseen by New Labour from 1997 came to an abrupt end however with the advent of the banking crisis in 2008. The resulting publicly funded bail-out added massively to existing public finance deficits and instigated calls, particularly from 'free-market' economists, for the government to implement significant reductions in public spending, immediately. New Labour chose instead to adopt more 'Keynesian' approaches by continuing to stimulate the economy and sustain investment in public sector services, a strategy supporting continued deficit expansion, while awaiting economic recovery, before cutting expenditure.

However, the general election of May 2010 saw a changing of political direction, as a coalition, Conservative led with Liberal Democrat support, embarked upon a largely monetarist approach of implementing immediate, significant and ongoing 'austerity' measures to eliminate public finance deficits by 2015. The emergency budget of October 2008 saw coalition Chancellor, George Osbourne, announce £18 billion cuts to welfare spending claiming these as 'necessary'. New Labour, proposing a phased, less intensive alternative, criticised the coalition approach, claiming the measures to be 'ideologically driven', unnecessary, resulting in severe harm to the economy and creating public hardship.

Within weeks, the implication of coalition 'political' choices began to impact across social work settings as local authorities struggled to balance budgets amid the first in a number of sharp reductions to central government funding for public sector services. Dunning (2010), for example, identified approximately 20 per cent of local authorities expecting to provide 'moderate needs' and above following the October 2010 Comprehensive Spending Review, a significant fall from the 53 per cent reported in 2006. The British Association of Social Workers identified, of 400 surveyed, around 75 per cent of social workers reporting changes to qualifying criteria being implemented within their services and around 90 per cent of respondents suggesting lives would be put at risk as a result of those changes (BASW, 2011). Cooper (2011) also reported pressures being placed on social work practitioners to reassess child protection referrals downwards in the wake of budgetary constraints. BASW research further identified significant workplace impact in response to measures being implemented, with both an inability for social workers to fulfil objectives and perform roles effectively being seen increasingly as the norm (BASW, 2011). One respondent reported social workers as being 'stressed and frustrated' with morale described as 'incredibly low'.

It can be seen therefore that the post-election landscape of social care provision has faced significant challenges resulting from political choices to implement immediate, extensive public expenditure cuts, challenges that may, or may not, have been as significant had different electoral choices been made. As such, this political episode serves to provide concrete evidence of integral links existing between political decision making and the activity of social work. Equally, any lingering doubt or misconception held by practitioners that such links are, to any extent, an irrelevance clearly faces challenge in light of that evidence.

Whatever the perception of recent political decision making, social workers remain bound to work within the legal duties and responsibilities placed upon them. Ultimately however, every social worker needs to balance those considerations with concerns as to the impact political decision making has for them, both in terms of threats posed to their profession and their ability to achieve the social justice they are committed to. Throughout their professional lives therefore, choices remain for the social worker to either adopt 'apolitical' approaches to practice, dismissing the relevance of political forces that surround them, or alternatively, to recognise the absolute relevance of such forces and contemplate what processes they themselves might need to engage with, political or legal, in responding to threats posed by 'politics' on their practice and profession. Those choices are yours.

Cross references: ethics, history of social work, social exclusion, social justice, values

SUGGESTED READING

Lavellete, M. (ed.) (2011) *Radical Social Work Today – Social Work at the Crossroads*. Bristol: Policy Press.

Rogowski, S. (2011) *Social Work: The Rise and Fall of a Profession?* Bristol: Policy Press.

REFERENCES

BASW (2011) 'Social workers express fears that cuts will "put lives at risk"'. Available from: www.basw.co.uk/news/social-workers-express-fears-that-cuts-will-%E2%80%98put-lives-at-risk%E2%80%99 (accessed 10 September 2011).

Cooper, J. (2011) 'Cuts causing child abuse to be downgraded, say social workers'. Available from: www.communitycare.co.uk/Articles/2011/04/14/116661/cuts-causing-child-abuse-to-be-downgraded-say-social-workers.htm (accessed 10 September 2011).

Coulshed, V. and Orme, J. (1998) *Social Work Practice: An Introduction*. Basingstoke: Palgrave Macmillan.

Dunning, J. (2010) 'Councils to deny social care support to all but most needy: most councils prepare to tighten care criteria to substantial or critical'. Community Care. Available from: www.communitycare.co.uk/Articles/2010/09/15/115321/councils-to-deny-social-care-support-to-all-but-most-needy.htm (accessed 10 September 2011).

Giddens, A. (1998) *The Third Way: The Renewal of Social Democracy*. Oxford: Polity.

Jones, C. (1996) 'Anti-intellectualism and the peculiarities of British social work education', in N. Parton (ed.), *Social Theory, Social Change and Social Work*. Abingdon: Routledge, pp. 191–210.

Jones, C., Ferguson, I., Lavellete, M. and Penketh, L. (2010) 'Social work and social justice: a manifesto for a new engaged practice'. Social Work Action Network. Available from: www.socialworkfuture.org/index.php/swan-organisation/manifesto (accessed 10 September 2011).

Merriam Webster Online Dictionary (2011) Available from: www.merriam-webster.com/dictionary/politics (accessed 10 September 2011).

Parton, N. and O'Byrne, P. (2000) *Constructive Social Work: Towards a New Practice*. London: Macmillan.

Rogowski, S. (2010) *Social Work: The Rise and Fall of a Profession?* Bristol: Policy Press.

White, S., Wastell, D., Broadhurst, K. and Hall, C. (2010) 'When policy o'erleaps itself: the "tragic tale" of the integrated children's system', *Critical Social Policy*, 30(3): 405–29.

40
Practice Education

Aidan Worsley and Lesley Littler

DEFINITION

Within the broad spectrum of professional social work, practice education takes on a particular hue. Qualifying students find that some 50 per cent of their studies are completed on placement in a work setting with a practice educator as a supervisor. Post-qualifying learning likewise draws on work-based learning notions and the current structure of the Approved Mental Health Practitioner Programmes still maintain a required placement element. Practice education is arguably *the* key component of professional training and development in social work. Requirement 6 of the Code of Practice for employees (GSCC, 2004) includes the notion that workers are responsible for maintaining and improving their knowledge and skills. This should include training towards professional development as well as the learning and development of others. Every social worker's introduction to practice education comes in their qualifying course, within the particular type of learning known as a placement.

As Walker et al. note:

> Each placement provides students with educational and learning opportunities to develop their professional practice through observation and experience of good practice and being able to engage in good practice alongside a practice educator. (2008: 28)

Practice education in a social work context thus refers to the development and assessment of professional knowledge, skills and values in (or for) a work-based setting. It normally includes a construct of professional supervision (from a mentor or practice educator) with an aim of professional development, often assessed against a competency framework.

KEY POINTS

- Practice education is an aspect of work-based learning.
- Knowledge, skills and values are key elements of the learning required to be evidenced.
- Competency frameworks are often used to assess development in practice, such as the National Occupational Standards (TOPSS, 2004) and the Professional Capabilities Framework (SWRB, 2011).
- Typical features of practice education in social work include supervision, autonomous learning and reflective practice.

DISCUSSION

Practice education is undergoing a significant process of change at the time of writing this chapter. The Social Work Reform Board (2011) is taking forward a significant series of changes to the nature of social work education and the profession itself. Not least of these is the suggestion that the number of days on placement should fall from the current 200 to 170. Furthermore, recent (2011–12) shifts in the requirements of practice educators mean that only qualified social workers with certain training completed and qualifications achieved can supervise and assess students. The erasure of the GSCC Post-Qualifying Framework means that at the current time of writing there is no nationally recognised accredited framework for practice educators in England. Typically, under current arrangements, qualifying students enjoy two or more placements (with a minimum of 200 days), with one of the final two placements being in a setting where students can experience 'statutory social work tasks involving legal interventions' (DH, 2002). This usually, but not always, means within a local authority setting. Prior to going out on placement, qualifying students will engage with some form of placement preparation and each university must satisfy itself that the student is fit (as in professionally suitable) to deal with service users and carers on placement. It is quite common for a short first placement to allow an opportunity to spend time observing practitioners. Practice education (in qualifying programmes) aims, within the full arc of the 200 days experience, to take students from beginner status to a state of readiness for practice commensurate with contemporary notions of social work.

Practice education, as its name suggests, is an educative process and should not limit itself to the more basic notions of 'on the job' training. Social work has few 'rote' learning elements due to its complex, uncertain nature. Understanding the difference between education and training is a key premise for a grasp of the concept and also the critical elements that are encouraged within the culture of social work practice education. This critical approach can be captured most easily in the concept of reflective practice which Schön (1983: 18) helpfully elaborated with the notion of the 'irreducible element of art' that is required to deal with the unconfinable complexity of contemporary professional practice. Schön envisaged the practitioner-learners questioning themselves in dialogue with the enabler. Authors such as Sue White bring this notion right up to date with her consideration of the need to 'educate for uncertainty' but also of the dangers of equating reflection and complexity with uncertainty (White, 2009). A challenge can become how practice education – learning in practice – can facilitate this complexity whilst operating within systems that seek the opposite:

> The more that the uncertainties of practice are acknowledged, the more fervent is the quest for technologies aimed at reducing them. There is a danger that we will become increasingly constrained as educators to focus exclusively on 'education for certainty'. (Taylor and White, 2006: 944)

Practice education and supervision go hand in hand. Supervision has core component elements, usefully captured by Kadushin (1976) as educative, supportive and administrative/managerial. This suggests an interesting tension as the practice educator can simultaneously carry the role of teacher, supporter and assessor – especially problematic when performance issues are identified. It is interesting to note that the social work degree (GSCC, 2003) talked exclusively of the 'practice assessor'. The profession largely refused to be drawn into this nomenclature and the phrase 'practice teacher' or 'practice educator' has prevailed – emphasising the developmental aspect of the role rather than assessment. Supervision within social work has not stayed immune to an increasing emphasis on risk management and bureaucratic procedures but there is some evidence that practitioners strive hard to ensure it remains a venue for reflective discussion and professional development (Beddoe, 2010).

Other typical features of practice education in social work include the production of a portfolio of work-based evidence – case notes, observation material, work products and reflective summaries. The exact make-up of these portfolios varies from course to course, but all will perform a vehicle for assessment against competency frameworks such as the National Occupational Standards (TOPSS, 2004). Students will create, as they work their way through the placement, a body of information which they will share with the practice educator in regular supervision to demonstrate competency and allow the assessment of practice against clear criteria.

Methods of learning and teaching within practice education can draw on a range of techniques but can include reflective journals, supervision discussion, direct observation of practice and, of course, ongoing actual case experience. But the process is not simply about training, rather:

> . . . ways of teaching and learning need to be scrutinised for their capacity to foster ability to learn from practice experience, to formulate contextual knowledge, to be open to differences and to reaffirm the broader values and missions of the social work profession (Fook, 2007: 38)

Fook reminds us of the role that practice education plays in 'enculturation' whereby we learn the norms, values and roles associated with the profession (Rynanen, 2001). By this process, the students' exposure to practice education helps shape their professional identity, offers them role models for their professional practice and helps the nascent professional learn to be who they are to become a professional social worker. It is also worthy of note that this isn't an insular, social work specific activity, but rather serves a function in helping to create a sense of identity in relation to other professional identities: the nurse, the teacher, the probation officer. Through practice education this sense of self both sustains social workers' professional identity for themselves but also in relation to others.

THE CONCEPT IN SOCIAL WORK PRACTICE

Case study

Thea is a third-year mature student on an undergraduate social work course. Having previously been dissatisfied with the stricture of work as a prison officer – and seeking a more directly helpful occupation, Thea elected to change career and become a social worker. She has enjoyed a first, short, mostly observational placement in a carehome setting. Her second, more substantial placement was in a NACRO youth offending community based team where she provided support to the local community by group activities and general social enhancement projects. She is now half way through her final placement in a community mental health team where she carries a small caseload of service users with a variety of mental and emotional health issues.

Thea is struggling with developing a more autonomous professional self. Her practice educator is picking up that without direct instruction on the next activity and independent learning on aspects of mental health, Thea becomes inactive, apparently unable to fully take responsibility for her own learning. Matters come to head when Thea is discussing the case of the Brady family in supervision. This is a complex family situation where Sheila Brady, a single mother, is a long-standing service user of the CMHT due to bipolar disorder – case notes indicate ongoing problems linked to housing, poverty and low-level theft. Thea has apparently intervened but focused almost exclusively on the school attendance of Sheila's 12-year-old daughter, Cher. The practice educator asks Thea to reflect in supervision on the scenario as a whole and what approach she might take to gain a fuller understanding of the Brady family situation. The practice educator then queries why Thea focuses so much on the matter of school attendance. It transpires that Thea finds this to be the most straightforward issue to deal with in a complex and challenging scenario. Thea also reflects that her background as a prison officer has encouraged a 'straightforward' approach to issues.

The practice educator works with Thea to broaden her awareness of the complexity of family dynamics by using spidergrams and case studies. Through extensive supervision discussion, Thea also begins to identify complexity and to make assessments as to what are the important 'levers' in the case that might facilitate the most beneficial effects – in addition to the priority given to the safeguarding issues. Thea realises that it is important to take responsibility for her own learning by ensuring she reads sufficiently around key areas of policy, legislation and practice (such as bipolar disorder) as they relate to her work. Thea goes on to pass her placement.

Cross references: anti-oppressive practice, critical thinking, social work, supervision

Beverley, A. and Worsley, A. (2007) *Learning and Teaching in Social Work Practice*. Basingstoke: Palgrave Macmillan.

Parker, J. (2010) *Effective Practice Learning in Social Work*, 2nd edn. Exeter: Learning Matters.

REFERENCES

Beddoe, L. (2010) 'Surveillance or reflection: professional supervision in the risk society', *British Journal of Social Work*, 40(4): 1279–96.

DH (Department of Health) (2002) *Requirements for Social Work Training*. London: HMSO.

Fook, J. (2007) 'Uncertainty: the defining characteristic of social work?' in M. Lymbery and K. Postle (eds), *Social Work: A Companion to Learning*. London: Sage, pp. 30–9.

GSCC (General Social Care Council) (2003) *Statement of Commitment*. London: GSCC. Available from: www.gscc.org.uk/page/130/Social+work+degree+documents.html (accessed 4 June 2012).

GSCC (General Social Care Council) (2004) *Code of Practice for Social Care Workers*. London: GSCC.

Kadushin, A. (1976) *Supervision in Social Work*. New York: Columbia University Press.

Rynanen, K. (2001) *Constructing Physicians Professional Identity – Exploration of Students Critical Experience in Medical Education*. Helsinki: Oulu University Press.

Schön, D. (1983) *The Reflective Practitioner: How Professionals Think in Action*. New York: Basic Books.

Social Work Reform Board (2011) *Proposals for Implementing a Coherent and Effective National Framework for the Continuing Professional Development of Social Workers*. London: SWRB.

Taylor, C. and White, S. (2006) 'Knowledge and reasoning in social work: educating for humane judgement', *British Journal of Social Work*, 36(6): 937–54.

TOPSS (Training Organisation for Personal Social Services) (2004) *National Occupational Standards for Social Work*. Available from: www.gscc.org.uk/page/130/Social+work+degree+documents.html (accessed 4 June 2012).

Walker, J., Crawford, K. and Parker, J. (2008) *Practice Education in Social Work: A Handbook for Practice Teachers, Assessors and Educators*. Exeter: Learning Matters.

White, S. (2009) 'Fabled uncertainty in social work: a coda to Spafford et al.', *Journal of Social Work*, 9(2): 222–35.

41
Professional Development

Elizabeth Harlow

DEFINITION

Development might be understood as growth, and professional development as growth in one's chosen profession. Such growth might involve the ongoing enhancement of pertinent knowledge and skill. The idea of ongoing development is well accepted for members of established professions such as law and medicine, but the idea is relatively novel for social work, which might be considered a semi-profession, a bureau-profession or a new profession. In the past, social workers could practise with a qualification which required a minimum of two years study and there was no requirement to update their knowledge and skill on an ongoing basis. Nevertheless, it is important to note that organisational and individual investment in principles of good practice may have meant that post-qualification education and learning did take place, albeit on a voluntary basis. The option of self-regulating professional development came to an end for social workers with the introduction of the Care Standards Act in 2000 (Blewitt, 2011). This legislation was part of the overarching policy of the (then) government of the United Kingdom (UK) which aimed to modernise and improve social services (see DH, 1998). In addition to being required to hold a degree in social work, practitioners had to be registered with a national regulatory body (a 'care council') and demonstrate their ongoing investment in professional development as a means of maintaining registration. There are a variety of means by which social workers might develop professionally and these are discussed below.

KEY POINTS

- Professional development requires ongoing investment in knowledge and skill.
- In the past, social workers invested in their professional development on a voluntary basis.
- Since the passing of the Care Standards Act in 2000 social workers have been required to demonstrate their ongoing professional development as a means of retaining registration with a care council.

DISCUSSION

Imogen Taylor (2004) discusses the modernisation agenda pursued by the New Labour Government in the UK at the turn of the 21st century. Although she focuses on the provision of mental health services and National Health Service as her example, the principles raised are pertinent to the requirement for social workers to engage in continuing professional development. For Taylor, the government's reforms were based on the idea of the 'learning organisation' (Senge, 1990), the 'learning society' (European Commission, 1995) and the 'learning age' (DEE, 1998). According to these ideas, the well-being of future society depends upon a population that is engaged in ongoing learning and development:

> The skills of the workforce are vital to our national competitiveness. Rapid technological and organisational change means that, however good initial education and training is, it must be continuously reinforced by further learning throughout working life. (DEE, 1998: 3–4, cited in Taylor, 2004: 76)

Taylor points to the ambition of the government to modernise services by encouraging multi-professional delivery and practice. However, government inspections indicated that structural re-organisation alone was inadequate, and attention had also to be given to personnel: for example, cultural issues, working practices and supervision (DH and SSI, 2002, cited in Taylor, 2004: 78). Finally, the increasing importance given to service users as consumers meant that health and social care professionals were being expected to work in partnership with and become answerable to, an increasing range of stakeholders. Social workers and their managers were therefore engaged in complex, dynamic networks of practice and accountability. This required a professionally 'nimble' workforce capable of learning on an ongoing basis and adapting to changing criteria for performance.

Whilst the above provides the policy backdrop to the Care Standards Act 2000, there have been additional influences specific to social work that encouraged, and continue to encourage, principles and practices associated with the concept of professional development. Since the 1990s there have been challenges to the recruitment and retention of practitioners. Whilst this is due to a broad range of factors, the problem of retention may be exacerbated because social workers as well as their line managers have experienced stress and 'burnout' (see Harlow, 2004). In general, insufficient training for the job and 'dead-end' careers have been identified as two of the possible causes of these conditions (Edelwich, 1980, cited in Sutton, 1994). In consequence, an investment in professional development and attention to career progression may help to offset the dissatisfaction and depletion of the qualified workforce (see below).

THE CONCEPT IN SOCIAL WORK PRACTICE

The Newly Qualified Social Worker Pilot Programme (CWDC, 2008) was introduced in an attempt to support and retain new entrants to the profession. In addition to a reduced workload, these new entrants were required to consolidate (in a structured way) the material learned on their qualifying course. In addition, they were to receive regular, good quality supervision. Supervision involving three main components – managerial, supportive and educational (Kadushin and Harkness, 2002) – has been a feature of social work since its charitable origins in the 19th century. It is through supervision that practitioners are managed and supported, but also enabled to reflect on their work as a means of learning and continuing their professional development. According to Hawkins and Shohet (2006), giving time to supervision is an important habit to develop:

> It [supervision] can give us a chance to stand back and reflect; a chance to avoid the easy ways of blaming others – clients, peers, the organization, society, or even oneself: and it can give us a chance to engage in the search for new options, to discover the learning that often emerges from the most difficult situations, and to get support. We believe that, if the value and experience of good supervision are realized at the beginning of one's professional career, then the 'habit' of receiving good supervision will become an integral part of work life and the continuing development of the worker. (Hawkins and Shohet, 2006: 3)

The habit of receiving good supervision is only possible if the line-manager is willing and able to engage in the process. In hard pressed social care organisations, line-managers may be less available than they and their team members may wish.

However, arrangements might be made for supervision to be purchased from independent or freelance providers. Furthermore, mentors or coaches might also be called upon to facilitate professional development. Within bureaucratic organisations, a mentor is frequently understood to be a more senior and experienced employee who, on an informal basis, offers help, advice and assistance to a junior colleague who is making his/her way towards career progression (Foster-Turner, 2006). In contrast, the services of a freelance coach may be purchased to work with an individual in order to improve his/her work performance. There are numerous approaches to coaching (see Peltier, 2001) and coaches are often contracted to help employees when problems in performance have arisen. However, this is not necessarily the case, and they may be contracted to work with 'high flyers', new recruits or those at mid-career who are seeking stimulation and possibly a new direction. Although social work practitioners are unlikely to have received bespoke coaching, this resource might have been made available to their line-managers (see Harlow et al., 2011). In practice, referring to structured systems of developmental and career support, organisations frequently use the terms mentoring and coaching interchangeably.

Social care organisations might offer in-house training or facilitate action learning as a means of encouraging a 'learning organisation' and the professional development of individual employees. Organisational members might form groups or networks for the purposes of 'research, critical reflection, studying, experimentation and evaluation' (Karvinen-Niinikoski, 2004: 38). According to Karvinen-Niinikoski, such approaches are based on the theory of experiential learning promoted by Kolb (1984) and reflective practice promoted by Schön (1983, 1987). Action learning of this kind might stand alone, or supplement taught courses that are provided by universities as part of the post-qualification educational framework. This post-qualification educational framework, which was revised in England in 2009 (GSCC, 2009), provides structured learning opportunities for social workers. Also in England, the responsibilities of practitioners and their employers in relation to professional development are guided by a code of practice issued by the General Social Care Council (GSCC, 2002). In 2009, the Children's Workforce Development Council introduced the new career grade of Advanced Social Work Practitioner (see www.cwdc.org.uk). Social workers would only be granted the status following a rigorous assessment. This initiative is in-keeping with the concerns of the Social Work Task Force (DCSF, 2009) which recommended not only increased emphasis on learning and development, but also opportunities for professional progression that did not require social workers to abandon front-line practice for management (Cooper, 2011), or another career altogether!

Cross references: accountability, critical thinking, reflection, supervision

SUGGESTED READING

Hawkins, P. and Shohet, R. (2006) Supervision in the Helping Professions, 3rd edn. Maidenhead: Open University Press.
Seden, J., Matthews, S., McCormick, M. and Morgan, A. (2011) Professional Development in Social Work: Complex Issues in Practice. Abingdon: Routledge.

REFERENCES

Blewitt, J. (2011) 'Continuing professional development: enhancing high quality practice', in J. Seden, S. Matthews, M. McCormick and A. Morgan (eds), *Professional Development in Social Work: Complex Issues in Practice*. Abingdon: Routledge, pp. 185–91.

Cooper, B. (2011) 'Careering through social work', in J. Seden, S. Matthews, M. McCormick and A. Morgan (eds), *Professional Development in Social Work: Complex Issues in Practice*. Abingdon: Routledge, pp. 178–84.

CWDC (Children's Workforce Development Council) (2008) 'Newly qualified social worker programme'. Available from: www.cwdcouncil.org.uk/social-work/nqsw-epd (accessed 2 December 2010).

DCSF (Department for Children, Schools and Families) (2009) *Building a Safe, Confident Future: The Final Report of the Social Work Task Force*. London: Department of Health/DCSF.

DEE (Department for Education and Employment) (1998) *The Learning Age: A Renaissance for a New Britain*. London: HMSO.

DH (Department of Health) (1998) *Modernising Social Services: Promoting Independence, Improving Protection*. London: The Stationery Office.

DH (Department of Health) and SSI (Social Services Inspectorate) (2002) *Modernising Mental Health Services, Inspection of Mental Health Services*. London: HMSO.

Edelwich, J. (1980) *Burn-Out*. New York: Human Services Press.

European Commission (1995) *Towards the Learning Society*. Brussels: European Union.

Foster-Turner, J. (2006) *Coaching and Mentoring in Health and Social Care: The Essentials of Practice for Professionals and Organisations*. Abingdon: Radcliffe Publishing.

GSCC (General Social Care Council) (2002) *Code of Practice for Social Care Workers and Employers*. London: GSCC.

GSCC (General Social Care Council) (2009) *The Post-Qualifying Framework for Social Work Education and Training*. London: GSCC.

Harlow, E. (2004) 'Why don't women want to be social workers anymore? New managerialism, postfeminism and the shortage of social workers in social services departments in England and Wales', *European Journal of Social Work*, 7(2): 167–79.

Harlow, E., Blunt, G. and Stanley, N. (2011) 'Evaluation of the children's workforce development council's support to front line managers project'. Available from: www.cwdc.org.uk/research/projects/completed (accessed 1 June 2012).

Hawkins, P. and Shohet, R. (2006) *Supervision in the Helping Professions*, 3rd edn. Maidenhead: Open University Press.

Kadushin, A. and Harkness, D. (2002) *Supervision in Social Work*. New York: Columbia University Press.

Karvinen-Niinikoski, S. (2004) 'Social work supervision: contributing to innovative knowledge production and open expertise', in N. Gould and M. Baldwin (eds), *Social Work, Critical Reflection and the Learning Organization*. Aldershot: Ashgate, pp. 23–40.

Kolb, D. (1984) *Experiential Learning: Experience as the Source of Learning and Development*. Englewood Cliffs, NJ: Prentice Hall.

Peltier, J. (2001) *The Psychology of Executive Coaching: Theory and Application*. Abingdon: Taylor and Francis.

Schön, D.A. (1983) *The Reflective Practitioner: How Professionals Think in Action*. New York: Basic Books.

Schön, D.A. (1987) *Educating the Reflective Practitioner: Towards a New Design for Teaching and Learning in the Professions*. San Francisco, CA: Jossey-Bass.

Senge, P. (1990) *The Fifth Discipline: The Art and Practice of the Learning Organisation*. New York: Doubleday.

Sutton, C. (1994) *Social Work, Community Work and Psychology*. Leicester: BPS Books.

Taylor, I. (2004) 'Multi-professional teams and the learning organization', in N. Gould and M. Baldwin (eds), *Social Work, Critical Reflection and the Learning Organization*. Aldershot: Ashgate, pp. 75–86.

42

Quality Assurance

Rachael Willis

DEFINITION

Quality assurance is most simply stated as being the assurance of quality. The challenge to achieve this becomes twofold – to describe what quality is, and then to determine what methods are employed to ensure that it is maintained or improved. As a measure it is considered to be both subjective and contextual. Moullin (2002) provides a definition of quality which emphasises a service or product's fitness for purpose and its conformance to specification. Moreover, the requirements of the customer must be met at an acceptable price. These terms clearly demonstrate the commercial and industrial origins of the concept.

From an historical perspective, diverse political and economic factors have contributed to the introduction of quality assurance within the social care sector and to its growing influence. Financial restraints in the 1970s prompted questions about both the cost to the economy and the contribution to society of the welfare state (Munro, 2004). Questions had also arisen regarding standards of social care following the public response to media coverage of inquiries and this prompted increasing challenges to the professional standing of social work. The government consequently placed an emphasis on the active performance and quality management of social care (Adams, 1998). They combined this with the political affinity at a national level for introducing the market mechanism into the provision of public services.

KEY POINTS

- The use of quality assurance to address perceived failings in social care by requiring basic service standards.
- Quality assurance as a precursor to greater managerial control of the provision of social care in an increasingly market oriented approach.
- Managers and professionals: a tension and a service dichotomy.
- The proliferation of processes and performance indicators to sustain a network of standards.
- The service user gaining a voice as a customer or stakeholder?

DISCUSSION

Though the terminology may vary, there is a general consensus amongst commentators that there are four main approaches to assuring quality. Each of these represents a step towards an increasing commitment to quality assurance, each has a different underlying emphasis – and each pursues a different quality ideal.

Quality control

Quality control is considered to be the monitoring and control of quality standards within first the 'production' and then the 'delivery' of products and services (Moullin, 2002). Quality assurance at this foundational level was introduced into social care provision in response to the demand for financial accountability. In 1983, the Audit Commission was instituted to report on public finances. This was a means by which a degree of financial transparency could be imposed on the public sector; it therefore became an instrument to maintain a downward pressure on the rising cost of social care (Adams et al., 2009). In parallel, a sequence of inquiries into social care cases caught the media's attention. The political reaction to this resulted in a call for minimum standards to be applied within care services (Hafford-Letchfield, 2007).

According to Adams (1998), quality assurance was considered to represent an objective standard to services and practice. It was intended to address the criticisms of failing standards and counteract what were also judged as the self-serving interests of the profession. He adds that adherence to standards, a compliance with the three 'e's – efficiency, economy and effectiveness – and the challenge to the professions – were all encapsulated in the policy of increasing managerial control. This approach was a corollary of the increasing adherence to market principles within the public sector, and more specifically within the provision of social care. Adams (1998) claims that it was these circumstances that placed the social work profession under increasing scrutiny, directly contributing to the determination of occupational standards and the introduction of competency based qualifications in the mid-1990s in the form of the Diploma in Social Work.

Critics of the quality control approach argue that a compliance with prescribed standards can only ever ensure that a minimum level of service is sustained (Moullin, 2002). It is also countered that such standards cannot reflect the complexity of work within a social care setting. Perhaps more disturbing is the suggestion that performance measures are not always representative and can have contradictory effects on services. This is illustrated within childcare, where measures designed to encourage longer foster placements in appropriate settings are said to be discouraging the termination of placements in adverse settings, with potentially negative impacts on the child (Munro, 2004).

Quality improvement

Quality improvement enhances standards by instituting improvements in the structure and processes within a service organisation. Based on the concept of a learning organisation, critical monitoring of standards is employed to modify the way in which the organisation functions. Munro (2004) suggests that having established service standards, an organisation will then invent processes to monitor each standard. Performance information therefore becomes central to managing the operation, and self-regulation is instituted through audits or inspections. However, an increasing concentration on process management risks an over-emphasis on tasks, activity and output, rather than on the actual experience of the service user as a 'consumer' (Seddon, 2008). A continuing concern is that it reduces the professional determination of practice. According to Munro (2004) there has also been an increasing sensitivity to risk within practice; this has resulted in growing attempts to generate procedural guidance. Tsui and Cheung (2004) claim that both the standardisation of processes and the documentation of procedures, which replicate approaches in the commercial sector, have – in social care – failed to deliver the expected improvements. Hafford-Letchfield (2007) suggests that the current management preoccupation with procedures and structure can often act as a barrier to service user led changes.

Quality management

Quality management extends the application of quality assurance to the people within an organisation. According to Moullin (2002), this seeks to further improve quality by addressing issues which relate to management and the workforce. Strategies can include the adoption of regular and increasingly structured supervision, as well as training development regimes and leadership approaches. Direct management and supervision thus become increasingly colonised by a performance and quality monitoring content. In an attempt to address this, contemporary thinking within social work suggests that a distinct and separate professional supervision should also be provided (Social Work Reform Board, 2010).

Total quality management

Total quality management (TQM) aims to achieve improvement by extending quality assurance to all aspects of an organisation's functioning. It attempts to orientate all elements of an organisation towards contributing to a quality service. The suggested re-orientation is expected to result in a refocusing of interest on the service user or consumer. TQM requires particular attention to service delivery. Those who are present at the point of service delivery (i.e. the workers, service users and carers) are therefore more directly involved in quality determination. This can represent an empowering of the 'customer'. However, the positive impact of such a shift in focus may be reduced if the form it takes is merely consultation by means of surveys and reviews (Adams, 1998).

THE CONCEPT IN SOCIAL WORK PRACTICE

Quality assurance approaches have had a profound impact on the experience of front-line practitioners. Past practices were characterised by greater levels of professional autonomy and more moderate levels of paperwork. This afforded the practitioner the flexibility to tailor the approach and style to each individual client (Munro, 2004). Embedded within what Mintzberg (1978) considered to be a 'professional bureaucracy', social workers would be less subject to management controls and more directed by values and practice theory.

Quality assurance has, since its introduction, been associated with the containment of cost to the public purse. The continued pressure placed on public expenditure has become a prominent feature of providing social care services in the wake of the 2008 banking crisis. Adams et al. (2009) argue that standard setting and quality indicators have tended in the past to mask cuts that have occurred in resources. The consequence, they claim, has been the gradual reduction of staff, and a resultant pressure on the remainder to work harder in order to maintain a growing range of services. Front-line social work practice is therefore increasingly associated with demands on capacity, and thus with proportionally higher levels of stress. Pressure is also expected to increase as procedures proliferate in response to perceived risk; whilst processes are more rigidly defined in an attempt to remedy failures in the activity management approach. According to Seddon (2008), the focus on process solutions continues to restrict the professional practitioner, who in response will use initiative to survive rather than innovate. By implication, processes become less diligently adhered to and thus ever less representative of activity within the service.

The rationale for applying such managerial controls to professional practice has been the pursuit of improvement – ostensibly in the quality of service provided. However, Munro (2011) argues that the course to set for improvement in practice is to instead increase the knowledge and skills required for addressing or resolving human problems. She goes on to explain that quality within social work practice, and by implication social care services, should be determined by a combination of evidence based practice and a degree of subjective professional wisdom. Munro noted as early as 2004 what is now commonly expressed in practice settings – that the face-to-face work with the service user is reducing as demands to both record and adhere to process tasks increase. Information technologies are ubiquitous in contemporary practice, and improvements in design can be expected as they evolve. However, records remain devoid of any measure or mention of quality.

Persistent change is a condition associated with TQM. Information technology and record systems are destined to remain. Should the future then be an increasing managerial commitment to move along the quality assurance scale to TQM? This may at first sight promise a democratising change in influence amongst the stakeholders in the service; but it is also to be noted that quality assurance is a commercial model, and that TQM gives greater emphasis to the customer – not necessarily to the service user.

As an alternative, the government tasked the Munro Review with addressing the increasing bureaucracy in childcare services, and recovering a measure of reliance on professional decision making (Munro, 2011) – undertakings of equal relevance to adults services and the wider profession. In parallel, the work of the Social Work Reform Board (SWRB) presents a mixed array of changes. These include further exercises in establishing standards, as illustrated by the Employee Standards and the Professional Capabilities Framework (Social Work Reform Board, 2010). Perhaps even more significantly, the establishment of a College of Social Work is intended to strengthen the profession and provide it with a voice. It is to be hoped that this voice makes a resolute case for funding future research, which informs and consolidates continued improvements in practice.

Cross references: accountability, leadership and management, the political context of social work, research and evidence based practice

SUGGESTED READING

Adams, R. (1998) *Quality Social Work*. London: Macmillan.
Munro, E. (2011) *The Munro Review of Child Protection: Final Report 'A Child-Centred System'*. London: Department for Education.

REFERENCES

Adams, R. (1998) *Quality Social Work*. London: Macmillan.
Adams, R., Dominelli, L. and Payne, M. (2009) *Practising Social Work in a Complex World*. Basingstoke: Palgrave Macmillan.
Hafford-Letchfield, T. (2007) *Practising Quality Assurance in Social Care*. Exeter: Learning Matters.
Mintzberg, H. (1978) *The Structuring of Organizations: A Synthesis of Research*. Englewood Cliffs, NJ: Prentice Hall.
Moullin, M. (2002) *Delivering Excellence in Health and Social Care*. Buckingham: Open University Press.
Munro, E. (2004) 'The impact of audit on social work practice', *British Journal of Social Work*, 34(8): 1075–95.
Munro, E. (2011) *The Munro Review of Child Protection: Final Report 'A Child-Centred System'*. London: Department for Education.
Seddon, J. (2008) *Systems Thinking in the Public Sector: The Failure of the Reform Regime and a Manifesto for a Better Way*. Axminster: Triarchy Press.
Social Work Reform Board (2010) *Building a Safe and Confident Future: One Year On – Progress Report from the Social Work Reform Board*. London: Department of Education.
Tsui, M. and Cheung, F.C.H. (2004) 'Gone with the wind: the impacts of managerialism on human services', *British Journal of Social Work*, 34(3): 437–42.

43
Record Keeping

Tom Parr

DEFINITION

Recording in social services is an everyday activity for social workers. (O'Rourke, 2010: 1)

It is almost taken for granted that record keeping is an important and indeed a key element of how any human service (health, social care, police, education, etc.) is delivered, but conversely, recording can be seen as a neglected and somewhat residual activity in social work practice (Preston-Shoot, 2003). The key drivers of accountability, efficiency and reform of recent years have changed both the way social work is provided and has had implications for social work practice. The pressure on social workers to justify their actions and decisions, and the requirement for social work agencies to demonstrate efficiency and effectiveness has meant that record keeping and recording practices are increasingly important.

Recording and record keeping could be defined as all forms of written information concerning service users and carers, including communication between different professionals. However, as O'Rourke (2010) has pointed out, this definition in itself does not sufficiently reflect the complexities of the process. She states that: 'Recording is less about writing ability and more about how we observe and listen, take in information, process it, and interpret it' (O'Rourke, 2010: vii). Recording, therefore, needs to be seen in the broader context of communication in social work. It is widely acknowledged that effective communication is a key aspect of social work and social care practice. This can involve verbal and non-verbal forms of communication within the provision of advice, guidance, support, counselling in the context of assessment, planning, and provision of care packages and services.

KEY POINTS

- '"If you haven't recorded it , you haven't done it" Interviewee 31' (O'Rourke, 2010: 48). Why record?
- Service users have the right to access their files (Data Protection Act 1998, Freedom of Information Act 2000) which has led to a far more collaborative approach to sharing information between service users and workers. Who is the record for?
- Recording in social work is a neglected area which requires greater emphasis on training support and guidance. What is the way forward?

DISCUSSION

Recording in context

O'Rourke (2010) provides an interesting analysis of the development of recording in social work dating back to the 19th century when 'The record was seen as incidental – it was important to record what was being done, rather than provide an account of how and why a decision was made' (O'Rourke, 2010: 2). The social work record was cast into the spotlight in the 1970s and 1980s when the inquiries into the deaths of children in the care of social services, most notably Maria Colwell through to Victoria Climbié, clearly highlighted poor and inadequate recording as a contributory factor to an overall systems failure that led to such tragedies. More recently, Lord Laming's review of child protection following the Baby Peter case made 58 recommendations which clearly indicated the need to examine current systems in order to raise standards within child protection. Within the context of improving communication both within and between agencies he stated that 'irrespective of the methods used for recording and managing casework, local leaders must ensure that children and young people's information is managed and recorded effectively to reduce their risk of harm' (House of Commons, 2009: 3.19). This acknowledgement, that systems are only as good as the information that is put into them, and that good recording is a product of face-to-face communication, observation, and engagement with service users and carers, was also highlighted in the Munro review of child protection (Munro, 2011). Whilst Munro is critical of the over-bureaucratic nature of social work, she nevertheless acknowledges that the written record has an important function in terms of providing a future reference point for the child. It provides a means of evaluating the actions that are undertaken, the effectiveness of those actions and can be a mechanism for examining accountability in relation to individual workers and service delivery. Munro acknowledges that the detailed assessment forms provide social workers with an implicit understanding of what essentially needs to be recorded, but she sees that the challenge for workers is in the area of how information and data is collected and analysed. Consequently, recording and record keeping needs to be seen in the wider context of engagement with service users and carers. It includes breaking down barriers, creating relationships within which information is shared between worker and families, being sensitive and having the ability to challenge evasiveness. As Munro states 'Above all, it is important to be able to work directly with children and young people and their families to understand their experiences, worries, hopes and dreams, and help them to change' (Munro, 2011: 6.10).

Why record?

The question of why is the documentation of practice through recording important can be argued on two levels:

- Accountability: there is an acceptance, on the one hand, that workers are responsible for their own practice and thus are accountable on an individual level for assessments, decisions made and work done (Lishman, 2009). As Parker frames this: 'If you were abducted by aliens tomorrow, would someone else in the office or agency be able to pick up your work and understand it?' (2004: 116). If contact is not accurately recorded, how do we know that work has been undertaken? (Moss, 2008). A theme to emerge from various inquiries is one of poor recording and ineffective passing of information between agencies, and whilst some of the spotlight was on individual workers it was also highlighted as an issue for the managers of services in terms of establishing policies for monitoring accountability.
- Can assist in planning, assessment, and decision making: good record keeping is essential in helping service users understand their situation and the processes that are undertaken to arrive at decisions. Significant progress has been made in recent years in the area of working in partnership with service users and carers particularly in the area of involvement in assessment, planning and the decision-making process. For many users of social work services the assessment

of risk is central to decisions made in relation to the planning of care. As O'Rourke (2010) cautions, service users and carers may interpret risk in different ways, as may the professionals involved. The rationale for decision making is as important as documenting the options chosen which might include a record of the service user's understanding and involvement, the options considered, choices made, factors that were taken into account, etc. It should describe not only what was done but why, how and how effective it could be (Lishman, 2009; Taylor, 2010).

THE CONCEPT IN SOCIAL WORK PRACTICE

Who is the record for?

It is clear that record keeping is important for both the individual worker and the organisation. It is important for the agency in terms of fulfilling certain 'legislative requirements, financial accountability for service delivery and its evaluation' (Lishman, 2009: 60). It is important for the worker in terms of individual accountability, personal evaluation and professional development. The move to a more participatory approach in social work in relation to the involvement of service users and carers combined with the right of access to information has resulted in many organisations practising the principle of 'openness' throughout their work. The Data Protection Act 1998 gives individuals the right to access information about them, and places an obligation on local authorities to operate good data protection practices. Generally speaking, formal access to files is less likely to be requested if service users or carers know records are being kept and what they contain. The efforts to standardise social work practice across the country with the introduction of common/single assessment frameworks has resulted in files and notes being more accessible to service users and carers. Critics of the frameworks have argued that recording has become very prescriptive and that assessments are more about form filling rather than the use of professional judgements. Alongside this social workers have also been encouraged to embrace the use of information technology systems. This has not had a smooth passageway and there is a legitimate area for debate as to how case records should be developed and how technology can improve practice. In an interesting newspaper article by White (2008) on the IT challenge facing social workers in child protection, she casts a critical eye over the current state of play:

> we are not arguing for a wholesale abandonment of new technology. Rather, the implications for practice are that the design of any system needs to be based on a thorough understanding of the needs of staff and their working practices. (White, 2008)

Finally, social work with people does not happen in isolation. It is undertaken in a world where multi-disciplinary working is the norm. The record is central to inter- and intra-agency working; it is the means by which information can be shared in relation to the needs of service users and how those needs can be best met.

The way forward?

What is clear is that good recording practices are essential for good social work practice. The following comments are a starting point for you to examine and reflect on key issues in your own and your organisation's attitude to recording.

- Recording is a complex activity and involves more than just writing up information.

Identify some of the skills and key issues that you feel social workers need to be aware of in relation to good recording practice.
    You may have identified some or all of the following issues:

- Self-awareness – appreciating how your own subjective perceptions can impact on your account of a given situation – it is important to distinguish fact from opinion.
- Need to be clear about why we are using the written word.
- The written word needs to be clear, relevant and use appropriate language.
- Have the ability to listen – recording is also about observing, listening, processing and interpreting information.

Some general tips for effective recording: before you start, be clear about why you are recording; record as soon as possible after the event or observation; avoid jargon; record in a way that you would be happy for the child or family to read what you have written; and sign and date each record.

- Recording is not simply an individual activity, it is important for the effective operation of the organisation. What are the implications for managers within social work organisations?

You may have identified some or all of the following issues:

- The culture of the organisation needs to acknowledge the importance of recording. Training in recording should be part of basic qualifying and should be continued at post-qualifying level.
- Managers need to rise to the challenge that the IT revolution presents in terms of more effective recording by individual workers and the potential for providing useful management information.
- Recording is not just an administrative task; it is complex, challenging and plays an essential part in defining the social work task. It is the means by which social work can become more accountable, service users and carers can become more empowered and the service provided and received can become more effective.

Cross references: accountability, communication, leadership and management, service user involvement

SUGGESTED READING

O'Rourke, L. (2010) *Recording in Social Work*. Bristol: Policy Press.
Lishman, J. (2009) *Communication in Social Work*. Basingstoke: Palgrave Macmillan.

REFERENCES

House of Commons (2009) *The Protection of Children in England: A Progress Report*. London: The Stationery Office.

Lishman, J. (2009) *Communication in Social Work*. Basingstoke: Palgrave Macmillan.

Moss, B. (2008) *Communication Skills for Health and Social Care*. London: Sage.

Munro, E. (2011) *The Munro Review of Child Protection: Final Report 'A Child-Centred System'*. London: Department for Education.

O'Rourke, L. (2010) *Recording in Social Work*. Bristol: Policy Press.

Parker, J. (2004) *Effective Practice Learning in Social Work*. Exeter: Learning Matters.

Preston-Shoot, M. (2003) 'A matter of record', *Practice*, 15(3): 31–50.

Taylor, B. (2010) *Professional Decision Making in Social Work Practice*. Exeter: Learning Matters.

White, S. (2008) 'Drop the deadline'. *The Guardian*, 19 November. Available from: www.guardian.co.uk/society/2008/nov/19/child-protection-computers-ics (accessed 4 April 2012).

44
Reflection

Mike Ravey

DEFINITION

I can't remember who told me that they '. . . like to talk about the past but not live in it'. This thought leads to the belief that we should not remain enslaved by events from our past but should use them to help shape our future. It is through this natural introspection and comparison of our memories and experiences that the majority of us adapt and change our reactions to the world around us. Dewey (1933), Kolb (1984) and Schön (1987) have drawn on these ideas to promote the examination of our learning through reflection. Their ideas instigated a movement towards a structured approach to learning from experience. It was Schön who coined the phrase 'reflective practitioner'. He also highlighted the distinction between 'reflection on action', which he perceived as a process that was undertaken after an event, and 'reflection in action', which occurs as a situation unfolds.

Reflection has become an integral tool in the development of both current and future professionals. However, it is useful to observe that precise definition and conceptualisation remain problematic (Gursansky et al., 2010; Mann et al., 2009).

Gursansky et al. perceive this as an irresolvable dilemma as the difficulty rests on the disparity between the need to define the concept while resisting the urge to develop a prescription that restricts individuality and creativity.

Dewey (1933), who has been awarded the accolade for the inception of reflection, defined it as an:

> . . . active, persistent and careful consideration of any belief or supposed form of knowledge in the light of the grounds that support it and the further conclusion to which it tends. (1933: 9)

This definition draws the idea of reflection away from the natural, passive experience that I alluded to earlier to a more active experience that evokes a process of critical analysis of a particular event. This notion is reinforced by a definition that describes reflection as a:

> . . . generic term for those intellectual and affective activities in which individuals engage to explore their experiences in order to lead to a new understanding and appreciation. (Boud et al., 1985: 19)

Some writers resist the temptation of producing definitions in favour of a more descriptive stance. Regardless of which approach is adopted to clarify understanding, there are underlying themes that underpin all of the above explanations. These themes are: the unearthing of deeper assumptions, beliefs and attitudes; development of critical thinking; and the improvement of practice. The most persuasive aspect of all of these descriptions is that it is a method that aids clarification of understanding, of seeing beyond the obvious to a deeper level.

KEY POINTS

- Reflection is a term used in common language to describe a process that occurs somewhere between learning and thinking. We might reflect in order to learn something and/or we might learn through the process of reflection.
- Reflection is viewed by many as a way of enabling, empowering and giving a voice to both practitioners and people who may be eligible for services.
- Theorists perceive reflection as a way of spanning the 'theory–practice' gap.
- There is a blossoming body of evidence that suggests reflection has positive effects for learners by enabling them to form associations and integrate information, which in turn leads to a deeper and more enjoyable learning experience.
- The diversity of definitions of, and frameworks and models for, reflection facilitate a unique and flexible approach to learning, which promotes individuality.

DISCUSSION

There is a growing body of evidence that illuminates how reflection has captured the imaginations of writers and in particular educationalists from within the caring professions, of which social work is no exception. The majority of these writers appear only too enthusiastic to convey the benefits of reflection. Maybe there needs to be a more considered approach to its use, as it would appear its adoption is often based on assumptions and anecdotes, with little or no empirical evidence to substantiate its use. As a body of literature it remains in the early stages of its development (Mann et al., 2009; Matthew-Maich et al., 2000). This is not a rejection of the use of reflection, but it is a fervent call for a rigorous examination of its benefits rather than what could be described as an 'evangelical' or certainly an unquestioning adoption of its qualities.

Reflection has gained significant favour within educational settings as a tool to bridge the 'theory–practice' gap. It has certainly helped to shape a pedagogical shift in the delivery of education from what could be described as the traditional positivist or reductionist stance of the lecturer being a guru or 'font of all knowledge' to a more inclusive approach. However, it would appear that this liberation of the learning process has experienced some resistance from government and employers, who have steered the practice of social workers to one of technical rationality. Gould and Baldwin (2004) suggest that this has been initiated as a response to the intertwining of issues of risk, case complexity, anxiety, efficiency and outcome measures. There is a risk that restricts the innovation and individuality of the practitioner, which is a crucial component of reflection. Ruch (2002) perceives this erosion of the flexibility associated with reflection as being enhanced by the adoption of evidenced based practice. It would appear that this perception is open to discussion as those models incorporating a vertical dimension would certainly see the analytical levels of reflection incorporating evidence and reflection being a facet of evidence based practice.

Graham and Megarry (2005) perceive reflection as an essential tool for social workers to deal with the increasingly complex and challenging role they have to adopt within society. Lay and McGuire (2011) describe its benefits as enabling the maintenance of a professional identify and allowing the practitioner to focus on social and economic justice while initiating social change and equalisation of power. They see it as enabling individuals to not only challenge society's beliefs and values but also their own. This view places a significant amount of power on the use of reflection as a tool to shape practice. With this power comes a certain amount of risk, which needs careful consideration in relation to the adoption of any form of reflection, be it critical reflection, journal keeping, or its use as an educational tool. The first of these focuses on the fact that reflection is not a natural skill and it would appear that reflection and certainly critical reflection need to be taught. This means that novices need support and education to engage with reflection, which is reinforced by the fact that unsupported exposure may leave the novice open to a level of distress as they face new situations, which is acknowledged by Graham and Megarry (2005) with their use of critical friends.

THE CONCEPT IN SOCIAL WORK PRACTICE

Case study

David was a third-year student on a joint nursing and social work degree programme in learning disabilities. He had never given reflection much thought and he had certainly never kept a diary or had the urge to record his experiences. In his first year on the programme he was introduced to the notion of critical reflection and the use of models and journals to facilitate this skill. He engaged with this process in the same way as he had with diary keeping before starting the programme, with a lack of interest and the view that the reflections in the portfolios were just a hoop to jump through. He maintained this ambivalence throughout the first two years of the programme. The only time he engaged with the reflective process was when he was on placement and the product of this was very sterile and minimalistic. Even though he displayed little passion for reflection he was fervently passionate about people with a learning disability and their rights. His academic work relating to this topic was of a very high standard.

Up until the third year his placements were well within his scope of experience as they were similar to his previous work place. In his third year, his practice placement was within a secure hospital setting. From the outset of the placement David was never at ease and he soon requested a change of placement, which was totally out of character. When his practice educator and mentor discussed this unease it soon became apparent that the restrictive environment the service users experienced was a significant challenge to his beliefs about how people with learning disabilities should be supported. As David was struggling to verbally express his feelings of unease his practice educator proposed the idea of a piece of critical reflection on his predicament. Initially David was resistant to this and certainly struggled to put pen to paper. His practice teacher supported David to select a model of reflection that he was comfortable with and with her help they deconstructed David's perceptions and beliefs and then explored them with relevant evidence. This was a 'light bulb' moment for David, as he not only gained a greater awareness of his self and practice, but he also became aware of the need for the secure environment. Not only did this process enable him to settle on the placement but it also brought a greater maturity to his academic writing.

CONCLUSION

This chapter has only touched the tip of the iceberg that is reflection. There is a small but growing body of evidence that supports the idea that reflection and reflective practice have beneficial effects for service users, practitioners and students within all social care, health and educational disciplines. The use of reflection has been embraced by educationalists, who perceive it as a tool to instigate deeper learning and the development of higher order skills essential for the increasingly complex world in which social workers find themselves. There is a risk that its use may be restricted to the academic arena. Therefore, there needs to be more robust evidence that its synthesis within both education and practice would enhance the service delivered to service users.

Cross references: critical thinking, ethics, managing change, supervision

SUGGESTED READING

Knott, C. and Scragg, T. (eds) (2010) *Reflective Practice in Social Work*, 2nd edn. Exeter: Learning Matters.
White, S., Fook, J. and Gardener, F. (2006) *Critical Reflection in Health and Social Care*. Maidenhead: Open University Press.

REFERENCES

Boud, D., Keogh, R. and Walker, D. (eds) (1985) *Reflection: Turning Experience into Learning*. New York: Kogan Page.
Dewey, J. (1933) *How Will We Think*. Boston, MD: Heath and Co.
Gould, N. and Baldwin, M. (eds) (2004) *Social Work, Critical Reflection and the Learning Organization*. Bodmin: MPG Books Ltd.
Graham, G. and Megarry, B. (2005) 'The social care work portfolio: an aid to integrated learning and reflection in social care training', *Social Work Education*, 24(7): 769–80.
Gursansky, D., Quinn, D. and Le Sueur, E. (2010) 'Authenticity in reflection: building reflective skills for social work', *Social Work Education*, 29(7): 778–91.
Kolb, D.A. (1984) *Experiential Learning: Experience as the Source of Learning and Development*. Englewood Cliffs, NJ: Prentice Hall.
Lay, K. and McGuire, L. (2011) 'Building a lens for critical reflection a reflexivity in social work education', *Social Work Education*, 29(5): 539–50.
Mann, K., Gordon, J. and MacLeod, A. (2009) 'Reflection and reflective practice in health professions education: a systematic review', *Advances in Health Sciences Education*, 14(4): 595–621.
Matthew-Maich, N., Brown, B. and Royle, J. (2000) '"Becoming" through reflection and professional portfolios: the voice of growth in nurses', *Reflective Practice*, 1(3): 309–24.
Ruch, G. (2002) 'From triangle to spiral: reflective practice in social work education, practice and research', *Social Work Education*, 21(2): 119–216.
Schön, D. (1987) *Educating the Reflective Practitioner: Towards a New Design for Teaching and Learning in the Professions*. Aldershot: Avebury Academic.

45
Religion and Belief
Philip Gilligan

DEFINITION

Anyone seeking universally accepted definitions of 'religion' or 'belief' faces considerable challenges, which are heightened when individualised and occasional expressions of religious feeling and spirituality are included (see Davie, 2007). However, a pragmatic and phenomenological/interpretive approach such as that adopted by Beckford (1992, 2001) seems appropriate in the context of social work. This sees 'religion' and 'belief' as being primarily what individual believers or communities say they are and avoids imposing any narrow 'substantive' or 'functionalist' definitions (see Hunt, 2005). Such definitions, inevitably, result in the boundaries of meanings becoming varied, inconsistent and changeable, but this serves to reflect experience in the real world. It also ensures that what service users see as their 'religion' or their 'beliefs', together with behaviours and practices that arise from them, are recognised and respected as such. At one end of the relevant continuum, expressions of 'religion' will include practices dictated by millennia of tradition and followed by whole communities, while, at the other, they may involve the relatively fleeting belief or practice of an isolated individual. What heightens the significance of both is their importance to someone as *religious* or *spiritual beliefs* or *practices* and their likely significant impact on behaviour, responses and understanding. Thus, they will be significant to what some individuals and groups need and to a variety of potentially positive resources they can potentially draw upon in meeting those needs. They include not only mainstream world religions, such as Christianity, Hinduism, Islam, Judaism and Sikhism and the many variations within them, but also numerous smaller groupings, as different as the Exclusive Brethren and 'New Age' spirituality. They are divergent in doctrines and ideas, but all have the capacity to impact significantly (for good and for ill).

KEY POINTS

- Religion and religious and spiritual beliefs are extremely significant to some individuals and groups as:
  - potential sources of emotional, psychological and practical support;
  - the origin of or factors contributing to the difficulties they experience;
  - concurrently positive resources and sources of difficulty.
- Social workers need to develop skills which allow them to:
  - assess when, where and how religion and belief are significant;
  - engage with service users in ways which take sufficient, appropriate and respectful account of religion and belief.
- Legislation, practice guidance and professional codes of practice require social workers to take account of religion.

DISCUSSION

Religion and belief play significant roles in determining the ways in which many people interpret events, resolve dilemmas, make decisions and view themselves, their own actions and the actions of others. In Britain, the proportion of individuals for which this is the case is particularly high amongst almost all BME communities, and particularly amongst those of African, Bangladeshi, Caribbean, Indian and Pakistani origin (O'Beirne, 2004). However, religion and belief may also be of profound significance (for good or for ill or for both) in the lives of individuals from white communities and social workers need to be alert to the fact that the religiosity of individual service users may be neither immediately obvious nor associated with public affiliation to particular religious institutions or faith groups. They also need to be aware of the existence of significant religious minorities amongst what may usually be seen as religiously homogenous communities; for example, Sikhs from Afghanistan or Christians from Iran and Pakistan. Members of such minorities may have particular needs.

Crisp (2010) encourages social workers to understand what really matters to those they are working with and to understand what spiritual resources may be available to them. She argues that this requires a dialogue between social work and broader spirituality literature that focuses on the context of 'lived experience' and acknowledgement that 'everyone is spiritual'. Crisp suggests that social work, as an ecologically based profession, needs to consider all aspects of a service user and their systems and, most especially, their need for transcendence, connectedness, identity, meaning and transformation. Like others (e.g. Furness and Gilligan, 2010), she suggests that social workers need to provide clear opportunities for discussion of specific religious practices or beliefs that are important to service users and that they wish to share. She notes the need for social workers to understand their own beliefs and to ensure that they do not project their own understandings onto service users.

Furness and Gilligan (2010) emphasise that social workers are unlikely to develop their understanding and awareness of issues of religion and belief unless provided with relevant tools. They argue that many are insufficiently engaged with reflection on these matters and are insufficiently aware of models from which to develop sound frameworks for culturally competent and religiously literate practice. Consequently, they offer an eight-point framework to be used by practitioners in undertaking assessments, intervention and evaluations. They suggest that social workers reflect explicitly on the following questions, as a matter of routine:

1 Are you sufficiently self-aware and reflexive about your own religious and spiritual beliefs or the absence of them and your responses to others?
2 Are you giving the individuals/groups involved sufficient opportunities to discuss their religious and spiritual beliefs and the strengths, difficulties and needs which arise from them?
3 Are you listening to what they say about their beliefs and the strengths and needs which arise from them?
4 Do you recognise individuals' expertise about their own beliefs and the strengths and needs which arise from them?
5 Are you approaching this piece of practice with sufficient openness and willingness to review and revise your plans and assumptions?
6 Are you building a relationship which is characterised by trust, respect and a willingness to facilitate?
7 Are you being creative in your responses to individuals' beliefs and the strengths and needs which arise from them?
8 Have you sought out relevant information and advice regarding any religious and spiritual beliefs and practices which were previously unfamiliar to you? (Furness and Gilligan, 2010: 47–8).

Furness and Gilligan (2010) provide case examples from contemporary practice which illustrate not only that the impact of religion and belief can be very significant in the lives of a variety of service users, but also the potentially varied and ambiguous nature of this impact. Religion and belief can provide essential support networks and sources of resilience, but they can also be the origin of major difficulties and may heighten the impact of other adversities and trauma. In some cases, particularly when religion and belief are of crucial importance to individuals and groups, they will do all these things to varying degrees at the same time. This can, perhaps, be clearly illustrated by the interaction of religion and experiences of child abuse in both religious and more general contexts.

Doyle (2006) suggests that religion can provide reassurance to victims of abuse who gain strength from a belief that God loves them unconditionally. She cites studies which identify 'religiosity' as a positive factor in survival and ongoing protection and reports interviewees as identifying religion as enhancing their ability to cope. Broader studies into resilience suggest similar patterns, while Kennedy emphasises that '. . . for a great many Christian children who have been abused, if they see God as loving, then the continuation of a Christian practice is essential for healing' (1995: 33–4).

However, membership of a faith community does not provide any protection from child abuse. Moules reminds us that 'Children can be abused in any environment . . .' (2006: 23), while Siddiqui suggests that: 'The Muslim community is at present in a state of denial – denial of the fact that child abuse takes place in places of worship including in mosques, *madrasas* (mosque schools) and families' (2006: 1). At the same time, beliefs in spirit possession and accusations of witchcraft, especially in the context of Pentecostal Christian churches, have played a major role in a small number of high profile cases of physical and emotional abuse of children (Stobart, 2006).

There is also compelling evidence from practice that abuse within the context of faith communities may have additional or specific impacts on victims and survivors. Writers such as Armstrong (1997) and Kennedy (1995) report that, while churches and other religious groups may offer abused children new hope, some aspects of Christian teaching can be extremely unhelpful to victims. Kennedy (1995) suggests that, for some, the experience of abuse, especially by clergy, is experienced, not only as betrayal by trusted authority figures, but as abuse by God. Farrell reports that a majority of participants in his research considered that God had been 'integral within the abuse' (2009: 39), while, in relation to the Roman Catholic church in England and Wales, Gilligan (forthcoming) suggests that the ongoing failure of the bishops to act on their commitment to initiate laicisation of priests convicted of offences against children (Nolan, 2001: 43–4) is likely to have an adverse impact on the recovery and survival of victims and survivors.

Social workers need to be alert to these issues and prepared to respond appropriately to how they impact on service users whatever the situation. It may be a child drawing positive emotional support from their belief in a loving God or trying to establish their identity through adoption of or rejection of a particular faith;

an adult expressing mental distress through desecration of religious symbols; parents seeking 'cures' for children through prayer or exorcism; or an older person arranging religious rituals associated with their impending death. Social workers do not need to share the religious or other beliefs of the individuals and groups they serve and must avoid promotion of their own religious viewpoints. However, they must recognise the potential for religion and belief to impact significantly on the lives of those they serve and prepare themselves to respond accordingly.

Cross references: equality and diversity, history of social work, looked after children, mental health, reflection

SUGGESTED READING

Crisp, B.R. (2010) *Spirituality and Social Work*. Farnham: Ashgate Publishing.
Furness, S. and Gilligan, P. (2010) *Religion Belief and Social Work: Making a Difference*. Bristol: Policy Press.

REFERENCES

Armstrong, H. (1997) *Taking Care: A Church Response to Children, Adults and Abuse*, revised edn. London: National Children's Bureau.
Beckford, J. (1992) 'Religion, modernity and post-modernity', in B. Wilson (ed.), *Religion: Contemporary Issues*. London: Bellew Publishing, pp. 11–23.
Beckford, J. (2001) 'The construction and analysis of religion', *Social Compass*, 48(3): 439–41.
Crisp, B.R. (2010) *Spirituality and Social Work*. Farnham: Ashgate Publishing.
Davie, G. (2007) *The Sociology of Religion*. London: Sage.
Doyle, C. (2006) *Working with Abused Children: From Theory to Practice*. Basingstoke: Palgrave Macmillan.
Farrell, D. (2009) 'Sexual abuse perpetrated by Roman Catholic priests and religious', *Mental Health, Religion and Culture*, 12(1): 39–53.
Furness, S. and Gilligan, P. (2010) *Religion Belief and Social Work: Making a Difference*. Bristol: Policy Press.
Gilligan, P. (forthcoming) 'Clerical abuse and laicisation: an exploration of rhetoric and reality in response to recommendations 77 and 78 of *A Programme for Action. Final Report of the Independent Review on Child Protection in the Catholic Church in England and Wales*', *Child Abuse Review*.
Hunt, S. (2005) *Religion and Everyday Life*. Abingdon: Routledge.
Kennedy, M. (1995) *Submission to the National Commission of Inquiry into the Prevention of Child Abuse*. London: Christian Survivors of Sexual Abuse.
Moules, S. (2006) 'The Catholic churches' response to allegations of child abuse', in *Child Protection in Faith-Based Environments: A Guideline Report*. London: Muslim Parliament of Great Britain.
Nolan, Lord (2001) *A Programme for Action: Final Report of the Independent Review on Child Protection in the Catholic Church in England and Wales*. London: Catholic Bishops' Conference of England and Wales.
O'Beirne, M. (2004) 'Religion in England and Wales: findings from the 2001 Home Office citizenship survey'. Home Office Research Study 274. Available from: www.mssl.ucl.ac.uk/~rs1/hors274.pdf (accessed 27 April 2011).
Siddiqui, G. (2006) 'Breaking the taboo of child abuse', in *Child Protection in Faith-Based Environments: A Guideline Report*. London: Muslim Parliament of Great Britain.
Stobart, E. (2006) 'Child abuse linked to accusations of "possession" and "witchcraft"'. Available from: www.education.gov.uk/publications/eOrderingDownload/RR750.pdf (accessed 27 April 2011).

46

Research and Evidence Based Practice

Emma Kelly

DEFINITION

Research in social work is one way to find out if action by a social worker has had an impact (positive, negative or none) with a service user. Behind this simple statement lies a complex range of issues about purpose, beliefs about knowledge and the role and function of social work itself. Whilst research is often seen as an academic preserve, the UK has seen a rise in service user research (Beresford, 2000) as well as by practitioners in the statutory and voluntary sectors (McLaughlin, 2011).

Research involves the collection of data/information and its analysis or interpretation to comment on an intervention, service or event, in order to produce findings. It can be applied retrospectively (looking at old case records) or occur simultaneously with practice (through observation) and can range from data about one individual to information about hundreds. Quantitative data is something that can be counted or is numerical in nature (e.g. the number of referrals made in a year) and qualitative data is the collection of opinions, feelings and actions 'emphasising interpretation and meaning' through techniques such as interviews and critical incident analysis. Social work research uses both approaches although qualitative methods are often more popular because they reflect the value base of the profession and encourage more participation from service users. Irrespective of the choice made, a researcher must be explicit about the ethics of the research, how it has been carried out (the methodology), how information has been interpreted and what claims they make about the findings (rigour); in doing so researchers acknowledge the limitations of their research and any possible bias. Clearly it would be wrong to make grand claims about the value of an intervention if the study has only considered its impact on one person; however, such a case study may indicate the need for further research. The role of research to produce 'evidence' of what works is contested despite the growing popularity of evidence based practice (EBP) in the UK (McEwen et al., 2008; Webb, 2001).

KEY POINTS

- Social work research is integral to exploring whether or not social work interventions achieve their intended outcomes.

- Anyone can do social work research from service user to academic and student to practitioner.
- Ethical approval is nearly always needed before research activity can begin. The ethics of social work research must comply with those of the profession.
- Research is evaluated by its methodology as well as the actual findings.
- EBP is a specific and currently fashionable approach to the collection, analysis and application of research findings.

DISCUSSION

Research is not a neutral activity and as such any results cannot be completely objective. Factors such as funding, organisational context, theoretical stance (of the researcher) and the design of the research will have an impact on the outcomes. Significant emphasis is placed on research design, as this is one way in which the potential for misleading findings can be minimised. The starting point is always 'what is it that is to be researched?' Specifically, 'what question is it that the researcher wants to answer?' Surprisingly, some published research is unclear what the actual question is or how relevant it is, making it hard to evaluate the findings against the stated aim.

A 'paradigm' underpinning the research; that is, a set of beliefs that you hold about how the social world operates and on the 'nature of reality', must be made explicit at the outset of any research (McLaughlin, 2011). A methodology is then chosen which is related to the theoretical position you take when designing and carrying out research; it will influence how you collect and analyse data and how you present your results. There are many different types of methodologies; those frequently used in social work include case studies, applied ethnographies, action research, and evaluation models.

One key aspect of the methodology is what type of data is to be collected, that is, quantitative or qualitative. Many arguments are made about the differences between quantitative and qualitative data and their respective merits. Some of these arguments are reductionist in nature, linking quantitative data with 'positivist' thinking and qualitative with 'interpretative' beliefs. The notion that knowledge can only be derived from direct experience lends itself to the so-called rational and unbiased collection of numerical data (McLaughlin, 2011). By way of contrast, an interpretive worldview that emphasises the significance of meaning can only be explored through thoughts, observations and feelings. In the social sciences, overstating the division is unhelpful as much research is likely to employ aspects of both approaches. If such an approach is undertaken conscientiously it is known as 'mixed methodology'. The advantages of mixed methodology for social work research are that 'each [methodology] offers a distinctive lens on a complex social phenomena' (Greene et al., 2010: 318).

EBP in social care is defined as 'the conscientious, explicit and judicious use of current best evidence in making decisions regarding the welfare of those in need' (Sheldon and Chilvers, 2000: 5). EBP is both a philosophy and a process where determining the type of evidence that leads to effective practice takes on primary significance. Traditionally, EBP in health has a clear position on what type of research can be considered to produce 'evidence', namely that derived from large-scale empirical studies using the preferred gold standard of a randomised control trial (RCT). Traditionally, RCT are placed at the apex of the 'hierarchy of evidence' (Qureshi, 2004) as they are said to produce data of 'clinical significance' by comparing a randomly allocated control group against a placebo group, usually involving large numbers of people. Whilst EBP and RCT are standard in medicine and nursing, there are very few RCT about contemporary social work practice, a gap first noticed by McDonald and Sheldon in 1992 (Qureshi, 2004).

THE CONCEPT IN SOCIAL WORK PRACTICE

Questions are often asked about whether there is such a thing as social work research, in other words, a body of knowledge distinctive from other related disciplines. Shaw et al. (2010: 3) suggest that there are four general features that characterise social work research: a broad range of methods; its contribution to theory and practice development; inclusion of stakeholders throughout; and 'a pervasive concern with social inclusion, justice and change'. There still exists a notion that social work research is valued less than research in other academic areas. In part, this is due to the complicated position that social work occupies – if we claim that all knowledge is valid then how can we begin to prioritise one form of knowledge over another? In addition, social work research is produced for a variety of purposes such as to improve practice, to contribute to policy development, to provide evidence for decision making and to promote social justice and change (Shaw et al., 2010).

Social work research also tends to be viewed quite suspiciously by practitioners. As with the gap between theory and practice, many social workers have a poor relationship with research, sidelining it to an activity that only takes place in universities and not something that is relevant to day-to-day practice (McEwen et al., 2008). Several studies show that academic research is rarely looked at by social workers for a number of reasons including: lack of time; limited access; lack of confidence in selecting good quality research; and no organisational culture that 'requires' ongoing learning (Moseley and Tierney, 2005). Partly in response to this gap, a number of research implementation institutes have been set up to promote easily accessible research and evidence in social work such as Research in Practice (www.rip.org.uk) and its adult-focused counterpart, RiPfA, the Social Care Institute for Excellence (SCIE) (www.scie.org.uk) and Making Research Count. Whilst these institutes can ensure availability of good quality research, studies evaluating specific partnerships between 'knowledge transfer organisations' and local authorities have reported mixed results (McEwen et al., 2008).

The emergence of EBP in social work is partly a response to the perceived vacuum of research use in contemporary practice, even though the model has many critics in social work (Webb, 2001). In the UK, the debate has focused on what counts as evidence for social work research. Marsh and Fisher (2005) stress that as well as research producing 'generalisable' knowledge, it must also produce research that is 'relevant and applied . . . that is, that it derives from and addresses practice concerns, and is potentially capable of translation into applicable ideas' (Marsh and Fisher, 2005: 3). This has led research institutes such as SCIE adopting a position which embraces empirical research evidence and the views and experiences of users and carers (preferably collected systematically).

Another way of bridging the gap between research and practice is to involve practitioners in research projects, so that social workers become the researchers. Both activities use core skills of interviewing, observation and analysis. One local authority study found that 39 per cent of social workers had been research participants and 31 per cent had helped to plan or design research (McEwen et al., 2008). These results suggest a good level of engagement with the research agenda in practice. However, the role of the social worker as researcher and the results of their studies tends to be sidelined.

Case study: the children's workforce development council (CWDC) practitioner-led research programme

Since 2006 the CWDC have supported over 190 local research projects 'to explore, describe, evaluate and report on ways in which services were being delivered within the children's workforce' (CWDC, 2011). Many of the practitioners who became involved had no prior experience of research and chose to explore a wide range of topics using a variety of methodologies. Their findings were published on the CWDC website to disseminate local social work and other children's workforce research to a national audience.

CONCLUSION

Professional registration requirements to demonstrate continuous learning, the ongoing public and political scrutiny into the state of social work and developments regarding the College of Social Work, all indicate that the role of research knowledge in social work is set to increase. Whilst meetings demands for the accountability and professionalisation of social work, the ongoing interest in improving knowledge provides opportunities to carve out a new model of research production.

Cross references: ethics, service user involvement, theory and social work

SUGGESTED READING

McLaughlin. H, (2011) *Understanding Social Work Research*, 2nd edn. London: Sage.
Shaw, I., Briar-Lawson, K., Orme, J. and Ruckdeschel, R. (2010) *The Sage Handbook of Social Work Research*. London: Sage.

REFERENCES

Beresford, P. (2000) 'Service users' knowledge and social work theory: conflict and collaboration', *British Journal of Social Work*, 30(4): 489–503.
CWDC (Children's Workforce Development Council) (2011) 'Practitioner led research program'. Available from: www.cwdcouncil.org.uk/plr (accessed on 16 June 2011).

research and evidence based practice

Greene, J.C., Sommerfeld, P. and Haight, W.L. (2010) 'Mixing methods in social work research', in I. Shaw, K. Briar-Lawson, J. Orme and R. Ruckdeschel (eds), *The Sage Handbook of Social Work Research*. London: Sage, p.315–31.

McEwen, J., Crawshaw, M., Liversedge, A. and Bradley, G. (2008) 'Promoting change through research and evidence informed practice: a knowledge transfer partnership project between a university and a local authority', *Evidence and Policy*, 4(4): 391–403.

McLaughlin, H. (2011) *Understanding Social Work Research*, 2nd edn. London: Sage.

Marsh, P. and Fisher, M. (2005) *Developing the Evidence Base for Social Work and Social Care Practice*. London: SCIE.

Moseley, A. and Tierney, S. (2005) 'Evidence-based practice in the real world', *Evidence and Policy*, 1(1): 113–19.

Qureshi, H. (2004) 'Evidence in policy and practice: what kinds of research designs?', *Journal of Social Work*, 4(7): 7–23.

Shaw, I., Briar-Lawson, K., Orme, J. and Ruckdeschel, R. (2010) *The Sage Handbook of Social Work Research*. London: Sage.

Sheldon, B. and Chilvers, R. (2000) *Evidence Based Social Care: A Study of Prospects and Problems*. Lyme Regis: Russell House Publishers.

Webb, S. (2001) 'Some considerations of the validity of evidence based practice in social work', *British Journal of Social Work*, 31(1): 57–79.

47

Risk Assessment and Risk Management

Shelley Briggs

DEFINITION

Risk assessment is a key element of social work practice that requires an understanding of risk, and the skills to assess and manage risk. Social workers' approach to the assessment and management of risk is fundamentally linked to social work values and professional standards. It is therefore essential to reflect on definitions of risk and how a definition informs the assessment and management of risk in practice. There is no agreed universal concept of risk, as views and perceptions of risk differ across organisations and professions. Risk is socially constructed and multifaceted with concepts of what constitutes risk evolving in cultural and historical contexts (Titterton, 2005). As the setting and environment in which risk operates can have a major influence on how risk is defined, it is essential that social workers uphold a holistic definition of risk informed by social work principles.

Risk assessment is a common term often associated with security, and health and safety, limiting the definition of risk to *the possibility of harm* and *exposure to danger*. This definition leads to a preoccupation with risk aversion in all aspects of our life (Green, 2007). Yet risk is a normal part of everyday life that is essential to enable learning and development (Barry, 2007). The positive nature of risk is evident in the development of children, where it is essential that children are given more independence as they develop. The increase in independence exposes children to more risk, which develops their capacity and resilience.

Risk can have beneficial outcomes as well as harmful ones. When one takes a risk in financial investment there can be financial gain as well as loss. The challenge for social workers working with vulnerable people is to have a holistic and balanced conceptualisation of risk. A good definition is provided by Titterton: 'Risk can be defined as "the possibility of beneficial and harmful outcomes and the likelihood of their occurrence in a stated timescale"' (2005: 25).

DISCUSSION

Risk assessment is a key component of social work practice as evidenced by the fact that the National Occupational Standards (NOS) (TOPSS, 2004) give risk management its own key role. The NOS and Codes of Practice (GSCC, 2010) also identify the need for the balance between rights and responsibilities, promoting service user's independence; and the associate risk and potential danger and harm of that risk. Walker and Beckett (2004) present two different perspectives on risk: the 'risk control perspective' where risk is viewed in a negative frame and the 'risk taking perspective', where risk is framed positively.

Social work risk assessment receives a lot of media attention with an emphasis on the negative, 'control' consequences of risk. High-profile cases such as the death of Baby P. provide a good example of the focus on the negative control consequences of risk. This media focus can have an impact on managers and social work agencies, directing attention toward negative consequences of risk with less consideration of the benefits of the 'risk taking perspective'.

The Social Care Institute for Excellence (SCIE, n.d.) has provided a very workable definition of risk assessment in their guidance:

> The role of risk assessment is to consider the situation, event or decision and identify where the risk falls on the scale in the dimension of 'likely and unlikely' and 'harmful or beneficial'. (SCIE, n.d.)

THE CONCEPT IN SOCIAL WORK PRACTICE

Risk assessment

Using the SCIE definition, how does one identify where something falls on the likelihood or unlikelihood scale? The key to determining likelihood is consideration of the risk factors. Factors can be perpetuating, in other words, increasing the likelihood, or protecting, decreasing the likelihood. Factors are also static, where they are set at that time and place and do not change with other variables, such as age, sex, offence history or health records; or dynamic, where the factors change with circumstances and the interaction of other variables, such as economic status, relationships, traumatic events, substance use, health condition, etc. (Barry, 2007). The perpetuating and protecting, static and dynamic factors can also be *internal* factors for the individual service user or family such as a health condition, ability to manage stress, substance use, relationship issues; or *external* factors such as environment, housing, employment rates, etc. (Barry, 2007). Social workers must approach risk assessment in an holistic way, identifying all the factors, the relationship between the different factors and how the factors apply to individuals or family at that time and place.

When working with a young person at risk of offending, factors which may perpetuate the risk could be *static* factors such as age and sex; with adolescent males having a higher risk of offending, and dynamic factors such as the use of substances, difficulties in the family, not being in employment or education and peer pressure (Youth Justice Board, 2005). External factors such as lack of employment in the area, limited recreational services and crowded housing may contribute to these dynamic, perpetuating risk factors. Equally, supportive peers and positive personal relationships could be protecting factors that would be further enhanced if education opportunities became available. The family could be both perpetuating and protecting and addressing some of the external issues could assist with enhancing the protecting factors within the family.

Considering the factors that contribute to the likelihood of an event happening, or reduce the likelihood of it happening, is only one part of the risk assessment continuum. The second part is whether the event or decision is harmful or beneficial. If the young person is led to offending by peers, there could be harmful effects to self and others. On the other hand, if the young person recognises the risk and is able to resist their peers and not engage in offending, they will develop a sense of control and independence. Individuals have agency over their response to different factors. Service users have their own risk management expertise which, with support, can be further developed and enhanced in the process of risk assessment (Standford, 2010). It is important to empower service users to enhance and strengthen their ability to manage risk situations.

Risk assessment tools

Social workers are engaged with the most vulnerable people in society and have a statutory responsibility to protect service users from harm. In those high-profile cases where there have been tragic consequences of risk, there has been a media focus on finding the person to blame; often the social worker. This has influenced the current managerialist climate with a focus on social work accountability and professional liability (Green, 2007). In part, this climate has also led to a drive to use more actuarial tools for risk assessment (Barry, 2007).

Risk assessment tools can be divided into three board types: clinical assessment, based on professional judgement; actuarial assessment, based on statistical analysis;

and structured clinical assessment which uses both actuarial tools and clinical judgement (Hothersall and Maas-Lowit, 2010).

The 'proceduralisation' of risk assessment has emphasised the use of actuarial tools (Hothersall and Maas-Lowit, 2010; Kemshall, 2010). Research studies have shown that social workers do not engage well with actuarial tools, using clinical assessment to override the results of the actuarial tools (Kemshall, 2010). While clinical assessment is an important part of practice, actuarial assessments have a role as well. Kemshall (2010) argues that when social workers fail to implement actuarial tools, it can lead to increased use of assessment frameworks. This can have adverse effects on practice, leading to a textbook mentality, reducing reasoning and privileging procedure over people (Kemshall, 2010: 1254).

Using actuarial tools to inform rather than replace professional judgement is key to best practice and social workers 'need to shift from seeing risk assessment as revealing the "truth" to risk assessment as ongoing hypothesis building' (Munro, 2004, cited in Barry, 2007: 31).

Whatever tools are used in risk assessment, sound assessments must:

- be analytical and proactive;
- demonstrate that reasonable steps have been taken to obtain and consider all information;
- use appropriate measurements;
- follow policies and procedures;
- and critically, show that the process has been accurately recorded (Hothersall and Maas-Lowit, 2010).

Risk management

When managing risk it is important to consider what the purpose of risk assessment is and what it can or cannot do. Titterton (2005) argues that risk management should not be about trying to anticipate every single potential risk but planning for risk taking strategies and for monitoring and reviewing these strategies:

> High quality risk management is marked out by the attention given to the needs and wishes of the individual and the agreed plan of action for reducing harm should respect the rights of the individual as a citizen. (2005: 92)

Consider work with older persons – where there has been a shift toward positive risk taking and a recognition that the risks associated with remaining in one's home are outweighed by the risk of maintaining independence (Titterton, 2005). Another example is working with service users who are at risk of self-harm. If service users are hospitalised every time they feel that they may harm themselves, they will not develop their own prevention strategies. Positive risk taking and building on service users' resilience and support networks can empower service users and enhance their sense of self-worth.

Clearly some areas of practice are more conducive to positive risk taking than others and in high-profile areas such as child protection and mental health, the potentially destructive consequences of the risk may require more intrusive interventions to manage risk. However, even in areas where the potential harm of risk is high, the social worker's perception of risk will impact on the assessment and management of risk. If social workers take a risk control perspective focusing on the negative aspects of risk, there is the potential to miss the service user's strengths and lose focus on service users' rights and independence. Using a risk-taking perspective, the social worker considers both the potential harm and the potential benefits of the risk.

CONCLUSION

Risk assessment and risk management present significant challenges in social work practice where the ever increasing risk aversion pressures of society need to be countered to enable a balanced reflection of risk, consideration of statutory duties and responsibilities, social work values, empowerment, and service users' rights.

Cross references: empowerment, law and social work, record keeping, safeguarding adults, safeguarding children, values

SUGGESTED READING

Hothersall, S. and Maas-Lowit, M. (2010) *Need Risk and Protection in Social Work Practice*. Exeter: Learning Matters.
Titterton, M. (2005) *Risk and Risk Taking in Health and Social Welfare*. London: Jessica Kingsley.

REFERENCES

Barry, M. (2007) *Effective Approaches to Risk Assessment in Social Work: An International Literature Review*. Edinburgh: Scottish Executive Social Reserarch.
Green, D. (2007) 'Risk and social work practice', *Australian Journal of Social Work*, 60(4): 395–609.
GSCC (General Social Care Council) (2010) *Codes of Practice for Social Care Workers*. London: General Social Care Council.
Hothersall, S. and Maas-Lowit, M. (2010) *Need Risk and Protection in Social Work Practice*. Exeter: Learning Matters.
Kemshall, H. (2010) 'Risk rationalities in contemporary social work policy and practice', *British Journal of Social Work*, 40(4): 1247–62.
Munro, E. (2004) 'A simpler way to understand the results of risk assessment tools', *Children and Youth Services Review*, 26(9): 873–83.
SCIE (Social Care Institute for Excellence) (n.d.) 'SCIE guide 18 assessment in social work better knowledge for better practice a guide for learning and teaching'. Available from: www.scie.org. uk/publications/guides/guide18/index.aspx (accessed 2 March 2011).
Standford, S. (2010) 'Speaking back to fear: responding to the moral dilemmas of risk in social work practice', *British Journal of Social Work*, 40(4): 1065–80.
Titterton, M. (2005) *Risk and Risk Taking in Health and Social Welfare*. London: Jessica Kingsley.
TOPSS (2004) *The National Occupational Standards for Social Work*. Leeds: TOPSS.
Walker, S. and Beckett, C. (2004) *Social Work Assessment and Intervention*. Lyme Regis: Russell House Publishing.
Youth Justice Board (2005) 'Risk and protective factors'. Available from: www.yjb.gov.uk/publications/ Resources/Downloads/Risk%20Factors%20Summary%20fv.pdf (accessed 29 July 2011).

48

Safeguarding Adults

Karen Owen

DEFINITION

The underlining principle of adult safeguarding is that 'all adults have the right to live free from abuse, harm and exploitation' (DH, 2000). *No Secrets* is government guidance issued to local authorities and has Section 7 status as defined in the Local Government Act 1972 which outlines the duties and responsibilities of local authorities to implement such guidance. Although it will remain as statutory guidance until at least 2013 it is recognised that it has shortcomings (DH, 2011).

Adult safeguarding work is also supported by the duty on public agencies under the Human Rights Act 1998 to intervene proportionally to protect the rights of citizens. Individuals have the right to respect for private and family life under Article 8 of the European Convention on Human Rights (ECHR). Citizens are safeguarded in Article 3 of the ECHR which includes the freedom from torture (including humiliating and degrading treatment).

The term safeguarding is a relatively new term which is used to describe all work to help adults who may be at risk to stay safe, to reduce significant harm and promote well-being. It is important for organisations that work with vulnerable adults to be able to differentiate between safety, protection and safeguarding as these terms are often used interchangeably; yet each require differing levels of strategic involvement.

KEY POINTS

- All adults have the right to live free from abuse, harm and exploitation.
- Adults are allowed to make risky decisions about their lives.
- While 'adult safeguarding' is an umbrella term that includes safety and protection it is most frequently used to refer to issues of adult abuse.
- There are many different types of abuse of vulnerable adults.
- Local authorities have the lead role in cases of adult safeguarding, although effective multi-disciplinary partnership working is essential to achieve best practice.
- In May 2011 the government declared its intention to legislate Safeguarding Adults Boards, making them a statutory requirement (DH, 2011).

DISCUSSION

Roles of professionals in adult safeguarding work

No Secrets states that local authorities are the lead authority in the protection of vulnerable people from abuse and significant harm. However, it recognises that this cannot be done unilaterally and that all agencies involved with the person must play their part. Most authorities have a strategic plan as well as operational duties under this guidance. The strategic structure involves having an adult safeguarding board which is made up of representatives from all the statutory authorities such as health, police (and other criminal justice agencies such as crown prosecution service/probation, etc.), fire service, and housing as well as representation from key voluntary/independent organisations in the local area. Social workers usually play a key role in safeguarding investigations along with colleagues in the police and health authorities where good communication is essential to safeguarding adults at risk.

Factors which may determine why some adults may be more at risk to exploitation and harm than others include:

- not having the mental capacity to make decisions about their own safety and well-being (some people may have fluctuating capacity due to illness or other conditions);
- communication difficulties;
- being physically dependent upon others for aspects of daily living and personal care;
- low self-esteem;
- having a history of abuse;
- social isolation/exclusion;
- stigma and discrimination from the wider society;
- being subjected to anti-social behaviour due to race, religion or learning disability amongst other things.

The Department of Health recommends the following principles of good adult safeguarding practice to assist local agencies in benchmarking their safeguarding arrangements:

- empowerment – presumption of person-led decisions and informed consent;
- protection – support and representation for those in greatest need;
- prevention – it is better to take action before harm occurs;
- proportionality – proportionate and least intrusive response appropriate to the risk presented;
- partnership – local solutions through services working with their communities. Communities have a part to play in preventing, detecting and reporting neglect and abuse;
- accountability – accountability and transparency in delivering safeguarding (DH, 2011).

Case study

Nadia Hassanali (52) and her family came to the UK in the 1970s as 'Ugandan Asians' fleeing Idi Amin's regime. Nadia has autism and Pica, which means that she will eat anything that she can. This includes anything that she sees on the floor and tearing loose wall paper from walls and eating it if she is left alone. She lives at home with her elderly mother, who only speaks Gujerati. Nadia attends a day centre four days a week. No-one there speaks Gujerati but Nadia responds to simple English. Jadwiga, a social work student, visits the family to review Nadia's care package as part of a cost-cutting exercise by the local authority. Jadwiga speaks English and Polish but not Gujerati. There is a shortage of interpreters in the local area but Nadia's case notes state that her sister-in-law usually acts as interpreter for such visits. Jadwiga notices that the house is dirty and that a bed is made up in the living room. During the interview it is revealed that Mrs Hassanali locks Nadia in this room with a bowl of crisps and a drink for five hours every Friday, while she attends mosque and visits her friend. On her return to the office Jadwiga goes to see Cindy, her team manager. Jadwiga is concerned that the family is at risk and services should be increased rather than reduced.

Using the benchmarking principles we can see that there are several potential instances of abuse of adults at risk. Nadia has been excluded from the review meeting and there is no evidence that her views have been sought. There is possible long-term institutional abuse on behalf of the local authority and the day centre because Nadia has been placed in a centre where no one has managed to learn a single word of Gujerati and her dietary requirements have been ignored. There has been an assumption that her sister-in-law could act as an interpreter even though this could compromise her ability to discuss her situation. Mrs Hassanali was not offered a carer's assessment nor was she offered an assessment in her own right.

Cindy arranged for a second visit, with Jadwiga and an interpreter. This resulted in a housing application being made so that the Hassanalis could move closer to their family and the mosque. Contact was made with the Imam who found a volunteer to support Nadia and her mother to attend the mosque together. The volunteer then spent the afternoon with Nadia, which allowed Mrs Hassanali to spend time with her friend. Mrs Hassanali was assessed as being in need of home support due to her own poor health.

An application was made to the Independent Living fund (ILF) and Nadia was granted a small allowance that enabled her to pay for 21 nights per year with a short breaks service. This enabled her to go on holiday with support and allowed her mother a rest.

Assessing the potential risks for the whole family, recognising that Mrs Hassanali and Nadia were both adults at risk, making links with her wider community and working in a multi-agency way prevented a family breakdown.

THE CONCEPT IN SOCIAL WORK PRACTICE

Unlike children's safeguarding work there is no one overarching piece of legislation which covers the work with adults at risk. While *No Secrets* (DH, 2000) is the key piece of guidance that professionals use it is widely recognised that the Human Rights Act 1998, the Mental Capacity Act 2005 and the Equality Act 2010 amongst others are used in support of adult safeguarding. These have helped to improve outcomes for adults who may be at risk and also have provided improved guidance to professionals in this field. *No Secrets* (DH, 2000) recognised that all adults have the capacity to feel vulnerable, and a strange environment or certain situations can lead to a loss of confidence and vulnerability. However, the law recognises that some people within society are more vulnerable or 'at risk' from abuse and exploitation than others. *No Secrets* defines a vulnerable adult as follows:

> A person who is or may be in need of community care services by: reason of mental or other disability, age or illness; and who is or may be unable to take care of him or herself, or unable to protect him or herself against significant harm or exploitation. (DH, 2000: 8)

Some organisations and individuals have questioned this definition 'because it seems to locate the cause of abuse with the victim rather than placing responsibility with the actions or omissions of others' (Association of Directors, 2005). The term 'vulnerable adult' in some authorities is being replaced by 'adult at risk' which recognises that there may be other adults at risk such as those forced into marriage, and trafficked women who may equally be vulnerable to significant harm and need to be given protection. 'Significant harm' is a key concept in safeguarding adults' work which helps practitioners to determine how serious or extensive abuse must be to warrant intervention.

What is abuse and how does it manifest itself?

Abuse can range from overt types of abuse such as sexual and physical assault, which are easily identifiable as crimes, to the more subtle forms such as psychological or discriminatory abuse. All forms of abuse can cause significant harm to the person who is being abused especially as in the majority of cases it is perpetrated by people who are not only known to the adult at risk but who are usually in a position of trust, for example, family members or staff employed to work with them.

Types of abuse

Types of abuse include: sexual, physical, neglect, financial, psychological, discriminatory (hate crimes come under this category) and institutional. *No Secrets* (DH, 2000) provides a useful overview of some of the indicators of abuse under each of these categories.

CONCLUSION

Risk assessments are key tools to use in safeguarding and are particularly important when working with adults who have the capacity to make their own decisions and who may choose to make what professionals may consider to be 'unwise decisions' (Mental Capacity Act 2005). Individuals should be involved wherever possible in their plans and any meetings about them. Some of the processes which organisations have developed to deal with allegations of abuse can in themselves be disempowering, for example, large meetings with a range of professionals discussing the most intimate aspects of a person's life can be very distressing. The individuals themselves should be central to everything you do and their views and wishes should be taken into account. Adults also have the right to live a life which involves a degree of risk and have the ability to make decisions about their lives providing they have the capacity to do so. Well-constructed risk assessments in conjunction with person-centred support plans are essential to good social work practice with adults at risk.

Cross references: domestic violence, ethics, law and social work, mental capacity, risk assessment and risk management

SUGGESTED READING

DH (Department of Health) (2010) 'A vision for adult social care: capable communities and active citizens'. Available from: www.dh.gov.uk/en/Publicationsandstatistics (accessed 22 May 2012).

Pritchard, J. (2009) *Good Practice in the Law and Safeguarding Adults: Criminal Justice and Adult Protection*. London: Jessica Kingsley.

Scragg, T. and Mantell, A. (2011) *Safeguarding Adults in Social Work*, 2nd edn. Exeter: Learning Matters Ltd.

REFERENCES

Association of Directors (ADSS) (2005) *Safeguarding Adults – A National Framework of Standards of Good Practice in Adult Protection Work*. London: ADSS.

DH (Department of Health) (2000) *No Secrets: Guidance on Developing and Implementing Multi-Agency Protection of Vulnerable Adults*. London: The Stationery Office. Available from: www.dh.gov.uk/en/Publicationsandstatistics (accessed 22 May 2012).

DH (Department of Health) (2009) *Safeguarding Adults: Report on the Consultation on the Review of 'No Secrets'*. London: Department of Health. Available from www.dh.gov.uk/prod_consum_dh/groups/dh_digitalassets/documents/digitalasset/dh_102981.pdf (accessed 28 May 2012).

DH (Department of Health) (2011) 'Statement of government policy on adult safeguarding'. Gateway Ref 16072. Available from: www.dh.gov.uk/prod_consum_dh/groups/dh_digitalassets/documents/digitalasset/dh_126770.pdf (accessed 20 May 2012).

Equality Act 2010. London: The Stationery Office.

49

Safeguarding Children

Noreen Maguinness

DEFINITION

'Safeguarding' was introduced into the lexicon of child protection in 1993 in the Home Office report, *Safe from Harm: A Code of Practice for Safeguarding the Welfare of Children in Voluntary Organisations in England and Wales* (Smith and Home Office, 1993). It was further underlined by Sir William Utting's 1997 report *People Like Us*, which located safeguarding as a minimum requirement for ensuring every child's physical and emotional health, education and social development (Frost and Parton, 2009). Parton (2005) also notes the seminal Laming Report (2003) and the equally significant but much less publicised, *Safeguarding Children: A Joint Chief Inspector's Report on Arrangements to Safeguard Children* (DH, 2002). It was unable to find a clear working definition of 'safeguarding' but for the purposes of the report defined it as: 'All agencies working with children, young people and their families (taking) all reasonable measures to ensure that the risks of harm to children's welfare are minimised' and '. . . where there are concerns about children and young people's welfare all agencies take all appropriate actions to address those concerns, working to agreed local policies and procedures in full partnership with other local agencies' (DH, 2002: par. 1.5).

The Children Act 2004 placed statutory obligations on agencies to co-operate in 'safeguarding' children. The language of policy and practice was changed, with 'safeguarding' replacing words and terms such as child protection, child abuse and risk. 'Safeguarding' was intended to capture the wider goals of promoting child welfare for all.

KEY POINTS

- Placing child protection in the broader context of child welfare has been 'deeply problematic and contributed to a systematic failure to focus on what child protection practice has to involve' (Ferguson, 2011: 36).
- The policy climate continues to call for joined-up working (Bell and Hindmoor, 2009; Frost and Robinson, 2007; Warmington et al., 2004) across and between agencies and their practitioners.
- Partnerships, joined-up working and inter-professional practice remain of critical contemporary relevance (Laming, 2009; Munro, 2010).
- There are early, encouraging signs recognising that more law and legislation may not be the answer.

DISCUSSION

The Children Act 2004 and *Working Together to Safeguard Children: Guide to Inter-Agency Working to Safeguard and Promote the Welfare of Children* (DfE, 2010) are firm policy exhortations in a 'congested state' (Skelcher, 2000) to organise collaborative efforts and 'set out' the complex, multi-layered inter-organisational domain that is children's services. Despite its prominence in policy and practice, 'working together' remains without clear definition (McLaughlin, 2004).

Safeguarding children and young people continues to take place within the dominant context of the Children Act 1989, its implementation and interpretation the domain of the street level bureaucrats (Evans and Harris, 2004; Howarth and Calder, 1998). The notion of the 'continuum of need' in relation to meaning, decision making and intervention is key to safeguarding. This continuum – from children in need and children in need of protection as defined by Sections 17 and 47 of the Children Act 1989 – is a fluid, non-binary concept and as such can illuminate professional difference at crucial points in the safeguarding process. Bainham (2005) and Fortin (2003) are clear that the concept of children in need is central to the operation of Part III of the Children Act 1989.

The post-Laming period has posited more law and policy as the answer but has failed to recognise the role of the individual. For the media, policy makers and public, the death of Peter Connelly (2007) raised questions about how it could 'happen again'. White et al. (2010) suggest that largely structural and organisational reforms had not helped practitioners in safeguarding children. It may be time for the policy maker to recognise that a 'top-down' prescriptive approach does not match the expectation that the practitioner will call upon professional judgement in a complex and unpredictable world. For instance, assessment is premised on discretion and decision making and routinely takes place against constant change. As such it is fallible. The top-down approach does not allow for the reality of the individual practitioner with their own autobiographical filter attempting to make decisions with and about children and young people and their families within 'grey areas'.

Safeguarding can be 'messy' and calls for the top-down policy maker to engage with the uncertainty and to entangle themselves in the disparate discourse that is inherent in practice. Jessop notes: 'It might seem odd to call for something that undermines clarities, envisions chaos and negates affirmation' (2003: 8). However, policy directives that recognise the fallacy that the service delivers just because the policy says it should are in a better position to deliver. The graphic analogy – 'Out in the swampy lowlands of practice' (Schön, 1983, cited in Braye and Preston-Shoot, 2006) – reflects the reality of the territory navigated by the street-level bureaucrat (Lipsky, 1980, 2010). This is the same street-level bureaucrat who will need to use discretion to assess and make decisions. Laming failed the practitioner and the reality of their practice.

THE CONCEPT IN SOCIAL WORK PRACTICE

Laming (2003) called for competent and confident practitioners but imposed a prescriptive and managerialist organisational structure underpinned with an expectation that increased and improved partnerships would automatically lead to a streamlining of human interaction. The policy believed practitioner behaviour would alter once organisational questions had been resolved. This did not take into account the ever-pertinent power of the practitioner to use discretion and authority case by case. The Munro Review (2011) provides early signs that there may finally be recognition that more law and legislation may not be the answer. The less prescriptive approach recommended by Munro will place an increased emphasis on professional and expert judgement.

Safeguarding can be encapsulated by reference to the Serious Case Reviews of Victoria Climbié (2003) and Peter Connelly (DfE, 2009). Each illuminates contrasting policy attempts to define what has become known as safeguarding. Climbié was characterised by the refocusing debate informed by Messages from Research (DH, 1995) which proved a watershed in shaping practice from the late 1990s. It concluded that too much of the work undertaken comes under the banner of 'child protection' (DH, 1995: 54) and that there was a bias towards assessment over prevention. Local authorities were encouraged to rebalance child protection and preventative family support services. The debate at ground level became characterised as the 'continuum of need', services and intervention aimed at embracing children in need and children in need of protection. Reder and Duncan suggest that whilst there was never an overt instruction to social services, 'it is common knowledge that they understood that was what was expected of them' (2004: 104). This policy shift was recognition that the central philosophy and principles of the Children Act 1989, particularly with regard to Section 17 and Part III, had been implemented only partially. Child protection had become a dominant concern at the expense of family support and children in need.

Victoria Climbié was defined from the outset as a child in need. This definition framed all subsequent activities; no child protection assessment took place and her name was not placed on the child protection register (in the current policy context she would not have been subject to a child protection plan). Reder and Duncan suggest a partial explanation for this in the influence of the refocusing debate:

> Increasingly, referred cases were dichotomized from the outset, based on limited information as either being a 'child in need' (therefore requiring supportive services) or 'child protection' (hence requiring a section 47 [Children Act 1989] investigation). (2004: 104)

Post Laming, the policy context became increasingly preventative, supported by the already existing assessment tool, *The Framework of the Assessment of Children in Need and their Families* (DH, 2000). The framework is based on an ecological model intended to place the child at the centre of the assessment or intervention, and to discourage the practitioner from being incident focused in order to address the holistic environment. It remains the core assessment tool used by practitioners yet fails to mention 'risk' (Calder, 2008).

Post Laming structural changes contained in the Children Act 2004 did not address the definition of what remain the core elements of work with children and families. Safeguarding denotes a child at risk of significant harm and a child in need requiring additional support services. It is for the practitioner, working in partnership with other agencies, to determine where and why the child needs to be located. The concern is that 'safeguarding' does not have the impact of child protection. There is a danger of losing sight of the distinctive nature of child abuse work and the specific nature of working with suspected abusive parents. The Executive Summary of Peter Connelly puts it well:

> The uncooperative, anti-social and even dangerous/parent carer is the most difficult challenge for safeguarding and child protection services. The parents/carers may not immediately present as such and may be superficially compliant, evasive, deceitful and manipulative and untruthful. Practitioners have the difficult job of identifying them among the majority of parents who they encounter who are merely dysfunctional, anxious and ambivalent. (DfE, 2009: pars 5.3)

Cross references: communication, critical thinking, multi-professional working, the political context of social work

SUGGESTED READING

Ferguson, H. (2011) *Child Protection Practice*. Basingstoke: Palgrave Macmillan.
Frost, N. and Parton, N. (2009) *Understanding Children's Social Care: Politics, Policy and Practice*. London: Sage.

REFERENCES

Bainham, A. (2005) *Children and the Modern Law*, 3rd edn. Bristol: Family Law.
Bell, S. and Hindmoor, A. (2009) 'The governance of public affairs', *Journal of Public Affairs*, 9: 149–59.
Braye, S. and Preston-Shoot, M. (2006) 'The role of law in welfare reform: critical perspectives on the relationship between law and social work practice', *International Journal of Social Welfare*, 15: 19–26.
Calder, M. (2008) 'Risk and child protection', in M. Calder (ed.), *Contemporary Risk Assessment in Safeguarding Children*. Lyme Regis: Russell House, pp. 206–23.
Children Act (1989) London: HMSO.
Children Act (2004) London: HMSO.
DH (Department of Health) (1995) *Child Protection Messages from Research: Studies in Child Protection*. London: HMSO.
DH (Department of Health) (2000) *The Framework for the Assessment of Children in Need and their Families*. London: The Stationery Office.
DH (Department of Health) (2002) *Safeguarding Children: A Joint Chief Inspector's Report on Arrangements to Safeguard Children*. London: Department of Health.
DfE (Department for Education) (2009) *Haringey Local Safeguarding Children Board Serious Case Review Child A*. London: HMSO.
DfE (2010) *Working Together to Safeguard Children: Guide to Inter-Agency Working to Safeguard and Promote the Welfare of Children*. London: The Stationery Office.
Evans, T. and Harris, J. (2004) 'Street-level bureaucracy, social work and the (exaggerated) death of discretion', *British Journal of Social Work*, 34(6): 871–95.
Ferguson, H. (2011) *Child Protection Practice*. Basingstoke: Palgrave Macmillan.
Fortin, J. (2003) *Children's Rights and the Developing Law*, 2nd edn. London: Butterworths.
Frost, N. and Parton, N. (2009) *Understanding Children's Social Care Politics, Policy and Practice*. London: Sage.
Frost, N. and Robinson, M. (2007) 'Joining up children's services: safeguarding children in multi-disciplinary teams', *Child Abuse Review*, 16(3): 184–99.
Howarth, J. and Calder, M. (1998) 'Working together to protect children on the child protection register: myth or reality?', *British Journal of Social Work*, 28(6): 879–95.

Jessop, B. (2003) 'Governance and meta governance: reflexivity, requisite variety, and requisite irony'. Department of Sociology, Lancaster University.

Laming, H. (2009) The *Protection of Children in England: A Progress Report*. London: The Stationery Office.

Laming Report (2003) *The Victoria Climbié Enquiry: Report of an Inquiry by Lord Laming*. London: The Stationery Office.

Lipsky, M. (1980) *Street-Level Bureaucracy*. New York: Russell Sage.

Lipsky, M. (2010) *Street-Level Bureaucracy Dilemmas of the Individual in Public Services*. New York: Russell Sage.

McLaughlin, H. (2004) 'Partnerships: panacea or pretence?', *Journal of Interprofessional Care*, 18(2): 103–13.

Munro, E. (2010) *Building a Safe and Confident Future: One Year on Detailed Proposals from the Social Work Reform Board*. London: HMSO.

Munro, E. (2011) *The Munro Review of Child Protection: Final Report A Child Centred System*. London: Department of Education.

Parton, N. (2005) *Safeguarding Childhood: Early Intervention and Surveillance in a Late Modern Society*. Basingstoke: Palgrave Macmillan.

Reder, P. and Duncan, S. (2004) 'Making the most of the Victoria Climbié inquiry report', *Child Abuse Review*, 13(2): 95–114.

Schön, D. (1983) *The Reflective Practitioner: How Professionals Think in Action*. New York: Basic Books.

Skelcher, C. (2000) 'Changing images of the state: overloaded, hollowed-out and congested', *Public Policy and Administration*, 15(3): 3–19.

Smith, D.R. and Home Office (1993) *Safe from Harm: A Code of Practice for Safeguarding the Welfare of Children in Voluntary Organisations in England and Wales*. London: Home Office.

Utting, Sir W. (1997) *People Like Us: The Report of the Review of the Safeguards for Children Living Away from Home*. London: HMSO.

Warmington, P., Daniels, H., Edwards, A., Brown, S., Leadbetter, M. and Middleton, D. (2004) *Interagency Collaboration: A Review of the Literature*. Bath: Learning in and for Interagency Working.

White, S., Wastell, D., Broadhurst, K. and Hall, C. (2010) 'When policy o'er leaps itself: the 'tragic tale of the integrated children's system', *Critical Social Policy*, 30(3): 405–29.

50
Service User Involvement

Clare Stone, Lisa Malihi-Shoja, Mick McKeown and the Comensus Writing Collective

DEFINITION

This chapter focuses on the involvement of service users – a particularly contested concept in social work practice. Authors such as Beresford (2005) have argued that the term 'service user' has currency and meaning and may be useful for advancing the aims of citizens who use services. There is also some controversy over a tendency in some quarters to conflate the interests of service users and informal carers. In this chapter we are concerned with both service users and carers (see also Chapter 8 on carers), but do not wish to suggest that there is a single user/carer perspective, rather that social work practitioners, planners and learners need to appreciate points of view from both constituencies. Service user involvement has been the subject of a huge amount of legislation and policy interest over the last two decades and, arguably, social work as a professional discipline has been in the vanguard of these changes (Kemshall and Littlechild, 2002).

This chapter draws on the experiences of a service user and carer involvement project called Comensus, based at the University of Central Lancashire (UCLan) which is a service user and carer led group that aims to incorporate the voices of those using health and social care services and their carers into the work of the Schools of Health and Social Work. The service users and carers who make up Comensus review teaching and learning materials; interview staff and students; carry out and plan research; help UCLan make important decisions; get involved in teaching; and help design courses from a service user and carer perspective.

KEY POINTS

- The term 'service user' is a contested concept with significant political implications.
- Service user involvement is important as they are the best judge of their own needs and quality of service.
- It is important that any involvement of service users in social work concerns is authentic and not tokenistic.
- Service users will require appropriate support for their involvement.

DISCUSSION

Recent national policy has promoted user involvement in social care and education. The 1998 White Paper *Modernising Social Services* signalled the government's 'intention to promote the perspective of service users in . . . social care' (Waterson and Morris, 2005: 654). Taylor (1996) cites the Children Act 1989 and the National Health Service and Community Care Act 1990 as examples of legislation emphasising user-led practice. The value of promoting greater levels of participation is reflected in some significant changes to social work practice, service delivery and education. Explicit reference is made to involving users in practice and policy development in the Code of Practice for Social Care Workers (GSCC, 2002) and the Requirements for Social Work Training (DH, 2002).

The General Social Care Council (GSCC) and Social Care Institute for Excellence (SCIE) share a commitment to putting service users and carers at the heart of all aspects of social work and social care, including social work education (GSCC and SCIE, 2004: 4).

The Social Work Reform Board embedded service user representation in their development of the 15 recommendations made by the Task Force to overhaul professional training and practice (SWRB, 2010).

Why involve service users?

User participation has historically been taken up by organised groups which have been described as a social movement for change (Brown and Zavetoski, 2005). In this light, the context of involvement can be considered in terms of the politics of user rights. A key argument for why it is worth pursuing is that service users themselves want greater involvement. Interestingly, the demands made by service user or disability movements focus on both large-scale, societal issues (for instance, around stigma and identity, oppression, discrimination or social inclusion), or on the micro level of everyday contact with services, especially their relationships with practitioners. If we view involvement from a movement politics model we can see how alliances between users and workers can develop, whether at the relational level or in terms of collective organising (Cox, 2009; McKeown, 2009).

The main reason we ought to be interested in maximising involvement is an acknowledgement of the notion that service users themselves may very well be the best judge of their own needs and of the quality of service provided. Similarly, the user of services is the best narrator of their own lived experience and practitioners who make efforts to listen and attend to these perspectives are arguably in a better position to begin to apply their professional judgements and skills to helping support these individuals. Social workers and students might care to reflect on relevant themes such as: how people have come to be users of services; their experiences of engagement with services and professionals; how to best elicit these user narratives; and how to make sense of them in ways that ultimately improve practice.

One specific example which relates to the interest in hearing the authentic voices of service users is in the arena of service user feedback. Many agencies give out compliments, complaints and comments questionnaires to service users which focus mainly on resources and information received. A more in-depth feedback method we have engaged in is 'customer journey mapping'. Lancashire County Council piloted the use of an unstructured/open interview technique to enable service users to talk about their experience of their contact with the council. The council analysed the narratives to inform service development and improvement. Final year MA social work students from UCLan fulfilled the role of researchers. In addition to experiencing empirical research they had the privilege of hearing first-hand how service users experienced contact with social services.

THE CONCEPT IN SOCIAL WORK PRACTICE

Once there is an interest in supporting user involvement, there need not necessarily be a limit to the imagination regarding where or how involvement may be enacted. There are a range of opportunities – some are at strategic levels, others operational and yet others are educational. Comensus participants have collectively developed their involvement in social work education to the point where they are involved in a range of different levels. One outcome has been the development of a completely user-led module for the BA social work programme at UCLan. This included the writing and development of the module, teaching it and involvement in the assessment of students. The teaching has moved beyond the simple re-telling of personal stories (though personal narratives are included) to engaging the students in critical thinking about general features of user involvement, how they can facilitate it in their own practice, and how they as professionals might relate to user movement demands for change.

Perhaps an obvious way for service users to help students and practitioners learn and develop their practice is by providing feedback. As a social work student or practitioner it is essential that you continually reflect on informal, verbal and non-verbal feedback. When requesting formal feedback from service users it is important to consider: who will facilitate obtaining the feedback (e.g. a practice educator or manager); when it is appropriate to ask; and the best format for each service user to use. One may wish to employ telephone interviews, face-to-face meetings or questionnaires. Below are some examples of questions designed to elicit feedback, for reflection, to guide professional development.

- Do you feel that X planned for the visit and had a clear understanding of the background to the visit?
- Was X aware of your support needs? (These may be disabilities, cultural needs, religious, gender, sexuality, etc.)
- Did X listen and understand what you said?
- Did X treat you with respect?

Stickley and colleagues (2010), with a focus on mental health nursing, describe some of the complexities of organising systems for user-led feedback for learners and raise some interesting points regarding professional resistance and the capacity of student practitioners to receive critical feedback from service users in the practice learning domain.

Beresford (2005) believes that access and support are essential for successful service user involvement. Tew et al. (2004) and a range of other authors all believe that support is essential for service users. This will ensure that they are prepared, feel confident, gain new skills and become empowered as part of the process of involvement. Braye (2000) also highlighted a range of characteristics necessary for involvement to move beyond mere tokenism. These include being clear about the level of involvement and its scope and remit. Braye highlights how people should be involved from the beginning and not as an afterthought. They should be given tangible goals, be involved by choice and not by coercion and should include both individual and collective perspectives.

CONCLUSION

Although there is a mandate for participation there are important considerations to be made regarding the complexities and challenges of realising *authentic* involvement. With careful planning we can maximise the potential for constructive alliances and be mindful of factors which either promote or hinder successful initiatives. This must involve a twofold awareness of the practicalities of working at both systems and individual levels of contact with service users. The system's level focus cautions us to consider the infrastructure of access and support, the individual level brings in consideration of personal motivations for involvement and how these may chime with mutual interests in making changes for better services. These views are aptly expressed in this comment by John Lunt, a member of the Comensus Writing Group: 'Infrastructure is important for service users to enable them to express their experiences with a view to inputting into strategies for the future benefit of others'.

Cross references: advocacy, carers, empowerment, partnership, personalisation, values

SUGGESTED READING

McKeown, M., Malihi-Shoja, L., Downe, S., Supporting the Comensus Writing Collective (2010) *Service User and Carer Involvement in Education for Health and Social Care*. Oxford: Wiley-Blackwell, pp. 156–60.

Warren, J. (2007) *Service User and Carer Participation in Social Work*. Exeter: Learning Matters.

REFERENCES

Beresford, P. (2005) 'Theory and practice of user involvement in research', in L. Lowes and I. Hulatt (eds), *Involving Service Users in Health and Social Care Research*. London: Routledge, pp. 6–17.

Braye, S. (2000) 'Participation and involvement in social care: an overview', in H. Kemshall and R. Littlechild (eds), *User Involvement and Participation in Social Care: Research Informing Practice*. London: Jessica Kingsley Publishers, pp. 9–28.

Brown, P. and Zavetoski, S. (eds) (2005) *Social Movements in Health*. Oxford: Blackwell Publishing.

Cox, P. (2009) 'Connectivity: seeking conditions and connections for radical discourses and praxes in health, mental health and social work', *Social Theory and Health*, 7(2): 170–86.

DH (Department of Health) (2002) *Requirements for Social Work Training*. London: Department of Health.

GSCC (General Social Care Council) (2002) *Code of Practice for Social Care Workers*. London: General Social Care Council.

GSCC and SCIE (General Social Care Council and the Social Care Institute For Excellence) (2004) *Living and Learning Together Conference Report*. London: General Social Care Council (GSCC) and the Social Care Institute for Excellence (SCIE).

Kemshall, H. and Littlechild, R. (eds) (2002) *User Involvement and Participation in Social Care: Research Informing Practice*. London: Jessica Kingsley.

McKeown, M. (2009) 'Alliances in action: opportunities and threats to solidarity between workers and service users in health and social care disputes', *Social Theory and Health*, 7: 148–69.

Stickley, T., Stacey, G., Smith, A., Betinis, J., Pollock, K. and Fairbank, S. (2010) 'The practice assessment of student nurses by people who use mental health services', *Nurse Education Today*, 30: 20–5.

SWRB (Social Work Reform Board) (2010) 'Building a safe and confident future: one year on: detailed proposals from the social work reform board'. Department of Education. Available from: www.education.gov.uk/publications/standard/publicationDetail/Page1/DFE-00602-2010 (accessed 17 May 2012).

Taylor, I. (1996) 'Reflective learning, social work education and practice in the 21st century', in N. Gould and I. Taylor (eds), *Reflective Learning for Social Work*. Aldershot: Arena, pp. 184–97.

Tew, J., Gell, C. and Foster, F. (2004) *A Good Practice Guide: Learning from Experience – Involving Service Users and Carers in Mental Health Education and Training*. Nottingham: Mental Health in Higher Education/NIMHE.

Waterson, J. and Morris, K. (2005) 'Training in social work: exploring issues of involving users in teaching on social work degree programmes', *Social Work Education*, 24(6): 653–75.

key concepts in social work practice

51
Sexuality

Julie Bywater

DEFINITION

In the English language sex can be used to categorise biological or anatomical differences between male and female. However, there is no longer a clear binary between male and female, as babies born inter-sexed account for 2–4 per cent of all births and there are ever increasing numbers of transsexuals and people who identify as neither male nor female (Fish, 2006). Transgender is another example of individuals who challenge the sex and gender division of men and women. The term 'gender', as opposed to sex therefore, more appropriately defines what it means to be a woman or a man in terms of their biological, psychological, social and cultural differences (Scott and Jackson, 2006).

Defining sexuality is difficult as it is not a simple, singular, measureable phenomenon (Gott, 2005). Living in a world rich with diversity, there is possibly the same infinite variety of sexual identities and preferences as there are faces. The terms sexual orientation and sexual identity are used to describe the direction of a person's sexual preferences, attractions and desires, which also encompass celibacy and sexual behaviours. For example, ten different sexual orientations/identities have been proposed: heterosexual male/female; lesbian; gay man; bisexual male/female; transvestite female/male and transsexual female/male (Lorber, 1994). But, there are further variations within these categories; for example, some men and women who may define their sexual orientation as heterosexual may be engaging in same sex activities, and in that sense may refer to themselves, for example, as 'men who have sex with men' or 'women who have sex with women' as opposed to defining themselves as gay or bisexual. This has recently been defined as 'queer heterosexuality' (Burdge, 2007). Sexuality has, however, been refined and channelled into specific representation and practices, and all cultures have produced specific mechanisms for regulating sexuality. For example, within social institutions such as religion, the family, and the criminal justice system, these mechanisms can be seen to promote monogamy and abstention from sex outside marriage, to criminalise incest and rape, to define the age of sexual consent, and criminalise sexual activity with children, animals and corpses. As such 'civilisation' and 'civility' are closely linked to sexual behaviour (Weeks, 2003).

KEY POINTS

- Sexuality is embedded in the social. Having an understanding of the meanings attributed to sexualities and how sexualities are constructed in a globalised world involves understanding the reflexivity between social structures and the personal in social and sexual theory (Weeks et al., 2003).
- Heteronormativity: is a globalised construct that serves to promote, regulate and maintain heterosexuality as the normal 'way to be'. These heterosexual norms subsequently construct people who are not heterosexual, or who are not heterosexual in the 'normal' way as 'deviant' or 'abnormal', and can often result in heterosexism.
- Sexual rights: basic human needs such as the desire for contact, intimacy, emotional expression, pleasure, tenderness and love which excludes all forms of sexual coercion, exploitation and abuse, should be the right of all human beings. Sexual rights include: the right for individuals to express their full sexual potential; the rights to sexual autonomy and integrity; to sexual privacy and intimacy; and to sexual equity with freedom from all forms of discrimination regardless of sex, gender, sexual orientation, age, race, social class, religion, or physical and emotional disability (Richardson, 2000; World Association of Sexology, 1999).

DISCUSSION

Essentially, two opposing perspectives have emerged to understand/define sexuality, that is, naturalist and social constructionist. The naturalist perspective defines sex and sexuality in relation to hormones, brain structures, drives and instincts which are seen to be grounded in biological functioning and appear devoid of sexual desires and pleasure (Weeks, 2003). An example of the naturalist definition is, 'sexuality is that which is concerned with the reproduction of the species' (Jackson, 2006: 5). This biological (essentialist/reductionist) perspective of sexuality has been traditionally located within school-based sex education, with images of the female and male reproductive organs to highlight the biological sexual goal of reproduction. Through the focus on genitals, the 'male sex drive' is associated with an erection, and 'active sex' is expressed in terms of penetration, penis in vagina. Within this context sexual identities are moulded into expected patterns of sexual activity: males are 'active' and females are 'receptive' and 'passive'. Although this tradition is now changing, discourses of 'natural' and 'normal', and of 'unnatural', 'wrong', 'bad', and 'abnormal' still provide the foundation for the '(hetero) normative' construct of (hetero)sexuality within society, where heterosexual expression is rewarded, and any non-heterosexual sexual expression is discouraged and/or regulated (Hawkes and Scott, 2005).

In contrast, the social constructionist definition of sexuality is presented as more complex, fluid and involving many facets of sexual behaviour whether the person defines themselves as heterosexual, gay or lesbian, bisexual, transgender or transsexual. In this definition, sexual behaviour and a sense of a sexual identity can include: emotional intimacy; sensuality; romance; sexual fantasies; desires; body image; masturbation; love; sexual activity with the goal of achieving sexual pleasure or orgasm rather than reproduction (mutual masturbation); oral sex; sex using contraception and condoms, etc. (Bremner and Hillin, 1994; Bywater and Jones, 2007). An emphasis within the social constructionist perspective is made on the influence that structural factors have in shaping our sexuality, factors such as: history; society; culture and politics; social relationships; sex and sexual practices; political identity; and spirituality in terms of beliefs, behaviours, relationships and identities. In this way, sexuality is seen to be linked to social powers that are, consequently, linked to social order. The social constructionist approach views all the different aspects of consensual; non-coercive; non-violent; or non-exploitative sexuality as acceptable, valid and equal (Bywater and Jones, 2007; Weeks, 2003).

'Queer' theory

'Queer' theory offers an additional social constructionist perspective on sexuality. Using the term 'queer' is an attempt to positively reclaim the offensive use of the word and is perceived as empowering for oppressed groups who then control the language representing them, 'As a theoretical perspective, it generally refers to any person who transgresses traditional categories of gender and sexuality' (Burdge, 2007: 244), that challenge the dominant sex/gender/sexual identity system (Richardson, 2000). The aims of queer theory are to: reject the terms 'lesbian', 'gay' and 'homosexual' because of the way that they consolidate and support the binary division between heterosexuality and homosexuality, and challenge the 'naturalness' of other binary divisions such as men and women, feminine and masculine that support fixed sex/gender/sexual identity systems, so as, 'to challenge and transform it in such a way that heterosexuality is displaced from its status as privileged, institutionalised norm' (Richardson, 2000: 43).

In addition, transgender and transsexual people are challenging the construction of the 'natural' sex/gender system. Challenges to the naturalist construct of parenting that assert that children require heterosexual parents in order to present appropriate gender role models for children have also been successful. Evidence from research studies comparing children with lesbian mothers and children with heterosexual mothers to explore a variety of areas with children, such as: gender identity (Golombok et al., 1983); personal and social development (Golombok et al., 1997; Tasker and Golombok, 1997); and the development of sexual orientation (Golombok, 2002; Golombok and Tasker, 1996) have found no significant differences or difficulties between the two groups of children in any of the areas researched.

Heterosexuality

Little attention has been given to theorising heterosexuality, and although it is deeply embedded socially and culturally, it is rarely acknowledged or problematised (Scott and Jackson, 2006). Heterosexuality is therefore treated as an unquestionable paradigm. By 'constructing' heterosexuality as 'normal', people who do not define themselves as heterosexual, for example, lesbians, gay men, bisexual men and women and transsexuals, are referred to as 'abnormal' or seen as 'other'.

This can be evidenced by the many privileges that heterosexual people can enjoy, for example: heterosexual people do not need to consider whether or not to tell someone that they meet for the first time about the fact that they are heterosexual; they will not be restricted in certain employments, for example as a clergy; and heterosexual teenagers will not have their sexual orientation dismissed as something that they will probably grow out of (Fish, 2006: 12–13). However, being heterosexual does not have the same experience, privilege or consequences for women as for men.

Gender and heterosexuality

Gender is a social division where men have more power than women, and are able to control women through political, economic, social and physical power (Abbott, 2006). This inequality is present within heterosexual relationships which are, it is argued, based on male dominance and female subordination with heterosexuality providing the linchpin for patriarchy (Scott and Jackson, 2006). Dominant discourses such as 'stud' and 'real man' for men, and 'whore' and 'slapper' for women are examples of how heterosexuality constructs, regulates and controls both men and women's sexual behaviour respectively (Abbott, 2006). For a heterosexual woman, her sexuality is defined and confirmed by her femininity and sexual attractiveness to men (Holland et al., 1998). There are also powerful pressures on men to conform in terms of their (hetero) sexuality and any non-conformity results in personal and social consequences. Being (hetero) sexually active confirms his masculinity. Within patriarchal societies, heterosexual men are the 'norm' and women along with non-heterosexual men and women are 'different', 'them', 'others' (Jackson, 2006).

The dominance of the naturalist (reproductive) perspective has resulted in sexuality being equated with youth, which in turn is equated with being fit, 'perfectly formed' and physically attractive. These are subsequently assumed to be the triggers to sexual desire, and can be seen to apply to all sexual identities and orientations, which are particularly proliferated by the media. Consequently, young men and women and adults with a disability, and older men and women may experience challenges with regard to their sexuality (Bonnie, 2004; Gott, 2005; Shakespeare et al., 1996). For example, the most commonly held assumption in western societies about older people is that they are asexual or sexually unattractive/desirable (Gott, 2005). These assumptions are also dominant in relation to disabled people's sexuality, and particularly impact upon people with a physical impairment (Milligan and Neufeldt, 2001). In addition, many disabled people are treated as eternal children, who need protection from sexual abuse (Shakespeare et al., 1996: 162). The association of sexuality with the young, fit and 'perfectly formed' body has also resulted in people with a visible impairment being regarded as asexual or repulsive if seen being sexual (Bonnie, 2004). There is also the perception that older people and disabled people will not be able to engage in 'normal' penetrative heterosexual sexual intercourse because of their physical frailty or impairment. And although people with a cognitive impairment or mental health problem are perceived as having the ability to 'perform' (hetero)sexually, they are thought to have, 'limited social judgement, and therefore, lack the capacity to engage in responsible sexual relationships' (Milligan and Neufeldt, 2001: 92).

Heteronormativity and heterosexism

Heterosexism is the term that best describes all the levels of prejudice and oppression experienced by non-heterosexuals. A powerful element of heterosexism is heteronormativity. Heteronormativity is the assumption that everyone is heterosexual unless someone indicates to the contrary, for example, incorrectly assuming that all pregnant teenagers are heterosexual. Heteronormativity and heterosexism are perpetuated through personal, cultural and structural levels of society (Thompson, 2006), such as: laws; media; education; religions; public services; cultural values; language; stereotypes; prejudices; and in extreme cases, violence and murder (Scott and Jackson, 2006). However, challenging heterosexual privilege and dominance (heteronormativity and heterosexism) can be very difficult as many heterosexual people deny, ignore or are not even conscious of the privileges they have from being heterosexual.

THE CONCEPT IN SOCIAL WORK PRACTICE

Social work has an important role in positively promoting sexual well-being for all service users (Myers and Milner, 2007). In doing so, practitioners should be aware of their own sexuality and how they have constructed their beliefs about others. If these equate to heteronormative assumptions and heterosexist attitudes, practitioners should address these personal issues to avoid conflict with equality legislation, diversity and human rights (Foreman and Quinlan, 2008), and in order to uphold social work values, principles of anti-discrimination, change and social justice.

Challenging heterosexism and questioning heteronormativity remains a neglected and marginalised issue within social work education and practice today. Whilst there have been significant developments over the last few years to address this, Hicks (2008) highlights the ways in which sexuality has been theorised within social work, and how anti-oppressive practice models and equality legislation have been constructed from an heteronormative perspective. It appears evident then, that within education, theory and practice, social work is implicit in the categorisation of people's sexuality and their subsequent marginalisation/'otherness'. It is imperative for social justice and self-determination that individuals are able to define their sexuality for themselves and this should be a respected and basic value within the social work profession.

Cross references: anti-oppressive practice, equality and diversity, social justice

sexuality

235

SUGGESTED READING

Bywater, J. and Jones, R. (2007) *Sexuality and Social Work*. Exeter: Learning Matters.
Dunk-West, P. and Hafford-Letchfield, T. (eds) (2011) *Sexual Identities and Sexuality in Social Work*. Farnham: Ashgate Publishing Ltd.

REFERENCES

Abbott, P. (2006) 'Gender', in G. Payne (ed.), *Social Divisions*, 2nd edn. Basingstoke and New York: Palgrave Macmillan, pp. 65–101.

Bonnie, S. (2004) 'Disabled people, disability and sexuality', in J. Swaine, S. French, C. Barnes and C. Thomas (eds), *Disabling Barriers-Enabling Environments*. London: Sage.

Bremner, J. and Hillin, A. (1994) *Sexuality, Young People and Care*. Lyme Regis: Russell House Publishing.

Burdge, B.J. (2007) 'Bending gender, ending gender: theoretical foundations for social work practice with transgender communities', *Social Work*, 52(3): 243–50.

Bywater, J. and Jones, R. (2007) *Sexuality and Social Work*. Exeter: Learning Matters.

Fish, J. (2006) *Heterosexism in Health and Social Care*. Basingstoke and New York: Palgrave Macmillan.

Foreman, M. and Quinlan, M. (2008) 'Increasing social work students' awareness of heterosexism and homophobia – a partnership between a community gay health project and a school of social work', *Journal of Social Work Education*, 27(2): 152–8.

Golombok, S. (2002) 'Adoption by lesbian couples: is it in the best interests of the child?', *British Medical Journal*, 234: 1407–8.

Golombok, S. and Tasker, F. (1996) 'Do parents influence the sexual orientation of their children?', *Developmental Psychology*, 32(1): 3–11.

Golombok, S., Spencer, A. and Rutter, M. (1983) 'Children in lesbian and single-parent households: psychosexual and psychiatric appraisal', *Journal of Child Psychology and Psychiatry*, 24(4): 551–72.

Golombok, S., Tasker, F. and Murray, C. (1997) 'Children raised in fatherless families from infancy: family relationships and the socio-emotional development of children of lesbian and single heterosexual mothers', *Journal of Child Psychology and Psychiatry*, 38(7): 783–91.

Gott, M. (2005) *Sexuality, Sexual Health and Ageing*. Maidenhead and New York: OUP/McGraw-Hill Education.

Hawkes, G. and Scott, J. (2005) 'Sex and society', in G. Hawkes and J. Scott (eds), *Perspectives in Human Sexuality*. Melbourne/Oxford: Oxford University Press, pp. 3–19.

Hicks, S. (2008) 'Thinking through sexuality', *Journal of Social Work*, 8(1): 65–82.

Holland, J., Ramazanoglu, C., Sharpe, S. and Thompson, R. (1998) *The Male in the Head: Young People, Heterosexuality and Power*. London: Tufnell Press.

Jackson, S. (2006) 'Heterosexuality, sexuality and gender: rethinking the intersections', in D. Richardson, J. McLaughlin and M.E. Casey (eds), *Intersections Between Feminist and Queer Theory*. Basingstoke and New York: Palgrave Macmillan, pp.38–58.

Lorber, J. (1994) *Paradoxes of Gender*. New Haven, CT: Yale University Press.

Milligan, M.S. and Neufeldt, A.H. (2001) 'The myth of asexuality: a survey of social and empirical evidence', *Sexuality and Disability*, 19(2): 91–109.

Myers, S. and Milner, J. (2007) *Sexual Issues in Social Work*. Bristol: Policy Press.

Richardson, D. (2000) *Re-Thinking Sexuality*. London: Sage.

Scott, S. and Jackson, S. (2006) 'Sexuality', in G. Payne (ed.), *Social Divisions*, 2nd edn. Basingstoke/New York: Palgrave Macmillan, pp. 233–50.

Shakespeare, T., Gillespie-Sells, K. and Davies, D. (1996) *The Sexual Politics of Disability: Untold Desires*. London: Cassell.

Tasker, F.L. and Golombok, S. (1997) *Growing Up in a Lesbian Family: Effects on Child Development*. New York: Guilford.

Thompson, N. (2006) *Anti-Discriminatory Practice*, 4th edn. Basingstoke: Palgrave Macmillan.

Weeks, J. (2003) *Sexuality*, 2nd edn. London: Routledge.

Weeks, J., Holland, J. and Waites, M. (eds) (2003) *Sexualities and Society: A Reader*. Cambridge: Polity Press.

World Association of Sexology (1999) 'Declaration of sexual rights'. World Congress of Sexology, 26 August 1999, Hong Kong. Available from: www.sexology.it/declaration_sexual_rights.html (accessed 17 May 2012).

52

Social Exclusion

Anne Keeler

DEFINITION

The term social exclusion originated in France in the 1970s and was used to describe those members of society not covered by the social security system. French social theorists recognised that the experience of multiple deprivations often resulted in poor social integration, with people feeling excluded and unable to participate in society (Barry and Hallet, 1998).

The term has been utilised by other European countries, with the UK Labour Party using the concept to underpin their social policies during the mid-1990s. At the time of New Labour's election in 1997, they created the Social Exclusion Unit (SEU) whose primary task was to develop policies to eradicate social exclusion and limit its effect in society (Taket et al., 2009).

Walker and Walker defined social exclusion as: 'the dynamic process of being shut out . . . from any of the social, economic, political and cultural systems which determine the social integration of a person in society' (1997, cited in Taket et al., 2009: 7). From this we can immediately see its relevance to social work practice as social work and discussions about social exclusion are interested in enabling individuals, groups and communities to participate in society as fully as possible.

A more developed definition by Pierson sees social exclusion as:

> . . . a process over time that deprives individuals and families, groups and neighbourhoods of the resources required for participation in the social, economic and political activity of society as a whole. This process is primarily a consequence of poverty and low income, but other factors such as discrimination, low educational attainment and depleted environments also underpin it. Through this process people are cut off for a significant period in their lives from institutions and services, social networks and developmental opportunities that the great majority of a society enjoys. (2010: 12)

This is particularly helpful to social work as it recognises the multi-faceted nature of social exclusion; not just who it affects or how it affects them but the consequences of being excluded.

KEY POINTS

* Social exclusion incorporates multiple disadvantages including: low income (poverty); unemployment; poor housing; lack of citizenship rights; and education.

social exclusion

- Debates on social cohesion see social exclusion as a personal failure. The existence of a 'moral underclass' that is dependent on welfare services and resistant to changing their circumstances supports this argument and is rooted in right-wing ideology and policy.
- Debates on social justice focus on people's rights to become full citizens. Individuals are encouraged to participate in society through full use of citizenship rights (civil, political and social). However, it is the individual's experience of diversity and disadvantage that often prevents them from becoming full citizens.
- Discussion in recent years has been more on social inclusion and developing strategies that enable people to fully participate in society. Social work aims to support people to feel included within society.

DISCUSSION

Debates about social exclusion include poverty, the underclass and social inclusion. The concept of poverty is based on 19th-century studies that focused on income poverty; a situation whereby a person does not have sufficient income to meet their basic needs. Despite attempts to address welfare issues in society, studies conducted in the 1970s and 1980s confirmed that poverty still existed. However, this was now seen as relative poverty rather than absolute poverty (Townsend, 1979, cited in Barry and Hallett, 1998).

The concept of the underclass stems from the United States and describes those people not in work and unlikely to seek work. This idea has two conflicting arguments; those who believe the underclass to be immoral and those who see them as being excluded because of structural difficulties.

Social inclusion has been defined as 'the attempt to reintegrate or to increase the participation of, marginalised groups within mainstream society' (Barry and Hallett, 1998: 5). The way to integrate people is through paid work, argue politicians, yet this may not on its own be sufficient. Paid employment may not be the most relevant way of including marginalised groups. There is an implied expectation that integration leads to conformity.

Levitas (2000) identified three key discourses central to the debate around social exclusion:

a A *redistributionist discourse* is concerned with the existence of inequality and poverty in society. Townsend (1979, cited in Barry and Hallett, 1998) studied poverty and introduced the concept of relative poverty; do people have sufficient resources to participate in ordinary life relative to what was expected from other members of society.

Taxation, benefits and services can redistribute wealth in society, thus reducing inequality and poverty. Policies that aim to redistribute wealth and income focus on improved social rights whilst recognising that a lack of social and economic power leads to structural inequality.

b A *moral underclass discourse* reflects views that the unacceptable attitudes and behaviours of individuals and groups in society have a direct influence on their experience of exclusion. Some decisions made by individuals and groups may reinforce or compound their experience of being marginalised.

Etzioni (1993, cited in Sheppard, 2006) believed that a shared moral commitment was an essential part of a good society and that an absence of these shared values would lead to 'social anarchy'. However, Etzioni was not necessarily arguing that these values needed to be based on traditional gender roles (Etzioni,1993, cited in Sheppard, 2006). To combat social exclusion at this level, it is important to deal with personal values as well as at a societal level.

c A *social integrationist discourse* views employment in paid work and participation in the labour market as key elements of a functioning society.

Tackling social exclusion can be seen as a political activity with social policies created to address social problems in society. These policies have a preventative objective; to reduce the likelihood of exclusion. Yet, it could be argued that social work activity in recent years has become reactive; its statutory functions of protection, safeguarding and managing risk dominating social work practice.

THE CONCEPT IN SOCIAL WORK PRACTICE

Social work is involved with those who are socially excluded in society; this includes those who are in poverty, unemployed or experiencing multiple disadvantages. Social work can be seen to provide resources which may increase people's opportunity for social inclusion. However, it could be argued that exclusion limits choice for people and restricts their opportunity for growth and change (Sheppard, 2006). Sheppard argues that social work operates between those that are marginalised and mainstream society which gives it a unique role.

However, Sheppard (2006) suggests that by the very nature of its statutory function, social work adds to the experience of exclusion by labelling and marginalising people. Social work acknowledges and takes account of social divisions within society but is not in a position to eradicate exclusion at this level. It is an ethical dilemma for social workers to balance these competing roles and tasks. This statutory and regulatory function may lead to coercion which in turn prevents people from making choices and participating on an equal basis in society. This authoritative role can lead to coercive behaviour which restricts people's actions and their ability to self-determine. Yet the GSCC Code of Practice (2002) encourages social workers to promote choice and empower individuals and groups.

Some excluded groups suggest that the debate about social exclusion does not include their perspective or analysis of the concept. This is not an inclusive debate and is seen as a devaluing concept with which some groups do not want to be associated. They argue that the concept of social exclusion defines people as deviant and that policies designed to tackle exclusion only reinforce the experience (Beresford and Wilson, 1998, cited in Barry and Hallett, 1998).

We may take Davies' (Sheppard, 2006) view that social work has a maintenance function in society in which the individual or family are able to become self-sufficient and live in a way that is accepted by society. Social workers aim to manage these excessive behaviours so that society is able to run smoothly. Social workers are torn between supporting those who are dependent on the state or encouraging self-sufficiency and independence from the welfare state. This is often described as empowerment; enabling service users to make choices and participate in society as fully as possible. However, in their attempts to be non-political, social workers are unable to challenge service users who may be seen by the rest of society to hold unacceptable values.

Successive governments' social policies are promoting employment as the solution to address exclusion. Social workers, through empowerment and challenging disadvantage, may seek to encourage service users to develop skills that make them more employable. However, is this for the benefit of the individual or society? It could support arguments for both social cohesion and social justice. On one level, the ultimate aim is for social inclusion or integration of those excluded. Encouraging work, strengthening networks and promoting citizenship are all ways to tackle social exclusion.

Underpinning social work practice is the concept of a strong value base which is reflected in the professional code of practice (GSCC, 2002). Biesteks' values (Biestek, 1961, cited in Pierson, 2010) emphasised the worker's relationship with individuals and formed the basis of casework. There is no coherent and agreed set of values that social work agrees on, rather different ideas which share some common themes. Clark (2000, cited in Pierson, 2010) summarises these as: recognising that everyone is of equal value; that people are entitled to equal treatment (justice); that everyone is entitled to their own beliefs; and that it is important to support the idea of community. Working with people who experience poverty is a central part of the social work task, and our beliefs about why this happens and how to help people make changes to overcome poverty are key aspects of social work. A commitment to equal opportunity enables workers to move away from an individualised response to one which recognises that barriers exist within society.

Tackling social exclusion is not just a social work task; the New Labour government believed this was a central aim of social policy. Yet there are things that social workers can do to promote social inclusion and tackle exclusion. Recognising social exclusion and the factors affecting an individual or family is the first step. Other steps are: seeking ways to maximise income; helping to develop a meaningful social network; working in partnership with other agencies and professionals; ensuring that people are enabled to fully participate in decision making as much as they are able to; and drawing on the strengths within the service user's neighbourhood (Pierson, 2010). Pierson called these the building blocks for tackling social exclusion. These are designed to help and support individuals and families yet move away from the personalised approach that can disempower and create dependency.

On the other hand, Jordan (2000: 110) felt that those experiencing multiple disadvantages lack choice and are 'shaped and constrained by the government's perception of their needs' so that social inclusion becomes a limited option. Whether we see social exclusion as a personal failing or as a structural issue there will always be those that argue that social work has a role to play in tackling inequality and promoting integration into society for individuals, families, groups and communities. However, we perhaps need to listen to those that are seen as socially excluded about the best way forward.

Cross references: empowerment, the political context of social work, social justice

SUGGESTED READING

Pierson, J. (2010) *Tackling Social Exclusion*, 2nd edn. Abingdon: Routledge.
Sheppard, M. (2006) *Social Work and Social Exclusion*. Aldershot: Ashgate.

REFERENCES

Barry, M. and Hallett, C. (eds) (1998) *Social Exclusion and Social Work*. Lyme Regis: Russell House.
GSCC (2002) *Code of Practice*. London: GSCC.
Jordan, B. (2000) *Social Work and the Third Way*. London: Sage.
Levitas, R. (2000) *The Inclusive Society? Social Exclusion and New Labour*. Basingstoke: Palgrave Macmillan.
Pierson, J. (2010) *Tackling Social Exclusion*, 2nd edn. Abingdon: Routledge.
Sheppard, M. (2006) *Social Work and Social Exclusion*. Aldershot: Ashgate.
Taket, A., Crisp, B., Nevill, A., Lamaro, G., Graham, M. and Barter-Godfrey, S. (2009) *Theorising Social Exclusion*. London: Routledge.

53

Social Justice

Bill Jordan

DEFINITION

As a value in social work's professional ethical code (BASW, 2002), social justice is rather different from the others (human dignity and worth, service to humanity, integrity and competence). Whereas those others are concerned with the intrinsic value of individuals, the ethics of practice, honesty and proficiency, social justice is about the relations between members of a society, the distribution of resources, and access to the protections of citizenship.

Whereas the other values involve actions which are under the direct control of practitioners, social justice concerns matters which are ultimately determined by political decisions and economic processes. While social justice is accepted as a human right, its interpretation is strongly contested. The concept features prominently in the social democratic political tradition, with social security schemes and public services for health, education, housing and social care as its main expressions, and equal rights as one of its chief goals. However, the philosopher most associated with the rival neo-liberal tradition, Friedrich Hayek (1976) described social justice as a 'mirage' which was also morally objectionable, because it involved the use of state power to impose an arbitrary pattern on society.

Social justice and injustice refer to ways in which members of a society treat each other, in families, communities and the polity as a whole. Usually these relationships are built into institutions and cultures, as in the subordination of women, the exclusion of disabled people, unequal access to resources, or the dominance of a ruling class (Jordan, 1990). These organised and habitual injustices are difficult to change, because they require shifts in consciousness, collective action and legal reform. The social work approach which attempts to embrace all these elements is called 'anti-oppressive practice' (Dominelli, 2004). It aims to include all citizens in roles and relationships of fairness, in which they receive what is due to them, and have the rights and responsibilities appropriate for their abilities and needs.

KEY POINTS

- Although social justice is ultimately the province of governments and courts, social workers are often operating at key points in social relationships, where injustices are most acutely experienced and implemented.
- Consequently, even when social workers cannot directly influence law and policy, they are likely to be complicit in social injustice unless they are aware of the wider significance of their practice.
- Social injustice concerns relationships of intimacy, kinship, community and political membership, involving the distribution of power and resources, so practice relevant to it involves several levels of awareness and action.
- To be effective, social workers need to be linked with ideas and movements outside their profession.

DISCUSSION

The literature informing debates about social justice can be traced to the Ancient Greek philosophers, and might indeed be regarded as a series of footnotes to them. One tradition, derived from Plato, seeks to define the abstract moral principles according to which society's institutions should be established, and in this way to lay down a blueprint for the just political system. The most influential example of this approach in modern times is the work of John Rawls (1971).

In recent years, Rawls' approach has been criticised from the standpoint of the tradition of Aristotle, in which the analysis of justice starts from the actual ways in which people live their lives, and the ways they create and distribute value in the various spheres in which they interact, from family to sport, from culture to politics (Sandel, 2009). It is necessary to identify specific injustices and reduce them by a process of challenge and negotiation, taking account of the cultures in which they have evolved and the purposes they have served (Sen, 2009). These latter approaches seem closer to what is required of and realistic for social workers.

Practitioners have direct contact with those most vulnerable to injustice, including groups who are largely invisible to the public and ignored (or treated with hostility) by the media. They are therefore in a position to inform debates about social justice, as well as acting to prevent unjust treatment by protesting against specific instances or advocating for those least able to defend themselves or implement their claims on others. In order to identify injustices, they need not only to be aware of current debates and issues, but also to develop a capacity for allowing themselves to become aware of their own complicity in unfairness, or worse – neglect, oppression or exclusion of people or points of view – in their everyday work.

One of the ironies of the emergence of anti-oppressive practice in the 1980s, drawing on arguments from social justice, was that it occurred when neo-liberal opponents of the politics of social justice were in the ascendant. Margaret Thatcher and Ronald Reagan were influenced by Hayek and his associates in their advocacy of free markets; but this was also the period when radicals such as Bailey and Brake (1976) and Statham (1978) began to influence social work education and training. Because the women's and anti-racist movements were emerging as important influences on organisational cultures at that time, it was these elements in the anti-oppressive approach which were most influential.

By contrast, the social democratic framework of welfare states was under severe strain at this time, as organised labour lost its dominant position in the governments of the affluent countries. As billions of new workers were drawn into industrial production in South and East Asia and Latin America, and Soviet socialism collapsed, global capital became the dominant economic power, and the incomes and job security of most citizens in these societies were threatened. Poverty and unemployment contributed to new phenomena of exclusion, and to the growth of whole districts with concentrations of social problems.

In most countries of Europe, North America and Australasia, social workers became involved in the practice of 'welfare discipline' (Schram, 2006) – the enforcement of work conditions around claims for means-tested benefits – or the rationing of social care, as governments redefined social justice in terms of self-responsibility in markets, and restricted state assistance to those unable to provide for themselves. All of these tendencies have been re-enforced by the economic crash of 2008–9.

THE CONCEPT IN SOCIAL WORK PRACTICE

If the basis for a practice derived from principles of social justice was originally found in the social democratic institutions of welfare states, then the economic weakness of labour in the affluent countries means that practitioners are going to have to look elsewhere for their inspiration and support. On the one hand, cuts in public services signal that vulnerable people cannot always rely on this source for their well-being or their empowerment, and the encroachment of business principles into social care further threatens the feasibility of professional commitment to this value.

Two alternatives now present themselves as possible emerging bases for a new practice of social justice.

The first of these is the idea that a better foundation for this value might be found in civil society and the associative principle, rather than either the state or the market. The philosopher and social theorist Phillip Blond (2010) argues that groups and communities have been subverted in their capacities to supply identity, respect and the sense of belonging, as much by the rise in the power of big business as by that of government and its agencies.

Accordingly he recommends a major transfer of power and resources to co-operatives, community groups, social enterprises and local authorities, as self-governing entities able to supply income streams and employment to their members. He claims that this would enable disadvantaged people to participate as full members of society, and supply a new version of social justice.

Some of his ideas have been taken up by David Cameron (2009), and were reflected in the Conservative Party's (2010) election manifesto, with its programme for the 'Big Society' (Norman, 2010). Citizenship would be expressed through collective action rather than individual self-realisation, and each locality would have an independent 'community organiser' to promote such participation. Social work staff would be encouraged to form co-operatives to take over aspects of service provision.

Independently of this, similar ideas have found expression through the organisation Participle Ltd (2011), which has pioneered social care projects such as the Southwark Circle, combining a membership system of skills exchanges with the provision of care services and volunteer support. Here too the intention has been to revive civil society through forms of community organisation which break down distinctions between service users, paid staff and unpaid workers.

However, the UK coalition government's cuts in public spending have not been matched by the kinds of redistribution recommended by Blond, arousing suspicions that the Big Society slogan is a cover for a further fragmentation of the social services. Unless resources go to those on the margins of society, such initiatives will merely consolidate the dominance of a global plutocratic elite.

The second alternative basis for social justice lies in the emergence of a new politics of resistance by the generation who are reaching adulthood in the aftermath of the crash. Guy Standing (2011) argues that young people are already exposed to far more powerful forces driving down their incomes, their security of employment and their prospects for developing careers with reliable pathways for professional development, incremental salary increases and pension entitlements. This 'precariat' is recognisable across the world, not only in high rates of youth unemployment but also in numbers of short term and part-time.

Not only was the 'Arab Spring' a manifestation of the frustration and idealism of this new generation, so also are the protests in Greece and Spain by young people in a similar situation. Standing (2011) suggests that demands for a universal basic income, supplying a secure foundation for the lives of all members of society, may (and should) supplant traditional social democratic politics, and allow the reconstruction of a set of institutions which will achieve social justice.

As yet there is no clear model of the forms which practice might take under any such development, but presumably in this version professional staff would be more accountable to service users and the wider community than at present.

In general terms, practitioners who take social justice seriously will want to look out for opportunities to find out more about social movements for emancipation, for democratic participation and for challenging oppression and exclusion. They will make themselves more open to ideas about how to help service users influence and participate in planning and providing services, and they will advocate on behalf of (or better still alongside) all those denied fair, open and equal treatment by authorities of all kinds.

Cross references: advocacy, anti-oppressive practice, empowerment, social exclusion

SUGGESTED READING

Dominelli, L. (2004) *Social Work: Theory and Practice for a Changing Profession*. Cambridge: Polity.
Fook, J., Ryan, M. and Hawkins, L. (2000) *Professional Expertise: Practice, Theory and Education for Working in Uncertainty*. London: Whiting and Birch.

REFERENCES

BASW (2002) *The Code of Ethics for Social Work*. Birmingham: BASW.
Bailey, R. and Brake, M. (eds) (1976) *Radical Social Work and Practice*. London: Edward Arnold.
Blond, P. (2010) *Red Tory: How Left and Right Broke Britain and How We Can Fix It*. London: Faber and Faber.
Cameron, D. (2009) 'The big society'. Hugo Young Memorial Lecture, London, 29 November.
Conservative Party (2010) *Invitation to Join the Government of Great Britain*. London: The Conservative Party.
Dominelli, L. (2004) *Social Work: Theory and Practice for a Changing Profession*. Cambridge: Polity.
Hayek, F.A. (1976) *The Mirage of Social Justice*. London: Institute of Economic Affairs.
Jordan, B. (1990) *Social Work in an Unjust Society*. Hemel Hempstead: Harvester Wheatsheaf.
Norman, J. (2010) *The Big Society: The Anatomy of the New Politics*. Buckingham: Buckingham University Press.
Participle Ltd. (2011) 'The Southwark Circle'. Available from: www.participle.net/projects/view/5/101 (accessed 17 May 2012).
Rawls, J. (1971) *A Theory of Justice*. Oxford: Clarendon Press.
Sandel, M. (2009) *Justice: What's the Right Thing to Do?* London: Allen Lane.
Schram, S. (2006) *Welfare Discipline: Discourse, Governance, Globalization*. Philadelphia, PA: Temple University Press.
Sen, A. (2009) *The Idea of Justice*. London: Allen Lane.
Standing, G. (2011) *The Precariat: The New Dangerous Class*. London: Bloomsbury Academic.
Statham, D. (1978) *Radicals in Social Work*. London: Routledge and Kegan Paul.

Malcolm Payne

DEFINITION

Social work is a range of practices associated with a profession (that is, a recognised occupational group) and informed by a discipline (that is, an organised body of knowledge, research, skill and values). Social work practice in any particular nation is adapted to conform with a legal, political, and social mandate in that country to provide services mostly to people considered to need help to manage deprivation, poverty and unfortunate life circumstances. Social work contributes to 'social care', a term used in the UK to refer to services led by social work disciplines; other countries call these 'social services'. Social care is in turn part of a broader range of services that have the objective of improving well-being, including education, healthcare, housing and social security.

The nature of social work practices defines social work in a more complex way. Social work practitioners work through interpersonal relationships with individuals needing help, their families and carers – and with colleagues, professionals and staff in other occupational groups providing related services. The practice is informed by social science disciplines, particularly psychology, social policy and sociology, used in combination. Social work aims to enhance the capacity and resilience of people in social relationships and social institutions to achieve personal goals and to reduce and manage the impact of problems that reduce their quality of life. More broadly, it aspires to achieve improvements in society through advocacy for social change, facilitating wide engagement in planning and management of social provision, particularly of those excluded from participation, and stimulating and supporting economic and social transformation that promotes human rights.

KEY POINTS

The previous two paragraphs cover social work as practices, an occupational group or profession and an intellectual discipline and describe:

- The source of the profession's mandate to exist and operate: Because the mandate originates from public concern, expressed through political decisions leading to a legal framework that expresses social objectives, social work will obviously be different in different countries. Scottish social work will vary from

English social work because the law and the framework are different. Social work in Surrey will vary from social work in Liverpool because the framework and context are different.

- Social objectives identifying the main social issues that social work tackles: Because these are generalised, they apply to many different countries. The nature of social work, the profession and discipline defines the characteristics of the service, social care or social services, in which it is the main profession.
- The activities themselves are interpersonal and worked out in interaction with related occupational groups; social work is not a stand-alone occupation.
- The main intellectual disciplines that contribute to social work; how they are combined says a bit more about the nature of social work.
- The main social objectives of social work set the direction and focus of these activities.

DISCUSSION

A series of statements like this, in trying to convey the complexity of a social entity, make the definition cumbersome. It is not succinct, as you might find in a dictionary. Dictionary definitions of social work '. . . present social work as official, mainly state, help with personal problems with deprived, aged or disabled groups, undertaken mainly by trained personnel with the aim of social betterment. They do not incorporate definitions related to radical social change or community work' (Payne, 2009). Therefore, they do not represent the aspirations of the 'International Definition of Social Work' produced at the beginning of the 21st century by various representative bodies of social workers:

> The social work profession promotes social change, problem solving in human relationships and the empowerment and liberation of people to enhance well-being. Utilising theories of human behaviour and social systems, social work intervenes at the points where people interact with their environments. Principles of human rights and social justice are fundamental to social work. (IFSW, 2000)

The IFSW definition focuses on social work's social objectives and its disciplinary sources and values. By neglecting the varying political, legal and social mandates of social work in different nations around the world, it sweeps the aims of social work within differing national welfare systems into its three broad social objectives. Another limitation is the generalised statement that social work methods involve intervening at the point of human interaction with the environment; the nature of that intervention, that interaction and that environment are unclear.

People have attempted definitions of social work throughout the history of its existence (Payne, 2005: Chapter 2). These demonstrate the variety of ways of constructing a definition of a complex social phenomenon such as social work. You can try to distil an essence or quality of the phenomenon, claiming that to be social work a practice must contain this essence or quality. For example, you could emphasise that social work is always carried out through interpersonal relationships with the aim of achieving improved social solidarity in society. Alternatively, you can try to define boundaries to it, identifying practices that are not included in social work. For example, you could say that social workers do not provide medical treatment, nursing care or physiotherapy and they do not educate or imprison their clients. A third alternative is to list a number of characteristics of social work, and claim a practice that incorporates most or all of these is certainly social work, while a practice that contains only a few is less likely to be social work. Therefore, as more of the characteristics mount up, we are more likely to identify an activity as social work. That reflects the reality that different professions with similar functions operate in a field of work, and that a particular profession is defined by the balance of roles and responsibilities that its practitioners take up, rather than some absolute boundary.

Another possibility is to use a process definition of a profession. This approach claims that social work is what is done by people who have gone through a defined process of personal development, education and socialisation. The British system for registering social workers works like this: its procedure requires registered practitioners to have completed a course that includes appropriate consideration of the role and nature of social work (Payne, 2011). Part of the guidance influencing the design of courses acknowledges that the nature of social work is contested and proposes that the contested views must be reviewed as part of the course (QAA, 2008). This means that qualifying social workers should be aware of the multifarious nature of activities and social institutions that contribute to how we understand the nature of social work. An alternative, rather similar, approach taken by Horner (2003), is to study the mandate for social work and the range of roles that social workers undertake in a particular country, the UK. This builds up a broad picture of the nature of social work, without simplifying that picture into a brief definition.

Defining social work therefore requires caution: an adequate definition must balance many factors. An implication of this complexity is that any definition is not for all time: it will shift as social expectations and contexts change.

THE CONCEPT IN SOCIAL WORK PRACTICE

Social work implemented in practice

Currently, however, the balancing of the various factors that define social work has produced four main types of social work around the world:

Social work: a practice where interpersonal skills are used with individuals, families and small groups to resolve interpersonal and social relationship problems. An example of social work is clinical social work in healthcare settings or social work in schools. Social work practice is strong in the US and contributes to social assistance and social care in developed countries. It may be available for particular services in less developed countries, for example, adoption, healthcare or to respond to social dislocation.

Social assistance, social care: services where social work disciplines lead the provision of services that help resolve social problems. This may include adult and child safeguarding, delivery of packages of social care services or access to care homes where people need help with everyday living. In some countries, social work is involved in providing social security, welfare services to school pupils, youth work and housing welfare. Social assistance and social care is an important part of social provision in most developed countries, where the state usually accepts wide responsibility for social provision.

Social pedagogy, social education, cultural education: social work disciplines that focus on the education and personal development of people who are disadvantaged or oppressed by social injustice. In some countries, social pedagogy works mainly with young people and primarily in group care settings such as residential, day and after-school care. Social pedagogy and similar practice is particularly strong in mainland Europe.

Social development: practice assisting people affected by economic development to come together in groups to identify and take action on issues of shared concern to them to enhance social solidarity and resilience in responding to social change. Most social development takes place in under-developed countries or regions.

Another way of understanding the different patterns of social work is by looking at theories of social work practice, which prescribe common approaches to social work practice. Some examples are as follows.

Psychodynamic practice focuses on correcting problematic psychological and emotional reactions to life.

Cognitive-behavioural practice focuses on modifying ways of thinking or behaving that are preventing an individual or group from functioning well in their social environment.

Task-centred practice focuses on helping people to specify problems in their lives and work out and implement programmes of activities that will enable them to overcome these problems.

Systems practice focuses on the interaction of social and personal factors in people's lives, helping people to adapt their social environment and their reactions to it so that they can live more harmoniously.

Humanistic practice focuses on developing people's understanding and awareness of their social identity in relation to others, so that they can increase their capacity to manage problems and meet their aspirations in life.

Critical practice, incorporating empowerment, anti-discrimination and feminist perspectives, focuses on identifying how patterns of social relationships and the role of social institutions form barriers to meeting their needs and then overcoming the difficulties that these barriers present to them.

All these descriptions of social work approaches are recognisably social work, in that they are concerned with how the social interacts with the personal. However, the different focuses draw out the range of possible factors that social work seeks to deal with. The earlier ones stress a search for problems or difficulties for individuals, while later ones emphasise adaptation, aspiration or personal development and place the source of barriers in society rather than the individual. Some approaches look at emotional and psychological reactions, or thinking and behaviour, while others look at adaptation, identity and patterns of relationships or institutional impacts on people's lives. These examples of different approaches to social work show how it balances the internal with the external, the psychological with the social, the positives and the negatives in people's lives.

Cross references: history of social work, international social work, the political context of social work, theory and social work

SUGGESTED READING

Horner, N. (2003) *What is Social Work? Context and Perspectives*. Exeter: Learning Matters.
Payne, M. (2005) *What is Professional Social Work?*, 2nd edn. Bristol: Policy Press.

REFERENCES

Horner, N. (2003) *What is Social Work? Context and Perspectives*. Exeter: Learning Matters.
IFSW (International Federation of Social Workers) (2000) 'International definition of social work'. Available from: http://ifsw.org/resources/definition-of-social-work (accessed 17 May 2012).
Payne, M. (2005) *What is Professional Social Work?*, 2nd edn. Bristol: Policy Press.
Payne, M. (2009) 'Dictionary definitions of social work'. Available from: www.scribd.com/doc/14979297/Dictionary-Definitions-of-Social-Work (accessed 22 June 2011).
Payne, M. (2011) 'Social work regulation in the United Kingdom', in A.A. Bibus and N. Boutté-Queen (eds), *Regulating Social Work: A Primer on Licensing Practice*. Chicago, IL: Lyceum, pp. 45–59.
QAA (2008) 'Social work. Mansfield: the quality assurance agency for higher education'. Available from: www.qaa.ac.uk/academicinfrastructure/benchmark/statements/socialwork08.pdf (accessed 22 June 2011).

55
Social Work in Healthcare Settings

Kate Bebe

DEFINITION

In order to define social work in healthcare settings it is necessary to consider briefly the history behind the need for health and social care professionals to work together.

The need for collaboration between social workers and healthcare teams was identified as long ago as 1959 (HMSO, 1959). Furthermore, the World Health

Organization (WHO), suggested in 1978 that different professionals should learn together the skills needed for working together to meet the needs of an individual (WHO, 1978: Vol. 1).

Social workers can be involved within the assessment, planning and discharge of vulnerable children and adults from a variety of healthcare settings. These can include liaison psychiatry, Child and Adolescent Mental Health Services (CAMHS), hospital social work for children and adults, mental health wards and learning disability teams.

This chapter aims to provide an insight into the complexity of hospital discharges and the social worker's role within the process. It will examine the practicalities of hospital discharge within the context of older people, the knowledge and skills required and the competing demands of the hospital environment.

KEY POINTS

- Working with healthcare professionals within hospital settings: understanding the system and acknowledging different priorities.
- When is someone ready for discharge? Understanding different definitions of readiness.
- Legislation, policy and reducing delayed discharge: an insight into the complexity of hospital social work.

DISCUSSION

Working with healthcare professionals within hospital settings

Tope and Thomas (2007) cite 59 reports produced by the Department of Health between 1920 and 2000, 24 of these reports date from the mid-1990s to 2000 and by the mid-1990s 'nearly every Department of Health publication has called for the health and social care workforce to overcome their reticence and put the needs of the patient, and their families first' (Tope and Thomas, 2007: 31).

A lack of communication between different agencies and professionals has been the main focus, highlighting a failure of collaborative inter-professional working. Terminology and abbreviations add to communication difficulties and it is necessary for any social worker to gain some knowledge regarding healthcare abbreviations and medical diagnoses. An understanding of continuing healthcare, palliative care and intermediate care are also essential.

A social worker assigned to hospital discharge needs to work in collaboration with a number of different professionals who all play their individual role within the assessment and discharge of a service user. These will include: consultants; senior house officers, (doctors); house officers; ward clerk; allied health professionals; discharge liaison; rapid response; intermediate care; district nurses; GP; palliative care team; community services; pharmacist; and transport.

It is necessary to understand the differing roles of professionals and the competing demands of the hospital discharge system. For example, Reed et al. note that medical staff 'feel their role is mainly making discharge decisions, (once someone is medically fit for discharge), and deciding the level of care required from a medical point of view' (Reed and Morgan, 1999, cited in Glasby, 2003: 79). Understandably, there is a need for beds to be made available and targets to be met, such as, Clinical Quality Indicators (DH, 2010) or the 18-week standard (DH, 2009). Assessments of need are undertaken at a fast pace within hospital settings; competing demand for beds and the capacity of the hospital all play a part in how fast the process needs to be.

The social workers' perspective, however, is to capture an holistic view, taking into account a person's physical, social, medical, psychosocial, functional and environmental needs. The term 'medically fit', does not necessarily take into account the time a person might need to come to terms with an illness or disability. When older people a   re admitted to hospital it is usually in situations of a crisis due to the sudden onset of an illness, a fall in the home, or stroke. Consequences of traumatic events can result in a lack of confidence and loss of independence.

Where disputes occur, it is the social worker's role to promote the rights of the service user whether the dispute is with the service user's family or hospital staff; the service user's choice is paramount. However, we also need to ensure that our inter-professional work is underpinned with respect, confidence, engagement, willingness to negotiate and a readiness to share.

When is person ready for discharge?

Simple discharges relate to at least 80 per cent of patients who will usually be discharged to their own home or place of residence. The person will have simple ongoing care needs that do not require complex planning and delivery. They no longer require acute care and can be discharged directly from Accident and Emergency, ward areas or assessment units (DH, 2004).

However, many older people have complex needs. The person may still be discharged to their own home, a carer's home, to intermediate care or to a nursing or residential care home. The person will have complex ongoing health and social care needs which require detailed assessment, planning, and delivery by the multi-professional team. Their length of stay in hospital is more difficult to predict. The terms 'clinical stability' and 'medical stability' mean the same thing. The person can be defined as clinically or medically stable when tests such as bloods and investigations are considered to be within the normal range for the person. However, 'fit for discharge' has a different meaning. People should not be discharged from hospital unless they are medically fit and have been formally discharged by a named doctor. Every hospital has a hospital discharge policy which should include details of how the hospital will arrange the discharge.

A person is 'fit for discharge' when physiological, social, functional, and psychological factors or indicators have been taken into account following a multi-disciplinary assessment, if appropriate. It is then safe for the person to be discharged or safe to transfer from hospital to home or another setting. The person who is 'fit for discharge' no longer requires the services of acute or specialist staff within a secondary care setting, and where review of the person's condition can be shared with the GP including adjustments to medication.

Legislation/policy and reducing delayed discharges

There is a wealth of legislation relating to the assessment, care planning and discharge of a person from hospital and further reading is necessary to fully understand its complexity (see Chapter 25 on law and social work).

The hospital discharge assessment should be carried out in line with the single assessment process, (National Service Framework [DH, 2001], Standard 2, person-centred care). The standards of the NSF embody fundamental principles ensuring care is based on clinical need, not age, and that services treat older people as individuals, promoting their quality of life, independence, dignity and their right to make choices about their own care. Members of the hospital multi-disciplinary team must work together to consider people's health and social care needs, and share assessment information in order to avoid duplication and delays.

In order to reduce the number of delayed discharges, the Community Care (Delayed Discharges) Act 2003 was introduced whereby a local authority makes a payment to the healthcare provider when an NHS person's discharge from hospital is delayed because the local authority has not put in place the community care services which the person needs from that authority in order to be safely discharged.

Specifically, social services must:

- Carry out an assessment in order to determine what community care services a patient will need in order for him/her to be safely discharged.
- Determine, following consultation with the NHS body, what services the authority will provide, irrespective of whether they have been subject previously to an assessment of their needs as assessed under Section 47 of the NHS and Community Care Act 1990.

The aim of the NHS and social services working together is to ensure that a complete package of care can be put in place smoothly and without duplication or omission of any particular service.

THE CONCEPT IN SOCIAL WORK PRACTICE

Arthur is a 75-year-old white British man who lives alone. He has never married. His older sister describes her brother's home as 'unkempt' and says that he self-neglects. He has no other family and appears to live in isolation. Arthur is admitted to hospital with breathing difficulties and reduced mobility. Following a series of tests, Arthur is diagnosed with lung cancer and is given a prognosis of two to four months to live.

A referral is made to the hospital discharge team and Sue, a qualified social worker, is allocated the case. Arthur has already been seen by members of the multi-disciplinary team and the discharge liaison nurse has completed a continuing care assessment. As Arthur's condition is now stable and only an overview of his healthcare needs is required, he does not meet the criteria for continuing healthcare funding. The staff nurse makes a referral to social services and faxes a Section 2 notification. The medical team has made the following recommendations:

- Consultant geriatrician reports that Arthur requires 24-hour nursing care.
- Registered general nurse agrees with the consultant and has spoken to Arthur's sister, suggesting she starts looking for a suitable nursing home for her brother.
- Occupational therapist reports that Arthur is very unsteady on his feet and is at high risk of falls. He is not safe to return home.
- Physiotherapist reports similar and agrees that Arthur is not safe to return home.

Sue makes arrangements to visit Arthur in hospital and undertakes an assessment of need within the single assessment process. She spends time talking to Arthur about his illness and what he wants to do. Arthur is adamant that he wants to go home. He is aware that he is dying, knows that he is at risk of falls and aware of the potential difficulties if his health deteriorates whilst on his own. He is agreeable to receiving home-care support. Although Sue recognises the risks identified by the medical staff she believes that Arthur has a right to make choices, to take risks and decide what he wants to do. She therefore liaises with the medical staff; therapists; community health and social care services and Arthur's family regarding Arthur being discharged home. Although the medical staff are not happy with the decision, Sue explains to them that Arthur has a choice. He has capacity and is, therefore, entitled to make a decision regarding his life.

Sue arranges a home-care package and agrees a discharge date and time with the multi-disciplinary team. There is no delay in Arthur returning home so no payment is incurred under Section 5 of the Community Care (Delayed Discharges, etc.) Act 2003.

Cross references: mental capacity, multi-professional working, older people, personalisation, safeguarding adults

SUGGESTED READING

Adams, R., Dominelli, L. and Payne, M. (2005) *Practising Social Work in a Complex World*. Basingstoke: Palgrave Macmillan.

Barrett G., Sellman, D. and Thomas, J. (2005) *Interprofessional Working in Health and Social Care*. Basingstoke: Palgrave Macmillan.

REFERENCES

DH (Department of Health) (2001) 'National service framework for older people'. Available from: www.dh.gov.uk/publications (accessed 21 May 2012).

DH (Department of Health) (2004) 'Achieving timely simple discharge from hospital: a toolkit for the multi-disciplinary team'. Available from: www.dh.gov.uk/publications (accessed 21 May 2012).

DH (Department of Health) (2009) 'Reviewing patients who have waited longer than 18 weeks'. Best Practice Guidance. Available from: www.dh.gov.uk/publications (accessed 21 May 2012).

DH (Department of Health) (2010) 'A&E clinical quality indicators'. Available from: www.dh.gov.uk/publications (accessed 21 May 2012).

Glasby J. (2003) *Hospital Discharge, Integrating Health and Social Care*. Abingdon: Radcliffe Medical Press Ltd.

HMSO (1959) *The Younghusband Report: Report of the Working Party on Social Workers in the Local Authority, Health and Welfare Services*. London: The Stationery Office.

Reed, J. and Morgan, D. (1999) 'Discharging older people from hospital to care homes: implications for nursing', *Journal of Advanced Nursing*, 29: 819–25.

The Stationery Office (2003) *Community Care (Delayed Discharges, Etc.) Act 2003: Royal Assent*, 8 April 2003 (Public General Acts – Elizabeth II).

Tope, R. and Thomas, E. (2007) 'Health and social care policy and the interprofessional agenda: creating an interprofessional workforce'. Available from: www.caipe.org.uk/silo/files/cipw-policy.pdf (accessed 21 May 2012).

WHO (World Health Organization) (1978) 'Personnel for health care: case studies in educational programmes', *Public Health Papers*, 1(70), World Health Organization, Geneva.

56
Stress in Social Work

Ashley Weinberg and Michael Murphy

DEFINITION

Stress is, 'the adverse reaction people have to excessive pressures or other types of demand placed on them at work' (HSE, 2009). Some would argue that to get the best out of ourselves we benefit from experiencing an optimal level of pressure. Yet where we have little control over that pressure, there are risks and symptoms. This chapter seeks to outline these in relation to social work practitioners.

KEY POINTS

Six aspects of work contribute to employee well-being if they are at optimal levels (HSE, 2004):

- demands – reasonable workloads and patterns of work and safety;
- control – having a say over decisions affecting one's own work;
- support – appropriate management practices and positive feedback;
- relationships – promoting positive relationships;

- role – job clarity;
- change – engaging and informing employees in times of change.

Taking these key issues into account, guidance exists for improving mental health at work, which could cut costs to employees and their organisations (NICE, 2009):

1 Promoting psychological well-being via policies and working practices, for example, better job design; engendering a 'culture of participation, equality and fairness'.
2 Adopting a structured approach to assessing and monitoring staff well-being.
3 Introducing flexible working conditions to manage workload and accommodate working patterns.
4 Supportive leadership styles and management practices, for example, clarifying roles and expectations, building staff confidence, providing constructive feedback, valuing and rewarding effort.

Whilst it is usually beyond the individual to influence the social work employer's business case, the issue of costs related to employee well-being is highly relevant to the organisation. This means there is scope for discussions, schemes and policies likely to promote positive psychological health at work on the basis of sound professional and organisational considerations. Those who also stand to benefit are the service users.

DISCUSSION

Individual signs and symptoms of stress

It is possible to view stress along a continuum which has positive well-being at one end and distress at the other. On the positive side, we enjoy meeting the challenges that life presents; for example, satisfaction in helping a client. In contrast, there is stress, which over time can lead to psychological health problems, such as depression and anxiety.

A continuum of psychological health

Positive Psychological Health → Eustress → Stress → Distress → Poor Psychological Health

Cognitive symptoms of stress

Our psychological capacity for everyday activities involves information gathering, memory, concentration, effective problem solving and decision making. Signs of cognitive strain include impairment of some or all of these and not surprisingly self-confidence can suffer too. Symptoms may be exacerbated by information overload especially where the individual has depleted coping resources.

Physiological symptoms of stress

The 'stress response' enables us to take 'flight or fight'. However, the psychosocial demands of modern work have replaced the threats faced throughout human evolution, so that the repeated activation of our age-old stress response can pose a threat to well-being (Clow, 2001). Physical signs of strain include: headaches; muscle trembling (e.g. eye twitch); excessive perspiration; decreased appetite; indigestion; sickness; shortness of breath; chest pains; and a decline in sexual interest. The chronic experience of physical symptoms can lead to health difficulties. A Europe-wide study of 6,467 pregnant women recorded higher risk of premature birth among those with low job satisfaction working more than 42 hours per week (Saurel-Cubizolles et al., 2004).

Emotional symptoms of stress

The transformation of a usually energetic and cheerful individual into someone with a gloomy, dejected or tense outlook affects their social performance; for example, withdrawal from social situations or displays of irritability. 'Burnout' comprises emotional exhaustion, including depersonalisation of clients and a lack of personal accomplishment (Maslach and Jackson, 1986). Where employees are trading in emotions, they can feel 'used up' over time, despite strong commitment to the job. Social and healthcare professions are prone to this and it is not uncommon for emotional strain to be linked to a depressed mood, encompassing a loss of interest and motivation, along with feelings of guilt. Whilst 20.5 per cent of the general population report high levels of psychological strain (Taylor et al., 2004) figures are comparably higher among social workers (Seymour and Grove, 2005).

Behavioural and organisational symptoms of stress

Sickness absence due to psychological and physical health problems accounts for 66 million working days at a cost of £3.4 billion in the UK public sector, with employees missing an average 8.5 days per year (CBI/AXA, 2006). In the UK working population, 40 per cent of all absenteeism is attributed to psychological ill health. Turnover of 25 per cent in UK social work has also resulted in skills shortages (Huxley et al., 2005). In contrast, presenteeism indicates behavioural strain as job security declines. This is 'impaired work efficiency' (Black Report, 2008), where the employee is unwell but continues to work. Alongside the negative effects of low morale, reduced commitment to the organisation and the potential for more mistakes and complaints, it is clear the organisation can also show symptoms of strain.

Stressors in social work

There are six contexts for categorising the sources of stress (stressors) experienced by the social work practitioner or manager:

1) The worker

Social workers deal with the most vulnerable members of society, often at times of crisis and distress. The first source of stress for the individual practitioner is their internal response to that work. Although their training tries to establish a personal/professional 'distance' from their work, social workers take their 'self' to work every day, which naturally involves a reaction to client trauma (Thompson et al., 1998).

2) Clients and their families

Because social workers meet their clients at times of significant vulnerability and upheaval, service users often respond to their practitioner with distress, anger or violence, seldom showing respect or gratitude. Clients find themselves ever closer to the involuntary end of the voluntary/involuntary continuum, creating an increasingly oppositional and stressful relationship with their practitioner (Spratt, 2008).

3) Team/colleagues

Most social workers practice in teams, which can provide an essential source of support, enabling the practitioner to operate to their maximum capacity. However, it can also be a potential source of stress, if the individual feels unsupported or isolated, or there is an unhealthy working culture (Thompson et al., 1998).

4) Supervisor/manager

The key skill of the social work manager is to mediate between the individual worker and the practice world (Fineman, 1985). The relationship between the practitioner and their supervisor/manager can vary from being a crucial source of support to potentially the largest source of stress, particularly when that relationship is experienced as neglectful or abusive.

5) Agency/senior management

The last two decades have seen significant changes in social care organisation with increased managerialism, bureaucratisation and performance management (Munro, 2011). This has caused many staff stress by significantly reducing the control that staff and their supervisors have over their work (Stanley et al., 2007). The unparalleled crisis in social work brought about by the UK Government's 2011 spending review and significant reduction in provision has led to structural re-organisations and fewer staff, with significant implications for staff stress.

6) Government/society

Largely influenced by critical media coverage of their role in child abuse and death, social workers are often portrayed as naive or inadequate (Munro, 2011), which adds to their stress burden. Occasionally the settlement of legal cases, such as that in favour of social worker John Walker against his employer in 1995, highlights the extreme nature of the job and the way in which it is administered.

THE CONCEPT IN SOCIAL WORK PRACTICE

Case study

Josie qualified three years ago, joining the children and families team of a large local authority. She had a supportive supervisor and with two other new team members formed a friendship group. Over the first two years her caseload built up

key concepts in
social work practice

with vulnerable families who were sometimes difficult to work with, including the Smiths. There was something about Mr Smith that Josie found very threatening. He was never violent, but always verbally abusive and extremely critical. As the Smith children moved from being children in need to becoming subject to care proceedings, Josie's dread of Mr Smith increased. Meanwhile, Josie's supervisor left and during a major re-organisation, both of her friends transferred to another team. Feeling unsupported, Josie entered a period where she felt very stressed, tearful and unable to face working with Mr Smith.

Coping with stress

A combination of coping strategies can help, but the first step is recognising the problem. Josie's distress might be pointed out by a colleague or family member, or she may spot it for herself. This could encourage her to talk to trusted colleagues who are able to offer advice. The ability to communicate our emotions to others can be integral to coping. Gaining social support is a buffer against the negative effects of stress, so Josie should establish her new manager's level of supportiveness and explore the possibility of passing on the case or regulating her exposure to the threatening behaviour until she is better able to cope. If the problems become too difficult, Josie might talk in confidence with her general practitioner or her employer's occupational health service.

Our choice of coping strategy may be strongly influenced by how much control we feel we have over a situation. Physically taking a break from work – even if this means simply not taking work home – can help reduce the activation of our body's stress chemicals (Sonnentag and Bayer, 2005), while relaxation techniques or working out at the gymnasium are also popular.

Cross references: accountability, managing change, mental health, reflection

SUGGESTED READING

Thompson, N., Murphy, M. and Stradling, S. (1998) *Meeting the Stress Challenge*. Lyme Regis: Russell House Publishing.

Weinberg, A., Sutherland, V.J. and Cooper, C.L. (2010) *Organizational Stress Management: A Strategic Approach*. Basingstoke: Palgrave Macmillan.

REFERENCES

Black Report (2008) 'Working for a healthier tomorrow.' London: TSO. Available from: www.workingforhealth.gov.uk/documents/working-for-a-healthier-tomorrow-tagged.pdf (accessed 21 May 2012).

CBI/AXA (Confederation of British Industry) (2006) 'Cost of UK workplace absence tops £13bn – new CBI survey'. Available from: http//:www.cbi.org.uk/ndbs/press.nsf (accessed 15 May 2006).

Clow, A. (2001) 'The physiology of stress', in F. Jones and J. Bright (eds), *Stress: Myth, Theory and Research*. Harlow: Pearson Prentice Hall, pp. 47–62.

Fineman, S. (1985) *Social Work Stress and Intervention*. Aldershot: Gower.

HSE (Health and Safety Executive) (2004) 'What are the management standards?' Available from: www.hse.gov.uk/stress/standards (accessed 8 February 2010).

HSE (Health and Safety Executive) (2009) 'Health and safety executive (HSE) stress at work: causes, signs and symptoms'. Available from: http://news.hse.gov.uk/2009/11/18/stress-at-work-causes-signs-and-symptoms (accessed 8 February 2010).

Huxley, P., Evans, S., Gately, C., Webber, M., Mears, A., Pajak, S., Kendall, T., Medina, J. and Katona, C. (2005) 'Stress and pressures in mental health social work: the worker speaks', *British Journal of Social Work*, 35: 1063–79.

Maslach, C. and Jackson, S. (1986) *The Maslach Burnout Inventory*. Palo Alto, CA: Consulting Psychologists Press.

Munro, E. (2011) *The Munro Review of Child Protection: Final Report*. Cm 8062. London: HMSO.

NICE (2009) *Public Health Guidance 22, Promoting Mental Wellbeing Through Productive and Healthy Working Conditions: Guidance for Employers*. London: NICE.

Saurel-Cubizolles, M.J., Zeitlin, J., Lelong, N., Papiernik, E., Di Renzo, G.C. and Breart, G. (2004) 'Employment, working conditions, and preterm birth: results from the Europop case-control survey', *Journal of Epidemiology and Community Health*, 58(5): 395–401.

Seymour, L. and Grove, B. (2005) *Work Interventions for People with Common Mental Health Problems*. London: British Occupational Health Research Foundation.

Sonnentag, S. and Bayer, U.-V. (2005) 'Switching off mentally: predictors and consequences of psychological detachment from work during off-job time', *Journal of Occupational Health Psychology*, 10: 393–414.

Spratt, T. (2008) 'The changing landscape of social care: implications for working with involuntary clients', in M. Calder (ed.), *The Carrot or the Stick? Towards Effective Practice with Involuntary Clients in Safeguarding Children Work*. Lyme Regis: Russell House Publishing, pp.12–24.

Stanley, N., Manthorpe, J. and White, M. (2007) 'Depression in the profession: social workers' experiences and perceptions', *British Journal of Social Work*, 37: 281–98.

Taylor, M.F., Brice, J., Buck, N. and Prentice-Lane, E. (2004) *British Household Panel Survey User Manual Volume A: Introduction, Technical Report and Appendices*. Colchester: University of Essex.

Thompson, N., Murphy, M., Stradling, S. and O'Neill, P. (1998) *Meeting the Stress Challenge*. Lyme Regis: Russell House Publishing.

57
Substance Misuse

Michael Murphy

DEFINITION

In this chapter, the term substance misuse includes the misuse of all substances including drugs, alcohol and prescribed medication. In most western societies individuals use substances for comfort, pleasure, to treat medical conditions, or to relax or energise themselves in the face of their daily routine. Individual clients often use a range of substances in the course of a normal week.

Traditionally three types of substance use have been established:

- *Experimental* use concerns the first time the individual uses that substance. Although very harmful in a small minority of cases, for most users and families experimental use is not problematic.
- *Social* use is where use occurs within a social group. This kind of use is within boundaries and the user can and does choose to go through periods of non-use.
- *Dependent* use is where the relationship between substance(s) and user has become essential to their well-being. The user begins to 'map' their day around the substance (obtaining, using and recovery) and does not seem to be able to choose not to use.

SCODA (Standing Conference on Drug Abuse) (1997: 35) offer a definition of dependence, 'a compulsion or desire to continue taking a drug, or drugs in order to feel good or avoid feeling bad. The compulsion or desire is usually initiated following previous, repeated use of the drug and is difficult to control'.

Harris (2006) claims that the *dependent* style of use is more complicated than it first appears, explaining that some users are dependent, but manage to protect their routines from the worst impact of their substance dependence. He claims that another group find it difficult to maintain their dependency without it impacting on all their roles and routines; he gives the label *addicted* to this group of substance users, indicating that their style of substance dependence implies a high degree of chaos.

In 2009, it was estimated that 6.4 per cent of the population of England were alcohol dependent (NHS, 2009) and in the financial year 2009–10, 206,000 adults were in treatment for drug problems (National Treatment Agency, 2010), although many more were using drugs without being in treatment.

KEY POINTS

- Social work is less concerned with the health or moral impact of substance misuse and more concerned with the psycho-social impact on the user and their living group.
- Involvement in the illegal drugs industry brings specific difficulties to the user, family and social work relationship. Alcohol misuse can be 'hidden' from view by its social acceptability.
- Substance misuse and mental ill-health can co-occur and potentially exacerbate both conditions.
- Between 250,000 and 300,000 children are brought up with at least one parent drug dependent (Advisory Committee on the Misuse of Drugs, 2003) and between 780,000 and 1.3 million children with at least one parent alcohol dependent. This leads to several distinct challenges to social work (Macrory and Murphy, 2011).
- Young people's substance misuse is a social problem on its own, but also as an exaggerating factor to youth crime, mental ill-health and familial problems.

DISCUSSION

The traditional perspective on substance misuse primarily concerns the medical and moral impact of the substance misuse on the user. Most treatment systems are tailored to deal with the user as a single patient. Some workers in non-treatment agencies may question whether substance misuse is strictly their 'business'. However, because of the significant psycho-social impact of substance misuse, it is a central concern to practitioners because it is impossible for one family member's substance misuse not to impact on their living group (Barnard, 2007; Kroll and Taylor, 2003). The nature and extent of that familial impact is often the key aspect of the social work intervention (Macrory and Murphy, 2011).

The illegality of most narcotic drugs adds a different dilemma to the social work role. How can they be honest about their use when that use is illegal? Clients who deny the extent of the problem are engaging in an entirely 'functional' activity. Conversely, alcohol is legal, socially acceptable and cheap. This brings its own problems. Because its use is so 'normal', it is easy not to recognise it until its use becomes chronic. We must acknowledge that social workers may also experience problematic relationships with alcohol in their own lives. Traditionally, treatment services for drug misuse have been far better funded than alcohol treatment services: 'The huge imbalance in funding that exists between drugs and alcohol often leaves the social workers not simply care planning but filling the gap' (Harris, 2007: viii–ix).

Co-morbidity occurs when the problems with mental ill-health and substance misuse occur at the same time. This phenomenon is not surprising as misuse of drugs can have an impact on the user's mood and sense of well-being. People who experience mental ill-health are often prescribed medication to help with their mood and affect, they may also self-medicate with other substances to try to alleviate symptoms:

> A clear association exists between mental illness and drug and alcohol dependence. Those experiencing mental ill-health have a higher risk of substance misuse. (HM Government, 2010: 7)

Parental substance misuse

The most pressing aspect in children and families' social work is not adult substance misuse per se, but the impact of parental substance misuse on children's well-being. The British government first acknowledged substance abuse as a parental problem in the *Hidden Harm* report (ACMD, 2003) then in 2008 the new drugs strategy (HM Government, 2008) included 'focus on families' as a distinct strand.

Young people's substance misuse

Forty years of research has suggested that substance use is a 'normal' part of adolescence (Parker et al., 1998); seeking hedonistic experience is part of growing up. Although social use of substances is not harmful for most adolescents, there are exceptions that are critical. In 2009–10 23,500 under 18s were in treatment in England for drug problems (NTA, 2010). For a minority of vulnerable adolescent users substance use can exaggerate other social problems:

- For some young people substance misuse is clearly associated with involvement in crime (Hammersley et al., 2003).
- Substance misuse and self-medicating for emotional distress by young people can lead to low impulse control for self-harm. If a young person is highly dependent on substances, it is easier to manipulate them into prostitution.
- For users who develop a dependence while still in adolescence (ACMD, 2006) it can radically impact on their relationships with family, friends and school.
- Significant misuse of cannabis has been linked to a greater occurrence of psychosis (Kuepper et al., 2011).

The challenge when working with adolescents is to try to address their substance misuse at the same time as their other social issues. Young people seldom seek help because they are worried about their substance use. When they do seek help it is often because their associated social problems are exacerbated by their use (Murphy et al., 2010). Adult workers struggle to 'join' the adolescent's understanding of the role of substances in their life, and their efforts to help are often misunderstood by the young person (Harris, 2006).

THE CONCEPT IN SOCIAL WORK PRACTICE

Case study

Sara was 16 years old. She had already left home several times, had short stays in residential care and two violent relationships with older males. Sara would say that she used 'everything'. She had committed a series of offences and had been admitted to hospital after two failed suicide attempts. Sara had been an open case to social workers from the youth offending team, the child and adolescent mental health service and the local authority, but they struggled to get to know her and to help her halt her downward spiral.

After her 16th birthday Sara was admitted to hospital following an (accidental) heroin overdose. She felt helpless, but contacted the social worker in a voluntary substance organisation. The assessment session took over three hours to complete. Her difficult road to change had begun. The worker saw Sara's substance problems as both a cause and an effect of her other problems. She was invited to join a group, where issues of substance, homelessness, domestic abuse and low self-esteem were worked on concurrently.

Substance abuse and social work practice

Assessment is about measuring the client's relationship with their substance(s) of choice. It explores how this relationship intrudes on to other areas of their lives. This is not simple, there is a desire to deny or minimise use of substances, particularly to practitioners who are not in treatment services.

We also need to include those factors that make a child (or adult) resilient to adversity:

- deliberate planning;
- high self-esteem and self-efficacy;
- ability to deal with change/problem-solving skills;
- feeling that they had choices and previous experience of success (Velleman and Templeton, 2006: 16).

CONCLUSION

Social work in this field can be crudely understood in terms of either assisting a person to control the effects of dependency or assisting them in abstaining and recovering from their dependency. A heroin dependent mother would be prescribed opiate substitutes (e.g. Methadone or Subutex). These would be taken once per day. This would reduce the amount of time she would spend getting the money to pay, use and recover. It might also improve her availability to meet the needs of her children. Although some utilise substitute prescribing to give up the substance altogether, for some substitute prescribing keeps harm at a controllable level but often does not lead to full recovery.

The abstinence/recovery model seeks to move quickly beyond substitute prescribing to a complete withdrawal. There are many recovery models available in substance treatment systems, but the most well-known one is the 12-steps model of Alcoholics Anonymous that uses medical, religious, psychological and social models to explain and combat dependence. The social worker role is to be a key part of the treatment system.

Cross references: family work, looked after children, mental health

SUGGESTED READING

Barnard, M. (2007) *Drug Addiction and Families*. London: Jessica Kingsley.
Harbin, F. and Murphy, M. (2006) *Secret Lives: Growing with Substance*. London: Random House.

REFERENCES

ACMD (Advisory Committee on the Misuse of Drugs) (2003) *Hidden Harm*. London: HMSO.
ACMD (Advisory Committee on the Misuse of Drugs) (2006) *Pathways to Problems: Hazardous Use of Tobacco, Alcohol and Other Drugs by Young People in the UK and its Implications for Policy*. London: HMSO.
Barnard, M. (2007) *Drug Addiction and Families*. London: Jessica Kingsley.
Hammersley, R., Marsland, L. and Reid, M. (2003) *Substance Use by Young Offenders: The Impact of the Normalisation of Drug Use in the Early Years of the 21st Century*. London: Home Office Research Series 261.
Harris, P. (2006) 'Where it all begins: growing up and the helping relationship', in Harbin, F. and Murphy, M. (eds), *Secret Lives: Growing with Substance*. Lyme Regis: Russell House Publishing, pp.110–25.

Harris, P. (2007) *Empathy for the Devil*. Lyme Regis: Russell House Publishing.

HM Government (2008) *Drugs: Protecting Families and Communities: The 2008 Drugs Strategy*. London: HMSO.

HM Government (2010) *Drug Strategy 2010 Reducing Demand, Restricting Supply, Building Recovery: Supporting People to Live a Drug Free Life*. London: HMSO.

Kroll, B. and Taylor, A. (2003) *Parental Substance Misuse and Child Welfare*. London: Jessica Kingsley.

Kuepper, R., Van Os, J., Lieb, R., Wittchen, H., Höfler, M. and Henquet, C. (2011) 'Continued cannabis use and risk of incidence and persistence of psychotic symptoms: 10-year follow-up cohort study'. *British Medical Journal*, March issue.

Macrory, F. and Murphy, M. (2011) 'Management of the effects of prenatal drugs in children of drug abusing parents', in M. Preece and E. Riley (eds), *Alcohol, Drugs and Medication in Pregnancy: The Long Term Outcome for the Child*. London: Ma Keith Press, p.197–216.

Murphy, M., Halligan, F. and Harbin, F. (2010) 'An evaluation of East Lancashire's early break service'. University of Salford.

NHS Information Centre (2009) *Statistics on Alcohol: England 2009*. Available from: www.ic.nhs.uk/statistics-and-data-collections/health-and-lifestyles/alcohol (accessed 15 June 2012).

NTA (National Treatment Agency) (2010) *Statistics for Drug Treatment Activity in England 2009/10 NDTMS*. Available from: www.nta.nhs.uk/publications (accessed 15 June 2012).

Parker, H., Aldridge, J. and Measham, F. (1998) *Illegal Leisure: The Normalisation of Adolescent Recreational Drug Use*. London: Routledge.

SCODA (Standing Conference on Drug Abuse) (1997) *Drug Using Parents: Policy Guidelines for Interagency Working*. London: LGA Publications.

Velleman, R. and Templeton, L. (2006) 'Reaching out: promoting resilience in the children of substance misusers', in F. Harbin and M. Murphy (eds), *Secret Lives: Growing with Substance*. Lyme Regis: Russell House Publishing, pp. 12–28.

58
Supervision

Simon Rogerson

DEFINITION

Convention dictates adopting some kind of definition and 'official' definitions at the very least provide us with a yardstick against which to measure departures from the norm. The Children's Workforce Development Council (CWDC) and Skills for Care define supervision as 'an accountable process which supports, assures and develops the knowledge skills and values of an individual, group or team. The purpose is to improve the quality of the work to achieve agreed objectives and outcomes' (CWDC, 2007: 5).

KEY POINTS

- Supervision finds itself at the center of discussions about the future of social work (Munro, 2011). What goes on in supervision reflects debates about what is going on in social work.
- Service user and social worker relationships are played out in supervision in the context of relationships between supervisors and supervisees and other relationships which exist within organisational hierarchies. These relationships are framed by theories of learning, theories of management and theories of social work practice. They are contained by policy, legal frameworks and at the agency level anything from performance targets, resource constraints, to payments by results.
- It may, then, be more useful to think about 'doing supervision' for this is a part of practice which is negotiated within a complex framework of contexts (micro, institutional and macro) and relationships.

DISCUSSION

The case study which follows raises a number of issues which will be briefly explored with reference to the supervision in social work literature.

- What is the *purpose* of supervision?
- *Process* – how does it best achieve these functions; what knowledge values and skills does it draw upon or demand of its participants?
- In what *contexts* is supervision taking place?

Purpose

Hughes and Pengelly (1997) refer to a triangle of participants in supervision: the supervisor representing line management and accountability; the practitioner bringing their experience of direct work with service users; and the service user with their own set of needs, demands and rights. Supervisory functions typically consist of: managing service delivery; focusing on a practitioner's work and facilitating the practitioner's professional development. In any supervisory relationship there are tensions around managing the competing demands of each participant and function. Each function is seen as being interrelated and practice becomes unsafe if one side of the triangle is ignored or avoided for any length of time.

Morrison's (2001) '4X4' model adds support and mediation to the educative and managerial functions. However, for Davys and Beddoe it is the supervisory relationship, as 'a medium through which all else is accomplished' (2010: 49), which incorporates but extends beyond support and mediation and which ensures that the three essential elements of supervision are accomplished, these being: service to clients; organisational policies and standards; professional knowledge and codes of practice.

Process

The Social Work Taskforce has recommended national requirements for the supervision of social workers as well as effective training for managers (DSCF, 2010). CWDC (2007) outline a series of units of competence for supervisors which cover: systems and processes; relationships; and practice and performance. Systems and processes refer to how supervision is integrated into organisational policies, performance management and workforce development. Supervisors and supervisees require clarity on the frequency, recording of, and agendas for supervision. These will usually be set out in a supervision agreement. All Newly Qualified Social Workers (NQSWs) should be offered weekly supervision in the first six weeks and fortnightly thereon for the first six months in post (CWDC, 2007).

Contexts

Macro

Traditionally social work supervision focused on the training of students and oversight of new practitioners (Davys and Beddoe, 2010). However, legalism has increased the public scrutiny of social work practice especially in respect to the management of risk in the context of public inquiries, and a wider critique of public welfare from the New Right and its associated media (see Ayre, 2001).

The uncertainty and fear that is subsequently generated is, at least in part, managed by the imposition of detailed control and audit mechanisms. Procedures, rules and regulatory frameworks have seemingly crowded out trust in professional relationships. This regulatory climate has culminated in an emphasis on task-centred models of practice and supervision (Davys and Beddoe, 2010). Here the focus is on the conscious, cognitive elements of the social work task of: collecting information; making plans; and completing detailed assessment forms which tell the social worker what data to collect and how quickly to collect it (Munro, 2011: 36). McDonald et al. (2008) note how these developments create barriers to the retention of professional knowledge. Taylor and White (2006) advocate an approach to social work education which calls for education for uncertainty. Their approach puts emphasis on the development of practical reasoning and the use of emotion to reflexively engage with practice dilemmas. There seems to be a growing recognition of the limits of managerialism. Munro has commented that 'managerial oversight often predominates and that too little attention is given to professional supervision' (2011: 53). Munro (2011) accepts that good records are important but recognises too the importance of relationships, practice wisdom, expertise, and communication skills.

Institutional

Where team members have expertise, engage in learning activities with one another, and are supportive of one another, supervision can go on outside the formal supervisory relationship in a learning organisation. The current fashion for 'hot desking', individual performance monitoring, together with the climate of insecurity engendered by cuts in welfare spending do not serve to facilitate the kinds of relationships between colleagues characterised by the interdependency and reciprocity advocated by Froggett (2000).

Micro

Tensions in supervisory relationships include care versus control, support versus challenge and proving competence whilst acknowledging difficulties. As such they mirror the contradictions at the heart of social work relationships where the simultaneous performance of tasks is required (Phillipson, 2002). Attitudes towards authority by each party may be a key variable in the underlying dynamics of the relationship which may be enacted through game playing.

THE CONCEPT IN SOCIAL WORK PRACTICE

Case study

Alan is an experienced social worker who works in a Community Mental Health Team. He values supervision to ventilate feelings, explore practice dilemmas, and to review his own professional development needs. More recently Alan has approached supervision with a degree of trepidation. A difficult case has left him feeling exposed and caused him to doubt his professional practice. Alan has worked with Peter – a mental health service user – for many years. Peter trusts Alan like he has trusted no one else in his life. Peter has complex needs involving a long history of alcohol-related problems, physical health needs, and difficulties with relationships. Alan lost his own father to alcohol.

Alan has never cared much for paperwork. Alan has, until recently, viewed himself as fortunate that his previous manager had little interest in monitoring his performance beyond lengthy critical case discussions which took up most of his supervision sessions. Alan found the psycho-dynamically informed conversations with his supervisor more helpful to the process of risk management than form completion.

Alan's supervisor of ten years retired recently. His new supervisor, a nurse, uses supervision to focus on unmet performance targets. Alan has been experiencing stress in his private life which has been impacting on and impacted by his work. He would normally have discussed these in supervision but he has yet to perceive his relationship with his manager as safe and supportive. Peter's risk-taking behaviour has escalated. Alan has been compensating by visiting outside his working hours. Other colleagues have accused him of being over-involved. He has not broached these issues with his new supervisor because he fears he will focus on his case recording which is weeks behind.

A number of weeks later Alan's partner leaves him. Alan is emotionally overwhelmed and takes a rare week off work. That week Peter is rushed to hospital after collapsing in the street. Peter is admitted to hospital dehydrated but soon stabilises. When Alan returns to work he feels guilty about letting Peter down but he also faces some difficult questions from his manager about the management of Peter's care and his case recording.

Commentary on case study

What was the purpose of Alan's supervision – what should have been going on here?

Alan's previous line manager had used supervision to explore professional knowledge and practice in relation to Peter's needs. However, supervision neglected any focus on organisational standards, accountability or professional codes of practice. Here the supervisor's corner of Hughes and Pengelly's (1997) supervision triangle – the management of service delivery – is neglected. This later has a significant impact on Alan as a practitioner when his next manager begins to assert the accountability function in supervision and when Alan is left exposed by his poor record keeping.

Within the more recent supervisory relationship there is little room for the service user who is perhaps crowded out by task-oriented and performance management tools. There is little room for Alan as a practitioner to consider how feelings from outside practice are being transferred into practice in the context of his professional relationship with Peter.

What was the process of supervision?

Supervision should have been a place where Alan's supervisor might try to work with Alan to unravel how Alan's feelings towards Peter were impacting upon his practice. Supervision would seek to recognise and contain Alan's fears of letting down Peter and not completing his paperwork, rather than avoid or deny them as each of his supervisors have done, albeit in different ways. At the point of risks associated with Peter escalating, Alan might have been encouraged to tell his story about Peter, identifying a goal – for example, improve risk assessment and management. He might have been encouraged to reflect upon the impact of risk escalation on himself in terms of thoughts, feelings, and values and the implications in terms of his role, professional practice standards and organisational protocol in order to generate contingency plans to be implemented and recorded.

CONCLUSION

That Alan's supervisor is from a different professional background raises issues about professional social work knowledge, skills and values and whether these can be recognised in the context of the blurring of roles resulting from inter-professional working (Banks, 2004). At a micro level, Tsui (2005) refers to the games of abdication or assertion of power played by supervisors. Here Alan's first supervisor abdicates their responsibility for organisational outcomes, presenting as 'one of the workers'. Alan as a supervisee may be playing games in order to redefine the supervisory relationship. Here 'evaluation is not for friends' and 'treat me don't beat me' may be strategies used at both conscious and unconscious levels.

Cross references: accountability, leadership and management, the political context of social work, quality assurance, team working

Davys, A. and Beddoe, L. (2010) *Best Practice in Professional Supervision*. London: Jessica Kingsley.

Tsui, M. (2005) *Social Work Supervision: Contexts and Concepts*. London: Sage.

REFERENCES

Ayre, P. (2001) 'Child protection and the media: lessons from the last three decades', *British Journal of Social Work*, 31: 887–901.

Banks, S. (2004) *Ethics, Accountability and the Social Professions*. Basingstoke: Palgrave Macmillan.

CWDC (Children's Workforce Development Council) (2007) 'Providing effective supervision'. Skills for Care and CWDC. Available at: www.skillsofrcare.org.uk/developing_skills/leader-ship_and_management/providing effective_supervision.aspx (accessed 4 June 2012).

Davys, A. and Beddoe, L. (2010) *Best Practice in Professional Supervision*. London: Jessica Kingsley.

Froggett, L. (2000) 'Staff supervision and dependency culture: a case study', *Journal of Social Work Practice*, 14(1): 27–35.

Hughes, L. and Pengelly, P. (1997) *Staff Supervision in a Turbulent Environment*. London: Jessica Kingsley.

McDonald, A., Postle, K. and Dawson, C. (2008) 'B arriers to retaining and using professional knowledge in local authority social work practice with adults in the UK', *British Journal of Social Work*, 38: 1370–87.

Morrison, T. (2001) *Staff Supervision in Social Care*. Brighton: Pavillion Publishing.

Munro, E. (2011) *The Munro Review of Child Protection: Final Report – A Child Centred System*. London: Department of Education.

Phillipson, J. (2002) 'Supervision and being supervised', in R. Adams, L. Dominelli and M. Payne (eds), *Critical Practice in Social Work*. Basingstoke: Palgrave Macmillan, pp. 244–51.

Taylor, C. and White, S. (2006) 'Knowledge and reasoning in social work: educating for humane judgement', *British Journal of Social Work*, 36(6): 937–54.

Tsui, M. (2005) *Social Work Supervision: Contexts and Concepts*. London: Sage.

key concepts in social work practice

59
Team Working

Sarah Kennedy and Valerie Houghton

DEFINITION

Øvretveit suggests that 'People in a team come together to achieve a common purpose which they could not achieve on their own' (1993: 55). There have been three influential policy drivers in recent social work practice that have led to the need for effective team working with other professionals, with service users and with families:

- the development of the learning organisation;
- the development of multi-professional working;
- increased service user involvement in design, delivery, and review of services.

A team can be defined as being:

> made up of individuals who see themselves and are seen by others as a social entity, who are interdependent because of the tasks they perform as members of a group, who are embedded in one or more larger social systems (e.g. community, organisation), and who perform tasks that affect others (such as customers or co-workers). (Guzzo and Dickson, 1996: 308)

A team differs from a group in relation to its size, selection, leadership, perception, style and spirit (Belbin, 2004). Within most organisations there are three main types of teams: work teams that do the day-to-day work of the organisation; task teams that address a specific problem or opportunity (such as case teams or development teams); and management teams who direct operational units. Often workers will be a member of more than one team.

KEY POINTS

- Much of what we consider to be social work is carried out in teams.
- Social workers need to be aware of the role they play in teams and develop team work skills.
- Teams can be with service users and families, or may be unitary, inter-professional, or multi-disciplinary; thus team members may have conflicting values and constraints.
- Effective teams reflect on their performance as well as their aims and outcomes – 'how' as well as 'why' or 'what'.
- Teams adopting a person-centred approach can improve care outcomes for service users.

DISCUSSION

What is teamwork?

Guzzo and Dickson (1996) highlight the difficulties of defining teamwork without resorting to identification of how a team works together towards meeting common goals and its adaptation to circumstances. They note that teamwork comprises activities such as: monitoring your own and other team members' actions; giving and receiving feedback to each other; effective communication between members; being willing and able to back up team members; and knowledge of each other's skills and roles within teams.

Forming a successful team

There are a number of conditions which need to be present in order for a team to work effectively:

- a clear and shared purpose;
- positive and effective leadership;
- awareness of each other's roles and remits;
- space and opportunity for reflection and feedback;
- excellent communication.

When joining a new team or existing team it is useful to have an awareness of how teams develop. According to Payne (1979), there are four stages, namely: orientation; accommodation; negotiation; and operation.

Benefits of teamwork

Teamwork benefits clients by improving the quality of care; making better use of resources; providing more holistic assessments and care delivery; and giving increased staff satisfaction. Within social care, teams involve the co-ordination of people whose role it is to provide a service to a person in need. This often means that different professionals work together in community multi-disciplinary teams and an individual's needs are 'matched' with the skills and resources available from within the team, highlighting the gestalt idea that the team is greater than the sum of its parts (Øvretveit, 1993).

Skills required for teamwork

All team members need to take responsibility for ensuring the team is effective. In this economic climate it is particularly important that team members develop creative skills; the ability to positively plan, challenge and meet the needs of service users in ways which do not always involve more resources but a more creative use of current resources – be they financial or through the use of community and people.

The move towards personalisation has increased the need for social workers to develop teamwork skills in order to participate in or co-ordinate teams or circles of support around individuals (Lunt et al., 2008). Working in partnership involves working co-operatively with service recipients and families. This can be considered another type of teamwork.

Skills around working collaboratively, such as co-ordination, taking responsibility and working autonomously, are essential for effective teamwork. Generalisations and misunderstandings about roles can sometimes be present within teams. Developing or acknowledging our own and therefore each other's roles and value base will enable more effective team working as recognition of the different challenges and responsibilities faced by various professionals can contribute to deeper levels of co-operation. It could be argued that some level of conflict within teams can be productive if accompanied by respect for each other's roles and avoidance of professional jealousy. Regular team meetings and reflection within formal teams will aid understanding and development of shared values.

THE CONCEPT IN SOCIAL WORK PRACTICE

It can be argued that social work comprises of three aspects: face-to-face clinical work; care management; and advocacy. Therefore, much of social work is carried out in teams. Although these teams may be *unitary*, consisting entirely of social work professionals, most consist of two professionals from different agencies working together – *interagency*, or increasingly, *multiagency*, involving participants from outside the social work organisation, such as allied health professionals, housing organisations, care providers, general practitioners (GPs), and so on. Øvretveit et al. note that it is the reality of modern health and social services that the support and care received by individuals 'depends as much on how professionals work with each other as on their individual competence within their own field of expertise' (1997: 1).

According to Belbin, every job:

> encompasses three possible roles . . . the professional role, the team role and the work role . . . and every person who enters a new job should consider his or her position from the point of view of these three forces. (2004: xvi)

She identified eight team roles useful to have in teams: company worker; chairman; shaper; plant; resource investigator; monitor evaluator; team worker; and completer/finisher (Belbin, 2004: 72). These team roles have been used throughout various disciplines to teach about teams and are worth exploring in order to gain increased self-awareness about one's individual contribution to teamwork. Research has identified that the team member most common to successful teams was the company worker, or implementer. There have been critiques of this typology but Belbin's work remains influential in a great deal of management training.

Working as a person-centred team can help to overcome some of the tensions that can inevitably occur when there are different dynamics and relationships present. There is much focus on the need to be person centred with individuals who we support, but being part of a person-centred team requires a change in thinking and a change in practice for professionals and organisations. It means that we also need to work in a person-centred way with staff and colleagues.

The person-centred team development model

Table 59.1 describes the sequence that a team needs to go through in order to operate in a person-centred way, thus aiding effectiveness of the operation of the team as a whole. The case below demonstrates some examples of how a successful team works together to achieve its purpose.

Table 59.1

Stages and questions to ask:	What do we have to do?
1 Why are we here?	Clarify values and directions; establish our purpose; think about what our successful team would look like?
2 Who are you? How can we support each other and work together?	Think about what are my strengths and where do I need support? Share this with my colleagues and learn the same about them. Clarify how much autonomy we have and how far we can use our own initiative. How will we make team decisions?
3 What are our goals?	Who are the individuals the team will be supporting? What is our role in the individuals' life? How can they best be supported by the team? Person-centred planning and team planning will help clarify the answers to these questions
4 Who does what, where and when?	Roles are clarified in relation to the goals of the team. Action plans are useful here.
5 How are we doing?	Review our actions regularly, both on a daily basis as individuals and during team meetings; actively create a culture where we are able to reflect on what we are doing and how effective it is? What is working and what is not working? Are we achieving our goals? Are we supporting people to get better lives?
6 What else can we try?	This is about ongoing learning – both of the individuals we are supporting, and of ourselves and the team we work within. We need to respond reflexively to enable growth and development.

Source: Adapted from Sanderson, 2002

Working as part of a person-centred team

Clare manages a team of workers who support individuals with learning disabilities and mental health needs to live independently. They have a team plan which details their overall purpose and roles within team meetings; this is put up at every team meeting and referred to. They have an 'away day' at least once a year. This gives them the essential opportunity to think about how they are operating as a team and consider what is working and what is not working. All team members have attended values based training and Clare uses a person-centred supervision process with the aim of ensuring all team members come away from supervision feeling listened to, supported, motivated and with a clear direction for action.

Not only does this approach lead to effective team working, but it also contributes towards the quality assurance process, and provides regulatory bodies tangible examples of how individual services and teams are meeting their aims and objectives.

CONCLUSION

Social work tasks such as care management involve purchasing from several different providers of housing, activities and leisure. According to Xyrichis and Lowton (2008), structure of teams (premises, size, composition) and team processes (having clear aims and objectives, regular meetings, and self-monitoring) are the two main tenets for effective team working in health and social care. In the light of recent reports into safeguarding issues (see DfE, 2011), teams need to find ways of working together often without the luxury of shared office space or shared paperwork.

Social workers need to develop team working skills in order to effectively work within and lead formal and informal teams so that individuals who are in need of support benefit from successful and cohesive team working. It is imperative that power differentials are examined in all social care interactions and this is particularly relevant when considering working in teams which involve service recipients and their families. The value base of social work demands self-awareness and acknowledgement of power differentials.

Cross references: communication, leadership and management, multi-professional working, partnership, reflection

SUGGESTED READING

Belbin, M. (2003) 'The Belbin team role model'. Available from: www.belbin.com (accessed 17 May 2012).

Øvretveit, J., Mathias, P. and Thompson, T. (1997) *Interprofessional Working for Health and Social Care*. Basingstoke: Palgrave Macmillan.

REFERENCES

Belbin, R.M. (2004) *Management Teams, Why they Succeed or Fail*, 2nd edn. Oxford: Elsevier.

DfE (2011) *The Munro Review of Child Protection: Final Report*. London: DfE.

Guzzo, R.A. and Dickson, M.W. (1996) 'Teams in organisations: recent research on performance and effectiveness', *Annual Review of Psychology*, 47: 307–38.

Lunt, J., Bassett, J., Evans, L. and Jones, L. (2008) 'People with learning disabilities planning for themselves', in J. Thompson, J. Kilbane and H. Sanderson (eds), *Person Centred Practice for Professionals*. Maidenhead: Open University Press, pp. 213–30.

Øvretveit, J. (1993) *Co-ordinating Community Care: Multi-Disciplinary Teams and Care Management*. Milton Keynes: Open University Press.

Øvretveit, J., Mathias, P. and Thompson, T. (1997) *Interprofessional Working for Health and Social Care*. Basingstoke: Palgrave Macmillan.

Payne, M. (1979) *Power, Authority and Responsibility in Social Services: Social Work in Area Teams*. Basingstoke: Palgrave Macmillan.

Sanderson, H. (2002) 'Person centred teams', in J. O'Brien and C.L. O'Brien (eds), *Implementing Person-Centered Planning – Voices of Experience*. Toronto, ON: Inclusion Press.

Xyrichis, A. and Lowton, K. (2008) 'What fosters or prevents interprofessional teamworking in primary and community care? A literature review', *International Journal of Nursing Studies*, 45(1): 140–53.

Pat Cox

DEFINITION

While numerous definitions of theory, including social work theory, are extant (for example, Payne, 2005), this chapter's author acknowledges that theories are coherent, explanatory frameworks; bodies of knowledge which constantly are expanding. In social work practice, theories (wherever they originate) are means of analysing and understanding a person (or family, group or community), a subject or an issue. Some theories applied or developed in social work are also paradigms, providing both a framework for analysis (or critique) and implicit guidance for action (Howe, 1987). Theories are context-bound; they are not independent of the nations and cultures where they are developed (Rojek et al., 1989). They are transferable between situations, but, as in any field of knowledge (including social work), no one theory explains everything.

From the inception of social work practice in the western world, workers sought to understand the 'person-in-situation' (Richmond, 1922) or 'person and situation' (Hamilton, 1940), through deploying existing theoretical knowledge or developing anew (Howe, 1987). Like these early social work thinkers, many social work educators today believe that service users and their carers deserve qualified social workers who can understand and analyse users' and carers' personal issues in addition to their circumstances as members of society (Cox, 2009); that is, consider the inter-relationships between personal, societal and political issues and the implications of all these factors for support or intervention. Theoretical knowledge of different kinds provides various frameworks for this.

KEY POINTS

- Theories have been adopted from other disciplines, including social and natural sciences.
- Theories have been developed within social work.
- Theory is directly relevant to practice and beneficial to practitioners, service users and carers.
- The use of theory is subject to a wide variety of influences that affect its development and direction.

DISCUSSION

Full details of theories adopted from other disciplines and applied to social work and theories developed within social work, require a book or two (Howe, 2009). Throughout its lifetime as a practice and an academic discipline, social work has used sociological (sometimes social) theories, particularly in understanding the material circumstances or outer worlds or 'situations', in which people live their lives. A complete list is not possible here: however, for example: theories of modernity which emphasise societies' structures; sociological theories of 'race' and racism; feminist sociological theories; social constructions of sexuality and disability; sociological theorising about class and about poverty (Cree, 2010), are all relevant in educating pre-qualifying workers. In addition are various modern and postmodern theories which centralise agency on the part of service users and carers and which emphasise their present and future 'situations' (Powell, 2012).

Social work has made use also of psychological theories, in order to understand 'the person' or the emotions and inner worlds of people with whom social workers engage, whether individuals, families, groups or communities. Theories used include: the work of Freud (2005), examining childhood development and its impact in our adult lives; Fanon (2008) on the impact of racism on the psyche; and work by Erikson and Erikson (1997) exploring adulthood and older age. The contribution of psychological theories to working with and within groups (Bion, 1998) is valued by educators and practitioners and aspects of theory from psychodynamic ego psychology underpin crisis intervention in social work practice (Parad and Parad, 1990).

Social work's adoption of psycho-social theory has waxed and waned. Psychosocial theory is not a combination of sociological and psychological theories; it is a theory in its own right, drawing from critical theory and psychoanalysis, endeavoring to understand how inner and outer worlds interact with and influence one another, and inter-connections and parallel structures between personal and social worlds (Miller et al., 2008). Its strength is its potential for understanding the feelings of service users and carers *and* their societal positions – 'person-in-situation' – and in analysing issues in relationships between service users and carers and social workers such as projection, projective identification, transference and countertransference (Froggett, 2002).

Social work has also built on theories first developed in the natural sciences; systems theory arises from general systems theory in biology (von Bertalanffy, 1971). Systems theory influenced the development of family therapy (Miermont, 1995), which explores familial relationships as system relationships. There are a number of family therapy 'schools', which have some commonalities and some key differences, but which all emphasise the importance of the whole family working together to resolve issues. Social work's application of family therapy often includes using techniques such as circular questioning, family sculpting and genograms.

Ecological systems theory was developed by Bronfenbrenner (1979), who argues that there are four significant inter-connected systems. These are (in ascending order): the micro; meso; exo; and macro and these surround the developing child. In Bronfenbrenner's original thinking, there is no focus on the child's internal world, so this theory was inclined more to 'situation' than to 'person'. It remains influential in social work; its influence can be discerned in the current 'Framework for Assessment'.

Theories which have arisen out of social work include task-centred theory, which focuses on defined problems or types of problems in people's lives; problems which social workers, service users and carers believe are solvable (Doel and Marsh, 1992). Thus while task-centred theory may address emotional concerns, it is less likely to address wider social issues (generally not amenable to speedy resolution) or interactions between the two. In earlier work, Howe (1987) provides a four-paradigm framework, arguing that social workers gravitate more towards theories of one paradigm than others. An ontological position – a position which each of us holds concerning the nature of the social world and human relationships and which leads us to seek explanations about the social world which 'fit' our ideas about it – influences social work practitioners' orientation towards a particular theory or theories and thus our practice is underpinned by theory from within a particular paradigm. Howe (1987) argues that this orientation is often unconscious and many workers will claim not to be using theory at all; those who claim to take an 'eclectic approach' also are choosing from within a limited range.

In the political and social climates of the 1990s in the UK, concerns were raised about the dwindling emphasis in social work on theory at the expense of competence (Jones, 1996). Howe's (1996) comments on the absence of theoretical frameworks which facilitate explorations of the feelings and material circumstances of service users and carers and the theoretical insights which workers bring to bear on them remain relevant today. Garrett (2009) notes the continuing undervaluing of theory in some quarters and the recent Capabilities Framework refers only to 'knowledge of social sciences, law and social work practice theory' (Social Work Reform Board, 2010: 7.)

Teaching theory is the responsibility of social work educators in academic settings and of practice educators in agencies. However, lack of updated theoretical works in some agencies, combined with workplace cultures of negative attitudes towards reading theory and research, may result in practice which is not securely supported by theory. Theories need to be re-read and reviewed in practice, so that practice develops. The focus in most theories applied in social work in the western world is the individual: child, young person or adult; families; or small groups. Theories of and about working with and within communities are not applied in the UK to the same extent that they are in other nations (Hugman et al., 2010). Increasingly challenges are made to the cultural hegemony of social work practice and education (including the development and deployment of theories) as they have been developed in the UK and North America (Mwansa, 2011). One limitation of UK social work's cultural hegemony is that social pedagogy – a theoretically informed practical and relationship-based approach to working with children and young people and well-established in mainland Europe – has been piloted in the UK only recently (Cameron et al., 2011). It is likely that some current theories will need to be updated in light of developing international understandings; some theories may become less frequently used.

The application of service user and carer 'knowledge through experience' within social work practice, education and research has enriched the discipline greatly (Branfield, 2009). Social workers' ability to explain the theory/theories underpinning their support for, or interventions with, service users and carers so that it can be easily understood, is essential. Research with service users and carers (previously 'clients') from the 1970s (Howe, 1987) to the present day, demonstrates that service users appreciate clarity of purpose and theoretical approach from their social worker.

THE CONCEPT IN SOCIAL WORK PRACTICE

Applying theory in practice

Ali began working with the Omar family when child protection concerns were raised around the death of their youngest child (a baby girl), although it was later agreed to be death from natural causes. The Omar family are refugees who have 'indefinite leave to remain' and their baby was conceived and born in the UK. Their older two children (a boy aged six and a girl aged eight) attend a local primary school. Having resolved the child protection concerns, Ali's involvement with the family should come to an end: everyone in his team carries an extensive caseload and he is under some pressure. However, there is a recent school report that both the older children have become emotionally withdrawn, with the boy having been subject to some racist name-calling. In Ali's professional judgement, Mr and Mrs Omar are depressed, appear to have difficulty grieving for their baby daughter and are distant from one another and from their older children. And while some of their neighbours, both English and of their own nationality, have supported them, others have cut off contact.

Ali's grandparents were migrants (but not refugees) with his parents as children to the UK during the 20th century and Ali remembers his parents' and his grandparents' stories about the excitements and the difficulties of settling somewhere different in the world and being determined to make new lives. Reflecting on psycho-social theory he is aware of the dangers of projective identification in relation to his own feelings about his family's experiences with those of the Omar family, and is determined to avoid this. So far, he hasn't discussed his family background with Mr and Mrs Omar, or their son and daughter, although it does inform his thinking about their feelings and their current situation.

Ali discusses the Omar family's situation with his social work colleagues and team leader. Everyone agrees that complete withdrawal of social work involvement at this stage would not help anyone and the school have indicated that they may soon make an official referral about their concerns for the older children. Despite the child protection investigation, Ali has managed to create and sustain a relationship with the family, who don't seem to want him to stop visiting but who currently find it difficult to say anything to him.

Reflecting on theory learned while qualifying and in discussion with his team leader and colleagues, Ali decides to draw from systems theory – in particular, family therapy. Previous practice experience has made him aware that some service users and carers are more comfortable working with theories that can be demonstrated actively – such as family sculpting (where each family member 'sculpts' the family relationships as they experience them) or drawing a geno-gram (a family tree which includes absent and present members). The advan-tage is that all four family members can be involved in both sculpting and genogram work and whatever the results of them are, doing both will lead to four-way discussions about family relationships (and indirectly feelings) between the parents and children. In addition, drawing from psychological theory about the impact of childhood issues in adult lives, Ali plans to ask the children to paint their feelings about their sister's death and about the racism at school, addressing both their emotional upheaval and their wider situation. He will continue using psycho-social theory to maintain his awareness of the impact of himself in the worker–Omar family relationship.

Cross references: carers, practice education, service user involvement, social work, supervision

SUGGESTED READING

Howe, D. (2009) *A Brief Introduction to Social Work Theory*. Basingstoke: Palgrave Macmillan.
Payne, M. (2005) *Modern Social Work Theory*, 3rd edn. Basingstoke: Palgrave Macmillan.

REFERENCES

Bion, W. (1998) *Experiences in Groups*. London: Tavistock.
Branfield, F. (2009) *Developing User Involvement in Social Work Education*. London: Shaping Our Lives Network.
Bronfenbrenner, U. (1979) *The Ecology of Human Development: Experiments by Nature and Design*. Cambridge, MA: Harvard University Press.
Cameron, C., Petrie, P., Wigfall, V., Kleipoedszus, S. and Jasper, A. (2011) *Final Report of the Social Pedagogy Pilot Programme: Development and Implementation*. London: Thomas Coram Research Unit at Institute of Education.
Cox, P. (2009) '"Connectivity": seeking conditions and connections for radical discourses and praxes in health, mental health and social work', *Social Theory and Health*, 7(2): 170–86.
Cree, V.E. (2010) *Sociology for Social Workers*, 2nd edn. London: Routledge.
Doel, M. and Marsh, P. (1992) *Task-Centred Social Work*. Aldershot: Ashgate.
Erikson, E. and Erikson, J.M. (1997) *The Life Cycle Completed*. New York: W.W. Norton and Co.
Fanon, F. (2008) *Black Skin, White Masks*. London: Pluto Press.
Freud, S. (2005) *The Unconscious*. London: Penguin.
Froggett, L. (2002) *Love, Hate and Welfare: Psycho-Social Approaches to Policy and Practice*. Bristol: Policy Press.
Garrett, P.M. (2009) 'The "whalebone" in the (social work) "corset"? Notes on Antonio Gramsci and social work education', *Social Work Education*, 28(5): 461–75.
Hamilton, G. (1940) *Theory and Practice in Social Casework*, 2nd edn. New York: University of Columbia Press.
Howe, D. (1987) *An Introduction to Social Work Theory*. Aldershot: Ashgate.
Howe, D. (1996) 'Surface and depth in social work practice', in N. Parton (ed.), *Social Theory, Social Change and Social Work*. London: Routledge, pp. 77–97.
Howe, D. (2009) *A Brief Introduction to Social Work Theory*. Basingstoke: Palgrave Macmillan.

key concepts in
social work practice

Hugman, R., Moosa-Mitha, M. and Moyo, O. (2010) 'Towards a borderless social work: reconsidering notions of international social work', *International Social Work*, 53: 629–43.

Jones, C. (1996) 'Anti-intellectualism and the peculiarities of British social work education', in N. Parton (ed.), *Social Theory, Social Change and Social Work*. London: Routledge, pp. 190–210.

Miermont, J. (1995) *The Dictionary of Family Therapy*. Oxford: Blackwell.

Miller, C., Hoggett, P. and Mayo, M. (2008) 'Psycho-social perspectives in policy and professional practice research', in P. Cox, T. Geisen and R. Green (eds), *Qualitative Research and Social Change: European Contexts*. Basingstoke: Palgrave, pp. 112–34..

Mwansa, L.-K. (2011) 'Social work education in Africa: whence and whither?', *Social Work Education*, 30(1): 4–16.

Parad, H.J. and Parad, L.G. (1990) *Crisis Intervention Book 2: The Practitioner's Sourcebook for Brief Therapy*. Milwaukee: Family Service America.

Payne, M. (2005) *Modern Social Work Theory*, 3rd edn. Basingstoke: Palgrave Macmillan.

Powell, J.L. (2012) *The Social Construction of the Lifecourse*. London: Routledge.

Richmond, M. (1922) *Social Case Work: An Introductory Description*. New York: Russell Sage Foundation.

Rojek, C., Peacock, G. and Collins, S. (1989) *Social Work and Received Ideas*. London: Routledge.

Social Work Reform Board (2010) *Building a Safe and Confident Future: One Year On*. London: HMSO.

von Bertalanffy, L. (1971) *General System Theory: Foundations, Development, Application*, 2nd edn. London: Penguin.

61
Values

Steven M. Shardlow

DEFINITION

Drawing on the work of Williams (1968), Reamer has offered this usable, albeit pragmatic, definition of 'values':

> Values have several important attributes and perform several important functions: they are generalised, emotionally charged conceptions of what is desirable; historically created and derived from experience; shared by a population or group within it; and provide a means for organising and structuring patterns of behaviour. (Reamer, 1999: 10)

Taking this definition uncritically, social work values may be regarded as a series of statements or beliefs, which the profession collectively regards as being desirable. Social workers have claimed that there is a universal set of professional values although it has proved notoriously difficult to enumerate these values in unanimously agreed form. At the global level, a statement of professional values has been developed by The International Federation of Social Workers (IFSW):

> Social work grew out of humanitarian and democratic ideals, and its values are based on respect for the equality, worth, and dignity of all people. Since its beginnings over a century ago, social work practice has focused on meeting human needs and developing human potential. Human rights and social justice serve as the motivation and justification for social work action. In solidarity with those who are dis-advantaged, the profession strives to alleviate poverty and to liberate vulnerable and oppressed people in order to promote social inclusion. Social work values are embodied in the profession's national and international codes of ethics. (IFSW, 2000)

This statement is clearly incontrovertibly noble and worthy; less clear is the extent to which the statement has directly influenced the day-to-day practice of social workers.

KEY POINTS

- Values are a set of ideas, principles, or statements, which people believe and to which they attach cognitive importance and have emotional attachment.
- Professional values are those held in common by a profession, either formally within a written code or informally as part of a collective approach to issues based upon practice wisdom.
- Professional values in social work are problematic, as while the overwhelming number of social workers assert their importance, there may be little consensus about the canon of social work values or their interpretation.
- Personal and professional values may be different, which may lead to tensions between the requirements of personal morality and a professional code of ethics.
- Professional values not only influence *what* is done in the name of social work but *how* professional practice is undertaken.

DISCUSSION

Social work is a highly normative profession. It is not solely concerned with the practitioners' technological skills; deeply embedded within the notion of social work is a belief that there is a set of ideals which collectively define professional aspirations. Assertions of the importance of 'values' are commonplace in social work writing; achieving consensus about an agreed meaning for the term or what kind of entities they may be remains highly problematic. There have been numerous attempts to enumerate lists of social work values during the history of the profession. The book, *Social Work Values: An Enquiry* by Timms (1983) has remained a seminal work on the subject of social work values. In this enquiry, Timms sought to uncover the nature of 'value talk' in social work by analysing the way that the terms 'value' or 'values' were used in everyday language: he cited evidence that there were no less than 180 different meanings of the word 'value' or 'values'.

Based on a review of the work of some 28 authors, Reamer (1999: 21) listed some 13 items as the most commonly cited social work values:

1 individual worth and dignity;
2 respect of persons, valuing individuals' capacity for change;
3 client self-determination;
4 helping individuals to realise their potential;
5 seeking to meet individuals' common human needs;
6 seeking to provide individuals with adequate resources and services to meet their basic needs;
7 client empowerment;
8 equal opportunity;
9 non-discrimination;
10 respect for diversity;
11 commitment to social change and social justice;
12 confidentiality and privacy;
13 willingness to transmit professional knowledge and skills to others.

This listing provides a good starting point for discussion about both the scope and extent of social work values and also exploration of detailed meanings, applications and implementation of each of the items in practice. Such a detailed analysis cannot be undertaken here.

THE CONCEPT IN SOCIAL WORK PRACTICE

Values in practice raise difficult and complex issues. To illustrate some of these difficulties four major areas of difficulty that confront practitioners have been explored where professional values conflict with: personal values; employer requirements; those of other professionals; the values of others (service users and carers). These are considered in turn.

When social workers' personal and professional values conflict, whenever possible, they should seek ways to ensure that the service user receives an appropriate service from another practitioner. For example, a social worker who is opposed to abortion for religious reasons, may receive a request to provide counselling to a pregnant service user about termination. In such cases, the worker should discuss her dilemma with her line manager and request that another worker might support the service user. In an ideal world a specialist agency will provide the necessary support. However the worker may feel pressure from her employer to support the woman, thus being caught with the dilemma of being true to her own beliefs and being true to her professional values of maintaining dignity and choice for the service user. Practitioners in such cases should not disclose their principled opposition to abortion; this may unduly influence service use. Such types of value conflict may engender profound stress for the social worker.

Many social workers are employed in large organisations. Suppose, for example, a social worker has witnessed what they believe to be unacceptable professional practice by a senior member of their employing organisation. The social worker considered that such an action both contradicted the professional value requirements and may have endangered service use; when reported, the employer may have refused to take further action. Having sought to persuade the employer of their position, the social worker may have reported the issue anonymously to the Children's Commissioner or the Care Quality Commission or may have maintained a principled objection – a course of action that could have cost their job. Each option would have demanded that the social worker confront how far they were prepared to go to maintain the integrity of their values.

It cannot be assumed that other helping professions subscribe to the same set of values. For example, at a hospital ward round, healthcare professionals and social work staff disagreed along professional lines about the discharge of a 90-year-old from hospital care to live on her own in the community. At the heart of the disagreement were different professional beliefs about balancing protection from harm and provision of independence. Where there is such a dispute, the reasons for disagreement should be explored in discussion across professional boundaries; the aim being not to win the argument but to explore what may be in the service user's best interest. Over time, through such discussion, team members may come to better understand each other's value position which may serve to strengthen team functioning.

On occasion, practitioners may find themselves in principled objection with the value position taken by a service user or carer; often this may be over an inconsequential matter. However, it may be fundamental as in the example below.

Case study

A male, aged 17 years, ten months, was expected by his family to return to a distant homeland to meet and marry a suitable female. He told his teacher that he did not want to follow this path but that he was worried that not to follow this culturally prescribed pattern would lead to his being ostracised by his community. He should be advised of his options not to conform to cultural norms and provided with alternative support structures. If he had been coerced legal action may have been necessary.

The principles underlying this example require detailed consideration. Tolerance of diversity is part of the canon of social work values even where values held by others may be distasteful or worrying. Where behaviours are perceived to be linked to religious or cultural practices there may be an extreme reluctance by social workers to intervene, justified by an acceptance of 'cultural relativism', in other words, no set of moral beliefs are superior to another. Therefore action may be deemed inappropriate. A significant number of religions do not accord equal status to men and women to: obtain a full education; participate in economic activity; or engage in social activity (for example, driving, walking on the street without following prescribed dress codes and such like). How is the social worker to respond to such situations, to accept a cultural relativist position and tolerate such behaviours without challenge? The problem may be perceived by the social worker as one of degree: practices grounded in religious or cultural practices are acceptable so long as they do not lead to harm. Such a stance places the social worker in the position of having to make a judgement about what is harmful and what is not, as in the example above.

However, cultural relativism is not the required position that follows from the professional commitment to diversity (see Reamer's list above). Rather, the espousal of a commitment to 'human rights' by social work practitioners provides an alternative basis for considered action. According to the United Nations:

> Human rights are those rights, which are inherent in our nature and without which we cannot live as human beings. Human rights and fundamental freedoms allow us to fully develop and use our human qualities, our intelligence, our talents and our conscience to satisfy our spiritual and other needs. (United Nations, 1987)

Human rights are *universal*, in other words, they apply to all people in all situations and *indivisible*, in other words, they cannot be separated and some promoted at the expense of others. They are located in the various declarations of the United Nations, notably the *Universal Declaration of Human Rights* (1948). Three broad areas of human rights are found: political (freedom of assembly, free movement free speech, right to vote and so on); standard of living commensurate with the level of economic development of the country of residence (education, housing, medical care and so on); and international social order that allows the rights to be realised (Reichert, 2006). In the difficult case above, the social worker could have explored the extent to which the 17-year-old's human rights were in danger of violation. Had he, for instance, had a learning disability, there may have been the added complication of his capacity to understand the full implications of marriage. This may have provided justification for immediate action, while acceptance of a position based on unbridled cultural relativism may have justified observation and inaction.

From these examples of the operation of social work values in practice it can be seen that professional values present many complex problems for the practitioner to address.

Cross references: anti-oppressive practice, empowerment, equality and diversity, ethics

SUGGESTED READING

Banks, S. (2006) *Ethics and Values in Social Work*, 3rd edn. London: Palgrave Macmillan.
Barnard, A., Horner, N. and Wild, J. (eds) (2008) *The Value Base of Social Work and Social Care: An Active Learning Handbook*. Maidenhead: Open University Press.

REFERENCES

IFSW (International Federation of Social Workers) (2000) 'Definition of social work'. Available from: www.ifsw.org/en/p38000208.html (accessed 14 March 2006).
Meinert, R.G. (1980) 'Values in social work called dysfunctional myth', *Journal of Social Welfare and Family Law*, 6(3): 5–16.
Reamer, F.G. (1999) *Social Work Values and Ethics*, 2nd edn. New York: Columbia.
Reichert, E. (2006) *Understanding Human Rights*. London: Sage.
Timms, N. (1983) *Social Work Values: An Enquiry*. London: Routledge & Kegan Paul.
United Nations (1948) *The Universal Declaration of Human Rights*. New York: United Nations.
United Nations (1987) *Human Rights: Questions and Answers*. New York: United Nations.
Williams, R.M.J. (1968) 'The concept of values', in D. L. Sills (ed.), *International Encyclopaedia of the Social Sciences*, Volume 16. New York: Macmillan/Free Press, pp. 283–7.

values

62

Welfare Rights

Neil Bateman

DEFINITION

Welfare rights practice includes advice and advocacy to maximise people's lawful entitlement to social security benefits. It may also include advice and advocacy on debts, housing and rights to community care services, but it usually refers to social security issues. The expression 'welfare rights' originated in the United States in the 1970s, where 'welfare' colloquially refers to the means-tested benefits systems administered by each state. The (American) National Welfare Rights Organisation was closely linked to the civil rights movement because of the levels of poverty among African Americans and the discriminatory and capricious application of welfare rules by public officials (Curtis and Sanderson, 2004).

KEY POINTS

- Welfare rights practice takes a variety of forms. It includes: advice about benefit entitlement; practical help with applications and providing supporting evidence; advocacy against benefit officials in support of an application or to challenge a decision about benefits; and direct advocacy before a First Tier Tribunal to try and alter an unfavourable benefit decision.
- Crucial to welfare rights practice is independence from the bodies which administer benefits, enabling advice to be given untainted by official 'interpretation' of the rules and without advocacy being compromised by allegiance to the organisation.
- Experience also shows that the quality of advice provided by organisations such as the Department for Work and Pension too often is incorrect or seriously deficient and in any event is increasingly difficult to obtain.
- Welfare rights practice often features in the work of many people with a helping role for those on low incomes and social workers are frequently asked for help with benefits issues by service users. There are also people who specialise in welfare rights practice – for example, welfare rights advisers employed by local authorities or the voluntary sector and advisers employed by some law centres and private solicitors.

DISCUSSION

Like any type of advocacy, welfare rights practice differs from many other activities carried out by social workers because it reverses power roles and involves the social worker challenging the welfare bureaucracy on behalf of service users, rather than rationing access to services. Advocacy can also generate conflict between organisations and it is important that employing organisations provide support and protection for their staff to act as advocates. This is particularly so when local authority staff advocate against another part of the organisation (such as the council's housing benefits service) or when people working in the voluntary sector challenge decisions about service users' entitlement by the body which funds them (again, this is most likely to be the local authority). This issue is particularly important because recent governments have encouraged a convergence of 'cash' and 'care' services.

Socio-economic context

It is stating the obvious that most people who use social work services are poor. While not all service users are poor and while not everyone living in poverty needs social work services, poverty worsens and even causes many of the interpersonal and care issues in which social workers are engaged. For example, there is compelling evidence to demonstrate the increased likelihood of children entering the care system when their families are in the poorest circumstances. Similarly, there is an increased likelihood of early death and disability is associated with low income, as well as an increased likelihood of offending and mental ill-health (see, for example, Anushree et al., 2010; Wilkinson and Pickett, 2010). Indeed, the link with poverty is why, for many decades, part of the UK government's funding formula for social care services has been based on the numbers of people receiving certain means-tested benefits in each local authority. Welfare rights practice is a practical response to the poverty experienced by service users.

The need for welfare rights practice has also become entrenched as a result of persistent economic inequalities and long-term poverty since the 1980s and the increased complexity of the benefits system as successive governments have tightened eligibility and conditionality while extending means testing as their preferred method of income maintenance. The administration of social security benefits has also become more remote as the Department for Work and Pensions has increasingly moved to regional benefit delivery systems. There is evidence of frequent failure in the administration of benefits which can often result in people being left without money they are entitled to – or even destitute.

Many benefit claimants increasingly experience the benefits system as punitive and stigmatising as a result of changes brought about by successive governments to make benefits more restrictive and conditional. Welfare rights advocacy is an important element of wider attempts to change this.

THE CONCEPT IN SOCIAL WORK PRACTICE

The complexity of the benefits system combined with the amount of time often taken to tackle even simple benefits problems (and the fear of making mistakes) has led some people to hold the view that welfare rights practice is not part of the social work task – particularly as social work has moved towards a more defined remit through the development of concepts like care management. Indeed, there is a concern that this may lead to a level of non-engagement in welfare rights practice by social workers.

However, because most service users are benefit claimants, the difficulty many have in accessing mainstream advice services and the effect of benefit problems on their lives, welfare rights practice should be one of the skills and areas of knowledge used by social workers as part of diversified practice. The key is having appropriate boundaries and good access to specialist support and referral systems. The real risk of the opinion that welfare rights practice is not for social workers, is that some very vulnerable service users' lives are made far worse as a result. On a practical level, the increased income from benefits can be used to help fund some care packages – either indirectly because of the way that people spend such money or directly through the legal rules for charging for adults' care services. Increased income also enhances independent living (see, for example, Noble et al., 1997).

Moreover, the role of being an advocate to tackle service users' benefit problems is an effective way to build professional credibility and trust as well as demonstrate empathy. It is also inherent in the social worker's professional duty to 'protect the rights and promote the interest of service users and carers' (GSCC, 2004). Benefit problems create 'stress and financial strain' (DWP, 2009). Non-engagement and failure to integrate into social work practice can pose risks to safe and effective practice – for example, benefits problems have formed a backdrop in some serious case reviews, including that for Victoria Climbié. There is also evidence that welfare rights work has positive effects on service users' mental and physical health and social well-being (Bateman, 2006; Wiggan and Talbot, 2006).

It seems essential for social workers to have good access to support from welfare rights specialists who understand the professional and organisational context that they operate within. This makes it far easier for social workers to tackle service users' benefit problems as well as to feel secure that they are doing so in the right way – and to be able to refer on a matter which really is too complex for a non-specialist to deal with. This is why many organisations employ in-house welfare rights specialists, most of whom provide second tier advice services to front line staff. This also is more likely to generate seamless referrals and engagement of social workers in the process. Employers therefore have a responsibility to ensure that support systems are properly funded and set up.

The boundaries which social workers can safely operate within include the ability to:

- understand the key eligibility criteria for social security benefits and to identify when service users may qualify;
- carry out basic benefit checks as part of social work assessments;
- know how to claim benefits and help service users make effective claims;
- resolve straightforward issues which arise in the claims process and support service users through this process, particularly where literacy, mental health, disability or lifestyle issues make claiming more difficult;
- obtain and supply relevant supporting evidence such as medical evidence or conclusions from assessments which can be particularly helpful for benefit claims by young people or people with a disability;

- understand the relationships between different benefits – for example, how disability benefits can affect means-tested benefits;
- understand the importance of appealing against benefit refusals, overpayments and sanctions;
- know how to appeal against such decisions and draft appeal notices;
- know when a benefits issue is complex and, how and where to seek help and if appropriate, refer service users.

The skills needed for effective welfare rights practice include:

- interviewing and not focusing on the presenting problem;
- legal research – knowing where to look and who to ask for independent information on benefit rights;
- communicating advice to service users in an appropriate way and summarising this in records;
- negotiation skills and knowing when negotiation is not appropriate;
- litigation skills – the ability to get your case over persuasively and using correct legal references, perhaps on the phone, in writing and by using formal appeals systems. Knowing which approach is best for each case.

Provided it is properly structured and supported, welfare rights practice is a legitimate and effective part of the social work role and can add value to the work of social workers.

USEFUL RESOURCES

WEBSITES

www.adviceguide.org.uk (Citizens Advice website covering a wide range of subjects)
www.direct.gov.uk (government web portal with access to benefits information and claim forms)
www.entitledto.co.uk (online benefits and tax credit calculators)
www.neilbateman.co.uk (personal website with a wide range of useful links)
www.rightsnet.org.uk (a website used by welfare rights specialists)

SUGGESTED READING

These are annual publications and the most up-to-date edition should be used.
Disability Rights Handbook. Published by Disability Alliance.
Guide to Housing Benefit and Council Tax Benefit. Published by Shelter and Chartered Institute of Housing.
Welfare Benefits and Tax Credits Handbook. Published by Child Poverty Action Group.
Young Persons Handbook. Published by Centre for Economic and Social Inclusion.

REFERENCES

Anushree, P., MacInnes, T. and Kenway, P. (2010) *Monitoring Poverty and Social Exclusion*. York: Joseph Rowntree Foundation.
Bateman, N. (2006) *Practising Welfare Rights*. London: Routledge.
Curtis, H. and Sanderson, M. (2004) *The Unsung Sixties*. London: Whiting and Birch.

DWP (Department of Work and Pensions) (2009) *Living with Poverty: A Review of the Literature on Children's and Families' Experiences of Poverty*. Department for Work and Pensions Research Report no. 594. London: HMSO.

GSCC (General Social Care Council) (2004) *Code of Practice for Social Care Workers*. London: GSCC.

Noble, M., Platt, L., Smith, G. and Daly, M. (1997) 'The spread of disability living allowance', *Disability and Society*, 12(5): 741–51.

Wiggan, J. and Talbot, C. (2006) *The Benefits of Welfare Rights Advice: A Review of the Literature*. London: National Association of Welfare Rights Advisers.

Wilkinson, R. and Pickett, R. (2010) *The Spirit Level: Why Equality is Better for Everyone*. London: Penguin.

Youth Justice

Chris Sheehy

DEFINITION

The Crime and Disorder Act (CDA) 1998, Part111, states precisely that the principal aim for youth justice agencies is to be the 'prevention of offending'.

At first sight the above statement might appear to be a clear and straightforward instruction, which assists us with definition. However, youth justice as a system is far from 'straightforward' to deal with conceptually. Children and young people implicated in the criminal justice system will have a 'need' and a 'right' to be assessed in a manner which focuses on their 'non-adult' status, and to have their legal rights respected. Social workers need to be educated and developed to assess, evaluate, and to advocate on behalf of children and young people in situations characterised by unmet need, vulnerability, and where there is simultaneously a stated or unstated expectation to intervene in a control and detention process.

For social workers there is a range of legislative priorities found in international and domestic law that compete with, or contradict, the CDA's stated principal aim. The Children Act 1989 reminds social workers of responsibility toward children 'in need', including the need to prevent children from entering the criminal justice system. The Act alerts social workers to the duty to protect children from 'significant harm'. Part 111 of the Children and Young Persons Act 1933, and Part 1 of the Children and Young Persons Act 1969, stress the importance of children involved in criminal proceedings requiring the protection of their welfare. A 'welfare' approach is also consistent with the recommendations in the 'Munro Review' (DfE, 2011).

The United Nations Convention on the Rights of the Child (UNCRC) was ratified by the UK in 1991, though not directly incorporated into domestic law. The UK is a signatory to the UNCRC and so reasonably there might be an expectation that the UNCRC will have a positive effect on judicial decision making. The UNCRC informs us in Article 3 that 'the best interests' of children should be a primary concern. Article 37 addresses the subject of 'detention' reminding us it should remain a 'measure of last resort'. The 'Beijing Rules', 1985, and the 'Riyadh Guidelines', 1990, emphasise 'safeguarding' and broader welfare issues. Cohen assists with the conceptual complexities for social workers:

> The closer you examine it the more it merges into its surrounding space. So it is with crime control . . . the parochial discipline of criminology, starts dissolving into much wider issues; political ideologies, the crisis in welfare liberalism, the nature of professional power, conceptions of human nature . . . we move into spaces which are not just amorphous, but imagined and imaginary. (Cohen, 1989: 197)

KEY POINTS

- Youth justice policy debates and service provision are heavily influenced by party political interest concerning youth and crime. Media reporting, if unbalanced or exaggerated, can prevent critical exploration, analysis, and debate into 'crime' and workable responses to crime. 'Moral panic' can encourage a disproportionate reaction, and political diversion (Cohen, 2002).
- Children as young as ten years old are deemed to be 'criminally responsible' (England, Wales and Northern Ireland). The majority of children entering custody have suffered from mistreatment or abuse, and have communication and literacy problems. A significant number (though not a majority) have been in care or have a physical disability, or complex mental health problems (Goldson, 2011).
- Social workers will generally access matters concerning 'youth justice' through 'youth offending teams' (YOTs), a feature of the CDA 1998. YOTs liaise with a variety of agencies, including the police, housing, health and education. The YOT will have access to information regarding the extent of unmet welfare need and any safeguarding issues. YOTs utilising local knowledge, listening to the aspirations of children and young people, collecting and disseminating valuable data could, if utilised, improve analysis and assist with change activity. Insights into 'race relations'; gender regulation; class differentials; the impact of labour market changes, high youth unemployment; reduced access to higher/further education and training; access to public space; urban underdevelopment; and intersectional issues, have the potential to engage wider debate.
- Statistical evidence from the 'official' crime surveys has shown crime figures as reasonably stable across the UK (Flatley et al., 2010; Goldson and Muncie, 2006). Austerity measures, worryingly high levels of youth unemployment and service cuts may impact upon crime statistics for the future. However, the last 15 years have seen a substantial increase in youth justice legislation, and

sentencing powers. Organisations such as the Standing Committee for Youth Justice have commented upon the high rates of children detained and released without appropriate aftercare provision.

- Restorative approaches can offer all of the individuals impacted upon by the 'offence' to jointly reach a mutual understanding. Van Ness and Strong list four key principles of restorative justice as: 'encounter, reparation, reintegration and participation' (Van Ness and Strong, 1997, cited in Goldson and Muncie, 2011: 111). Importantly, the mental capacity of a 'young participant' and their ability to give 'informed consent ' to the process will be crucial.

DISCUSSION

Cohen encourages us to think critically about the tendency to associate change with improvement:

> . . . all reform is motivated by benevolence, altruism, philanthropy and humanitarian-ism, and the eventual record of successive reforms, must be read as an incremental story of progress . . . (and additionally) . . . Early forms of punishment, based upon vengeance, cruelty and ignorance give way to informed, professional and expert inter-vention. (Cohen, 1989: 18)

The last decade and a half of policy changes and the haste in which they were introduced denoted a political shift for Labour policy. The 'tough on crime' agenda produced the Crime Sentences Act 1997, and was consistent with the earlier intro-duction of Secure Training Orders by the Conservative government's Criminal Justice and Public Order Act 1994. From 1998 onwards explicit reference has been made to the 'repeat offender'; fast tracking was encouraged to reduce the time from investigation to sentence to half of what it was in 1996. Increasingly, 'victims' are mentioned in policy, but without adequate attention being given to collecting data on children and young people as victims, including 'young offend-ers'. Simultaneously, the wider 'responsibility agenda' argued that families and communities increase their responsibility for current and 'future' offenders. The CDA 1998 'Framework Document' was aimed at agencies and individuals working within youth justice. Agencies were instructed to participate in YOT structures, and the policy initiatives. Clearly stated objectives for each area team and indi-viduals were introduced to enable performance and cost to be monitored and assessed (Home Office, 1998).

Youth justice legislation substantially increased following on from the Crime and Disorder Act 1998. The same year the Human Rights Act (1998) received Royal Assent; it is likely that the HRA (1998) will produce challenges to the CDA (1998). The Youth Justice and Criminal Evidence Act 1999 was followed by fur-ther examples of similar legislation throughout the next decade including the 2010 Crime and Security Act.

Welfare approaches, though not omitted, were being replaced by a host of orders, which according to Haydon and Scraton amounted to 'Adultism' (Muncie et al., 2009: 15). Judge Mumby, in the High Court, in a Howard League for Penal Reform case commented:

> . . . the State appears to be failing, and in some instances failing very badly, in its duties to vulnerable and damaged children . . . [he goes further adding] . . . which, on the face of it, ought to shock the conscience of every citizen. (Mumby, 2002: para 175, cited in Goldson and Muncie, 2006)

A shift to targeting 'non-offenders', who happen to share a similar identity, or 'disadvantages' with 'convicted offenders', was aimed at preventing crime through prediction techniques. An 'actuarial' process, aimed at predicting 'risk of criminality' which uses tools more suited to assessing deficit, will not be as effective for children with complex needs. Assessing for deficit can risk low expectation, stigma, and self-fulfilling prophecy, all well recognised in social work. Goldson and Muncie helpfully articulate the contradictions and lack of clear policy direction in youth justice:

> . . . it is difficult to identify any consistent rationale and/or philosophical core to the reforming zeal. A new rhetoric of youth crime prevention, restoration and social inclusion is uncomfortably located alongside the targeting of 'non offenders' as well as 'offenders' within formal systems of justice (criminalization); an increased tendency to responsibilize children, their families and communities, and a reliance on an expanding control apparatus to 'manage' poverty, structural disadvantage and systematic inequality. (Goldson and Muncie, 2006: 92)

Similarly, Feely and Simon comment that children 'are grasped not as coherent subjects, whether understood as moral, psychological or economic agents, but as members of particular subpopulations' (Feely and Simon, 1992, cited in Goldson and Muncie, 2011: 96).

THE CONCEPT IN SOCIAL WORK PRACTICE

Case study

Joe is ten years old; he was 'picked up by the police', at 10pm in a city centre train station. He was taken to a police station (he had failed to turn up for court the previous day). Allegedly Joe had stolen a box of teddy bear stickers from a local shop. The custody sergeant was unable to locate Joe's mother and they believed she 'worked nights'. Joe will appear in court the next day. On arrival at the station you ask to see Joe. You are directed to a cell (the 'juvenile' rooms you are told were already full). Joe has a standard blanket and a thin mattress, and he looks reasonably clean and nourished, but small for his age. The cell door is left open and the custody sergeant has let one of his staff sit outside in case Joe wakes up frightened. The station is almost full, and they are preparing for the arrival of drunken, injured, disturbed prisoners to arrive. All professionals concur, though lawful, a police station is no place for a young child.

Comment

Joe is a child in a cell, though he may be formally referred to as a 'youth in custody', the risk here being that language can serve to 'anaesthetise' the punitive reality (Cohen, 1989). Whilst the lower age of criminal responsibility continues to be ten, if essential social and mental capacity factors relating to children are ignored, then surely holding children 'responsible' for behaviours becomes illogical, and thereby unjust. It is therefore important for social workers to resist forms of practice which are 'punitive' and are not consistent with a value base which takes seriously a duty to advocate for vulnerable children and ensure justice and proportionality.

It will be essential for social workers in cases concerning children to ensure that proportionate and protective principles enshrined in law are utilised particularly at times of 'riot' and 'panic'. This position does not condone 'criminal activity' which damages individuals, property and communities, neither does it dispute the associated suffering, loss, or anger of those affected by crime. Rather it acknowledges the need to investigate the conditions which give rise to such behaviour with a view to preventing further harm.

Cross references: anti-oppressive practice, looked after children, safeguarding children

SUGGESTED READING

Brown, S. (2005) *Understanding Youth and Crime*. Oxford: Oxford University Press.
Muncie, J., Hughes, G. and McLaughlin, E. (eds) (2009) *Youth Justice, Critical Readings*. Oxford: Oxford University Press.

REFERENCES

Cohen, S. (1989) *Visions of Social Control*. Oxford: Polity Press and Basil Blackwell.
Cohen, S. (2002) *Folk Devils and Moral Panics*, 3rd edn. London: Routledge.
DfE (2011) *The Munro Review of Child Protection: Final Report*. London: DfE.
Flatley, J., Kershaw, C., Smith, K., Chaplin, R. and Monk, D. (eds) (2010) *Crime in England and Wales 2009/10: Findings from the BCS*. Home Office National Stats.
Goldson, B. (2011) '"Time for a fresh start"; but is this it? A critical assessment of the report of the independent commission on youth crime and antisocial behaviour', *Youth Justice*, 11(1): 3–27.
Goldson, B. and Muncie, J. (eds) (2006) *Rethinking Youth Justice: Comparative Analysis, International Human Rights and Research Evidence*. London: Sage.
Goldson, B. and Muncie, J. (eds) (2011) *Youth Crime and Justice*. London: Sage.
Home Office (1998) *Crime and Disorder Act Home Office Framework Document*. London: HMSO.
Howard League for Penal Reform, 11 May 2011, press release. Available from: www.howardleague. org/childarrests (accessed 5 September 2012).
Muncie, J., Hughes, G. and McLaughlin, E. (eds) (2009) *Youth Justice, Critical Readings*. Oxford: Oxford University Press.
United Nations (1985) Standard Minimum Rules for the Administration of Juvenile Justice ('The Beijing Rules'). Available from: http://www2.ochr.org/english/law/beijingrules.htm (accessed 5 September 2012).